The Gaumont Palace Wood Green in 1934. Right, "This Way In" photograph courtesy of Graham Rumble.

GAUMONT
BRITISH
CINEMAS

Above: the Gaumont Palace Doncaster in 1934. Opposite: drawing of Gaumont Palace Frome from opening programme (1939) (courtesy of John Hickey).

GAUMONT BRITISH CINEMAS

BY ALLEN EYLES

CINEMA THEATRE ASSOCIATION

Distributed by BFI PUBLISHING

BFI PUBLISHING

First published
in January 1996 by the
Cinema Theatre Association
5 Coopers Close
Burgess Hill
West Sussex RH15 8AN

Distributed by
BFI Publishing
British Film Institute
21 Stephen Street
London W1P 2LN

The CINEMA THEATRE ASSOCIATION was formed in 1967 to promote serious interest in all aspects of cinema buildings, including architecture, décor, lighting, music, film projection and stage facilities. The CTA campaigns for the preservation and, wherever possible, the continued use of cinemas and theatres for their original purpose, and maintains an archive of historical material. Visits to cinemas and theatres in the UK and overseas are regularly organised, as well as lectures, talks and film shows. The CTA publishes the magazine *Picture House* and the bi-monthly *CTA Bulletin*, a members' newsletter. (Enquiries/Membership Secretary: Bill Wren, Flat 30, Cambridge Court, Cambridge Road, Southend-on-Sea, Essex SS1 1EJ.)

The BRITISH FILM INSTITUTE exists to promote appreciation, enjoyment, protection and development of moving image culture in and throughout the whole of the United Kingdom. Its activities include the National Film and Television Archive; the National Film Theatre; the Museum of the Moving Image; the London Film Festival; the production and distribution of film and video; funding and support for regional activities; Library and Information Services; Stills, Posters and Designs; Research, Publishing and Education; and the monthly *Sight and Sound* magazine. (Membership details: Membership Department, South Bank, London SE1 8TL.)

ISBN: 0 85170 519 7

Printed in Great Britain by
The KPC Group
London and Ashford, Kent

CONTENTS

The Gaumont Holloway (now Odeon) in 1958.

ACKNOWLEDGEMENTS

I am greatly indebted to several experts who kindly read the text of this book in a near-final draft and made many valuable comments and suggestions. They were John Fernee, whose enthusiasm was invigorating; Elain Harwood, who also kindly provided some biographical data on W. E. Trent, W. Sydney Trent and Newbury A. Trent; Tony Moss, who also contributed the history of Gaumont organs and many elusive photographs from his collection; and David Trevor-Jones, who also accompanied the author all the way to Colindale in a joint attack on outstanding research queries at the British Library's Newspaper Library, then pursued matters further in distant parts of East London.

In addition, Stan Fishman, recently retired marketing director and former chief booking executive for the Odeon circuit, generously checked the post-World War Two text against his own memories of working with Odeon and Gaumont for forty-eight years and gently helped me avoid a few errors and amplify a few points. He also showed me some very useful material from the time when he ran live shows.

Paul Archer, the highly regarded manager of the Odeon Sheffield, gave me access to the weekly returns of the town's Gaumont cinema in the late Forties and Fifties, providing a unique source of detailed information on which I have drawn extensively. I greatly regret that he died before I was able to thank him in person.

Information regarding Gaumont projection equipment was generously supplied by Mike Taylor in Liverpool and Dan Ford in Enfield, both members of The Projected Picture Trust.

Other members of the CTA Committee who provided particular help were Oliver Horsburgh, Tim McCullen, Brian Oakaby, Bill Wren and, not least, Alan Richardson who pitched in with much rare material on Salisbury.

This book is only possible because it is assured of efficient distribution to the members of the Cinema Theatre Association by Jeremy Buck, the CTA's Sales Officer, whose sterling work on the author's earlier *ABC The First Name in Entertainment* is much appreciated.

My wife Lesley Eyles contributed extensive technical assistance.

Harold Ackroyd, an admirable cinema historian and former ABC manager, provided me with some valuable insights into the Liverpool scene.

David V. Cheshire provided many useful press cuttings and updates along with general encouragement.

Carl Chesworth sent me many interesting bits and pieces.

Terry Creswell loaned a rare opening programme and sent photocopies of many vintage examples of Gaumont advertising. Sally McGrath rushed me a copy of the Gaumont Palace Taunton opening programme with her usual efficiency.

Andy Garner was helpful as always, as were Ken George and Terry Staples with regard to children's shows, while Bruce Peter came up with some Scottish details.

Gil Robottom communicated some valuable information on Coventry.

Graham Rumble provided copies of some valuable illustrations from his collection on Holloway.

David Sharp eased access to copying material at the BFI Library and Information Services. Bridget Kinally of BFI Stills, Posters and Designs helpfully expedited the copying of some rare photographs.

D. W. C. Sparke, former CTA social secretary, long ago provided some of the information on postwar Gaumont sites.

The late Leslie Wilkinson allowed me to borrow some precious newspapers to copy their cinema advertising, with Stuart Smith kindly acting as intermediary.

Jason Williams (as manager of the Odeon Doncaster) kindly responded with some important information. Graham Dilks at the Odeon Salisbury sent me information and photographs on recent changes.

I asked in the *CTA Bulletin* for up-to-date information on the current use of many former Gaumonts or on what has replaced them where demolished, plus a few other elusive details. Besides many of the individuals previously named, I was delighted with the response and express my sincere thanks to the following members: David Baker (Bridgwater)(also, through him, Bill Chidgey), Michael D. Blakemore (Birmingham), Fred Burgoine (Luton), Jim Carter (Bridport), Barry Chandler (Harpenden), John Duddy (Walsall), Bill Fleckney (Portsmouth), Peter Foreman (Ringwood), Alan Glover (London N.W.2), Mervyn Gould (Loughborough), Bob Grimwood (St. Osyth), Peter Hamer (Plymouth), Tom Hamill (Kendal), Alan Hodson (Birkenhead), Brian Hornsey (Stamford), R. Howland (Swindon), Frank Manders (Sunderland), John Matthews (Wolverhampton), Thomas Maxwell (London), John J. McKillop (Wishaw), Alan Moore (Gloucester), Chris Plaister, John Platford (Surbiton), John Potter (Anglesey), David Reeves (Chippenham), Ken Roe (South Tottenham), Tom Ruben (London), Clifford Shaw (Sheffield), Stuart R. Smith (Sheffield), Barry Stevenson (Tooting), Ron Whitehead (Bayswater), H. T. Willis (Barkingside), Fred Windsor (Worthing), John Yallop (Weymouth) and Malcolm Young (Oxted). I hope the list also includes all those who communicated by telephone.

At Odeon Cinemas, technical executive Andy Robertshaw dug out some missing dates of recent conversions despite a hectic work schedule. Mike Robinson of Top Rank Clubs/Mecca Social Clubs supplied several photographs and a current list of clubs.

Odeon Cinemas have been generously indulgent towards my research activities for a great many years (Chris Moore, former public relations executive, could not have been more helpful when I started).

In connection with this book, I am glad to acknowledge the substantial assistance given by Andy Robertshaw and Odeon managing director Hugh Corrance with regard to the illustrations.

INTRODUCTION

My introduction to the Gaumont circuit was not a favourable one. The Gaumont at Balham in South London was no picture palace. Known to locals as "The Hole in the Wall", it had a long, narrow entrance, the width of a shop front, leading to a converted swimming baths. (Many years later, a relief manager, unaware of the building's history, recalled his surprise when a patron complained that his foot had gone through the floor. The pool had never been filled in when a sloping wooden floor was inserted.)

The Gaumont had a smallish auditorium, long and straight, with a gallery down the side. From the street, part of the screen could be glimpsed every time the doors to the auditorium were opened, but not enough of the picture to amount to anything. Although well placed in the centre of the shopping area, this Gaumont was no match for the yellow-tiled Thirties Odeon which sat somewhat remotely (if you came from the Tooting Bec side) at the top of Balham Hill. Even so, the Gaumont offered a good, bright picture without any technical hitches and I enjoyed many films there from my introduction with *Where No Vultures Fly* (for which there were small queues) to *Heller in Pink Tights* in its final years.

By the railway bridge in Balham stood the ruins of another cinema — the frontage lingered, looking none too safe, but the roof and auditorium had gone, except for the lower part of the side walls. From the high platforms of the railway station and from trains passing by, a pool of water could be seen at the foot of the slope where the screen had stood. As a schoolboy, I never knew anything about this building, which had in fact been another Gaumont house, regarded as superior to the one that survived.

I did learn something about another Gaumont cinema one day when I was exploring Victoria. Walking down Wilton Road in the morning, I found a side exit from the New Victoria half open. Slipping inside, I was surprised to find myself at the front of the balcony rather than on the stalls floor. I couldn't really see the decoration and at age twelve was more interested to find a film running in the deserted auditorium — evidently the projectionists were testing the print. Unfortunately, it was no action-packed adventure but a tearjerker called *Little Boy Lost* with Bing Crosby, so I was soon on my way...

Then, when I was moved to Streatham, there was a mysterious building at Streatham Hill, a huge cinema that sat closed and apparently abandoned. This was the war-damaged Gaumont, giving no indication from the front of its injuries and offering no announcement of its future. Streatham had its cavernous Astoria playing the Odeon circuit programmes and its relaxing Regal offering the ABC release. To catch the weekly Gaumont release, a journey was necessary, usually down to Brixton Hill and the creaky Clifton, but otherwise to the Regal West Norwood (a large but old-fashioned Gaumont theatre), the slickly-run Granada Thornton Heath, or back to the hole in the wall at Balham.

Then, in 1955, the closed Gaumont at Streatham Hill came back to life with a splendid new auditorium cunningly inserted inside the old one. Its major drawback to an impecunious youngster was that its cheapest seats were confined to the front three or four rows of the stalls, uncomfortably close the screen, while everywhere else on that floor was at a single, higher price. It seemed spitefully mean to have so few seats available at the lowest price, but of course this section could be expected to fill up first, encouraging patrons to pay more rather than queue.

In fact, apart from a near capacity crowd for the Melina Mercouri-and-hit-tune sex comedy *Never on Sunday*, which really brought the place alive, I don't think I ever saw a huge audience at the Gaumont Streatham, although those front rows were often well occupied. Unfortunately, because of the sea of empty seats behind, I discovered that it was impossible to slip further back without attracting the attention of the usherettes.

The bombed-out cinema at Balham was the Palladium, seen here circa 1915. (Courtesy of David Francis.) (Now office block.)

The Gaumont Balham, "the hole in the wall", in November 1960. (Photograph by Allen Eyles.) (Demolished.)

Of course, the films I saw at the Gaumont weren't necessarily crowd-pullers anyway, but I did get the distinct impression that the Gaumont's programmes were far weaker overall than those at the Astoria or Regal. And now I know I was right. Even so, it was very annoying when the Gaumont closed less than six years later to become a bowling alley. It had a wide auditorium with excellent sightlines, ideal for CinemaScope, whereas the Astoria had to drop its top masking and reduce the size of image whenever it had a 'scope picture. I never found the Astoria very inviting as a building, although it had a classier location and could certainly draw the crowds.

By the time the Gaumont closed, I had begun to care about cinemas and made an effort to visit more of them, especially those that were threatened with closure. With no way then of knowing which were architecturally interesting and which were not, I was utterly astonished to catch the huge shell-like interior of the Gaumont Bromley on its final day, after so often being reminded of its presence by the large red neon sign on the back of the building glimpsed from the main railway line. The Rose Hill Gaumont was another amazing interior with its cutaway sides and dramatically layered ceiling. The Elephant and Castle Trocadero, a prominent Gaumont house (although not built for the circuit), lasted many months after its demise was first announced, and I went there whenever the programme was tolerably interesting to savour the still extraordinary sense of occasion, of potent atmosphere, that this popular but excessively large cinema managed to evoke. On the other hand, the West Norwood Regal never felt very inviting – especially on a winter Saturday afternoon when the heating had failed to come on.

It was only in later years living in North London that I came across the fading splendour of the Gaumont Wood Green (by then renamed Odeon) and the still smart and immense Gaumont Camden Town (also by then an Odeon) and really started to appreciate the many magnificent buildings erected by the circuit. My founder membership of the Cinema Theatre Association paid dividends. One of the CTA's earliest trips was to catch the Gaumont Bournemouth in 1968 before the original auditorium was destroyed in twinning, although I have to say in all honesty I was more taken then by the modern lines of the huge ABC which we also visited. A CTA visit to the Regent Stamford Hill, North London, just before its closure as a cinema in 1972, revealed another astonishing interior, hardly

*Top: the war-damaged Gaumont stood at Streatham Hill "temporarily closed"
for many years. Photograph taken circa 1945. Below: the new auditorium
that appeared in 1955 with "floating" ceiling. (Now bowling alley.)*

altered since the day it opened. In 1981, a CTA weekend concluded with an inspection of the Odeon (ex New Victoria) Edinburgh with its starry ceiling and watching muses. And, in more recent times, the CTA gained access to a further jewel, the former Regent at Hanley, just before that closed, having been made redundant by a multiplex.

In later years, courtesy of the Rank Organisation, I was able to make my own tours of the former Gaumont Palaces at Cheltenham, Derby and Doncaster, among others. Doncaster was the only disappointment (because of heavy modernisation) and I came to regard the Gaumonts as being just as interesting, in their different way, as the Odeons that were then my prime quarry and that were more plentiful on the ground.

As indicated in Chapter 15, there is just enough left today to indicate the glory that was Gaumont and the very real achievement of the circuit's chief architect, W. E. Trent, and his associates. But it is not just its best cinemas that make the circuit's story worth telling.

Although the Gaumont name has vanished in Britain, it was once a potent force on the cinema scene, and this book describes the circuit's strong start and later decline. It is a very complicated story — I had not fully appreciated when I started just how complex the structure of the Gaumont-British Picture Corporation was, and I can only hope that the following excavations make it reasonably clear. There are many lists and facts and figures in this book (which those interested in the broader picture should skip) — but they are included because such lists do not exist or are not readily accessible anywhere else.

I have also attempted to describe purpose-built cinemas as they looked when they opened. This was the only consistent approach I could find. Virtually all of them have been subjected to drastic alterations or total demolition, and I have referred to their present status in the captions to the accompanying illustrations (this information is also in the A to Z of Gaumont cinemas). The final chapter surveys the best of what remains to be seen today.

Perhaps for those raised in the multiplex era, the Gaumont story will seem too remote to be interesting. But there is, I hope, a nostalgic appeal for those of us who remember the heyday of cinemagoing and the excitement of choosing between the various programmes on offer for the one week they were around. Quite often, it was true, as the slogan put it: "Your week is not complete without a visit to a Gaumont theatre."

1 : IN THE BEGINNING

The Gaumont name is, as most readers will know, derived from the French film pioneer Léon Gaumont (1864-1946). He established the Société Léon Gaumont & cie on 10 August 1895, taking over an optical company called Comptoir Général de la Photographie to set up his own business manufacturing and selling photographic equipment. That year the Lumière brothers showed their Cinématographe and Gaumont decided to make film projectors. In 1896, he offered his first model, the Demeny Chrono built by George Demeny. The following year the Gaumont organisation started making films to help sell its projectors.

Films were supplied to Britain and Léon Gaumont personally visited the offices of a certain Mr. Le Couteur in Brook Street, Mayfair, to collect some money owing. Le Couteur had been showing Gaumont's films in a hall, said to have been in Regent Street. In spite of his name, Le Couteur was unable to speak French and a young member of his staff, A. C. Bromhead, stepped in to act as interpreter. From this first meeting it was but a short step for Bromhead to become Gaumont's British agent.

"On a visit to Paris in 1897," Bromhead recalled in 1923, "he took me over the workshop where he was then constructing various photographic and mechanical appliances. I suggested to him then the possibilities of a business in England. In 1898 the business was started, with myself as his agent and manager, at 25 Cecil Court. The first member of the staff was T. A. Welsh ... and we opened for business on September 12. We had little else than a small stock of photographic odds and ends and a large stock of hope and courage." (Cecil Court would soon become known as "Flicker Alley" for its concentration of film company offices.)

Léon Gaumont had manufactured an advanced projector made of aluminium alloy with spool boxes of the same metal which held 200ft. of film (approximately the length of three of the short films of that era which made up a programme). Bromhead gained the British rights and offered this machine to British exhibitors for seven pounds and ten shillings.

"In the early part of our business career," Bromhead further recalled, "I persuaded M. Gaumont to let us have a few films for sale. We fitted up one of the machines...in the basement, and there, on an old sheet, we showed a small but by no means imperfect picture to those who represented the exhibiting side of the business. We sold outright our pictures of various small scenes averaging 60 feet in length... The chief, if not our entire, outlet, in the first place, was to exhibitors who were giving music-hall turns. The topical [newsreel] side of the business very quickly developed to meet this condition of things. It was, in fact, our mainstay, and other subjects were only introduced by degrees. Curiously enough, a great fillip to this side of the business was given by the film of Queen Victoria's funeral, of which we sold large numbers."

Another "topical" included film of troops from the Boer War disembarking at Southampton at 9am one morning that was being shown to audiences at the London Hippodrome by 3pm the same day. Around 1899, Bromhead set up a small open-air studio in a field at Loughborough Junction, South London, but Léon Gaumont disapproved of films being made there, no doubt preferring that Bromhead confined his efforts to selling the French output, and it was closed down, although the production of topicals continued.

In 1906 a British Gaumont company was formed to take over and absorb A. C. Bromhead's operations, with Bromhead gaining a minority shareholding in the new organisation. During this year, Bromhead had opened up one of the first full-time cinemas. A former shop in Bishopsgate in the City of London was converted into a cinema called the Daily Bioscope. This was usefully located between the police station and the fire station, opposite Liverpool Street railway station.

With upholstered chairs and a lushly decorated waiting lounge, the Daily Bioscope offered 120 seats at twopence and fourpence, running from noon to 9pm with a special show for office workers between 1pm and 2pm. Here, for example, the Derby could be seen on the same day it was run. A. C. Bromhead has left an account of his motives in establishing the cinema. "I made many efforts to induce private showmen themselves to start permanent theatres. I tried hard to persuade some of the music-hall exhibitors to open continuous shows, and some of them subsequently did — but it was not until we had opened the first continuous show in London in Bishopsgate Street early in 1906 that the continuous show really started on its conquering way. This show was opened largely as a demonstration and for the purpose of leading the way for other exhibitors to whom we hoped to sell our apparatus and our films."

This venture can claim to be both the first newsreel cinema and the first Gaumont British cinema. On Bromhead's own admission, "it paid its way and little more, and it was sold to ... Arthur Gale and his partner after a few months' operation. It had the distinction, however, of being the first — and the last — kinema within the confines of the City of London."* Gale's partner was William H. White who in 1909 opened the Vaudeville in Reading, which many years later took the Gaumont name.

Keeping out of exhibition in France, Léon Gaumont had frowned on the venture, leading to its disposal. But in 1910 Gaumont began operating cinemas in France, laying the basis for a circuit which is still in operation — in fact the second largest in that country today.

In 1907 the British Gaumont company moved to 5 and 6 Sherwood Street, near Piccadilly Circus, and opened a branch office in Glasgow. Around this time, film sales were flagging and Bromhead began hiring out some of his titles instead of selling them outright. Gaumont offered film of such events as the 1907 Shackleton expedition and the Johnson-Burns boxing match of 1908. These were sold to particular exhibitors as "exclusives" in their area, a method of selling originated by Bromhead. New branches were opened in Manchester, Liver-

*Top: Léon Gaumont, demonstrating one of his early projectors.
Below: staff assemble for a photograph outside the Gaumont premises in
Cecil Court, off Charing Cross Road, circa 1906.*

*It had become known as the Bishopsgate Picture Palace or Theatre by 1914 and was operated by the Bishopsgate Theatre Co. Ltd. As for being the only cinema in the City of London, Bromhead could not have anticipated the Barbican Centre and the cinemas included there.

pool and Cardiff and, when Gaumont opened a New York office in 1908, A. C. Bromhead was the vice president. He was also put in charge of expanding into the British Empire and in 1909 and 1910 formed companies in Canada and Australia with ten separate branches, being allotted shares in the new companies in proportion to his own cash investment. He spent most of his time travelling, leaving T. A. Welsh and H. D. Wood to run the British operation with the help of a Mr. Gent. A member of staff from 1910 was William J. Gell.

More space was needed and a move was made to premises at 5, 6 and 7 Denman Street, round the corner from Sherwood Street, in November 1910. This followed the start of a regular newsreel, the Gaumont Graphic, on 25 October 1910, for which a laboratory was soon established in Orange Street. In 1913 it was a Gaumont Graphic cameraman who captured on film the death of Emily Davidson, the suffragette who threw herself in front of the King's horse during the Derby.

The next year the Gaumont company opened a studio at Shepherds Bush just before the start of the First World War and expanded considerably on the production side. When contact with France became difficult, it began a long-standing association with the Kalee company.

The French Gaumont company emerged from the War in bad shape, having lost much of its overseas market to American producers. Annual production was slashed to less than a dozen films a year aimed at the domestic market. The British company was left more or less to fend for itself. In 1921 French Gaumont had piled up huge debts and its bank began to exercise control. This was the last straw for A. C. Bromhead and his younger brother, Reginald, who had become managing director of the British company. They saw it as an opportunity to sever ties with France and in the middle of the year started talks offering to acquire the entire French holding in the British operation.

Negotiations were protracted but in December 1922 the Bromheads succeeded and the Gaumont company here became entirely British-owned, although Léon Gaumont remained a member of the board and there were reciprocal agency arrangements with the former parent company. The buy-out was achieved with the financial backing of a merchant bank, Ostrer Bros., headed by Isidore Ostrer. William J. Gell became managing director. Isidore and his brothers Mark and Maurice joined the Gaumont board.

The company expanded to ten branches, improved its production facilities, and employed over 500. But it had not achieved independence after all. The real power lay with Isidore Ostrer. The oldest of five sons born to a impoverished Polish shoemaker at Bow in East London, he was nicknamed "Mephi", short for Mephistopheles, because of his rather sinister appearance. However, for several years the Bromheads and Ostrer saw eye to eye.

2: ISIDORE LEADS THE WAY

It was Isidore Ostrer who decided to build the company into a powerful organisation which would acquire cinemas to supplement its activities in production and distribution. The steadiest profits were to be made in exhibition and the ownership of cinemas guaranteed outlets for the films that Gaumont produced and distributed. In November 1926 the Ostrers acquired from E. E. Lyons the fifteen cinemas of the Biocolour circuit, located as far apart as Glasgow and Plymouth. Rumours of circuits being courted for acquisition had been rife and cinema owners were disturbed by the implications of a producer/distributor invading the exhibition sector but there was relief that none of the big American companies was behind the take-over.

Then in March 1927 the Ostrers announced a new £2.5 million combine to be known as the Gaumont-British Picture Corporation (GBPC) that would be made up of the old Gaumont company, the Ideal and W&F Film Service distribution companies, and the Biocolour cinemas. GBPC was registerd as a public company on 24 March. This was the first major combine to take in all three segments of the film business — production, distribution and exhibition — and it would encourage many others to follow suit, most notably John Maxwell who started British International Pictures in April 1927 and created the Associated British Cinemas circuit from three existing chains as a subsidiary in 1928.

In taking over the old Gaumont Company Ltd., GBPC obtained the Shepherds Bush studios, which were at that moment being more than doubled in size, and distribution branches in Manchester, Liverpool, Newcastle, Birmingham, Leeds, Cardiff, Bristol, Glasgow, Dublin and Belfast, as well as a business selling cinema equipment. The purchase price of £605,000 included The Theatre (Grimsby) Ltd., which owned the Savoy Grimsby. A separate contract provided that A. C. Bromhead and Reginald Bromhead would receive £40,000 in exchange for surrendering the rights they held to 15% of the Gaumont

Co.'s profits and would work for the new company for five years at an annual salary of £5,000 each.

Ideal Films Ltd. was headed by Harry Rowson and Simon Rowson and, under the deal to take it over, Simon Rowson became a director of GBPC.

The W&F Film Service Ltd., along with C&M Productions Ltd., formed a prominent production and distribution outfit which released the output of Gainsborough Pictures, source of such hits as *The Rat* and *The Lodger*. The companies belonged to Charles M. Woolf and M. Woolf, and the former became a director of GBPC.

The freehold or leasehold of twenty-one cinemas was acquired, including the previously mentioned Savoy Grimsby. Under contracts dated 18 November 1926, fifteen properties, which had been operated as the Biocolour Picture Theatres circuit, were taken over from E. E. Lyons and Thomas Underwood (with the agreed price in brackets):

Bradford Empire (£14,997 15s. 7d.)
Brighton Academy (£45,210 1s. 5d.)
Bristol Palace (£48,953 1s. 11d.)
Burslem Coliseum (£13,707 18s. 7d.)
Cardiff Hippodrome (£1,885 1s. 3d.)
Colchester Hippodrome (£41,913 5s. 5d.)
Dalston (North London) Picture House (£111,291 0s. 7d.)
Glasgow New Savoy Picture House (£90,640 0s. 4d.)
Hanley Empire (£38,721 18s. 5d.)
Holloway (North London) Empire (£11,155 5s. 11d.)
Hoxton (North London) Britannia Theatre (£6,007 2s. 0d.)
Newport (South Wales) Coliseum (£7,897 18s. 1d.)
Peckham (South London) Hippodrome (£20,937 13s. 3d.)
Plymouth Savoy (£38,644 2s. 6d.)
Stoke-on-Trent Hippodrome (£24,413 4s. 6d.)

These figures included substantial amounts totalling £70,200 as compensation to the directors for loss of office as well as the

GAUMONT-BRITISH PICTURE CORPORATION
LIMITED
(Incorporated under the Companies Acts, 1908 to 1917.)

CAPITAL - - £2,500,000

DIVIDED INTO

Authorised.   Already Issued or to be Issued.

1,250,000 7½ per Cent. Cumulative Preference Shares of £1 each - 1,000,000 Shares £1,000,000
2,500,000 Ordinary Shares of 10/- each - - - - 2,000,000 Shares £1,000,000

The Corporation has also created £1,000,000 of 6½ per cent. First Mortgage Debenture Stock. Arrangements have been made to issue £500,000 of this Stock at 97 and to place the whole of such issue privately. The Stock is redeemable at 102 per cent. by a Cumulative Sinking Fund of 2 per cent. each year, commencing in the year 1929. Any portion not so redeemed to be repayable at a like premium in the year 1953.

The Preference Shares are entitled to a fixed Cumulative Preference Dividend at the rate of 7½ per cent. per annum and in the event of a winding-up to priority as to repayment of capital and arrears of fixed cumulative dividend (whether declared or not) up to the commencement of the winding-up, but to no further right to participate in profits or assets.

The Articles provide that on a show of hands every Shareholder present in person shall have one vote, and on a poll every Member present in person or by proxy shall have one vote for every Share held but that the Preference Shareholders shall have no right to attend or vote at any General Meeting unless their Preferential Dividend shall be six months in arrear or a Resolution is proposed affecting the rights or privileges of the holders of Preference Shares.

It is proposed to pay the first half-year's Preference Dividend on the 30th September, 1927, calculated on the amounts paid up on the Preference Shares from the due dates of payment, and thereafter to pay such Preference Dividend half-yearly on the 31st March and the 30th September.

The Articles of Association provide that the amount for the time being remaining undischarged of moneys raised or borrowed by the Directors for the purposes of the Corporation otherwise than by the issue of share capital shall not without the sanction of a General Meeting exceed in the whole the amount of the nominal share capital for the time being of the Corporation.

The **L.O.G. Syndicate, Limited,** have applied for 1,900,000 Ordinary Shares at par which will be allotted in full against payment for cash and 100,000 Ordinary Shares are offered for subscription as below.

ISSUE AT PAR
OF
1,000,000 7½ per Cent. Cumulative Preference Shares of £1 each
AND
100,000 Ordinary Shares of 10/- each.

Applicants for Preference Shares have the right to apply for and have allotted to them one Ordinary Share in respect of every ten Preference Shares allotted. Applications for Ordinary Shares alone will not be accepted.

Directors :

LIEUT.-COL. A. C. BROMHEAD, C.B.E., 6, Denman Street, W.1, *Chairman and Managing Director* of the Gaumont Co., Limited (Chairman).
REGINALD C. BROMHEAD, F.C.A., 6, Denman Street, W.1, *Managing Director* of the Gaumont Co., Limited (*Managing Director*).
COL. H. A. MICKLEM, C.B., C.M.G., D.S.O., 7, King Street, St. James's, S.W.1, *Director*, Bankers' Investment Trust, Limited.
S. ROWSON, 76 and 78, Wardour Street, W.1, *Joint Managing Director* of Ideal Films, Limited.
CHARLES M. WOOLF, 74/6, Old Compton Street, W.1, *Managing Director* of W. & F. Film Service, Limited.
C. H. DADE, 88, Kingsway, W.C.2, { *Director*, Electrical and Industrial Investment Company, Limited. } { *Director*, Ever-Ready Company (Great Britain), Limited. }
ALFRED DAVIS, The Marble Arch Pavilion, W.1, *Director*, Electric Pavilion (Marble Arch), Limited.

Bankers :
NATIONAL PROVINCIAL BANK LIMITED.
MIDLAND BANK LIMITED.
LLOYDS BANK LIMITED.

Brokers :
MYERS & CO., 19, Throgmorton Avenue, London, E.C.2, and Stock Exchange.

Solicitors :
LAWRANCE, MESSER & CO., 14, Old Jewry Chambers, London, E.C.2.

Auditors :
NICHOLSON, BEECROFT & CO., 1/4, Paternoster Row, London, E.C.4.

Secretary (pro tem.), Registrar and Registered Office :
W. B. ROBINSON, 25/31, Moorgate, E.C.2.

Messrs. OSTRER BROS., 25-31, Moorgate, E.C.2, are authorised for and on behalf of the Corporation to receive Applications for the above Shares through their Bankers,
NATIONAL PROVINCIAL BANK LIMITED, 15, Bishopsgate, E.C.2, and Branches,
MIDLAND BANK LIMITED, 5, Threadneedle Street, London, E.C.2, and Branches, and
LLOYDS BANK LIMITED, 72, Lombard Street, London, E.C.3, and Branches.

PAYABLE AS FOLLOWS :—

PREFERENCE SHARES.	ORDINARY SHARES.
2s. 6d. per share on Application.	2s. 6d. per share on Application.
7s. 6d. ,, ,, ,, Allotment.	2s. 6d. ,, ,, ,, Allotment.
10s. 0d. ,, ,, 30th April, 1927.	5s. 0d. ,, ,, ,, 30th April, 1927.
20s. 0d.	10s. 0d.

Payment in full (for either class of share, by separate cheque) may be made on allotment under discount at the rate of 5 per cent. per annum, which discount will be refunded by the Company.

From the prospectus for the launching of the Gaumont British Picture Corporation

Early Gaumonts. Above: the New Savoy Glasgow (seen in 1954 as the Savoy). Below: King's Hall Penge (late 1945). (Both demolished.)

value of "other assets", a standard phrase added principally to cover any attached property, such as shops.

Under a contract dated 26 January 1927, GBPC arranged to take over the four Pavilions in the London area owned by Alfred and Minnie Davis (with the agreed price in brackets):

Lavender Hill Pavilion (£60,000)
Marble Arch Pavilion (£210,000)
Shaftesbury Avenue Pavilion (£40,000)
Shepherds Bush Pavilion (£240,000)

Alfred Davis became a director of GBPC and a contract provided that his brother Basil was to receive an amount equivalent to that earned by Alfred as a director and that both of them, as well as two other brothers, Edward and Stuart, would be employed by GBPC for three years at £2,000 each per annum.

Finally, a contract dated 3 February 1927 added the Colchester Empire at a cost of £8,200, payable to William Williams, John Pritchard and Richard Pritchard.

These, then, were the first cinemas in the Gaumont circuit. The purchase prices are a good indication of the hugely varying value of the properties. The Marble Arch Pavilion gave Gaumont a strong West End outlet, while the Shepherds Bush Pavilion and Dalston Picture House were two vast London suburban cinemas. The Savoy Grimsby was the leading cinema in that town. The Brighton Academy gave Gaumont a significant hall in that town. The acquisition of the Colchester Empire on its own is perplexing as the Hippodrome had been obtained earlier and would be the key Gaumont cinema in the town. The Bristol Palace, built as a music hall, must have been in a bad state as it was closed three months later and entirely rebuilt behind its facade to plans drawn up by Frank T. Verity, reappearing in 1928 as the New Palace. Most of the other cinemas in this first batch were also converted music halls and would become of minor significance as time went by.

Denman Picture Houses

A year later, in March 1928, an amalgamation of ninety-six further cinemas under a new umbrella company called Denman Picture Houses Ltd. was announced as part of the GBPC empire (the name came from GBPC's head office location in Denman Street). A prospectus was issued, offering £2 million of seven per cent debenture stock to the public. Of the properties, sixty-eight were freehold and twenty-eight leasehold, and in some cases a majority interest had been acquired rather than full ownership. The take-overs included several long-established regional circuits, whose founders and owners were in some cases given directorships in the new company.

Purchased outright for £250,000 were the seven cinemas of Thompson and Collins' Enterprises in the Newcastle-on-Tyne area:

Byker Grand Theatre
Gateshead Scala Theatre
Gateshead New Palace Theatre
Newcastle Pavilion
North Shields Borough Theatre
Sunderland King's Theatre
Wallsend Borough Theatre

Thomas Thompson became a director of Denman Picture Houses.

Then there were the six London-area cinemas making up the Hyams circuit, with the purchase price in brackets:

Hoxton Cinema and Ye Olde Varieties (£60,000, mortage debt of £3,925 taken over)
Penge King's Hall (£32,000)
Stratford Broadway Super Cinema (£240,000)
Stratford Imperial Playhouse (£40,000)
Westminster Bridge Road Canterbury Music Hall (£120,000)

Phil Hyams and Sid Hyams became directors of Denman Picture Houses.

The Gale and Repard circuit (sometimes referred to as the Exchange circuit), comprising three London suburban cinemas and three in Lincolnshire, came with a price tag of £260,000:

Canning Town (East London) Cinema
Canning Town (East London) Grand Theatre
Gainsborough Electric (closed)
Gainsborough Grand
Lincoln Corn Exchange
Palmers Green (North London) Palmadium

Major Arthur J. Gale was retained by GBPC in some capacity.

In addition, two cinemas in Southeast London, the New Cross Kinema (and Dance Hall) and Rotherhithe Lion Electric, were fully acquired as a cost of £180,000, with a mortgage debt of £40,000 also taken over. Also brought into the Gaumont empire were the West Kensington (West London) Super Cinema (for £47,500) and the Newcastle-on-Tyne New Westgate

(£72,500), plus seven cinemas in the Liverpool area purchased from T. Halliwell Hughes:

Aigburth Rivoli (£15,000)
Dingle Beresford (£33,850)
Dingle Picturedrome (£14,800)
Great Crosby Corona (£15,000)
Sefton Park Grand (£16,350)
Tue Brook Empress (£27,000)
Wavertree Magnet (£18,000)

Turning to the cinemas in which the Denman company took a controlling interest, these included New Century Pictures, the circuit headed by Sydney H. Carter, who became a director of Denman Picture Houses. An outlay of £338,696 15s. brought in:

Barnsley Empire
Barnsley Princess
Bradford Morley Street Picture House
Bradford St. George's Hall
Gorton (Manchester) Corona
Harrogate Scala
Leeds Assembly Rooms
Leeds Coliseum
Liverpool Mount Pleasant Picture Hall
Saltaire Picture House
Sheffield Albert Hall
Wakefield Carlton
Wakefield Empire

In addition, Gaumont inherited booking agreements with a number of cinemas including the Holbeck (Leeds) Queen's, Hull Majestic and Princes Hall, Shipley Princes Hall and Scarborough Londesborough Theatre. These were terminated in late 1928 or early 1929, although that for the Hull Holderness Hall continued and resulted in Gaumont acquiring the property in 1931.

Another pioneer circuit that now became part of the Denman/Gaumont group was National Electric Theatres, contributing nine cinemas at a cost of £148,099:

Balham (South London) Pavilion
Burton-on-Trent Electric
Chatham National Electric
Finchley (North London) New Bohemia
Halifax Electric Theatre
North Finchley (North London) Grand Hall
Sowerby Bridge (Yorkshire) Electric

York Electric
York Scala

Then there was North of England Cinemas, a further interest of Thomas Thompson, who relinquished control for £105,000 (but gained, as previously mentioned, a seat on the board on Denman Picture Houses):

Hunslet (Leeds) Pavilion
Middlesbrough Cleveland Hall
Middlesbrough Grand Opera House
Middlesbrough Hippodrome
Middlesbrough Pavilion
Middlesbrough Theatre Royal
Thornley Hippodrome
West Hartlepool Picture House
Whitley Bay Empire

Thomas Ormiston's interest in eleven Scottish cinemas was acquired in exchange for a seat on the board of Denman Picture Houses plus the sums indicated in brackets:

Alloa La Scala (£3,440)
Bellshill Picture Theatre (£739 10s.)
Edinburgh Cinema House (£7,200)
Falkirk Pavilion (£9,000)
Hamilton La Scala (£22,382 10s.)
Kirkcaldy Rialto (£21,862 10s)
Kirkintilloch Pavilion (£3,182 10s)
Lanark Picture House (£3,450)
Motherwell Pavilion (£11,512 10s.)
Perth Alhambra (£34,350)
Wishaw Cinema (£11,850)

Two London suburban halls were obtained from Catwood Cinemas for £127,251:

Cricklewood (North London) Queen's Hall
Rushey Green (Southeast London) Queen's Hall

Two inner South London suburban halls were acquired from Newington Electric Theatres for £75,957 10s.:

Kennington Prince's
Newington Butts Queen's Hall

In another deal, the Leeds Scala was added at a cost of £47,118.

The E. C. Shapeero interests in the Midlands were purchased by Denman (Midlands) Cinemas for £125,000 cash, £110,000 debenture stock and 5,000 shares of £1. This consisted of:

Cape Hill (Smethwick) Electric

More early Gaumont halls. Left: Corona Gorton, Manchester (circa 1945). (Demolished.) Centre: Electric Burton-on-Trent (shown in 1932). Right: Electric York (circa 1945).

The Scala South Shields (part of the GTC take-over in 1928), showing at back left the Mile End Road entrance, at right the main entrance on Ocean Road. Composite photograph taken c1945 for Gaumont by photographers Frank & Sons who were based in the Scala Buildings on Mile End Road. (Building stands in other uses.)

Dudley Empire
Handsworth (Birmingham) Villa Cross
Harborne (Birmingham) Picture House
Hyson Green (Nottingham) Grand
Kettering Electric Pavilion
Mansfield Empire
Mansfield Rock
Nottingham Electra House
Nottingham Mechanics' Hall
Redditch Public Hall
Smethwick Rink

Then came an intriguing partnership with the Bernstein interests under which a separate new company, Denman (London) Cinemas, took a controlling interest (fifty-one per cent) in the Bernstein theatres, leaving the Bernstein family with the rest of the shares (forty-nine per cent). Most remarkably, Sidney L. Bernstein remained in charge as managing director with an annual salary of £5,000. Other directors were E.(Ernest) G.(George) Bygrave, the Bernsteins' accountant, and, representing Gaumont, A. C. Bromhead (Chairman) and R. C. Bromhead. Apparently, Bernstein needed the money he received (said to have been £250,000) for other family businesses (or perhaps the development of the first Granada cinemas at Walthamstow, Tooting and elsewhere) and also felt his small chain would prosper from being part of such a large and powerful new combine as GBPC, which also provided administrative services. The seven cinemas involved*, all in North and East London, were:

East Ham Empire
Edmonton Empire
Enfield Rialto
Leytonstone Rialto
Plumstead Empire
West Ham Kinema
Willesden Empire

Bernstein's loss-making Willesden Hippodrome (actually in Harlesden) was soon grouped with the Denman (London) Cin-

*These cinemas would never be directly operated by Gaumont and became part of the Granada circuit that Sidney Bernstein established in 1934. However, even after the Second World War, any expenditure on the buildings above a very low limit had to be approved by Gaumont. It was not until March 1965 that Granada bought out the Gaumont holding and took full control.

emas properties until it could be quickly sold off, but whether this was for booking and operating convenience or whether there was a financial link is unclear.

Over the remaining months of 1928, the main Denman company added several more cinemas:

Dennistoun (Glasgow) Parade
Edgware Road (London) Grand
Morecambe Tower
Newcaste upon Tyne New Westgate
Plymouth Palladium

and three of the four "Bright and Beautiful" cinemas operated by the late J. J. Bennell in Scotland:

Coatbridge B. B. Cinerama
Eglinton Toll B. B. Cinerama
Perth B. B. Cinerama

General Theatre Corporation

In March 1928, another amalgamation of existing circuits had been launched as the General Theatre Corporation (GTC) by Sir Walter Gibbons and F. A. Szarvasy with Gibbons as managing director. But this had been hit by a poor response to its £3.5 million shares issue. It would seem that the almost simultaneous flotation of Denman Picture Houses was more attractive to the investor and GTC suffered as a result. Gibbons resigned as managing director in April, offering his services in an honorary advisory capacity. The following month, GBPC stepped in to acquire the ordinary share capital, appointing its own directors in August, retaining only George Black from the original Board.

With GTC, GBPC now controlled another fifty-seven properties, although this included the following music halls:

Birmingham Hippodrome
Boscombe Hippodrome
Brighton Court Theatre and Billiard Room
Brighton Hippodrome and Palm Court
Holborn (London) Empire
Leeds Hippodrome
Liverpool Royal Hippodrome
London Palladium (then operating as a cinema)
Newcastle upon Tyne Hippodrome
Paris (France) Alhambra (in course of construction)
Penge Empire

Portsmouth Hippodrome
Sheffield Hippodrome
Southampton Hippodrome
Southend Hippodrome
Wolverhampton Hippodrome

The GTC cinemas included two first-run houses in the West End of London:

Charing Cross Road Astoria
Haymarket Capitol

Then, in the London suburbs, there were:

Balham Palladium
Clapton Rink
Crouch End Hippodrome
Highbury Picture House
Islington Blue Hall
Islington Blue Hall Annexe

And in the rest of the country:

Abbeymount (Edinburgh) Regent
Allerton (Liverpool) Plaza
Anfield (Liverpool) King's Hall (and Billiard Hall)
Birkenhead Park
Birkenhead Queens
Birkenhead Super
Bootle Broadway (and Billiard Hall)
Bootle Strand
Chester Glynn
Chester Music Hall (operating as a cinema)
Chester Majestic
Edinburgh St. Andrew's Square Picture House
Edinburgh Rutland (in course of construction)
Egremont (Wallasey) Lyceum
Gosforth Globe
Heaton (Newcastle upon Tyne) Scala
Kensington (Liverpool) Casino
Leith Capitol (in course of construction)
Little Sutton King's Hall
Liverpool Rialto
Liverpool Savoy
Luton High Town Electric
Luton Palace
New Brighton Trocadero
Newcastle upon Tyne Grey Street Picture House
Newcastle upon Tyne Queen's Hall

Seacombe Marina
Sefton Park (Liverpool) Cameo
Shildon Hippodrome
Southport Palladium
South Shields Scala
Sunderland Palace
Walton (Liverpool) Bedford

Gaumont now had a total of 182 properties, making it by far the largest circuit in the country. Yet, looked at now, the overwhelming impression the cinemas on these lists give is of an accumulation of mostly outmoded properties, including former music halls that adapted poorly to film use.

Had Isidore Ostrer known of the prize that would next come within his grasp, it seems highly questionable whether he would have bothered to make any of these acquisitions.

3: PROVINCIAL CINEMATOGRAPH THEATRES

It was in December 1928 that the news first came out: Gaumont had offered to purchase Provincial Cinematograph Theatres (PCT), the leading national chain of ninety-six cinemas (controlled through a holding company, Standard Film).

PCT was in no difficulties at the time. Indeed, it was steadily expanding under the skilled management of Will Evans. In the recent past, three American companies had expressed interest in buying PCT and some discussions had taken place with First National in the winter of 1927. But stories of a take-over had subsided and when the Gaumont bid became known there was general surprise that PCT that was being bought rather than expanding itself. In fact, Isidore Ostrer had persuaded Lord Ashfield, chairman of PCT, and prominent shareholder Lord Beaverbrook to sell their interests.

However, events did not proceed smoothly. Ostrer offered fifty shillings a share and the newly emerged rival Associated British Cinemas, headed by John Maxwell, made a bid of fifty-two shillings and sixpence. The directors of PCT were divided over which suitor to accept. Ostrer, on behalf of Gaumont, raised his bid to fifty-five shillings and a majority of the shareholders accepted the offer, including Lord Ashfield, who then resigned with the other directors. The new directorate consisted of A. C. Bromhead (chairman), R. C. Bromhead (vice-chairman and joint managing director), Will Evans (joint managing director), Isidore Ostrer, Mark Ostrer, and Sir William Jury. Only Evans and Jury had been part of PCT before the take-over. Jury's presence on the board related to PCT's acquisition of the Tivoli in the Strand from Jury-Metro-Goldwyn. Evans had been sole managing director and was now required to share the position with Gaumont's R. C. Bromhead.

The acquisition of PCT included other companies under its control: Associated Provincial Picture Houses, the West Country circuit of Albany Ward Theatres, the Jersey and Guernsey Amusements Company, and the small Scala Theatres chain in London.

A list of the cinemas that became part of the Gaumont empire from February 1929 should indicate the high overall quality of the circuit, especially compared to those acquired previously. In the West End of London, the PCT properties were:

> Regent Street New Gallery (the circuit headquarters were in New Gallery House, the office block incorporating the cinema)
> Strand Tivoli

Next, in the London suburbs, PCT's circuit comprised:

> Acton Globe
> Clapham Majestic
> East Ham Premier Super
> Holloway Marlborough Theatre
> Hackney Pavilion
> Ilford Super
> Kentish Town Palace
> Peckham Tower
> Peckham Tower Annexe
> Stamford Hill Regent (opened February 1929)
> Sydenham Rink
> Tottenham Palace
> Walham Green Red Hall

The Ilford and Tottenham Palais de Dances and Les Gobelins restaurant in Regent Street were also owned by the company.

In the rest of England, PCT's theatres were:

> Ashton-under-Lyne Majestic
> Birmingham West End (plus dance hall)
> Brighton Regent (plus dance hall, cinema temporarily closed by fire)
> Bristol Regent
> Darlington Alhambra
> Darlington Arcade
> Darlington Court

Doncaster Majestic
Glossop Empire
Glossop Palace
Hanley Regent (opened February 1929)
Leeds Majestic (plus dance hall)
Leicester Picture House
Liverpool Trocadero
Northampton Exchange
Nottingham Picture House
Nottingham Hippodrome
Peterborough Broadway
Plymouth Andrews Picture House
Preston New Victoria
Sheffield Regent
Sunderland Havelock Picture House
Worcester Arcade
York Picture House
York St. George's Hall
In Scotland, the PCT halls comprised:
Dundee King's
Edinburgh New Picture House (plus surrounding Royal Hotel)
Glasgow Picture House
In Ireland, PCT's sole (but important) holding was:
Belfast Classic
In the London area, the cinemas of the subsidiary company Associated Provincial Picture Houses (APPH) were:
Finsbury Park Cinema
Islington Angel
Kings Cross Cinema
Sutton Surrey County Cinema
There was also a Palais de Dance at Finsbury Park.
These were APPH's other English halls:
Dudley Criterion
Dudley Regent
Halifax Picture House
Leigh Palace Theatre
New Brighton Tivoli
Walsall Picture House
Wednesbury Picture House
Willenhall Picture House
Wolverhampton Agricultural Hall
Wolverhampton Queen's
Wolverhampton Scala
There was one APPH cinema elsewhere, in Scotland:
Aberdeen Picture House
The Albany Ward subsidiary consisted of:
Barnstaple Theatre Royal
Bridgwater Bijou
Bridgwater Palace
Calne Palace
Chepstow Palace
Chippenham Palace
Cinderford Palace
Cirencester Picture House
Dorchester Palace
Easton Palace
Exeter Palladium
Frome Palace
Ilfracombe Alexandra Hall
Ilfracombe Scala
Lydney Picture House
Monmouth Picture House
Portland Palace
Salisbury New Theatre
Salisbury Palace
Salisbury Picture House
Stroud Palace
Stroud Picture House
Swindon Palace
Treharris Palace
Trowbridge Palace
Weymouth Belle Vue
Weymouth Palladium
Weymouth Regent (plus dance hall)
Yeovil Palace
The Jersey and Guernsey Amusements Company added:
Guernsey St. Julian's Theatre
Jersey King's Hall
Jersey Opera House
Jersey Picture House
Lastly, there was Scala Theatres, which operated the following London halls:
Ealing Broadway Palladium
Kilburn Grange
Maida Vale Palace

Gaumont took over ninety-six functioning cinemas (including the temporarily closed Regent Brighton). A figure of 116 was mentioned in the trade press, and the difference no doubt can be explained by PCT cinemas yet to open and sites held. Cinemas being planned or actually constructed included Regents at Bournemouth and Ipswich, New Victorias at Bradford, Edinburgh and London (Victoria), and Albany Ward's Regent Swindon.

PCT alone would have made Gaumont the dominant force in British film exhibition. The importance of the deal was not just that the company operated well-sited and popular cinemas in almost all of the big cities (Manchester notably excluded) but also that its Regents at Bournemouth, Brighton, Bristol, Dudley, Hanley, Sheffield, Stamford Hill, Swindon and Weymouth, along with its New Victoria at Preston, were large (but not excessively large, usually seating a little over 2,000) modern cinemas that would remain valuable assets like the new halls in the pipeline, all of them able to stand up to the vast amount of competition that would arrive in the Thirties. Several other cinemas, such as the Belfast Classic, Kilburn Grange and Leeds Majestic, would also remain highly lucrative. Of course, PCT had its dregs, particularly among the Albany Ward group. But very few of the GTC, Denman and original Gaumont halls matched up to the many leading PCT properties.

PCT continued as a separate company within the GBPC group for many years, maintaining its own headquarters at New Gallery House throughout the Thirties. As PCT became such a major part of the Gaumont empire, with its influence spreading through the appointment of its chief architect W. E. Trent to design and oversee all new Gaumont cinemas, it seems appropriate to backtrack and describe the evolution of the company.

The Rise of PCT

Provincial Cinematograph Theatres was formed in November 1909 with a capital of £100,000 to open fifteen cinemas in cities and towns with a population of at least one quarter of a million. It was the brainchild of Dr. Ralph T. Jupp, who had studied medicine at Birmingham and practised in South Africa until deafness forced him to give up the profession. He returned to England where he was inspired by the cinema building activities of Montagu A. Pyke to establish a circuit of his own. He gained his financial backing from his uncle, J. J. Newbould, and from Sir William Bass, Captain Aubrey Meares and Stanley

Ball. He recruited a former fellow medical student, Walter Grant, who dropped his East Coast practice to join in the new venture which started with one room, a typist and an office boy. Jupp was the managing director with Sir William Bass as chairman.

The company took the bold step of establishing a chain of cinemas far removed from each other, with consequent administrative difficulties, instead of concentrating on dominating a particular region. In part, this was dictated by Pyke's rapid expansion which had been confined to the London area. A gentleman's agreement was reached with Pyke under which he restricted his circuit to the capital while PCT built elsewhere.

The first PCT cinema opened in Dublin on 9 April 1910, seating 220. Before the end of the year, others had followed in Edinburgh, Manchester, Birmingham, Glasgow and Leicester, all called the Picture House and seating from 350 to 850. At the first annual general meeting in February 1911 a dividend of 10 per cent was declared. Profits in the year ending 31 January 1911 had been £4,334. During 1911, further PCT cinemas were opened in Leeds, Belfast and Bristol, plus second halls in Dublin and Manchester. For the year ending 31 January 1912, trading profits had soared to £47,104 and more than four million people had bought tickets from PCT. From the start, PCT offered continuous performances, then practically unknown, and sought expensive city centre locations, providing a standard of luxury and elegance designed to attract the "carriage trade" — affluent middle and upper class patrons who wouldn't have been seen within miles of the average early picture house. PCT provided seats throughout — there were no benches at the front. It was soon joked that if you wanted to reach a PCT cinema all you had to do was to ask for the centre of the town and you would find it at that very spot. In 1914, the *Bioscope's* Birmingham correspondent sought to indicate the high class of patronage at the Picture House there: "It is interesting to note that a string of fashionable cars is always to be seen outside."

In 1912, PCT entered Nottingham and Liverpool (the Prince of Wales, retaining the name of a converted theatre). Profits for the year ending 31 January 1913 leaped to £61,652. The thirteen cinemas operating by April 1913 were valued at £380,080. Under Ralph Jupp as managing director, Captain Meares was the general manager, Stanley Ball ran the film department and Walter Grant was in charge of catering arrangements. J. R. Naylor and G. H. Sale were the company's appointed architects.

PCT's cinemas were so successful that many were enlarged, replaced, or supplemented by more capacious new cinemas within a few years. In 1913, for example, the Grafton in Dublin closed to be doubled in size in six weeks. Demand on the catering side led to the Wedgwood Café area at the Birmingham Picture House being similarly enlarged, although there was no room to increase the auditorium and queues were frequently seen even in the afternoons.

In 1913, PCT arrived in Portsmouth and Halifax, and added a second Edinburgh hall, the New Picture House. PCT became the first exhibition company to be quoted on the Stock Exchange. During 1913, Ralph Jupp started a production company, the London Film Company, and arranged for PCT to invest £10,000 in its initial year in exchange for first call on the output. The arrangement started well with the commercial success of *The House of Temperley*.

PCT also began planning cinemas costing 40 per cent less for smaller towns (with a population of 150,000), making more of the seats available at lower prices. To build these, a new company, Associated Provincial Picture Houses (APPH), was promoted in January 1914 by PCT. It was legally distinct but had the same directorate and was even bigger in capitalisation than its parent. APPH opened Picture Houses in Aberdeen, Wednesbury and Willenhall, and took over the PCT cinemas in Wolverhampton and Halifax. Further expansion was curtailed by the First World War, as was further production by London Films. However, in October 1914, it was reported that all the company's theatres and cafés were profitable and that business had improved since the outbreak of war.

After the First World War started in 1914, Dr. Jupp, Captain Meares and Walter Grant volunteered for service. Jupp's cousin, F. E. Adams, took over temporary control of the company, while A. E. Newbould, son of J. J. Newbould, also became involved. Quite apart from the newcomers' inexperience, profits were hit by a number of factors shared with other cinemas: programmes were becoming longer and cost more to hire while reducing the number of shows, war newsreels or "topicals" were very costly, revenue was down because servicemen paid only half price, donations were made to help the war effort, and staff costs were higher because of the call up and the expense of temporary replacements.

In April 1917, PCT attracted unwelcome attention when the company secretary, Mr. Macauley, left without notice and later criticised the activities of the directors and management. A shareholders' committee appointed a committee of investigation which largely rejected Mr. Macauley's case. In March 1918, Ralph Jupp, who had resumed his role as managing director, resigned because of ill health and Sir William Bass left, referring to the pressure of his military duties. The shareholders installed a new board with F. E. Adams appointed managing director and A. E. Newbould as the only survivor of the previous directorate. Jupp went into business as an estate agent in London's West End and retained a connection with PCT as he handled sites for the company.

In 1919, PCT increased its capital with a heavily oversubscribed issue of new shares and Lord Beaverbrook took a £400,000 stake in the company, becoming a director and then making a £300,000 investment in APPH early in 1920. During 1919, the London Film Company made eight films, all of which were booked by PCT and all of which proved to be flops, returning only a third of their total cost. Production was halted.

PCT issued more new shares in March 1920, and used the new capital to take over existing cinemas. During this year, it acquired (for £226,207) almost all the ordinary shares of Albany Ward Theatres, the biggest circuit in the West Country, comprising some twenty-five properties. PCT retained the services of Albany Ward himself, with his great knowledge of the area, to continue running the cinemas. It purchased the New Gallery in London's Regent Street to gain its first West End cinema (Montagu Pyke was no longer in the picture) and it also invested £280,296 in APPH for expansion. Excluding the Albany Ward circuit, PCT was recording twenty million admissions a year in its seventy-two cinemas and showing a profit in the year ending 31 January 1921 of £224,913.

In 1921, Lord Ashfield was elected Chairman and PCT opened the huge Regent Brighton at a cost of £400,000. Ralph Jupp did not live to see the opening of the Brighton cinema, first of the PCT supers — he died in June as a result of pneumonia, aged only 45. Nor did he witness the hard times on which the circuit soon fell, although he knew that things were not going well: PCT were no longer purchasing sites for expansion but sitting on the fence while the film trade attempted to ride out a severe drop in attendances following a postwar boom. This had been exacerbated by a coal strike, an industrial slump leading to a shortage of disposal income, a high rate of Entertainments Tax, and the abnormally hot summer and autumn of 1921.

The slump continued in 1922 and 1923 with high unemployment. No progress was made on using the company's stock of sites at Belfast, Dundee, Liverpool, Preston, Sheffield, Southampton and West Hartlepool, although some work had been done at Preston during the War. At Portsmouth, PCT had taken over the building of which the existing Picture House formed a small part, with a view to erecting a larger cinema. PCT's fortunes declined so much that F. E. Adams resigned as managing director and by 1923 it was effectively bankrupt. The dividends were in serious arrears — ordinary shareholders had received nothing since 1920.

Lord Ashfield recruited William Evans to take over as managing director. Will (or Bill) Evans had begun his career opening skating rinks like the Canadian Rink Tottenham in North London, and then converting them to cinemas when the skating boom had passed. He had recently sold his circuit, North Metropolitan Theatres, to PCT. Evans accepted Ashfield's offer, reputedly specifying that he would take no salary until he had made £80,000 for the company.

During this crisis, the Albany Ward circuit had broken away from PCT to operate on its own under Ward's control. But Ward was in ill-health and resigned as managing director of the circuit in September 1924, letting PCT take back nineteen cinemas but retaining seven for himself.*

Under Evans' astute management and a general improvement in economic conditions, PCT soon recovered. In 1925, the New Gallery was rebuilt to provide a modern West End cinema and PCT acquired the huge Majestic Leeds and the West End Birmingham among many others. (The West End replaced the Picture House, giving a much needed cinema of larger capacity.)

During this year, rumours of an American take-over, hinting in particular that Metro-Goldwyn were interested in the company, surfaced and then died down. Evans decided to expand the circuit with a number of new cinemas, using some of the

Two important PCT take-overs. Top: the Majestic Leeds at time of opening in 1922. Restaurant entrance is closest to camera on the curve, cinema entrance at far end. (Now Top Rank bingo club.) Lower picture: the West End Birmingham, circa 1945. (Demolished.)

---

*In September 1927, PCT took over from Albany Ward the seven cinemas he still operated, together with two that he had recently opened, further consolidating its presence in the West of England where it was the strongest circuit.

The Regent Sheffield in 1927. (Outline of main name sign on exterior photograph has been crudely reinforced by pen.) (Demolished.)

sites it had acquired years earlier, and he appointed W. E. Trent as PCT's chief architect.*

Trent's initial task was the reconstruction of the Weymouth Royal Jubilee Hall, which re-opened in August 1926 as the Regent (using the name PCT had introduced at Brighton). Here he provided a completely new auditorium of modest size (1,234 seats) and limited interest within the shell of the old building.

The architect's first major opportunity was provided by a site at Sheffield, which PCT had bought during the War. PCT were taking a chance by proceeding, as many in the trade viewed this as a risky undertaking. But here, during 1927, arose a vast cinema that was a worthy successor to the Regent Brighton. Though less flamboyant, the Regent's frontage was conspicuously similar with a large, deeply recessed central window and coffered surround echoing a proscenium arch and screen.

The name Regent appeared no less than three times on the frontage: largest across the very top in an illuminated sign, then immediately above the recess in a smaller size, and finally, smaller still, mounted in lights on top of the front edge of the canopy which carried details of the current attraction. Cartouches with monograms of the PCT name appeared on each wall alongside the central recess, above small windows, brackets holding three lantern-like light fittings, and ground-level display cases with film stills. The PCT monogram also appeared at each end of the canopy front.

The base and much of the façade around the entrance was faced in white faience, while the rest was in mottled red bricks,

---

* William Edward Trent (1874-1948) was articled in 1892 to Henry Poston of Lombard Street, London, with whom he remained as an assistant until 1905. While in this office, he studied at the Architectural Association evening school. In 1905, he established a City practice. In 1909, he was responsible for converting a shop in Kingsland Road, Dalston, North London, into a cinema, but little is known of other work as a cinema architect before he gained this important position with PCT. So why did Evans choose him? He had been responsible for the large Super at Ilford, East London (1922), although he did not design the interior decoration: this was now an important PCT hall and could have impressed Evans. (Trent is often credited with the 1921 Premier Super at East Ham, East London, but this seems doubtful — he certainly did not handle the interior decoration. However, he was responsible for some mid-1930s modernisation of the frontage.) When Trent joined PCT, his existing practice was taken over by his son, W. Sydney Trent.

an unusual colour for Sheffield. Horizontal stone bands and a large panel for film posters helped to break up the brick wall extending to the corner of the site. Behind this wall lay, at a slight angle, the back of the auditorium, for the main entrance had been placed on one side to make the fullest use of an awkward site. As at Brighton (and most later cinemas), there was a separate entrance to the front stalls at the screen end of the building to speed up admissions during busy periods.

At the Regent Sheffield, the spacious foyer offered imitation stone walls above a broad Roman marble plinth. The floor had a pattern of white and dove marble squares, while the ceiling was coffered in plaster. Richard Ward's book *In Memory of Sheffield's Cinemas* recalls: "Other decorative features included a large sculptured chimney piece, mirrors, cut glass candelabra and antique terracotta vases. A broad staircase led to the rear stalls and another flight of marble stairs led to the first floor." This was a typically lavish entrance space in the manner of the Brighton Regent and PCT halls that followed.

The American idea of the atmospheric cinema, in which audiences sat in an outdoor setting under a "sky" ceiling, seems to have inspired the wall treatment to one side of the mezzanine lounge: patrons looked out past a carved-wood balustrade to a painted view of an Italian garden with cypress trees and buildings. However, a different treatment prevailed nearby. Ward notes: "The tea room was in Georgian style with panelled walls, fluted pilasters and ornate ceiling. The colour scheme was ivory with various shades of green and it seated about 150 people." The chairs were roundbacked with a wicker pattern and had well-cushioned seats. The floor was covered in a carpet with an elaborate design incorporating the PCT name.

The auditorium, generally in neo-classical style, was dominated by a shallow dome with lighting concealed behind the rim, and by an elaborate proscenium arch, similarly illuminated. The dome had become a standard feature of auditorium design, superseding the early barrel vault ceilings. Here Trent added a taller inner dome. Projection was from the back of the outer dome, in what would become the favoured position in PCT cinemas of this period. It resulted in a shorter throw but at an awkward angle, and added to the isolation of the projection room staff, but proved perfectly satisfactory from the audience point of view and sometimes allowed more seating space at the rear of the auditorium. A separate box, also set in the back of the dome, housed the spotlights for the stage.

The curved proscenium arch had a ribbed surround decorated with three medallions while the splay walls offered decorative grillework in the style of gates, painted gold with a backing of rose silk. There were single boxes to either side, between the grilles and the balcony front, while a series of roundheaded arches separated the stepped side passages from the mass of balcony seating.

This was an impressively detailed auditorium very much of its period. Both externally and internally, the Sheffield Regent was one of the few cinemas in Britain to that date to bear comparison with the best work done in America by Thomas Lamb (a Scotsman by birth) and others.

The cinema included a huge, fully-equipped stage, 27 ft. deep and 32 ft. wide, with seven dressing rooms. As this was the silent period, there was a live musical accompaniment to the films. The orchestra numbered twenty-five players in matching uniforms who also performed as an attraction in their own right during the stage shows that supported the screen offerings. And there was a Wurlitzer organ on a lift to relieve the orchestra and provide its own distinct interludes.

The Sheffield Regent has been described in some detail because it set the style for the PCT cinemas that would follow, both designed by W. E. Trent and by other hands.

In 1928, the new Bristol Regent was the work of local architect W. H. Watkins. This had a relatively plain front elevation with the name Regent seemingly confined to the top front edge of the canopy. In the auditorium, the decorative treatment of the proscenium arch and splay walls was rather more florid than at Sheffield, while the ceiling of the auditorium was another double dome. The shallow outer dome was largely plain and lit in a blue colour while the taller inner dome was surrounded by sunburst decoration. Side and rear passages were again separated from the seating area by a line of columns.

W. E. Trent himself was responsible for the Dudley Regent and the Preston New Victoria, both of which opened later in 1928. The Dudley cinema was a modest-sized cinema on a fan-shaped stadium plan for the APPH branch of PCT.

The much larger Preston cinema was to have been called the Regent but the town already had a place of amusement (not a cinema) using the name, and so a few days before opening it became the New Victoria, after the new flagship cinema being planned in London.

The huge foyer was dominated by a vast dome with a central

glass panel admitting daylight and a chandelier suspended from the centre. This led to a long, straight auditorium seating 2,100 with columns extending down each side from ceiling to stalls floor, behind which lay the side passages. Another double dome was set in the ceiling, with the projection portholes placed in the back of the shallow main dome. The proscenium surround was again illuminated by concealed lighting from the rim, while there were paintings of Chinese figures on the splay walls above exits, surmounted by the letters "PCT" in an Oriental style.

Besides new cinemas, there was undoubtedly much work going on to improve older properties. One instance, noted from 1928, is of substantial improvements to the Rink Sydenham, Southeast London, which took three months.

In February 1929, the month that Gaumont control of PCT became effective, the Regents at Hanley and at Stamford Hill, North London, opened a week apart.

Plans by W. E. Trent for the Hanley cinema date back at least to October 1927. The site was an awkward one, resulting in a rather inconspicuous main entrance on Piccadilly, set back from the existing building line, no doubt a requirement of the local authorities to facilitate any future street widening. The recess was covered by the standard canopy, which projected slightly over the pavement, with the name "The Regent" mounted as usual above its front edge. The name also appeared in larger letters horizontally alongside masks of comedy and tragedy on the set-back elevation of white faience, high up above the windows to the restaurant.

Far more conspicuous than the Piccadilly entrance were the rear and side elevations on other streets, in Italianate style with faience at ground floor level. Both carried the Regent name while the stage end wall also had cartouches with the letters of PCT intertwined, as at Sheffield.

At Hanley the main entrance hall had suspended light fittings in rectangular art deco style. The tall auditorium lay at an angle to this entrance, with the righthand side of the stalls nearest the foyer and the balcony set further back. This space was unmistakably the work of W. E. Trent. There was a double dome with projection from the back rim of the lower dome, a proscenium arch lit from the rim, square moulded piers with simple capitals and uplighters extending round the edge. However, the mouldings were in more of an art deco style, as were the line of light fittings across the coffered ceiling at the rear of the circle.

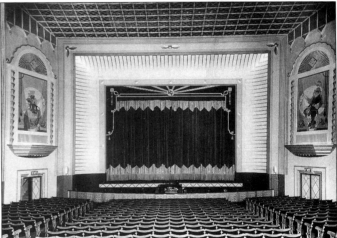

The New Victoria Preston in 1928. (Closed.)

The Stamford Hill Regent was credited to W. E. Trent's son, W. Sydney Trent*, under the supervision of his father. This was a very unusual location for PCT to build, being in a North London suburb rather than a city centre. However, it was as lavishly designed as other Regents, with a full-sized stage for cine-variety, 35 ft. or 40 ft. deep (sources vary) behind the 45 ft. proscenium opening.

The corner site seems to have been so large that there was no need to build an entrance block more than a single storey high. (Cafes were usually built over entrances: this Regent had one, but it was located elsewhere). The canopy projected in a curve, with the name of the cinema mounted on top. There was a low, faience-faced bay above and behind the canopy with the cinema name repeated in larger letters. Behind this lay the huge entrance hall, 70 ft. long by 36 ft. wide, which had the customary polished marble floor (with chequer-board pattern), with a large dome of coloured glass (admitting daylight) and a fountain-like light fitting suspended from the centre. Steps led up to the back stalls, while passages to the side led to the front stalls.

From the outside, the auditorium loomed high above the entrance block. This had a front section with the cinema name mounted horizontally at the top above tall windows and stone gryphons at the corners. Inside, the auditorium ceiling was dominated by a central dome (with projection once again from within it) with a very extensive moulded surround which reached almost to the side walls. There was no colonnade

*William Sydney Trent was born in 1903, the only sone of W. E. Trent. He took a three-year course at the Architectural Association School and gained the AA Diploma in 1923. He then served in the office of Henry Smart (Messrs. Davis and Emanuel) for a short period before joining his father's practice in the City of London. As previously stated, when his father was appointed chief architect of PCT in 1925, he carried on the practice, designing the Keats Memorial Library at Hampstead, several hotels for Charringtons and other breweries, and private houses. Although he is credited with the Stamford Hill Regent in 1927 and others later, apparently it was not until 1932 that he actually joined the GBPC architects' department to work directly under his father. During World War Two, working for the Ministry of Aircraft Production, he designed and superintended the erection of six large factories and two dispersal camps among other buildings. He died suddenly and peacefully in his sleep at age 41 on 22 October 1944, survived by his father.

Above and facing page: the Regent Stamford Hill. Exterior photograph from 1945, others from opening in 1929. (Demolished.)

around the proscenium but the very wide circle was in this instance supported by slender round columns to the sides of the rear stalls. Bas-relief heads of comedy and tragedy were alternated across the balcony front. The fluted proscenium arch had a curved top while the splay walls were dominated by glass fittings in the design of a cascade above elaborately decorated side exits. To each side, high up, were panels in bas relief showing naked females cavorting with strips of film, the first apparent use of what would become a favourite decorative motif. The name of the sculptor has not emerged, but later work of this kind was attributed to Newbury A. Trent.

Trent at Gaumont

Following the take-over of PCT in February 1929 by Gaumont, W. E. Trent soon became chief cinema architect to the parent company. He would design and supervise projects for the various subsidiary chains while seeing through PCT cinemas in the pipeline. The first of these, the Bournemouth Regent, opened in May 1929. Here Trent worked with local architects Seal and Hardy.

The exceptionally wide frontage on Westover Road had a canopy running the entire length with the cinema name mounted as usual on top in the centre, above the flight of steps leading into the main foyer. A front stalls entrance was reached down a passage alongside the cinema on the left-hand side. Above and behind the canopy there was an arcaded loggia in white terracotta, crowned by a red brick attic storey and a roof of bright red tiles. In the centre of the roof was a copper dome, an unusual external expression of the dome over the auditorium. This was a very dignified exterior, hardly suggestive of a cinema at first sight, with posters confined to the front wall at each end of the loggia. At night, floodlights inside the gallery made the arches stand out in sharp silhouette. In later years, the name Regent and the words Restaurant and Cinema were mounted on the edge of the roof. The rear elevation on Hinton Road had elaborate stone dressings with roundheaded arches on the back wall and over the side passages (with urns mounted above the latter). As also at Hanley and later, PCT/Gaumont cinemas made a good impression wherever their sides were exposed.

The main foyer was very wide, with a floor of marble (black, but covered with white squares), an illuminated double dome over the centre, suspended light fittings to each side, and

Above: the Regent Bournemouth in 1929. (Interior now converted to six-screen Odeon.)

The Regent Ipswich. In view of inner foyer, note on the left the doors to boxes at the rear of the stalls. Photographs show original light fittings (undated but probably circa 1960). (Live theatre in 1995.)

payboxes to either side of steps leading up to both stalls and circle. The restaurant was over the main foyer, with seating for 300 and access to the open air in the gallery above the entrance.

Seating 2,267, the auditorium was treated in the Italian Renaissance style and dominated by a large coffered dome, lit as usual from the rim. The wide proscenium arch with gently curving top had a moulded criss-cross pattern brilliantly lit from the rim. Panels over the front side exits and between pilasters on the side walls of the circle showed painted views of distant landscapes in a faint bow towards the atmospheric school of design. This was the work of Frank Barnes, who became Gaumont's full-time chief artist (and may have been working in a similar capacity for PCT). A further landscape scene filled the safety curtain.

The Bournemouth Regent opened with a silent feature, *Two Lovers*, but was fully equipped for talking pictures as well as for stage shows, a regular feature of which were the Nine Regent Girls.

This debut was followed by the re-opening of the Regent Brighton after a major fire at the stage end. The opportunity was taken to provide a more modern design of proscenium arch, which was no longer curved but straight-edged, while the boxes to each side gave way to pilasters and decorative grillework with a vertical emphasis.

Then came the modest-sized single-floor Swindon Regent, designed by W. Sydney Trent for the Albany Ward division of PCT. In no way comparable to his work at Stamford Hill, this was an exceptionally plain building, externally and internally, the frontage only being completed in 1931 (by W. E. Trent and Ernest F. Tulley). The Albany Ward department seems to have restricted expenditure on most of its new cinemas, and this is the likeliest explanation of why the people of Swindon did not fare better.

Their cinema was in stark contrast to Trent senior's splendid Ipswich Regent, opened a few weeks later. Here the front elevation was in the modern Georgian style, and there was a Georgian treatment to the main entrance hall which had a floor of Roman stone.

In the 1,775 seat auditorium, the ceiling was again dominated by a dome, with the projection room and spot boxes situated at the back, but this dome was of octagonal shape with a small light fitting suspended in the centre. The auditorium was semi-stadium with only a slight overhang of the balcony. At the rear of the stalls floor were fourteen boxes, each seating five and grouped between the three passages into the auditorium. Each box had its own door from the spacious lounge and waiting room underneath the balcony.

A decorative feature of the auditorium was the grillework in a repetitive vertical pattern, illuminated from below, on the splay walls over the side exits, The fluted proscenium frame was, as usual, coloured by concealed lighting from the rim and it had a scalloped inner edge. The panels on the side walls featured large paintings by Frank Barnes.

There were neo-classical touches, as in the festoon cornices and coffered ceiling of the lounge, but the light fittings here and in the auditorium were unmistakably art deco and the horizontal banding of the stalls dado (interrupted by radiators) was also a new touch. In general, the interior of this PCT cinema had a far more modern feel that its predecessors.

Despite its relatively modest number of seats, the cinema had a large stage and a number of dressing rooms. There was a cafe or restaurant over the entrance hall with barrel-vaulted ceiling, old gold carpet, and blue furniture, that seated over 100.

In April 1930, the Gaumont-controlled GTC completed and opened the Edinburgh Rutland Cinema. This had been initiated by a local promoter, F. R. Graham-Yooll, and delayed by difficulties in placing the foundations owing to a railway tunnel beneath. Entered at the screen end, this 2,187-seater designed by T. Bowhill Gibson was internally rather bizarre, combining a ponderous theatrical arrangement with atmospheric touches: landscape paintings on the extensive surround to the proscenium arch and on the side walls at stalls level, plus chunky art deco light fittings.

In July 1930, PCT's impressive new Rink Smethwick opened to the plans of William T. Benslyn, retaining only the name of the former roller skating rink turned cinema that had occupied the same site. The 120 ft. wide curved front elevation was in sandfaced brick with small towers at each end, crowned with glazed cupolas. Portland stone surrounded the five main windows, each capped by a carved peacock with its feathers arranged behind it like a conch. The name of the cinema appeared both high up on the front elevation and, as usual, mounted on the front of the canopy.

The foyer at Smethwick was in Italian Renaissance style displaying scenic paintings by Frank Baines. The auditorium was enormously wide in a semi-stadium style, reducing the ceiling height and providing improved sightlines from the balcony. Projection was from a box built over the back of the balcony and supported by two columns within the auditorium.

Benslyn was an incisive designer who went in for bold, vigorous decorative schemes in his auditoria. Most eye-catching at Smethwick were the sets of twelve alcoves along each upper side wall, the rear four reduced in height by the rise of the balcony, all illuminated from below by lights concealed in large shell fittings. Forward of these alcoves, the vertically ribbed splay walls featured unusual grilles, projecting out like cages (there were no exits below to provide a base). These grilles were of plantlike design, capped by circular rosettes resembling sunflowers. The proscenium opening was unusually wide at 45 ft., with a depth of 30 ft. Concealed lighting at the outer edge of the splay walls, extending across the ceiling, created a break from the rest of the auditorium — in effect, an outer arch echoing the proscenium.

The Rink was followed a month later by the Edinburgh New Victoria, on which W. E. Trent collaborated with J. Jordan. This was the first time the New Victoria name had been used since Preston and may again have been dictated by the more usual Regent name already being used by a cinema, as it happened one at Abbeymount that was already part of the Gaumont empire. Seating just under 2,000, the New Victoria was located well out of the city centre, so that it played films concurrently with one of the other smaller, better located PCT properties.

Externally, the New Victoria was clad in faience with four Doric columns in antis above the entrance while the only large name sign appears to have been on top of the canopy. The foyer was on the plain side with a more modern floor pattern and design of pay box than earlier PCT halls, plus numerous art deco light fittings suspended from the coffered ceiling. A restaurant was located above, with the same fittings but with the standard round-backed chairs and PCT design of red carpet. There was a curved vestibule at the back of the stalls with a further wide expanse of the circuit carpet pattern covered by sets of wicker chairs. This area was flanked by engaged Ionic columns, and had a line of art deco lights suspended from a central band of decorative plasterwork. Steps led up to the doors of twelve boxes placed across the back of the stalls in the same manner as Ipswich. The balcony extended over the rear stalls by a few rows, rather more than at Ipswich, and here the total seating capacity was higher.

Above: the New Victoria Bradford, exterior from 1933, interior from opening in 1930. (Now three-screen Odeon plus Top Rank bingo club.)

Left: two views of the auditorium of the New Victoria Edinburgh on opening in 1930. Note boxes at rear of stalls floor and sky ceiling. (Now converted to five-screen Odeon.)

The extremely wide auditorium was in an original, semi-atmospheric style, creating a restrained, relaxing atmosphere. The ceiling was completely plain to represent the sky while the matching side walls each featured five top-lit niches alternating the muses of art, music and drama (the work of a sculptor called Beattie). An Ionic-style colonnade ran across the back of the circle, interrupted in the centre by the projection portholes on the back wall above the rear entrance. This colonnade extended the side wall treatment of slender, fluted engaged columns between the niches.

There was a wide pedimented proscenium with a coffered frame. The safety curtain displayed a view of classical buildings and mountains. The dado was strongly banded horizontally with a series of art deco light fittings just above it, providing the only direct illumination.

As customary, there was a substantial stage, 32 ft. deep (the proscenium opening was 40 ft.) and five dressing rooms were provided. The organ was the usual Wurlitzer.

In September of that same year, the Bradford New Victoria, designed by local architect William Illingworth, opened its doors. Seating 3,318, this was, at the time, the third largest cinema in the country, beaten only by Green's Playhouse in Glasgow and the Davis' Theatre at Croydon. It remained the largest cinema opened by PCT and could have seated more, but was provided with huge lounges and a large stage.

Built in a prominent central location, the New Victoria had a brick and stone frontage dominated by twin towers which marked the entrances. A large restaurant and lofty ballroom above were attached to the main auditorium with a separate entrance on a side street (there was a further tea lounge in one of the two towers).

The Bradford auditorium reverted to the style of earlier Regents with a huge dome, 70 ft. in diameter, three-cove proscenium arch with concealed illumination, rounded arches along the side walls of the balcony (the columns extending down to the rear stalls floor), and a decorative scheme generally in the Italian Renaissance style. Only the balcony and projection arrangements were markedly different, perhaps unique, the balcony being split into a front section and a much higher rear section with the projection room placed halfway back, taking advantage of the break in height. This effectively gave two separate circles but without any overhang (at the Davis' Theatre, as at several others, the main circle extended over a small circle which had the projection room at the back).

As chief cinema architect to GBPC, W. E. Trent expanded his workload to undertake the replacement of the Palladium at Southport, Merseyside, for GTC, a sister company within the Gaumont organisation. Fire had destroyed the auditorium in March 1929, leaving the front of the building intact. A completely new auditorium, approximately double the width of the old one, was created by taking over the former car park, adding a third more seating for a total of 2,124.

It was decided to retain the colonnaded frontage, dating from 1914. This had to be extended in line with the increased width of the building, and Trent (who was assisted here, as on many other occasions, by Ernest F. Tulley) matched the existing style. (The original architect, George E. Tonge, was still busy designing cinemas but seems never to have been considered for the task: the initial choice of architects, before Trent, was the Liverpool firm of Gray and Evans.)

Here at Southport, Trent returned to the dome, lit from the richly ornamented rim, as the central decorative feature of an otherwise basically flat ceiling. This was a single dome, not as dominant as those in earlier PCT cinemas, with a small pendant light fitting in the centre. It was ringed to the sides and front by a line of large cylinder-shaped light fittings (shorter over the balcony), suspended from a slightly raised, decorated band across the ceiling. The ring of hanging lights was to be repeated by Trent in many subsequent cinemas and was probably inspired by a similar feature at the London New Victoria, planned much earlier but opened two weeks after Southport. The splay walls and proscenium frame alternated horizontal and vertical patterns in a simple, repetitive, modern pattern.

Costing £100,000, the New Palladium (as it was originally called) was transitional between the past Italian Renaissance schemes and the more modern, forward-looking cinemas to come. It had a fully equipped stage to feature cine-variety.

Undoubtedly, the most celebrated cinema associated with PCT was the New Victoria at Victoria, London. This was the last to use the New Victoria name and had been painfully slow to arrive, for reasons recalled in a valuable reminiscence, published in 1972, from Ernest Wamsley Lewis, then a young architect:

"In 1928 I was interviewed by William Evans, managing director of Provincial Cinematograph Theatres, at his office over the New Gallery Cinema in Regent Street. He told me that he had read a report in a newspaper of my return from the U.S. where I had been working on super cinemas; that he had to build one in London where the site had cost £250,000, and that money was lost every day until it was built. He supposed that American practice would suggest that I could get a move on.

"He had received several sketch designs from some of those who considered themselves to be well-known theatre architects, but none of their designs gave a sufficient number of seats to make it a paying proposition. He pointed out that his firm had built a number of cinematograph theatres in the provinces where there had always been irregularly shaped sites, where the big area could be filled with the auditorium and the entrance foyers and ancillary rooms could be planned in the odd spaces.

"On this site there was just one rectangular block for the auditorium and stage entrances, foyers, exits, toilets, offices, etc., and he would like to know what I could do with it. A vaudeville stage was required.

"I went to see the site which was between parallel streets, Vauxhall Bridge Road and Wilton Road, just opposite Victoria station, with a frontage of about 167 feet, with the distance between the streets just over 100 feet. I found hoardings behind which were terraces of houses with basements, front areas, and vaults under the pavements. It occurred to me immediately that the stalls floor should be down in the basement, and that the entrances, foyer, offices and lavatories should go in the triangular section forming the balcony. I then drew a sketch scheme, and thought 3,600 seats could be got into it.

"Mr. Evans seemed pleased with this; we had a long chat about aesthetics and I learnt that on first leaving school he went to Art School. I think he went to the Royal Academy school. He won a prize, but gave it up, because he did not think it would bring in enough money. For my part, I was very happy to find that he did not expect the usual architectural tripe which was usually plastered over the English theatres."

Lewis was then introduced to W. E. Trent, who took over the financial aspects of the project as it went forward. Contracts worth £600,000 for the cinema's construction were finally placed in February 1929, but the cinema did not open until October 1930.

The two matching frontages were very severe in style, with horizontal bands contrasting with the strong vertical emphasis over the two entrances. The walls were faced in slabs of cast Portland stone, except for the ground floor with cast slabs of

The New Victoria London in its year of opening, 1930. Wilton Road entrance. (Now Apollo Victoria theatre.)

grey granite. Vertical signs showing the words "Exit" and "Stage Door" were cast in stone and inset in the walls, as was a tiny figure of Charlie Chaplin. Above each main entrance there were two vertical grilles in pierced stone alongside two upright columns faced in shiny black Swedish granite. Between the top of the columns the name New Victoria was placed. The horizontal bands were picked out in neon at night while the name of the theatre also lit up. The current programme was mounted in a frame over the vertical ribs above the canopy, using letters of the alphabet with stud lighting. The canopy was split level, with a higher section over the entrances, overlapping the lower sections to each side. On the Wilton Road side, two bas-relief panels to each side of the entrance displayed audiences in an amphitheatre watching a film. These were the work of Newbury A. Trent.*

As E. Wamsley Lewis states, the entrance hall was ingeniously placed in the space beneath the balcony. Stairs with mermaid finials led to the rear of the circle past another decorative panel by Newbury A. Trent on the back wall, depicting the spirit of cinema through a nude female surrounded by spiralling strips of film. Stairs on this side of the entrance hall also led down to the stalls while doors on the other side admitted to the centre and front of the circle. As mentioned in the introduction, the front side exits of the circle were at street level, giving an indication of the extraordinary amount of excavation undertaken.

The auditorium was unique. "Imagine a fairy cavern under the sea, or a mermaid's dream of Heaven; something one has never seen or thought of before; huge submarine flowers against the walls that branch up and out and throw mysterious light towards the realms above, and glassy illuminated stalactites hanging from the ceiling; and a proscenium like a slender host of silver trees, and silvered organ pipes that shoot up to the roof; while over the whole the lights change from deep-sea green to the colours of the dawn, and from these to the warm comfort of sunlight." Thus ran the description in the company's house journal, *Gaumont-British News*.

W. E. Trent described it similarly in *The Bioscope* (15 October 1930): "The idea of the interior decorative scheme is a fairy palace under the sea — a place of one's dreams, fantastic, mystical, unlike any place of one's waking experience, built in unusual form, lighted by mysterious and beautiful lights...to produce in the spectator the proper frame of mind for relaxation."

The marine theme was reinforced by decorative features above doorways and around light fittings — mermaids, fish, shells — while a green carpet of wavy design replaced the usual red of PCT halls. The seats were covered in green, blue and grey material, patterned to evoke sea waves. The side walls had columns formed of a series of plaster shells with concealed lighting. The under-balcony ceiling was decorated with a huge shell-like shape with more concealed illumination.

The auditorium ceiling recalled earlier PCT cinemas with its huge dome and rim illumination, plus projection from the back of this space. There was an angular central light fitting and the rim had a valance from which were hung huge silver glass witch balls. Around the outside of the dome were eighteen glass stalactite fittings (more than half of them 12 feet long). Part of the dome could slide open to admit daylight and fresh air. As well as the projection room, the boiler house, heating and ventilation plant were placed on the roof of the building.

The scheme of the auditorium was inspired, as Lewis himself declared, by Hans Poelzig's Grosses Schauspielhause in Berlin, but it was a stunningly original and thorough design for a British cinema.* Although it would have echoes in some later

---

* Newbury Abbot Trent, the younger brother of W. E. Trent, was born on 14 October 1885 at Forest Gate, London. He trained in art at the Royal College of Art and the Royal Academy and as a sculptor under Percy Wells. Besides his work on PCT and Gaumont cinemas, he designed and executed the memorial to King Edward VII at Brighton, and created war memorials at New Barnet, Beckenham, Ilford, Tredegar, Wallsend and Wanstead, as well as the recumbent effigy of Dean Pigon in Bristol Cathedral and, in the centre of London, plaques at 3 St. James's Square (a 1933-34 building by Alfred and David Ospalek) and large plaques of sailors (dated 1938) to each side of the Adelphi main entrance on John Adam Street. His hobby was furniture making. He died on 2 August 1953, aged 67, survived by his wife and two daughters.

* E. Wamsley Lewis did not work on any further Gaumont schemes. The New Victoria became the only cinema ever built to Lewis's designs, although he submitted plans early in 1938 for a 1,450 seat cinema in King Street, Weymouth. I am indebted to Elain Harwood for the information that he designed many houses in the Weymouth area as well as a school in Folkestone, and that, after the Second World War, he became a conservationist, restoring old buildings for the Civic Trust.

cinemas, it was too controversial and offbeat to be a widespread influence. Sidney Bernstein of Granada openly thought it would put audiences off. While the New Victoria did not fulfill expectations as a West End house, its fringe location and booking difficulties seem more to blame than its design.

The New Victoria should perhaps have been called Gaumont, but it never was. The introduction of the Gaumont name came four months later with the beginning of a series of Gaumont Palaces. These are described in Chapter 5.

PCT Organs

Tony Moss notes: "PCT and APPH had standardised on Wurlitzer organs from 1925 onwards, installing Model 'F' organs of 8 ranks — diaphonic diapason, tibia, concert flute, violin, violin celeste, clarinet, vox humana and tuba horn in their principal theatres, such as the Regent Street New Gallery, Glasgow Picture House and Edinburgh New Picture House. Further Model 'F' organs followed in 1927 at the Belfast Classic and the Sheffield Regent, and in 1928 at the Bristol Regent and the Tivoli in London's Strand, the latter replacing a straight Jardine when PCT took over the theatre from MGM.

"After the amalgamation of PCT with GB, further theatres under construction, all Regents, opened at Bournemouth, Hanley and Stamford Hill with 9-rank Wurlitzers, the extra being a krumet, a very fine reed stop. At the end of the year, another Regent opened at Ipswich, but with a smaller Model 'D' (6 ranks). Also in 1929, a 9-ranker was installed in the Brighton Regent, rebuilt after a fire, the new organ replacing a straight model by Hill, Norman and Beard.

"1930 saw a change of name to New Victoria at Edinburgh, Bradford and London. Edinburgh had a 10-rank Wurlitzer (secondhand from Baltimore) and Bradford a 10-ranker with a 3-manual console, not large enough for that giant theatre. But they were the last: the organ at the London New Victoria was a Compton, the first in a GB/PCT theatre, and specially designed by the principal organist, Reginald Foort. However, it was badly placed, above the stage in chambers behind dummy pipes and above a shelf, with the result that the 15 ranks were barely heard, except at the back of the circle! Reginald Foort came up from the Bournemouth Regent to open it, but is reported to have been so disappointed with the result that he hurried off to a giant Christie at the Regal Marble Arch.

"The fourth New Victoria, the renamed Regent Preston, had opened in 1928 with a 2/9 Wurlitzer similar to those at Bournemouth, Hanley, Stamford Hill and Brighton.

"PCT's managing director, Bill Evans, had taken a keen interest in PCT organ policy. He liked the Wurlitzer, particularly the sweet Model 'F' at the New Gallery. He was very fond of Florence de Jong, who in 1928 became the principal organist when Reginald Foort went off to the new Empire Leicester Square (returning the following year to open the Bournemouth Regent). It was Evans who asked Florence's sister, Ena Baga, to join her at the New Gallery after he heard them 'duetting', and the musical director, Ernest Grimshaw, was strongly influenced by Evans.

"Why did Comptons replace Wurlitzers? Was it partly the departure of Bill Evans? Partly the impression made by the large Compton at the Shepherds Bush Pavilion? The influence of Reginald Foort? I suspect it was mainly a matter of cost as all the Wurlitzer pipework was made in the U.S.A. and had to be shipped across, while Compton were beginning to make an impression with their theatre organs in the late Twenties.

"Following the installation of the first Compton at the New Victoria in London, the second was installed at the New Palladium Southport when it re-opened in October 1930. The organ was a 3/10 Compton with a new design of console with straight tops, unique to Gaumont-British, in place of the curves of the French style adopted by PCT."

4: BOARD WARS

Shortly after the take-over of PCT, the affairs of the Gaumont-British Picture Corporation became racked with financial disputes. Although Isidore Ostrer and his brothers always emerged on top, these rows would continue to hamper both the reputation and the expansion of the company throughout the Thirties. Whether Isidore was being devious rather than clever but misunderstood and whether the poor returns to investors were the result of bad management or bad luck are matters that have never been clearly resolved. Certainly, many shareholders felt powerless with the huge majority of the shares being non-voting and control of the company held by the Ostrers who may have been interested in selling or merely leading others on. The jewel in the GBPC crown, the profit centre, was the cinema circuit. The various battles for control were fought with that prize in mind. Therefore, a description of the parent company's difficulties has a place in the narrative.

The Fox Affair
In order to fund all the recent Gaumont acquisitions and find operating capital for such matters as the installation of sound equipment in the cinemas now that talking pictures had come to stay, Isidore Ostrer visited the United States in the spring of 1929 offering to sell an interest in GBPC. He found a willing listener in William Fox, head of the Fox film company. At this time, Fox productions were not doing that well in Britain for lack of showing time, especially on the Gaumont circuit which was returning only $500,000 a year to the London office. This was a serious matter when, by one estimate, twenty-five per cent of the total gross of a Hollywood movie came from this country.

Ostrer was prepared to sell forty-nine per cent of the Metropolis and Bradford Trust, which controlled GBPC, for $20 million. According to William Fox's biographer, Upton Sinclair, the film magnate calculated that he could recover an investment of $20 million in less than five years, thanks to increased revenues of $5 million per year from the showing of his pictures in Gaumont cinemas and the dividends on his shares. Fox's American investment advisors arranged for London banks to lend Fox $8 million. He paid $14 million in cash and $6 million in notes due in six months. It seems that Fox had, or thought he had, acquired control of GBPC, either then or through exercising a future option. In addition, Fox believed that he had arranged for Fox pictures to be given preferential treatment on the Gaumont circuit and shown for about twenty weeks of the year.

The Bromheads had always opposed any American investment in GBPC and were alarmed by the Fox deal and by Fox's claims to have taken over. An extraordinary general meeting of GBPC was held on 18 July 1929 at which resolutions were unanimously passed altering the articles of association to ensure that the company remained under British control. A. C. Bromhead was worried because the Ostrer Bros. were to buy a huge block of unissued shares which they planned to sell as a block and not offer them to the public. In August 1929, Isidore Ostrer shocked the Bromheads by demanding that they resign from all their positions in the Gaumont companies. They held out for two weeks until the resolution preventing foreign control was confirmed and the Ostrers were committed to taking up the new share issue, ensuring the company had sufficient capital to meet forthcoming commitments. Then the two brothers resigned in what the *Kinematograph Weekly* called a "bombshell".

Isidore Ostrer himself took over as chairman of GBPC and Mark Ostrer became vice-chairman. C. M. Woolf and PCT's Will Evans were appointed joint managing directors. Woolf also took the position of deputy chairman. According to Woolf, the Bromheads were removed for sound business reasons: they had sold their shares and were no longer entitled to run the company. However, A. C. Bromhead declared that he had been increasing his own holding in GBPC.

At this time, William Fox was temporarily out of action, having been seriously injured in a car accident on 17 July. Then, in October, the Wall Street crash precipitated the Fox company into a state of financial crisis. After a few months of struggle, Fox lost control of the company. If any option to purchase control of Gaumont did exist, Isidore Ostrer took the view that the arrangement was with Fox himself and did not apply to the Fox company.

By April 1931, it was clear that if the Fox company did not control GBPC, neither did Isidore Ostrer as far as share ownership went. The situation was that the Fox company and the three Ostrer brothers both owned 4,950 voting shares in the Metropolis and Bradford Trust, while the balance of 100 shares was held by an independent chairman, Lord Lee of Fareham, who had been nominated and appointed by both parties. M&BT owned sixty-five per cent of the ordinary share capital of GBPC.

On 22 May 1931, Isidore Ostrer through his solicitors wrote to the British government offering to give to the nation his voting shares in M&BT or, alternatively, create a special voting trust. There was much speculation in government circles over "this curious and intriguing proposal", as it was described in official papers preserved in the Public Record Office. Attempting to analyse his motives, officials came up with four possible answers.

First, that the offer was intended to demonstrate Isidore's patriotism. He wanted GBPC to compare favourably with his principal rival, British International Pictures, which was run without any noticeable foreign involvement by Scotsman John Maxwell. (Ostrer may have felt at a disadvantage as a Jew. A civil service minute surviving in Foreign Office files noted: "The Gaumont-British is, like any other film company, essentially commercial. Indeed, it is known in the trade as Gaumont-Yiddish." Though this is dated 20 September 1934, anti-semitism no doubt coloured the government's viewpoint in this earlier period when controversy over GBPC was at its height.)

The second line of thought was that Ostrer expected the government to refuse his offer. He was seeking some favourable publicity. He said, through his solicitors, that he might not be able to resist a future offer for his shares. He was preparing the way to sell them later at a profit without being blamed if GBPC then went into foreign hands.

The third motive attributed to Ostrer was to relieve the pressure from America to acquire control of GBPC.

Fourthly, Ostrer's offer was intended to make it more difficult for Fox to sue him.

The Government remained highly suspicious of the whole business. It didn't want to become involved in running a film company. It felt that Ostrer could form a special voting trust by himself. In a letter dated 29 July 1931, the President of the Board of Trade rejected the offer. In any case, it would have been difficult for the Government to legislate for an industry in which it had a part share.

The Gaumont deal had not panned out as Fox had intended. The Fox company's annual report, issued in June 1931, declared to "no fewer than 395" of the 1,013 theatres it owned were in Great Britain. The Fox investment in M&BT shares was put at £3,806,185, with further outlays in British property totalling £292,832.

In May 1932, Fox engaged Sir William Jowett, the former Attorney General, to sue Isidore Ostrer for misrepresentation and to recover his investment, which he put at $20 million. It was suggested that the current widespread showing of Fox films in Gaumonts was an attempt to weaken Fox's case. Apparently, Gaumont offered a derisory $3m to take the shares back.

Peace finally came in August when the Fox company agreed to drop its financial claims against GBPC in exchange for a better showing of Fox pictures on the circuit, the appointment of Fox's Sidney R. Kent and a banker to the Gaumont board, plus the production by Gaumont of half the quota films that Fox needed to handle as a distributor. It should be remembered that Gaumont was at this time a profitable company, issuing dividends, and so Fox had a worthwhile investment.

Exit Will Evans

In March 1931, Will Evans, the man who had made such a success of PCT, resigned as joint managing director of GBPC and severed all connection with the company. Like the Bromheads before him, he did not see eye to eye with the Ostrers. C. M. Woolf continued as joint managing director, now sharing the post with Mark Ostrer who had also replaced Isidore as chairman. Isidore had become president of the company. Evans was appointed managing director of the Moss Empires theatre circuit at the instigation of a leading shareholder, Lord Beaverbrook, and was soon heading a group negotiating to buy the Fox interest in GBPC with the support of Lord Beaverbrook and a leading bank. However, these negotiations got nowhere and Evans soon found himself in trouble running Moss Empires, in which the Denman Trust, a GB subsidiary, had a substantial holding. The theatres were doing badly and Evans experimented with turning the two Empires at Cardiff and Southampton into cinemas. The GB nominees on the board opposed in vain his plans to convert twelve of the thirty-two Moss Empire theatres to cinemas because it would create unwelcome competition for Gaumont halls. The Cardiff and Southampton properties continued as cinemas booked by Gaumont.

Without Woolf

In May 1935, another key figure left. Like the Bromheads and Evans before him, the strong-minded C. M. Woolf, deputy chairman and joint managing director of GBPC, had found it difficult to work with the Ostrers, and they had become fed up with him. The official reason for his departure was "ill-health" but the compensation he received revived him enough to set up a new company, General Film Distributors. He soon gained more financial backing from J. Arthur Rank, who was no fan of the Ostrers after the dismal results from Gaumont's distribution of a film he had backed, *Turn of the Tide*.

Production woes

Gaumont's policy had long been to try to make films that would appeal to the American market, spending more on its productions than could be justified without success there. Much of its output had American players: Richard Dix had starred in *The Tunnel* (1935) and Walter Huston had taken the title role in *Rhodes of Africa* (1936). But the American market proved impenetrable.

In the middle of 1936, the company changed its policy on film production, cutting down on budgets and concentrating on pictures that might cover their costs on the domestic market. The Shepherds Bush studios was closed, with production being concentrated at Islington, home of the now fully-owned Gainsborough Pictures. Gaumont's distribution company was shut down and the Ostrers, who had evidently not lost their respect for C. M. Woolf's business acumen, arranged for Gaumont productions to be handled by General Film Distributors.

Mark Ostrer now closely supervised the progress of films,

upsetting Michael Balcon who resigned as head of production. Balcon's right-hand man, Edward Black, took his place.

A later solution to Gaumont's production problems lay in agreements with Fox and MGM by which Gainsborough made films for these companies to distribute, helping them meet their quota obligations. Thus Alfred Hitchcock's *The Lady Vanishes* (1938), the Jessie Matthews comedy *Climbing High* and the Will Hay comedy *Ask a Policeman* (both 1939 releases) were handled by MGM which opened the films at its West End flagship, the Empire Leicester Square, before they went out on Gaumont circuit release. Pictures made by the Gainsborough team for 20th Century-Fox as 20th Century Productions included another Will Hay comedy, *Where's That Fire?* (1939).

The Fox shares and John Maxwell

Without Woolf, the Ostrers were, briefly, in unchallenged control of GBPC. The ordinary shareholders remained none too happy as profits were insufficient for them to receive any dividends. With both production and distribution showing huge losses, the cinema circuit was the only source of profit.

At this time, it seemed that the Ostrers were intent on selling control of GBPC. They were reported to be asking £2.5 million for the key M&BT shares. Fox and MGM — or the Schenck brothers, Joseph and Nick, who controlled the companies — were said to be interested. There was a huge uproar in the press and Parliament over the prospect of Hollywood gaining control. John Maxwell, head of the rival Associated British Picture Corporation, stepped in with an offer that was accepted by the Ostrers in October 1936. ABPC purchased 250,000 non-voting M&BT 'B' shares for £600,000 plus — more importantly — a five-year option to buy the majority of voting shares (at a cost of around £900,000) held by the Ostrers and with them control of GBPC.

However, Maxwell had failed to fully consider that the transfer of the Ostrers' shares required the consent of 20th Century-Fox, the successor to the old Fox company. Now it was Maxwell's turn, after William Fox, to think he had gained control of GBPC and to find himself sadly mistaken. Fox's Sidney Kent blocked the deal because there was widespread concern in Hollywood over the power Maxwell would have if he controlled both the big British circuits and could therefore dictate the terms on which American films would be played. In fact, Fox made the situation more complicated by selling half its voting shares to Metro-Goldwyn-Mayer so that the consent of both companies would be required. While Maxwell still held the option, however, no-one else could bid for the Ostrers' shares.

Maxwell did gain a seat on the board of GBPC and still hoped he could oust the Ostrers to take control. He disputed the amount of profits claimed by GBPC in its most recent accounts, suggesting dividends were being paid only to ensure that the Ostrers held on to control. The Ostrers stood by the figures and Maxwell initiated a law-suit in March 1937, demanding £600,000 in compensation, and was thought to be behind a small group of dissident shareholders headed by C. L. Nordon and W. H. J. Drown.

The management responded by suggesting that Drown's public campaigning was responsible for the huge drop in the value of the company's shares which, in two years, had plunged from a price of 36 shillings to four shillings and ninepence. Nordon complained that even the profits from the cinemas represented a feeble return on the investment involved and in November 1937 he put forward a motion that the latest set of accounts should not be adopted and that the Board of Trade be asked to investigate them. The accounts showed that the cinema chain had made a profit of £561,702 but there had been losses of £766,809 in production and distribution. Reserves that had stood at £2.5 million had been reduced to £85,000.

Eight hundred shareholders packed themselves onto the stalls floor of the New Gallery cinema on Friday 15 October 1937 and heavily defeated the motion on a show of hands after shouting and barracking Nordon and Drown while they were speaking. The pair pointed out the huge profits that Associated British was making and indicated that they would be pleased if John Maxwell were running Gaumont. As a director of Gaumont, Maxwell was present. In fact, most of those in attendance were Gaumont employees who had been recently given small amounts of stock with instructions to attend the meeting and support the directors. Although the leading trade paper, the *Kine Weekly*, did not mention this, even that publication criticised Gaumont for the lack of detail in its accounts.

In fact, holders of over eleven per cent of the shares applied to the Board of Trade in January 1938 for an inquiry — by far the greatest number ever to make such a request. It was suggested that some of the applications had been falsified while one Member of Parliament, speaking in the House, accused Maxwell of instigating the demand as a way of taking over the company.

However, Maxwell came unstuck in his suit for misrepresentation against the Ostrers. He resigned from the board of GBPC on 7 July 1938 when his case finally came to court and was adjourned after the first day's hearing. The action was withdrawn in October 1938. Judgment was entered in favour of the Ostrers, who were also awarded costs.

The Board of Trade seemed to have delayed initiating an investigation while Maxwell's suit was pending. It managed to drag its heels for some further months before appointing an inspector in February 1939. At this time, there were strong rumours of a merger of Gaumont and Odeon, but any detailed negotiations had to wait until the BoT investigations, which could take more than a year, were completed. The Ostrers were as obstructive as possible. In the summer of 1939, the President of the Board of Trade, Oliver Stanley, said in Parliament that the Gaumont directors had been slow to provide books and accounts and described them as "not as helpful to my inspector as I should have expected them to be." In fact, Mark Ostrer was ordered to pay High Court costs after he refused to give evidence to the inspector in the presence of a shorthand writer. His grounds were that the sensitive information he provided would appear in the inspector's report. This would be given to the minority shareholders, providing useful data for John Maxwell, who was, he alleged, the prime mover behind the whole affair.

With the start of World War Two, the inquiry slowed down even further. Its report was still awaited at the end of 1941 when new developments made any conclusions it might put forward largely irrelevant.

5 : THE GAUMONT PALACES (1931-35)

Both the parent company and various companies within the Gaumont empire built new cinemas, replacing older ones or filling in gaps in the spread of the circuit. PCT and its related companies were by far the most active of these, continuing their expansion programme with chief architect W. E. Trent, as previously noted, now in charge of all GBPC's new builds and improvements. For four years, these new cinemas were usually called Gaumont Palaces. Several of them were among the most lavish and striking cinemas ever built in this country. Most were very well equipped for live use with huge stages: they usually included variety acts in their programmes.

1931
Birmingham

The first cinema to be built and opened by the Gaumont British Picture Corporation of its own accord was the Gaumont Palace in Steelhouse Lane (later Colmore Circus), Birmingham.

This was the first time the Gaumont name had been used on a British cinema. The Palace appendage became standard for the series of new cinemas that followed until late in 1935 when it was dropped. The full name was clearly suggested by the huge Gaumont Palace in Paris (which was being totally reconstructed on ultra-modern lines at this time).

The site had been eyed for cinema use in 1929 when George Coles submitted a scheme for a 3,072-seater on behalf of an unidentified client. But, in the event, the Gaumont Palace that opened on 9 February 1931 was designed by local architect William T. Benslyn, who had been responsible for the Rink opened seven months earlier in nearby Smethwick. The main sign giving the name of the cinema was in upper and lower case scroll lettering that was not used on subsequent Gaumont Palaces (the same style of lettering also spelled out the word Cinema on the curving corner of the building). The Gaumont Palace name was also mounted in plain capital letters on top of the canopy, continuing the way that names had been displayed on preceding PCT cinemas. For the first time, the initials "GB" were displayed, on two stone roundels high on the brickwork.

The most prominent feature of the front elevation was a deep recess above canopy level that could be likened to a proscenium opening, recalling some of the PCT Regents. The architrave consisted of Istrian marble (on which the main Gaumont Palace sign was mounted) with an outer rim of black marble. The scrolls at the corners formed a link with, and probably suggested, the scroll lettering of the name.

At the back of the recess was a 35 ft. wide set of convex windows. Usually in PCT and Gaumont houses, the windows above entrances served to admit light to upper floor restaurants but here daylight shone through into the lofty main entrance hall. At the back, this had steps down to the stalls in the centre and flights of stairs to either side that curved inwards and joined outside the balcony foyer. This was very similar to what became the standard approach to foyers in the ABC cinemas of W. R. Glen. Teas and light refreshments were available in the balcony foyer.

In the auditorium, the balcony overlapped the rear stalls by only a few rows yet had nearly as many seats as the lower floor. Figures of 972 and 1,120 respectively were issued (although this gives a total of 2,092 and other sources indicate the seating was 2,034 — varying figures for Gaumont cinemas have been a recurring problem in the compilation of this book).

While the auditorium followed the basic pattern established at the Sheffield Regent and other earlier PCT halls, Benslyn's decorative approach was characteristically incisive and forthright, and here without any classical touches. The space was dominated by a huge, shallow double dome extending to the side walls of the auditorium with concealed lighting from both rims. Within the dome, Benslyn introduced some decorative features inspired by the astronomical societies which had met

Above and right, the Gaumont Palace Birmingham. Exterior from c1945 when an advertising display blocked the central window above the canopy as a war-time safety precaution. Dome and auditorium shots undated but post-war. (Demolished.)

Below, the Gaumont Palace Chester in 1931 (Tony Moss collection). (Gutted for bowling alley, now bingo club.)

in the preceding building on the site, Galton House. In the centre was a representation of the points of a compass, carefully placed to show accurate directions and resembling a sunburst. The flat edge of the inner dome displayed the twelve signs of the Zodiac. Silver stars and coloured planets were to be seen on the ceiling outside the dome.

At the back of the circle, the auditorium was 150 ft. wide. It narrowed to a proscenium opening of 50 ft. The fluted proscenium frame was strongly lit by concealed lighting. As was invariably the case, the lighting here and in the domes could change in colour — in this case between red, blue and "flame", or a blend of colours. The splay walls had overlapping vertical bands curving upwards to meet the rim of the dome. There were five fountain-like fittings mounted on the bands on each wall, casting light upwards.

The original screen could be expanded by movable masking to the full width of the proscenium and a height of 30 ft. This enabled spectacular sequences to be enlarged by a special Magnascope lens on one of the three Kalee projectors.* The projection box and associated rooms were placed at the back of the outer dome and reached by crossing the flat roof. The stage was 20 ft. deep with dressing room space for twenty-five performers. A Compton organ with walnut console on a 6 ft. lift was installed (details of the organ in this and other Gaumont Palaces are given at the end of this chapter). A separate entrance to the front stalls, for use in peak periods, was provided from the side street.

This first Gaumont Palace was rapidly followed by nine more before the end of the year, including two major reconstructions of existing properties and four built on the sites of old cinemas.

Chester
The Chester Gaumont Palace was for PCT and another contribution from William T. Benslyn. Opened in March with nearly 2,000 seats, the cinema had a large stage, 30ft. deep, and nine dressing rooms.

*Three projectors were a feature of key houses, enabling shows to continue if one broke down or, in this case, switch straight over to a larger image. Magnascope facilities were to be found in many large cinemas of this period. The system was still used for newsreel events like the Grand National in the late Forties at the Regal Edmonton (a Gaumont cinema).

There was a mock half-timbered, gabled front elevation to blend in with the local architecture (including the Tudor-style frontage of the Majestic, one of three Gaumont halls already in the town). In further deference to the historic character of the town, the Gaumont Palace name seems to have confined to the top of the canopy with details of films showing restricted to the display frames on the sides of the deep, stepped entrance area below the canopy.

According to contemporary descriptions, the entrance hall offered a change of theme, being in the style of an Italian palace. Three arches on one side led to the circle and to the Tudor-style restaurant behind the bay window of the front elevation. On the other side of the entrance stood a large fireplace between two arched recesses.

The fan-shaped auditorium had a more conventional distribution of seats than at Birmingham, with 800 in the balcony and 1,200 on the stalls floor. The width at the back of the balcony was 142 ft., narrowing to 41 ft. at the proscenium opening. Here the ceiling was dramatically lit but the familiar double dome arrangement was varied by a hexagonal outer frame while in the centre was a diamond-shaped decorative grille that extracted stale air. Two supplementary bowl-shaped light fittings were suspended over the back of the balcony. Projection here was from the back wall, not from the back of the dome.

The proscenium frame was ribbed and cove-lit with variable colours that covered the full range of the spectrum. Two vase-like light fittings were mounted on the fluted splay walls. The side walls of the auditorium were dominated by five large recesses with curving pediments: these were lit from below behind decorative features and contained drapes. The predominant colour in the auditorium seems to have been orange, with a black dado.

Middlesbrough, Guernsey, Barnstaple
The 1,700-seat Middlesbrough Gaumont Palace, opened in April, was not a new building but the result of a nine-month transformation of the Grand Opera House by W. E. Trent and Ernest F. Tulley for the Denman Picture Houses division of GBPC. The exterior was little altered. While the time interval suggests that a modern auditorium was inserted, no photographic record has been located to confirm this. As in Chester, the circuit had three other halls in the town and soon closed one.

The reconstruction of the St. Julian's Theatre at St. Peter Port

The Gaumont Palace Middlesbrough showing a hit film of 1945. (Demolished.)

The Gaumont Palace Barnstaple, in late 1930s or 1940s: name sign on canopy has been shortened to Gaumont. (Now split for films and bingo.)

(on Guernsey in the Channel Islands) was another Trent and Tulley undertaking, this time for Albany Ward/PCT. It led to a completely new auditorium seating a modest 758 that opened in June. Again, the exterior was not modernised while the interior treatment, to judge from a poor photograph, seems to have been very dull and uninspired, one of several Albany Ward economy jobs.

Another Albany Ward/PCT addition was the Gaumont Palace Barnstaple, designed by the W. H. Watkins practice and opened in August as a replacement for the Theatre Royal. This was a modest-sized small-town cinema on a cramped site on a narrow street. It had a towering frontage with fluted pilasters, and a wide but cramped foyer. There was a circle lounge above the entrance but no space for a cafe. The auditorium had a curved, old-fashioned ceiling giving a tunnel-like appearance. It did, however, make elaborate use of concealed illumination through a rectangular three-cove proscenium surround. The interlocked initials "GP" appeared high up in front of this area as the centerpiece of a decorative feature. No stage facilities seem to have been included.

Salisbury

W. E. Trent alone is credited with the now celebrated Gaumont Palace in Salisbury, opened in September as part of the Albany Ward/PCT division. This cinema was attached to the historic Ye Halle of John Halle, which was used as the entrance area. The name Gaumont Palace was mounted in Gothic lettering vertically on each side of the narrow mock-Tudor facade dating from the 1834 restoration of the hall by Pugin. In a stroke of genius it was decided to recreate the Tudor style of the old building for the entire new cinema: inner foyer, restaurant and auditorium. (One imagines that, at the time, this must have seemed arrogant or impudent and been resented by purists: or was the skill with which it was done appreciated from the first?)

The first scheme for a cinema on this site was by architects O'Donoghue and Halfhide, when it was to be called Ye John Halle Cinema and Restaurant, and this was approved by Salisbury Council on 6 May 1929. It is more than possible that the idea of a Tudor scheme originated there. Gaumont already had three cinemas in Salisbury and obviously decided that a take-over was the best way of handling the threat of a large new competitor. By May 1930, W. E. Trent became the sole architect, submitting plans for a slightly enlarged site.

When, as a listed building, the cinema came under threat of demolition in 1986, architectural historian David Atwell summed up its significance: "The auditorium is a classic example of design acknowledging the need to combine and equate sympathy for the adjacent 'real' Tudor building with cheapness and speed of construction. Like most other cinemas of its time, it is essentially no more than a brick box with corrugated asbestos roof, supported on steel trusses. Inside, the box was decked out in the most lavish and exuberant way, making it an uniquely valuable survival in the chronology of cinema design. The chosen style is Tudor Gothic to suit John Halle's hall, and there is rich oak panelling and fibrous plaster ornament in the foyer. The auditorium, originally seating 1,675, has an elaborate fibrous plaster ceiling, grained to imitate heavy oak timbering. There are a number of framed canvas murals on the walls, painted by Frank Barnes to imitate tapestries. The walls themselves are plastered and lined to imitate ashlar stonework. There is much carved oak and ornate fibrous plasterwork elsewhere, carried though with a rare degree of precision, completeness and academic care. The whole effect was to create an interior of rare integrity and unified style."

The Tudor-style decorative scheme extended to the cafe/restaurant with oak chairs and tables, and inglenook fireplaces. In the auditorium, the main curtain and safety curtain displayed period themes, the latter showing a portcullis, armed figures, and the quotation "For Thine Own Especial Safety" attributed to *Hamlet*, Act 4, Scene 3. There were in all nearly forty murals of different sizes on the various walls.

A separate entrance for the front stalls was provided on Catherine Street. As usual, the scheme included a full stage and flytower. After the opening, two older Gaumont properties in Salisbury were soon closed.

Interior views of the Gaumont Palace Salisbury auditorium and cafe in 1931. (Now five-screen Odeon with cafe as one cinema — see Chapter 15.) See front cover for general auditorium view.

Coventry, Plymouth

Seating over 2,500, the Coventry Gaumont Palace was the largest cinema in the Midlands when it opened in October 1931. The architect W. H. Watkins had submitted the first plans for this cinema at the end of 1928, which may explain why in many respects it was a throwback in design to the PCT openings of that period (although it was actually opened by the parent company rather than PCT). Percy Bartlett was the member of the practice primarily responsible for the Coventry scheme which integrated parts of the adjacent Coliseum Theatre.

The front elevation in cream terracotta was very respectable but on the dull side. The large area of windows above canopy level was only slightly recessed, a band of light green tiles forming an architrave. A further splash of colour was provided by the red in the two capitals to columns breaking up the window space, which linked up with red and green decorative "capitals" placed alongside the top corners of the architrave. There was a separate entrance to the front stalls from Whitefriars Street and a huge ballroom, originally part of the Coliseum, which re-opened as the Gaumont Palace Ballroom two months after the cinema. Two cafes were provided — one for the cinema, one for the ballroom.

Internally, this was a most impressive cinema and the most striking achievement of Watkins' practice, excepting perhaps its collaboration on the Forum at Bath. The main foyer with its huge art deco laylight feature led to wide, curved, enclosed corridors across the rear of stalls and balcony with art deco light fittings in the ceilings amid ornate decoration.

The vast auditorium was confidently arranged with neo-classical details including mock-marble pilasters along the side walls. It was dominated by a single huge dome (85 ft. in diameter) which extended through the pitched roof and so was expressed externally, like that at the Regent Bournemouth. The projection box was at the back of the dome which had a flat-based, richly decorated circular light fitting at the centre. Illumination also highlighted the freize above the architrave along the side walls of the balcony. The proscenium arch was gently curved with three coves of concealed lighting that seems to have been graduated in strength, increasing towards the opening.

Watkins' Gaumont Palace at Plymouth, opened a month later, replaced a smaller cinema and was altogether stiff in comparison to the Coventry cinema. The main elevation was over 100ft. wide and rather lumpish in design, mainly in brick with some stonework, as used to face the blunt octagonal tower set back on top of the structure. The theatre name seems to have been displayed only on top of the canopy, although by the early Forties a Gaumont sign was mounted on the side of the tower and by the late Fifties a smallish Gaumont sign had been mounted across the vertical ribs in the brickwork above the entrance.

This cinema had a very wide foyer with much pine panelling and an art deco light fitting awkwardly superimposed on fussy ceiling decoration. A shallow flight of marble stairs led to both

The Gaumont Palace Coventry. 1931 photographs. (Now converted to five-screen Odeon.)

Foyer and auditorium of the Gaumont Palace Plymouth in 1931. (Subdivided auditorium now in nightclub use.)

stalls and circle and had payboxes to each side, where they were frequently found in PCT and Gaumont cinemas of this period. A very wide lounge also combined art deco light fittings with more traditional decoration — although it provided plenty of space, no cafe seems to have ever operated here.

The huge and lofty auditorium was dominated by another massive dome, 65ft. in diameter and lit from the rim. The circular grille in the centre, covering an air extract, was surrounded by a decorative sunburst. The double proscenium frame had the usual cove lighting. Decorative panels over the front side exits and along the walls of the circle above the side passages seem to have been rather ponderous in design. Projection was from the back of the circle rather than from the dome. There was a fully equipped stage with a floor area of over 1,200 sq. ft. and several dressing rooms.

Redditch, Anfield

William T. Benslyn came back on the scene with the modestly sized Gaumont Palace for the small town of Redditch, opened in November through Denman Picture Houses as a replacement for the ancient Public Hall cinema. The vigorous design of the auditorium was unmistakably the work of Benslyn with the side wall and splay wall treatment recalling aspects of the Smethwick Rink and Birmingham Gaumont Palace. The central recess in the ceiling with the usual concealed lighting was not dome-shaped but long and angular, creating a more modern look.

In December, suburban Liverpool gained a Gaumont Palace on the site of the King's Hall in Anfield. This was a 1,600-seater designed for GTC/Gaumont by local architects Gray and Evans who also designed GTC's Alhambra music hall which had opened in Paris three months before. The practice's earlier work included the Rialto, another Liverpool cinema closer to the town centre, also operated by GTC/Gaumont. The exterior is illustrated but photographs of the interior have proved elusive. Although a stage and dressing rooms were included, they do not seem to have been put to any regular use.

1932

This was a year of substantial expansion in the suburbs of the capital, with three Gaumont Palaces in South London and one in West London, while the Albany Ward division was again very active in the West Country, opening three new Gaumont Pal-

Left and above, the Gaumont Palace Redditch in 1931 (from Tony Moss collection). (Now bingo club.)

Below left, the Gaumont Palace Anfield, Liverpool, in 1931.
Below right, 1931 auditorium of the Gaumont Palace Streatham.

Above: extension to Gaumont's Lime Grove (Shepherds Bush) studios under construction in 1931.

Opening of Gaumont Palace Peckham in 1932. Below left and right, exterior and auditorium (Tony Moss collection). (Now heavily altered as Top Rank bingo club.)

aces. In all, nearly 16,000 seats were added to the circuit by the seven cinemas, giving a high per site average of 2,259 seats. Four of the cinemas were among the most outstanding built in Britain. Furthermore, the extended Gaumont studios at Shepherds Bush (for which Nicholas and Dixon-Spain were the architects) opened on 29 June at a cost of £250,000, while a staff sports club was also inaugurated at Norbury, South London.

Peckham, Streatham

The first Gaumont Palace in the London area was opened by PCT in February at Peckham, south of the Thames, with just over 2,000 seats, replacing an old theatre which had been demolished in 1928 to make way for it. It was the only new Gaumont designed by the prominent team of Frank Verity and Sam Beverley, although Verity had handled the reconstruction of the Bristol Palace. Building work at the Peckham site did not properly start until April 1931. Problems with the foundations of the old theatre necessitated revisions in the final plans that eliminated a proper stage. Variety was presented there, but with some difficulty: given the very limited space, it was impossible to store sets, or even the seats and instruments for the band to perform, and all this had to be brought in from outside while the audience was entertained by a special interlude on the Gaumont "Super Organ", a Compton.

The excavation problems may explain why the auditorium was set diagonally across the rectangular site. (This does not seem to correspond to the space occupied by the former theatre as photographs suggest it was set squarely on the site with fly tower across the back.) The building had two matching corners, one the main entrance, the other seemingly only an exit (but possibly once a cafe entrance?). The main entrance was unprepossessing and failed to hide the end of the auditorium and pitched roof. The auditorium was very wide and dominated by another vast, oval-shaped dome with an outer rim that reached the side walls. Projection was from the back of this dome. The proscenium arch consisted of decorated, receding splays. Decorative grillework was placed unusually far back on the side walls, meeting the balcony fascia.

A reminiscence of working at the new cinema as a page boy appears in the book *Enter The Dream-House*. Asked about uniforms, Sid Cove, who was a page boy at the time of opening, recalled that the female uniforms were "red dresses with just little press studs down the front" while male ushers were dressed in blue with gold epaulettes.

Next came the Gaumont Palace at Streatham, also in South London, with around 2,400 seats. The policy here initially was of films alone, without vaudeville acts, although it soon fell in line with other new theatres in offering cine-variety if only because the rival Astoria provided live support. This cinema was designed by Nicholas and Dixon-Spain, whose previous cinema work included the 1924/25 reconstruction of the New Gallery in Regent Street.

The auditorium was uninspired and had acoustic problems: an echo could be heard at the back of the circle from certain positions. There was an open-air terrace for teas over the main entrance. No match for the Astoria or the later Regal Streatham, the Gaumont Palace was, curiously, a replacement scheme by the parent company for a PCT Regent: plans had been approved in April 1929, just two months after Gaumont gained control of the circuit, for a 3,234 seater, designed by W. E. Trent, but progress was suspended around the end of the year for reasons unknown. Its construction had then been linked to that of the new Streatham Hill Theatre, which went ahead on an almost adjacent site.

Hammersmith

The largest new arrival of 1932 was the Gaumont Palace at Hammersmith, West London. Architect Robert Cromie's first plans for this site dated as far back as mid-1925. In January 1929, the Davis family (whose circuit had become part of Gaumont) formed a new company with GBPC to build a huge Davis Theatre in Hammersmith (A. C. and Reginald Bromhead sat on the board as Gaumont representatives). The Davises had just opened Davis' Theatre Croydon with 3,725 seats, designed by Robert Cromie, in which Gaumont had taken a financial interest of around twenty per cent (with the Bromheads again as directors), also booking its films for a while. In July 1930 the Hammersmith scheme was taken over entirely by GBPC and the cinema opened as the Gaumont Palace, seating 3,560 and retaining Cromie's design, which was strikingly similar to that of the earlier Croydon cinema.

John House noted in his article "3000 Plus" (*Picture House*, no. 16, Winter 1990/91): "...the 190 ft. facade in red brick and stone was probably the widest of any cinema in the country and had no less than nine pairs of vestibule entrance doors

Gaumont Palace Hammersmith in 1932. Bas relief murals above entrance doors are just visible. Cafe spreads around well on first floor. (Now concert hall.)

leading to a wide foyer with cafe restaurant above the staircases at either end. The auditorium was a true fan-shape with a balcony no less than 165 ft. wide at the rear wall and laid back over a stalls area converging to a simple proscenium opening of 64 ft. covered by gold tableaux curtains. Above was the decorative organ grille and the ceiling had two lighting coves, the larger of which concealed the ports of the projection room within the lip. Decorative features in the splay walls were reminiscent of the same architect's work in Croydon and Kingston [Regal/ABC] and enhanced by plaster colourings in green, grey, mauve, silver and gold."

The foyers and auditorium were well supplied with light fittings and plasterwork decoration in art deco style. Newbury A. Trent provided the bas relief panels of nude figures above the doorways in the main foyer. The cafe area was situated around the well looking down on the ground floor foyer. The intricate, old-fashioned, traditional design of Gaumont carpet, inherited from PCT, clashed with the modern design of cinemas such as this. The stage was a massive 35 ft. deep and there were twenty dressing rooms.

Exeter

Built for the Albany Ward division of GBPC and the last cinema designed for the circuit by W. H. Watkins, the Exeter Gaumont Palace occupied a most unusual site with only a narrow gateway on the main street leading to a forecourt with the cinema building at the back. The entrance was flanked by two towers, set at an angle and containing exit staircases.

This auditorium was a stadium with a narrower section of seating at the back, raised in tiers and extending over the main foyer. The wider front and centre areas were dominated by a huge dome with a central light fitting and concealed illumination from the rim. Six lantern-like fittings in art deco style were suspended from the ceiling around the dome and over the rear seating in a manner reminiscent of the New Victoria in London and several Trent Gaumont Palaces to come. High on the side walls, lit from below, were a series of frescoes in alcoves, depicting medieval life.

Seating 1,500, this was a most attractive auditorium, with a substantial stage having a floor area of over 1,000 sq. ft. The site was not only set well back from any main road but also a peculiar shape. There were triangular-shaped extensions behind the walls of the front and centre stalls on both sides, con-

Gaumont Palace Exeter in 1932. (Now Top Rank bingo club.)

Gaumont Palace Taunton. Exterior and auditorium (right) in 1932 (both from Tony Moss collection). Below, accurate drawing of auditorium by its architect (from opening programme, courtesy of Sally McGrath) and 1973 photograph by John Fernee. (Now Top Rank bingo club.)

taining a separate front stalls entrance for peak period use, dressing rooms, staff rooms and lavatories.

Taunton

The Taunton Gaumont Palace was one of the most lavish cinemas ever built in a small town. As at Salisbury, the Albany Ward people seem to have abandoned any financial restraints. It dominated its surroundings with a pleasingly handled brick exterior in a Dutch idiom, and looked as though it ought to seat far more than 1,476. Inside, the auditorium was truly palatial. It was indeed a major asset to the town both in its appearance and in its much utilised capacity to handle live shows as well as films. This too little-known building was probably the master work of its architect, William T. Benslyn.

The front elevation on Corporation Street was of local bricks of golden brown colour which harmonised with other buildings in the vicinity. It made a dignified impression with a broad architrave of Ham Hill stone around the central section and a proscenium frame effect around the windows to the restaurant behind the canopy. The name Gaumont Palace could only be found discreetly arranged in neon-lit letters on the balcony in front of the windows. Above the windows, like a crest, appeared a sculpture by Newbury A. Trent in the Ham Hill stone, symbolising love and life caught up in a reel of film. Floodlights were placed on the canopy to accentuate the facade at night. On the side street at the stage end there was a separate stalls entrance protected by a long canopy.

At the front entrance, considerable space was taken up by two sets of double doors before one reached the wide foyer with its deeply coffered ceiling and sculptures by A. Hinton. The restaurant above had decorative friezes of flowers and birds of brilliant plumage, designed and painted by Frank Barnes who, as the Gaumont company's own artist, had a studio base at the Acton Globe cinema. The balcony, which stretched over only a few rows of the rear stalls, had seats in straight rows, angled slightly at the sides, rather than arranged in the usual curve.

The auditorium was decorated with an extraordinary amount of vigorously and intricately patterned plasterwork. In the ceiling, concealed light issued from a rectangular frame interrupted at the corners by roundels from which four glass fittings giving a glittering direct light were suspended. Placed at the centre of the ceiling was a conspicuous elliptical multi-faceted fitting con-

taining coloured lighting and an extract grille. The edge of the ceiling carried a richly decorated band with jewel-like features spaced at intervals of 7ft. 6ins. Over the front exits to each side of the proscenium opening and high along the side walls were featured flower-like light fittings of fibrous plaster, reminiscent of those seen at the Birmingham Gaumont Palace but here more prominent. Between these lighting features were hung sound-absorbing fawn-coloured velours.

There was the usual concealed lighting around the ribbed proscenium cove. The proscenium opening was a wide 50 ft., behind which lay a stage 74 ft. wide and 21 ft. deep, with eight dressing rooms and a music room.

This was the last Gaumont cinema designed by an outside architect. In future, except for schemes that were taken over by the company, all its buildings were the work of company architect W. E. Trent and various assistants.

Wolverhampton

The Wolverhampton Gaumont Palace was another of the year's notable contributions to cinema architecture. In this APPH development replacing an old property at a cost of over £100,000, W. E. Trent, here assisted by Ernest F. Tulley, designed a completely modern cinema in the spirit of the London New Victoria.

The bold horizontal banding of the two elevations of the London cinema was adapted to a single frontage on a sharply curving site, with horizontal bands of stone on brickwork to each side of an imposing entrance area. As at the London New Victoria, there was a higher section of canopy over the entrance, which had a strong perpendicular emphasis, with two black columns and wide bands of light-coloured stonework rising into the air to either side of a recessed central glazed area. The glazing bars here continued the horizontal emphasis, as did the main sign, while the wide panel of changeable letters giving the current attraction ingeniously tied the two sides of the frontage to the centre. The name of the cinema and the film could be seen from a considerable distance away, especially at night when the exterior was spectacularly enticing.

The main foyer was also striking with its two lines of globe light fittings attached to a ribbed structure curving up into the ceiling.

In the auditorium at Wolverhampton, the side walls were unusually plain, faced in fabric with a perpendicular pattern in

Gaumont Palace Wolverhampton. Exterior in 1973 on day of closing as Gaumont (photography by Terry Creswell). See front cover for night exterior in 1932. (Demolished.)

shades of green, fawn and gold. A line of semi-cylindrical lights stretched along the sides, just above the dado with its thin horizontal bands that turned at right angles at the screen end to join the vertical bands to each side of the proscenium arch. These bands, suggestive of columns, were matched by columns and bands painted on the safety curtain. Above the proscenium arch, a ribbed canopy splayed out to a rim from which concealed lighting illuminated the whole proscenium area. The rear stalls were lit by a band of cove lighting that stretched across the auditorium as well as by lights in suspended shallow bowl fittings further back.

The high ceiling of the auditorium had a flat, undecorated central recess lit by concealing lighting from the rim, a highly simplified version of the domes of earlier cinemas. This recess was fringed by a series of pendant lights linked by a decorative band across the ceiling and consisting of three globes suspended one above another, reducing to two and then one across the back of the circle to match the decrease in height. Projection was from the back of the circle.

This theatre was yet another with full stage facilities and a fly tower. The stage was 23 ft. deep and there were eight dressing rooms.

Lewisham

At the Gaumont Palace at Lewisham, Southeast London, W. E. Trent was assisted by James Morrison (Keith P. Roberts, who later designed many important Odeons, was also on the design team). Seating 3,050 and costing more than £150,000, it was the biggest cinema ever designed by Trent and continued the modern look of the Wolverhampton cinema opened three months earlier, but with a far more elaborate auditorium scheme. Sidney Bernstein had originally been partnered with Gaumont British in this site but sold his interest. After Birmingham, Coventry and Streatham, this was the last of the Gaumont Palaces to be opened by GBPC itself rather than through a subsidiary.

The horizontal banding of the front elevation at Lewisham again recalled the London New Victoria, as did the high canopy over the entrance steps. There were eight narrow bands in blue and gold mosaic projecting from a background of cream-coloured terrazzo slabs. A large central window with predominantly horizontal glazing bars admitted light to a restaurant area with 200 places. The name Gaumont Palace was mounted

Gaumont Palace Lewisham in 1932. Note standard "wheel" back chairs in restaurant over main foyer.

Gaumont Palace Lewisham in 1932. Note half-visible mural above circle entrance doors in right centre picture. (Demolished.)

between the top two projecting bands. Smaller, changeable letters with stud lighting were mounted to each side of the central window spelling out the week's attractions.

The main entrance hall, directly below the restaurant, had walls lined with polished macassar wood and walnut around the display cases. Circle patrons paying the higher prices ascended a centrally placed staircase while stalls customers were deflected to either side. Payboxes were situated to either side of the stairs. Decorative panels on subjects such as "The Cinema Show" (above doors to the circle) were the work of an unidentified artist, probably Frank Barnes.

The site at Lewisham was an excellent one that, like Hammersmith, allowed a fan-shaped auditorium which concentrated attention on the proscenium opening. In fact, sightlines from every part of the auditorium were exceptionally good. The main ceiling stepped down towards the screen in five broad, outward-curving ribs that contained concealed lighting. These curves connected with columns supporting seven tall arches on each side wall, beyond which were wide staircases leading from the circle to ground-floor exits and illluminated by art deco pendant light fittings suspended high above, in the shape of superimposed cones, which gave off a rose-coloured light. The illumination was otherwise almost entirely concealed, apart from further cone-shaped fittings over the rear stalls, suspended from deep recesses.

The lower side walls were decorated with thin bands which stepped down toward the screen. Statues sculpted by Newbury A. Trent were mounted on each side in the arches closest to the proscenium opening which was 56 ft. wide by 36 ft. high. As usual, a three-colour system enabled the proscenium area to be flooded with any tone or shade. Curtains were in graduated shades of orange, while the proscenium frame was in silver and blue.

One curiosity of the design was the rotundas occupying the rear corners of the back stalls. These were crush halls (so named for good reason) that held patrons waiting for seats to become available. In most cinemas, crush halls did not eat into space that could have been easily used for further seating. Two more rotundas fulfilled a similar function for the circle, but these were fitted into the void under the stepped circle and so did not impinge on auditorium space.

The cinema was provided with a fly tower and full stage facilities. The stage was 85 ft. wide and 36 ft. deep while a 75 ft.

grid enabled any piece of scenery to be flown. The exterior side and end walls were on public display along roads at the back and, while unavoidably overpowering, were well finished, with tall windows set in the side walls to break up the mass of brickwork. A block of dressing rooms filled the rear apex of the site.

With its location close to a key shopping centre and a major road junction, this was the outstanding cinema for a wide area, challenged (from 1937) by the Woolwich Granada.

1933

This was a quiet year generally for cinema openings. Gaumont inaugurated only two Palaces and the rival ABC circuit also managed a mere two debuts, although Oscar Deutsch did launch his Odeon circuit with five cinemas, mostly modest in size and design.

Cheltenham

In March, the Gaumont Palace Cheltenham, designed by W. E. Trent for the Albany Ward side of GBPC, opened on the site of the Highbury Congregational Chapel which had been acquired in September 1931. Work started on the cinema in March 1932 so it took a year to finish construction, about average for Gaumont.

The main elevation was dominated by a vertical sign flanked, between two sets of horizontal windows, by sculptures in bas relief from Newbury A. Trent depicted dancing figures holding up strips of celluloid, capturing "the spirit and the romance of the film". The sign announced the Gaumont Palace name on each side and jutted up awkwardly into the air above roof level. Vertical bands on the sign made a right angle turn at the base to ingeniously connect with the glazing bars on a wide window belonging to the first floor cafe (which seated 100). With other long windows cut into the corners of the front elevation, a striking, clean-cut streamlined effect was intended but the result was rather too ponderous and plain, stuccoed where tiles would have helped.

Like the exterior, the overall effect of the auditorium was rather coarse compared to Trent's preceding work. The side walls of the auditorium had horizontal bands in alternating textures and colours of warm orange and beige. Every other band was raised and reached the columns of the proscenium arch with the top band turning into a curved canopy over the open-

ing. The intermediate recessed bands stopped short of the proscenium arch, giving way to large fluted scrolls in gold that
curled out from the frame. Slit vents like sunrays occupied the
ceiling near the proscenium. The fire curtain carried an
ornate design painted by Frank Barnes. The proscenium
opening was 45 ft. wide by 30 ft. high, while the stage measured 65ft. wide by 22ft. deep and was equipped for full theatrical use.

The circle front was rather deeply curved and the fascia joined
up with one of the bands across the walls. Lines of pendant
light fittings hung from the sides of the ceiling which rose in
steps to a long central cove. From this was suspended a trough
which cast light upwards. The steps in the ceiling extended to
the back wall of the circle so that this was higher in the centre,
enabling the projection box to be positioned there with sufficient clearance.

Egremont (Wallasey)

It was not until November that the second new theatre of 1933
opened, at Egremont, Wallasey, for the GTC division of GBPC.
This was only built because the chain's cinema on the site was
destroyed by fire. W. E. Trent's scheme adopted a stadium plan
with the stepped rear portion being designated the circle. A
customary overhanging balcony would have been included but
for height restrictions dictated by the "ancient lights" of adjacent buildings. As a result, this Gaumont Palace seated a modest 1,209.

The frontage was unremarkable and not tall enough to
conceal the pitched roof of the auditorium. There were three
panels of carved stone placed above the main windows, designed
by Frank Barnes (not Newbury A. Trent), showing the top half
of naked male and female performers (left and centre panels)
being filmed by an equally naked cameraman (right panel). Even
for a cinema of this size, there was a separate front stalls
entrance on the side street with its own small canopy.

A modest foyer and a wide lounge (underneath the raised
rear section of seating) led to the auditorium which was entered from the sides. Here the decorative work generally led
towards the screen and the walls were mainly covered in tapestry which helped absorb the sound. Light fittings were rather
unusually suspended from poles leaning at an angle from the
side walls. Other light fittings in the ceiling were of linear art
deco design. There were vertical decorative grilles to each side

Gaumont Palace Cheltenham in 1933.
(Now subdivided as five-screen Odeon.)

Gaumont Palace Egremont (Wallasey) in 1933. Note old-fashioned circuit carpet design in centre aisle. (Now subdivided as six-screen Apollo cinema.)

The Hippodrome is Now Closed.

GAUMONT PALACE

A GAUMONT BRITISH THEATRE

MANAGER
T. FITZGIBBON

Telephone
MARINE 6633.

NEW DECORATIONS
NEW FURNISHINGS
NEW LIGHTING
NEW SEATING

OPENS MONDAY
AT 1·30   PERFORMANCE COMMENCES:- 2 P.M.

TOM WALLS
RALPH LYNN
in
"A CUCKOO
IN THE NEST"
with
YVONNE ARNAUD

CLIFFORD MOLLISON
CONSTANCE SHOTTER
in
'MEET MY
SISTER"

A WALT DISNEY
COLOURED SILLY SYMPHONY
THREE LITTLE PIGS

REDUCED MATINEE PRICES up to 3.30 except S.		EVENINGS			Continuous Performance
CIRCLE	1/-		FRONT CIRCLE	1/6	DAILY 2 to 10.30 Doors Open 1.30
STALLS	7d.		CIRCLE	1/4	SUNDAYS 6 to 11 at 1 to an 5 Open 5.30
FRONT STALLS	9d.		STALLS	1/-	Seats May Be Booked for the Sunday Performance
BALCONY	5d.	REDUCED PRICES FOR CHILDREN	FRONT STALLS	1/-	
REDUCED PRICES FOR CHILDREN			BALCONY	6d.	

Gaumont Palace Southend. Re-opening announcement from 1934 (courtesy of Bill Wren). Exterior from 1945. (Demolished.)

of the proscenium. Medallions featuring full-length naked females in bas relief twirling strips of film formed capitals to the vertical bands on either side of the proscenium frame. The stage was a mere 9 ft. deep. This cinema was one of the few new ones not to include an organ, although a chamber was provided.

1934

The Gaumont Palaces this year were on a much larger scale and included four major works by W. E. Trent, all super cinemas seating over 2,000. First, though, came a modest reconstruction.

Southend

Improvements to the Hippodrome Southend resulted in its re-opening with the name of Gaumont Palace. This came into the Gaumont net as one of the GTC live theatres and had operated as a music hall until 1933 when films had been successfully introduced, probably using back projection. It was then decided to smarten up the theatre and adapt it for permanent cinema use.

The front of the building was raised by two floors that incorporated a new projection box, and gained a new canopy and name sign. Photographs of the interior are elusive, apart from the poor image incorporated in the advertisement for the re-opening, but the alterations are firmly recalled by CTA committee member Bill Wren as being very slight. It still retained the look of a theatre, keeping the top gallery with its forms, while the old entrance hall and side passage to the front stalls remained little changed. The upper boxes of the two to each side of the proscenium arch were demolished and replaced with grilles while the lower boxes were filled with banks of flowers. "The original swag house tabs remained for a long time, unused, and silk tabs were used for the screen, billowing out over the stalls when opened too fast. The new feature was the twenty-eight or thirty amber bulbs set in small compartments around the arch over the stalls. Main lighting came from three 'up-turned umbrella' fittings."

Holes were cut in the ceiling at the back of the gallery for projection ports while the box itself was built on the roof, extending to the front of the building. This created a very steep throw and required the screen to be set at an angle facing it, creating a distorted view of the picture from the front stalls. Sightlines generally were bad, but such was the pull of the pro-grammes and the building's central location that it was a money spinner for many years.

Wood Green

The Gaumont Palace at Wood Green was very much the North London equivalent of the Lewisham cinema south of the Thames. It stood on a site that had been originally reserved for another giant Astoria to follow those at Brixton, Finsbury Park, Old Kent Road and Streatham. The site was acquired by the APPH division of GBPC in September 1931 and work began on constructing the cinema in April 1933, with a gala after-noon opening eleven months later. Ernest F. Tulley collaborated with Trent on the scheme.

This Gaumont Palace was a spectacular achievement, all the extensive foyers and lounges as well as the auditorium itself being handled with consistent flair. Only the exterior was disappointing, and this was largely because there was insufficient width to make a great impression. In fact, the parade of shops to either side had been built already, leaving a gap until the cinema operator was settled. The front elevation was appreciably higher than the adjacent property and, in a manner similar to Lewisham, carried the name Gaumont Palace in a slot across the top. There was the usual central set of windows above the canopy while the temporary illuminated letters for the current attraction were mounted above them in the absence of space at each side as at Hammersmith or Lewisham.

The main block of the building was set almost at right angles to the entrance some way back, so that there was a long entrance hall and foyer to be crossed, with the restaurant accommodating 170 diners stretching back at first floor level overhead. The entrance hall had a stepped ceiling and suspended light fittings reminiscent of the main auditorium ceilings in this and other Gaumont Palaces. The foyer had linear floor patterns and ribbed ceiling with flush tube light fittings that led patrons forwards, past three payboxes to a long central staircase to the circle or steps to the stalls. These were marked by backlit signs with modern san serif capitals. The circle and stalls lounges were impressive, with art deco mirrors, further backlit signs over the doors, and other streamlining effects, the only discordant element being the fussy standard circuit carpet design.

The auditorium — seating 2,256 — was long and essentially rectangular, not fan-shaped like Lewisham, with parallel side

The Gaumont Palace Wood Green in 1934. Note GB motif in centre of floor in entrance hall. (Now Top Rank bingo club.)

Gaumont Palace Wood Green in 1934 with its painted safety curtain and view to rear with globe fittings in centre on ceiling. See also auditorium view on first page of this book.

walls until the curve of the ante-proscenium area was reached. The main ceiling rose in steps towards the centre, as at Cheltenham, with the same placing of the projection ports on the back wall, but there was altogether richer decoration at Wood Green. Seven globe-shaped lights were suspended along the centre of the ceiling, each from a ribbed dome-like recess. These were matched along the side walls by more spherical fittings mounted one above another in niches that became taller further forward. The rear stalls were lit by coves extending across the soffit.

The steps in the ceiling, incorporating ventilation grilles at the edges, curved round above the proscenium arch. The side walls, featuring thin horizontal bands interrupted by the niches, leaned inward at the top as they curved round to meet the proscenium arch.

The arch itself was dramatically curved in two semi-circles, the space between — which was wider at the crown — being illuminated by concealed lighting from inner and outer rims. Round-headed, forward-leaning niches, called lunettes, were placed above the side exits to each side of the proscenium opening. These carried the organ grilles and discreet clocks, the latter added almost as an afterthought (clocks were rarely prominent in Gaumont Palaces). The niches were lit with variable colours from the rim and moulded in vertical bands curving at the top.

The whole proscenium area offered a supremely well-balanced blend of curving forms. The semi-circular shape of the proscenium was very unusual and, along with the inward lean of the walls in this area, seems to have been derived from the much publicised 1926-27 scheme at the Titania-Palast, Steglitz-Berlin, designed by Schöffler, Schloenbach and Jacobi. (In other respects, the cinemas were very different.) The Radio City Music Hall had incorporated a series of round arches, but this opened too late (December 1932) to have had any likely influence on Wood Green. The round shape was, of course, not well suited to surround a rectangular screen but the arch at Wood Green was so enormous (54ft. wide and 40ft. high at maximum) that the picture remained well clear of the rim.

The stage was 80ft. wide and 30ft. deep with a fly tower and eight dressing rooms. Initally there were live shows accompanying the films, plus of course an organist for the Compton. On the safety curtain was a striking painting by Frank Barnes showing the signs of the Zodiac. As was also the case at Lewisham, a flat was provided for the manager.

The Gaumont Palace Doncaster in 1934.
(Now three-screen Odeon, heavily modernised.)

Doncaster

The Gaumont Palace at Doncaster opened in early September with 2,020 seats as the largest cinema in South Yorkshire, replacing a smaller picture house which had lasted less than thirteen years. On this corner site W. E. Trent collaborated with his son W. Sydney Trent for PCT. The entrance was set squarely on the main street — Trent senior never went in for corner entrances. The Gaumont Palace name was displayed on two vertical signs as well as above the entrance doors, atop the wall down the side road, and on the back of the fly tower: everyone in Doncaster must have known what it was called and where it was. Again there was the distinctive high canopy over the entrance. Above it were the convex windows of the restaurant and a freize of posed figures in bas relief sculpted by Newbury A. Trent depicting "the progress of a film from its conception, the writing of the scenario, the building of the set, to the shooting and completion." Higher still came a large GB neon sign with a floral border.

The canopy had separate lower extensions to each side of the entrance, one curving down the side street. Another stretch of canopy at the stage end of the side street protected patrons queueing at a front stalls entrance. Considerable effort was made (as at Lewisham) to relieve the plainness of the huge area of brickwork exposed to view.

On the side walls of the entrance hall, murals were to be seen in panels depicting such film stars as Greta Garbo, Ralph Lynn and Laurel & Hardy, while, at the head of the first flight of stairs to the balcony where it divided into further flights left and right, another panel, painted by Frank Barnes, showed a youth on horseback in front of a curved proscenium arch. The doors to the front circle were on the next level directly above this mural.

The wide auditorium narrowed towards the screen with curious vertical undulations of the side walls. Horizontal bands in alternating colours and textures led the eye towards the screen, as did the stepping down of the ceiling in broad curves, culminating in a canopy over the proscenium arch with decorative grillework on the underside. As in many other Gaumont Palaces, the principal colour of the interior decorative scheme was green. Illumination came not from concealed sources but from sets of spaced-out ovoid light fittings suspended from the ceiling in a line close to each side wall. These were supplemented by clusters of similar light fittings hanging from small recessed domes in a line down the centre of the ceiling. There was further decorative grillework in a horizontal band along the side walls above an exceptionally tall dado.

The safety curtain displayed more of Frank Barnes' artistry, showing Doncaster's principal industries, coal mining and the manufacture of railway locomotives, with the local race course in the background. For some unexplained reason, RCA sound was installed here when the usual equipment for Gaumont Palaces was the British Acoustic system marketed by a sister company, G.B. Equipments. While standard Gaumont carpet was still laid in the lounges, the floor of the restaurant was covered in a modern, angular design although the customary old-fashioned round-back chairs were used.

The stage at Doncaster became one of the most used on the circuit and in the Sixties was 67 ft. wide and 54 ft. high behind a proscenium opening 45 ft. wide by 28 ft. high. There were eleven dressing rooms.

Derby

The Gaumont Palace at Derby, with 2,175 seats, opened in the same month as Doncaster. A further collaboration of the Trents, father and son, this was totally different but overall the less interesting of the two, partly because of site problems.

The site was on a rising hillside, so that 8,000 tons of earth had to be removed before work could begin. Even so, the back of the auditorium was many feet higher than street level — patrons had to climb a flight of steps to enter the foyer and then ascend more stairs at the back of the foyer to reach even the stalls. This helps explain the appearance of the frontage with its unusually deep central recess flanked by two large staircase blocks, and also why the top of the auditorium's pitched roof was not too well hidden from view.

The massive frontage in red brick and cream-coloured terracotta carried the cinema's name in a slot at the top, as at Lewisham and Wood Green, on what was in fact the back wall of the auditorium. Decorative freizes carved by Newbury A. Trent and representing active figures of a clown, pantaloon, harlequin and columbine appeared in panels to each side of the name sign, but were too far away to be properly appreciated. The main sign was also hard to see past the tall corner blocks and in later years additional Gaumont signs were mounted over the rounded vertical glazing on the inner front corners of both brick blocks. The canopy was again staggered — high above the en-

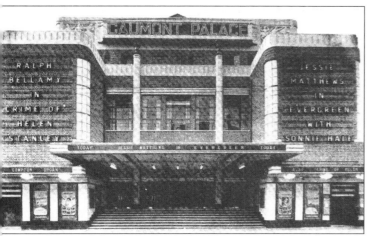

Gaumont Palace Derby. Exterior in 1934 and, above right, safety curtain depicting local industry and original light fittings above front exits (both from Tony Moss collection). Below, foyer and auditorium (suspended light fittings are not original) in 1962. (Subdivided building stands.)

The Gaumont Palace Chadwell Heath, formerly Embassy. Exterior with wartime grime in 1945. Auditorium in 1934 with peacock fan attachment to organ. (Now Top Rank bingo club.)

trance, low to each side. At the back of the central recess were the windows of the café, which here seated 150. On the flanking blocks were mounted letters detailing the current attractions.

In the auditorium at Derby, the side walls featured vertical bands and recesses in contrast to the horizontal emphasis at Doncaster. The three recesses on each side were in fact windows draped with green curtains, with a tall crystal lamp in front. The colour scheme was predominantly a soft warm brown, relieved by touches of green, pink and silver. The walls curved inward slightly at the top edge to meet and "support" the flat ceiling. This had a long, shallow central recess with stepped sides and a richly ornamented rim, while down the centre was suspended a long trough casting light upwards. A line of nine pendant light fittings and the decorative bands and layers in the ceiling all extended forward and then curved round in front of the proscenium arch.

The long central recess created a much modern look than the huge domes of earlier cinemas and directed attention towards the screen. (The dome was far better suited to horseshoe-shaped theatre auditoria, where it could occupy most or all of the ceiling, than to cinemas which usually extended much further back and were rectangular or fan-shaped rather than circular.)

The ribbed proscenium frame (45 ft. wide by 29 ft. high) was swathed in light from behind the rim, as in the earliest Gaumont Palaces. There was a canopy with a boldly-moulded edge over the proscenium that linked up with two round decorative features that carried vertical lighting. The canopy was said to reflect sound but, if it was so useful acoustically, one wonders why it wasn't featured at many other cinemas. Decorative grillework was to be seen above the dado and between the proscenium frame and canopy. As at Doncaster, the safety curtain had a superb design reflecting local industries: a steam locomotive was back by a fan-shaped depiction of industries like coal that were linked to the railways.

Stage dimensions are lacking, but there were fourteen dressing rooms.

Chadwell Heath

A 1934 addition to the circuit was the Embassy at Chadwell Heath, Essex, which opened in May with 1,806 seats and was put up for sale or lease by August. Taken over by Gaumont through PCT, it was immediately renamed the Gaumont Pal-

The Gaumont Palace Chelsea in 1934. Far corner display announces variety acts and organist. (Space redeveloped, old circle in cinema use.)

ace. The deal introduced the architect and part-owner Harry Weston to Gaumont and led to several partnership arrangements.

The cinema itself was altogether too brash to be mistaken for a genuine Gaumont Palace. Its exterior was in cream faience and black; the entrance hall featured a floodlit glass column of crystalline rods; the auditorium had a saucered floor, parallel horizontal fins on the splay walls, extending across decorative panels and grillework, leading towards the proscenium arch which was backlit from the rim; and an organ console with an illuminated fan attachment that opened up at the back like a spread of peacock feathers. The stage was 24 ft. deep and there were four dressing rooms.

Chelsea

A site in Kings Road, Chelsea, on part of which had stood film pioneer William Friese-Greene's studio and laboratory, was first acquired for cinema use by A. E. and David Abrahams and cleared for a scheme from the drawing board of Clifford Aish. Gaumont/PCT made a deal to take over in February 1932 and first lodged new plans in December. However, it took two years before the cinema opened as the Gaumont Palace Chelsea to become the fourth of W. E. Trent's major contributions to the circuit in 1934, working again with Ernest F. Tulley.

The front elevation incorporated a sculpted bas relief head of Friese-Greene by Newbury A. Trent with masks of comedy and tragedy to either side, placed just beneath the main Gaumont Palace sign — once again, too high on the frontage to be properly appreciated. Trent also created two panels to either side of the canopy (and just below it), depicting "The Awakening of Science to the Force of the Elements" and "The Harvesting of the Elements in the Film". The wide centre section of the frontage, faced in Portland stone, was flanked by two slightly lower brick wings on each of which were mounted neon-lit floral GB signs (the most prominent use of the device on any Gaumont) and a frame within which the names of the week's films and their stars were mounted. There was a separate entrance down the side street to the first floor cafe (seating 150).

The wide main foyer was provided with settees and wicker chairs at each end. Globe light fittings in a circular arrangement were suspended from the ceiling. Two payboxes were placed near the back walls, with the stalls entered in the centre between them and the circle reached by staircases to each side. Although the auditorium was carpeted in the traditional design, the staircases, cafe and lounges featured a jazzy pattern of stripes and rectangles.

With 2,502 seats, the wide auditorium had fluted, beige-coloured walls above dado level. There was a striking proscenium arch of unusual, shallow curves, with coloured lighting concealed behind the rims. Filling the 52ft. wide opening, screen curtains with a pattern of vertical folds continued the vertical emphasis of the side walls. The ceiling was treated with a mother of pearl effect and was slightly stepped with decorated edges while the large, flat central recess, reminiscent of the shallow domes of earlier cinemas, was indirectly illuminated from the rim and a suspended central trough.

At intervals, on each side wall, were decorative panels fronted by three globe fitments suspended from the ceiling. One surmounted exits from the front of the circle. Another, alongside the front stalls, was additionally lit from its base while underneath it, above the dado but not specially lit, was a substantial mural of a half-naked female figure. The balcony fascia and front half of the soffit were also furrowed like the side walls.

The Gaumont Palace had a stage 26 ft. deep, 80 ft. wide, and with a height of 70 ft. to the grid. There was a large scene dock, property room, rehearsal room and eight dressing rooms. This was yet another Gaumont thoroughly equipped for live entertainment. As a key cinema, almost in the West End of London, it was provided with three projectors to overcome breakdowns.

Yeovil

A week after Chelsea, the Gaumont Palace at Yeovil, a fifth W. E. Trent scheme of the year (and the third with Ernest F. Tulley), made its debut for the Albany Ward division of GBPC, replacing an old cinema. This was a pleasant but unremarkable building that pales into insignificance compared to Trent's other recent work. One suspects that budget restrictions may have been imposed on new Albany Ward cinemas once more as nothing as lavish as the Gaumont Palaces at Salisbury and Taunton would appear again.

The restrained frontage of the Yeovil cinema was on Georgian lines, with red brickwork and stone dressings. Seating 1,384, the auditorium was of the stadium type with a tiered back section replacing the balcony. An opening description speaks of "the novel treatment of the wide proscenium open-

Auditorium of Gaumont Palace Chelsea in 1934.

Gaumont Palace Yeovil in 1945 (revival of Moon Over Miami*). (Now bingo club.)*

ing, with its shaped overhanging canopy, flanked on each side with a tapering fluted column terminating in an elliptical-shaped lighting bowl; concealed in the backs of the columns are a series of coloured lamps which illuminate the lighting cove and thus throw the columns into bold relief." The walls were covered in tapestry of blue and gold with fluted pilasters at intervals. There is no indication of any stage facilities.

1935
Rochester, Stroud...

Shortly before its debut in April, the Majestic at Rochester, Kent, became attached to the Gaumont circuit. Plans for the cinema had been passed nearly two years beforehand when it had been expected to open by Christmas 1933. The owning company, Southern Proprietary Holdings, involved the co-architect Harry Weston and was joined by two directors representing GBPC. This was the second Weston project to become part of the Gaumont circuit, following the Chadwell Heath Embassy.

Weston was associated with Arthur W. Kenyon in designing this large (2,002 seat) hall which opened as the Majestic and would not change its name until 1950 when it became the Gaumont, by which time it had been fully taken over.

From the snake-skin pattern of its auditorium carpet upwards, in no way did this look like a Gaumont cinema, being generally much less intricate in design but, in some respects, quite innovative. It had a mainly brick, cliff-like frontage that was never its best feature, with a name sign that could be seen from the other side of the Medway. The entrance was wide and draughty with circular windows to the payboxes. There was a dance hall on the first floor.

In the auditorium, the ceiling was dominated by three lighting coves that extended the entire width. The underside of the balcony stepped up to the front in an attempt to avoid the oppressiveness of many back stalls areas. The side walls between balcony front and proscenium opening were decorated with tiles in a modern, repetitive pattern with a horizontal emphasis, illuminated from lights set in thin horizontal bands mounted in front. The arrangement dramatically guided the eye towards the screen. This seems to be the first instance of what became a fairly popular decorative device, copied for the Wrexham Odeon (opened in March 1937) and adapted (in a pattern of individually lit squares rather than strips) for the Oldham Gaumont (as described in Chapter 7). There was no decorative

Majestic Rochester in 1935. Later renamed Gaumont and Odeon. (Demolished.)

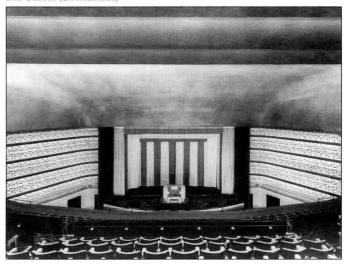

Crowds await guests Jessie Matthews and Sonnie Hale (both contracted to Gaumont) on opening day of the Gaumont Palace Stroud. Below: the auditorium. (Both from Tony Moss collection.) (Building survives.)

proscenium arch at all — just a plain opening. Full stage facilities were not provided. Seats were upholstered in horizontal shaded lines, rose-coloured fading into beige, with grey arm rests.

At Stroud, Gloucestershire, W. E. Trent and W. Sydney Trent designed a small Gaumont Palace for the Albany Ward section of GBPC. This replaced both an earlier hall on the site and another picture house which closed at the time of the August opening. The stone-faced frontage was unremarkable, with the Gaumont name set vertically down one edge of a small tower feature matched by the word Palace round the corner (except that Palace was one letter shorter and left a blank space at the bottom). The GB emblem was also recessed into the stonework. Seating just under one thousand, the auditorium was on stadium lines with a central laylight and other lights mounted at intervals on the side walls against vertically ribbed plasterwork. Between these lights, the walls were covered with graded tones of blue silk arranged in horizontal bands. The main curtains were also designed with horizontal bands of different shades of colour, continuing the pattern.

This was the twenty-eighth and last of the Gaumont Palaces. When the circuit's next new cinema opened a few weeks later in the centre of Manchester, it was named simply Gaumont — although, by any definition, it was a palace.

Gaumont Palace Organs

Tony Moss writes: "The first theatre built purely by Gaumont British, the Gaumont Palace in Birmingham, had a Compton 3.10, but with the top manual (keyboard) only as a coupler and having no stops of its own. The Compton at the Shepherds Bush Pavilion was rebuilt at the same time and modernised with a lift and a new console.

"The Chester Gaumont Palace opened with a similar Compton, but with 8 ranks rather than 10 (economy already?), and the rebuilt Grand Opera House at Middlesbrough had a similar instrument.

"Albany Ward Theatres, a subsidiary of PCT, had no organ policy at all and when the Salisbury Gaumont Palace opened in September 1931, no organ was ordered or installed.

"The Gaumont Palaces at Coventry and Plymouth had 9 and 8-rank Comptons respectively, the difference perhaps dictated by their variation in size. Redditch and Anfield, Liverpool, Gaumont Palaces were both organless, but Peckham's in 1932 had a 10-ranker, the same size at the standard Comptons installed in later Paramount theatres. As Peckham was by Paramount architects Verity and Beverley, it makes one wonder if originally this could have been a scheme for Paramount.

"A month later came Streatham, with another 3/10 model, followed in March by Hammersmith, a different kettle of fish altogether. As a scheme for Davis designed by Robert Cromie, it had many echoes of Davis' Theatre Croydon, not least the organ chambers being sited above the stage and the organ a large, reedy model. At 15 ranks, it was not as big as Croydon's but had a similarity of tone. The console was of the standard Gaumont-British pattern, but with four manuals rather than three.

"The Exeter Gaumont Palace had a small 6-rank Wurlitzer transferred from the former PCT library at Regent Street and, before that, in Les Gobelins restaurant. Also in the West Country, the beautiful Taunton theatre followed in July with understage organ chambers but, alas, no organ — the theatre was built above a stream and dampness was the reason given for no installation.

"For the particularly fine Gaumont Palace at Wolverhampton, the size of organ dropped dramatically to only 6 ranks. But it doubled to 12 for the 3,000 seater at Lewisham. A compromise of 8 ranks was reached for the only organ installed in 1933, at the Cheltenham Gaumont Palace, but a similar instrument to Lewisham's appeared at the magnificent Wood Green theatre in March 1934.

"A major change came in 1934 with the opening of the Gaumont Palaces at Derby, Doncaster and Chelsea, in that Gaumont-British introduced the illuminated console surround to the circuit, in the form of the 'rainbow' design new at the time. The company was perhaps influenced by ABC, Union and Odeon, all of whom were installing illuminated consoles from 1933 onwards. Derby and Doncaster both had 3/10 Comptons, whereas Chelsea was a bit larger at 13 ranks."

Above: Felton Rapley at the console of the Compton at the Gaumont Palace Birmingham. He played there in 1939-40, and was later circuit supervisor and a prolific composer. Below: Con Docherty at the Gaumont Palace Derby. He was resident organist 1934-36. (Both from Tony Moss collection.)

6 : NEW GAUMONTS (1935-39)

Manchester

It was to have been Granada's first venture in the North — a huge new cinema in a prime site in Manchester with a particularly elaborate interior design by Theodore Komisarjevsky lifting it well above the average run of new Granadas, if not quite to the level of Tooting. Back in December 1934, Bernstein Theatres had arranged to buy the Hippodrome from Oswald Stoll and it closed on 2 March 1935 to be almost entirely demolished to form the site for the new super cinema. Jessie Matthews and Sonnie Hale laid a foundation stone on 2 September 1935. Work proceeded and then, to general surprise a month before opening, it was announced that Bernstein Theatres had arranged to sell the cinema when completed to Gaumont-British and that it would open as the Gaumont, not the Granada.

The official announcement given to the Press stated: "The deal has been governed by the fact that the Gaumont-British Picture Corporation have not hitherto possessed a key theatre in Manchester although they have key theatres in every other big city." The cinema was said to have cost £300,000. The price paid by Gaumont was not disclosed. (According to Tony Moss, Gaumont acquired the owning company, Granada Manchester Ltd., and Sidney Bernstein remained a director.)

In fact, the deal is not so surprising when the existing partnership of the two circuits in Denman London Cinemas is taken into account. They were in close contact already and had a year earlier announced joint plans to build new cinemas at Enfield and East Ham. Gaumont certainly did need a city centre outlet as it had stated, and would have no difficulty programming it with its national release, while Granada may have had doubts about its ability to secure top product in competition with local exhibitors.

It has been suggested that the cinema was called Gaumont rather than Gaumont Palace because the shorter name contained the same number of letters as Granada and was easier to substitute at such a late stage. By this time the Palace appellation must have seemed old-fashioned and theatrical, even a handicap in competing with the spread of sleek new Odeons, and perhaps the ease of change at Manchester was a deciding factor. It would certainly have been a squeeze to fit the longer name.

The capable architects of the building were William T. Benslyn and James Morrison (the assistant on the Gaumont Palace Lewisham), who had gone into partnership and previously collaborated on the Granada Bedford. But, as at Bedford, they did not contribute to the interior decoration. The tall frontage was clad in faience and had a rounded corner but was otherwise little suggestive of the Odeon style as the arches, balconies and other details were in Italian Renaissance style to correspond to the interior. There was no large window: the space above the main entrance was filled with an enormous announcement panel, 38 ft. high by 26 ft. wide, with a triple border in blue and green. This accommodated up to twelve rows of 18-inch-high letters which lit up in red, announcing the current attraction. The front really came alive at night, its shape accentuated by three lines of neon tubing on the canopy and two lines on the cornice. The main Gaumont sign above the panel was in red letters 4 ft high outlined in blue neon. In all, about 3,000 ft. of neon tubing was mounted on the exterior of the building. In an odd touch, at the rear corner of the cinema down the side street, the heating and ventilation plant could be viewed through a large window at ground level, and was even floodlit at night.

Inside the building, there was a vast double-height foyer with red non-Gaumont carpet and Granada-style chandeliers backed by a curved grand staircase with gold-fluted walls leading to the balcony foyer, which overlooked the main foyer for its entire length. Each arched recess in the balcony foyer was fitted

The Gaumont Manchester. Exterior from roadshow era, circa 1960. Note the Oxford to right, which became a Rank cinema around this time. Interior from opening in 1935. (Gaumont demolished.)

with a mirror, balanced by mirrors on the opposite wall of the entrance foyer — an adaptation of the hall of mirrors theme at the Granada Tooting and elsewhere.

The auditorium had three arched grilles on each of the side walls, as at standard Granadas, with a railings pattern in dull gold, plus a fourth matching arch containing doorways to the front of the balcony. The ceiling had a coffered design, particularly rich for a Granada with heavily moulded flower decoration, but no main central chandelier — instead, a series of smaller fittings. The proscenium was boldly treated with pilasters that had gold-highlighted Corinthian capitals. As usual with Granadas, the walls to the back of the auditorium were plain, but looking forward — as audiences did — the general effect was sumptuous (it needed to be to compete with the Paramount across the road).

Total seating capacity was a large (but less than colossal) 2,250. The stage was 23 ft. deep with a proscenium opening of 50 ft. Projection was from over the rear balcony with a throw of 132 ft., using Ross machines adapted to Western Electric Wide Range sound equipment. In the basement was a 60 ft. long licensed bar, the longest in the North of England, and a buffet restaurant. The Long Bar was the only part of the cinema treated in a modern style. Refreshments were also available from the balcony foyer.

Worcester

A week after the Manchester opening, the Gaumont Worcester made its debut. This was another Trent-Tulley collaboration, but one of their weakest. Externally, this PCT house was unprepossessing with large areas of plain brickwork in a modern Georgian style plus a base in Portland stone. The design cried out for the Gaumont name to appear centrally on the brickwork above the five sets of windows to the 100-seat restaurant, but instead it was mounted vertically in red neon at an angle at each end of the central section where it would be more visible along the straight length of Foregate Street. Extensions to the frontage provided space for large posters rather than changeable lettering.

Beyond the wide foyer lay an auditorium in semi-stadium style with a separate raised rear section that did overhang the stalls. Seating 1,740, the auditorium was rather plainly decorated with sets of three vertical bands close together at intervals along the side walls and horizontal bands on the splay walls

The Gaumont Worcester in 1935. (Now bingo club.)

leading into the wide proscenium opening. The basic colour scheme was tones of warm beige with sparing use of blue-green and silver. Backlit decorative grillework above the front side exits added some interest. Art deco light fittings were set close to the ceiling, spaced along the sides of the auditorium and clustered in the centre within an ornamented rib leading to the top of the proscenium arch.

The stage was 70 ft. wide and 14 ft. deep, with a height of 45 ft. to the grid. The proscenium opening was 50 ft. wide and 28 ft. high. Contemporary reports note that the male staff were uniformed in brown material with gold braid while the ladies wore light beige with blue trimmings. This contrasts with the colours described for Peckham earlier.

1936

It was more than year before any further Gaumonts opened, but four came along in November. During this gap, main rivals Odeon and ABC inaugurated twenty-eight and twelve new cinemas respectively.

Chippenham

Work started in March to build the Gaumont Chippenham, which succeeded the Palace Theatre elsewhere in the town as another example of upgrading the Albany Ward group of cinemas in the West Country. Here, on a more central site, W. E. Trent combined with his son W. Sydney Trent to produce a pleasant but unremarkable small town cinema seating 1,084. The exterior in Georgian style was far more interesting than Worcester's, incorporating two stone urns mounted on brick columns and panels in carved stone above three large windows, representing the spirit of the cinema (in the centre), light and sound.

As at Worcester, the auditorium was semi-stadium with a low ceiling. The rear section extended over the main foyer which had a rather low, partly sloping ceiling as a result. In the auditorium, horizontal bands of silk on the side walls graduated in colour from light fawn at the top to deep orange at the bottom. The banding idea continued through the decorative grillework of the ante-proscenium area and onto the pattern of the main screen curtains. In the centre of each grille was a vertical tubular-shaped light fitting, while other illumination came from pendant lights along the side walls and an elaborate central trough and laylight fixture in the middle of the plain ceiling.

By this time, all the carpeting was of the more modern circuit design. Chippenham lacked a restaurant and full stage facilities.

Bromley

In contrast to Chippenham, W. E. Trent's work on the Gaumont Bromley for PCT was a major undertaking with a vast and astounding auditorium. The town, with a population of 45,348, had two out-of-date Gaumont cinemas threatened by the impending arrival of a brand-new Odeon. Gaumont decided to compete by building its own new cinema, on a more prominent site with a much larger seating capacity. The Gaumont opened two months after the Odeon, and the two added 4,075 seats, creating what must have been a severe case of over-seating. It would be fascinating to know how well each cinema did but individual admission figures for any cinemas in the Thirties are virtually non-existent. Certainly, one of the two older Gaumont halls soon stopped showing films and went over to live theatre. Of course, catchment areas were wider than the town itself, and the new Gaumont must have drawn some patrons away from the Lewisham cinema to the north.

Externally, the Gaumont was faced in brick with horizontal banding, with a flat-topped corner tower clad in faience tiles. This carried a vertical fin on which the Gaumont name was placed on each side, plus a GB sign at the very top where the fin rose above the tower. Space was allocated to set up changeable lettering for the week's programme on a dark background lower down the tower and in a matching space to the other side of the entrance. There was a short canopy over the entrance and another running down the side of the building to shelter queues with a separate entrance for the front stalls at the far end, used during busy periods. The windows of the cafe-restaurant were, as usual, placed over the entrance, but were slightly recessed and far less prominent than on most of the Gaumont Palaces. (Keith P. Roberts may have been the assistant who designed this exterior as there survives an accurate, detailed drawing signed by him. Roberts would soon be designing some of the best Odeons at Andrew Mather's practice.)

The ground floor foyer had a central stalls entrance and side staircases to the circle with two payboxes set into the wall between them. In the ceiling, six parallel lines of neon tubing ran across the centre of the foyer towards the stalls doors.

The Gaumont Chippenham. Exterior photograph from c1945, interior from opening in 1936. (Now nightclub.)

The Gaumont Bromley in 1936. See also back cover.
(Converted to department store.)

The auditorum resembled the inside of a giant shell in graded mother of pearl tints and was immense, seating a very substantial 2,583. The elliptical proscenium arch was embellished with further shell-like shapes containing lights that changed colour from orange to green or red as the house lights dimmed, while there was a valance with a wave-like edge. Ventilation openings were arranged in triangular patterns beyond the edge of the round proscenium arch which carried concealed lighting in its rim. The light fittings suspended from the ceiling were sponge-shaped. The general shape may have owed something to the Radio City Music Hall, but the handling of the nautical theme was quite original. Mirrors in the lounges reinforced the acquatic motif with etched fish and seaweed shapes. Unusually, the organ lift was placed at the left hand side of the stage rather than in the centre of the orchestra pit.

At Bromley, the Gaumont had an unusual feature recalled by CTA member Malcolm Young. This was an illuminated display box set against the masking on the floor of the stage, underneath the screen, which carried stencil lettering that lit up the words SUNDAY NEXT, MONDAY NEXT or TOMORROW while trailers were being shown. Although recalled from a later period, this was presumably a feature of the cinema when it opened.

Full stage facilities with a fly tower were provided. The cafe-restaurant accommodated a maximum of 150 persons.

Chatham

In the Chatham area, Gaumont bought a controlling interest in a company called Kent Proprietary Holdings which was building the Palace. This was one of a series of deals with similarly named companies, usually associated with architect Harry Weston. However, the Palace was the work of Arthur W. Kenyon, who had collaborated with Weston on the Majestic Rochester. (I am indebted to Elain Harwood for a note that Kenyon was not a regular cinema designer but a noted architect, town planner and journalist best remembered for his housing at Welwyn Garden City and the church of St. Albans, North Harrow, 1938. Tony Moss informs me that the original architect's drawing, held at the local library, shows the building named as the Gaumont Palace.)

Here was a totally modern cinema. Externally, it boasted a flat-topped Dudokian tower in Dutch brick that was a landmark for miles around and carried clocks on each side and the front. The long facade lacked any windows but was relieved by deep niches. A 200 ft. canopy ran the entire length of the building. There was the novelty of a roof garden.

The auditorium was an astonishing break with tradition, as was to some extent acknowledged at the time. In its simplicity, it looks extraordinarily like a Fifties or Sixties design. There was no pronounced proscenium arch, just a deeply curved opening, to each side of which was vertically ribbed plasterwork that resembled the folds of the main curtains. A horizontal grille replaced the orchestra pit and there was no barrier or orchestra rail. A flight of curved steps led up to a narrow platform in front of the curtains for announcements and personal appearances. Downlighters, set in a canopy or hood over the screen opening, illuminated the area. Whether this starkness of design was approved by audiences is not known.

There was a 20 ft. deep stage and seven dressing rooms. A cafe with dance floor was also provided. The Palace was on the Chatham side of Watling Street, which allowed it to open on Sundays, and for several years it drew huge audiences from Gillingham where cinemas were closed. Its tower proved a disadvantage during the war as audiences feared that so prominent a landmark would be a bombing target.

East Ham

On 20 August 1934, Mark Ostrer, C. M. Woolf and Sidney Bernstein had made a joint announcement as the heads of Denman (London) Cinemas that they would build new cinemas at Enfield and East Ham to replace old-fashioned existing properties. The new buildings would have almost identical designs by W. E. Trent. It was said that contracts had been placed with builders and the new Enfield cinema would open in September 1935, to be followed a month later by the East Ham one. In fact, the Enfield redevelopment never took place and it was not until 30 November 1936 that the new Granada East Ham opened with W. E. Trent as the architect and Theodore Komisarjevksy as the interior designer. Actually, property had been acquired behind the Empire East Ham as far back as October 1929 with a view to rebuilding on an enlarged site.

At East Ham, Trent's main elevation offered a slimmer version of the Bromley tower, with the Granada name set on each side of a vertical fin that projected above the flat top. The letters in the Granada name were spaced to line up between horizontal bands that carried neon tubes across the light tiles covering the tower and across the frontage above the main en-

Above left and centre: the Palace Chatham in 1936. (Gutted for bowling alley, now church.)

Modernised frontage of Premier East Ham in 1936. (Now Top Rank bingo club.)

Below: the Granada East Ham in 1936 with Trent exterior and Komisarjevsky interior. (Now bingo club.)

trance. The area above the entrance had a very slight recess but was curiously blank apart from a row of three small windows low down, suggesting that it might have been originally designed to display programme information. The brasher Granada influence could be detected in the three parallel strips of neon that outlined the vertical fin and the roof sign facing east along Barking Road, while the three shop units to the right of the entrance were not a typical Gaumont feature.

Internally, the 2,468-seat cinema was very much a standard Komisarjevsky job in Renaissance style with the usual light fittings, coffered ceiling, and sets of three grilles on the splay walls of the auditorium.

Correspondence in the Sidney Bernstein papers held by the British Film Institute reveal that there was considerable discord over Komisarjevsky's participation. It seems that W. Sydney Trent was to have been responsible for the auditorium scheme and in August 1936 he submitted various designs in "modern" style as arranged with Sidney Bernstein. Then Bernstein decided he wanted a "classical" look but disapproved of several submissions by Trent, who arranged for an outside company, Maples, to come up with some further ideas. However, Bernstein turned to Komisarjevsky, who had been providing Granada interiors to his complete satisfaction, leaving Trent to complain in writing: "You took the matter out of my hands without either explanation or apology". Describing himself "in complete disagreement" with Komisarjevsky's scheme, Trent insisted, "It must be made perfectly clear that I am not responsible for the interior decorations." Bernstein responded with an apologetic letter.

Besides building new cinemas, it should not be overlooked that the Gaumont circuit was steadily improving many old ones. In East Ham, for example, it had the Premier a half mile away which, to help it compete with the new Granada, was given a modern facade with a new vertical sign that curved over the top of the building like that of the Granada.*

*Because of the Premier, the Granada East Ham could not normally play the Gaumont circuit release. One wonders if its construction made economic sense. It was also blocked by nearby ABC cinemas and from July 1938 by the new East Ham Odeon, so it was soon confined to independent programmes. Live shows helped support weak films. It did of course gain Fox CinemaScope pictures in the Fifties during the booking dispute with Rank and also obtained a small proportion of the Rank releases in its final years of cinema operation.

1937

This was the peak year for cinema bows by the major circuits. While Gaumont opened only ten brand-new outlets, ABC managed twenty-two and late-starter Odeon romped ahead with thirty-five. However, one of the new Gaumont halls, the Gaumont State at Kilburn, North London, was the most spectacular addition to the circuit of the entire decade, even though it was a development of a partly owned subsidiary, Gaumont Super Cinemas, and more to the credit of the Hyams Brothers and Major A. J. Gale, who originated it, than to GBPC. It is considered in more detail in the next chapter on Gaumont Super Cinemas, along with Gaumonts at Watford and Oldham that also opened during the year as part of GSS.

In October 1937, the complete reconstructon of the Glasgow Picture House was contemplated, using extra land at the rear. The auditorium would have been reversed to provide seating for around 3,000. The cinema had already been enlarged twice, but this new scheme never went ahead.

Camden Town

The Gaumont Camden Town was another major addition to the circuit in the populous London inner suburbs. Seating 2,742, this was one of the largest Gaumonts, previously exceeded in seating capacity only by the Hammersmith and Lewisham Gaumont Palaces. Built for PCT, it was known for its first few years as the Gaumont Regents Park. Designed by W. E. Trent, W. Sydney Trent and Daniel Mackay, this had a comparatively modest entrance on Parkway, fitted into a line of older buildings with a narrow canopy the width of two shop fronts. The Gaumont's frontage rose slightly higher than its neighbours, with a round-headed projecting fin that displayed the GB sign on top and the Gaumont name lower down alongside a large panel on which the current film show and live acts were announced in changeable lettering. Several bands of neon extended round the cinema name and display box on the left-hand side and underneath.

Inside, Trent and his associates made a thrilling job of the entrance hall with its island paybox, bowl-shaped light fittings susepended from small domes, hardwood panelling on the side walls extending outwards slightly over the ceiling to form troughs of concealed lighting, long central staircase leading to stalls and cafe, and passages to either side leading to the stalls below a curved drop in the ceiling that seemed to sweep one

This page and next: the Gaumont Camden Town (Regent's Park) in 1937. GB monogram may be just visible in design of carpet for lounge. (Stalls area now used for Top Rank bingo club. Upstairs disused in 1995.)

along (see front cover). The slightly curving stalls foyer was another rich area with plaster varnished and grained to resemble white wood panelling and a central band of illumination with ribbed plaster bands to either side. The cafe seems to have been a comparatively dull area but at least the seats were of a modern design to match the carpet. There was a spacious circle lounge with distinctive pendant light fittings and concealed light issuing from the top of two central pillars.

The enormously high auditorium had a ceiling which stepped down in wide curves towards the proscenium in a manner reminiscent of Lewisham. Here the side wall treatment was much simpler with plain columns marking the side gangways and horizontal bands leading the eye towards the proscenium arch. Each step in the ceiling had two pendant light fittings suspended from small dome-shaped recesses. There were large backlit grilles of plain design on the splay walls. Principal colours on the walls and ceiling were pink and beige. The overall effect was much less elaborate than Lewisham but nevertheless the auditorium would inspire an important painting, "Interior, Gaumont Camden Town", by Frank Auerbach.

The cinema was fully equipped for live shows with a 31 ft. deep stage, twelve dressing rooms and the luxury of one bathroom. There were three Gaumont Magnus II projectors with British Acoustic Duosonic sound apparatus. The organ console here emerged from an archway at the side of the stage rather than rising from the pit.

Haymarket
The Gaumont Haymarket was the only cinema in the West End of London ever to carry the circuit name (the next nearest was at Chelsea). The Haymarket theatre involved a complete internal reconstruction of the Capitol for the GTC branch of GBPC, the auditorium being deemed too old-fashioned after just eleven years. The Kit Kat club in the basement area had been acquired and operated by Isidore Ostrer since 1931. Now it became part of the redevelopment, providing the new entrance and allowing the new stalls floor to be set 12 ft. lower. The steeply-raked upper balcony was discarded and the new auditorium seated 1,328, nearly 400 fewer than before. This low capacity would prove to be a handicap in later years. The Compton organ was installed here with the console on a plinth that emerged from the righthand side wall in a similar arrangement to Camden Town.

The Gaumont Haymarket in 1937. (Auditorium replaced.)

Gaumont Dingle (Prince's Park) in 1937. Note rounded corners of screen favoured by the circuit. (Top Rank bingo club in 1995.)

W. E. Trent gave a vertical emphasis to the narrow space with perpendicular bands on the fawn-tinted walls and with sculptures in rim-lit recesses to each side of the proscenium arch showing a female above a male. (A further naked female dancing figure, designed by Sigmund Pillitzer, was etched in glass for a foyer alcove.) There was more indirect lighting in an oval dome just in front of the proscenium arch and from stepped coves in the ceiling. Three projectors were installed to minimise the effect of a breakdown. The 144 seats in the front circle were particularly roomy and luxurious, suitable for the celebrities attending premieres.

Although the entrance now occupied the full width of the frontage onto Haymarket, the main Gaumont sign and an announcement of the current attraction were placed on the rounded northeast corner where the old entrance had been, facing Piccadilly Circus. Floral-edged GB neon signs were placed on the sides of the tower on the same corner. A cafe was included.

Dingle (Princes Park)

The Gaumont at Dingle (Princes Park), a southern district of Liverpool, opened on Easter Monday 1937. Here Daniel Mackay assisted W. E. Trent on a Denman Picture Houses project that replaced the long-shut Picturedrome. In fact, a sign announcing "A Super Cinema Will Be Erected" was prominently placed on the closed cinema in November 1929. However, the circuit had the Beresford and Rivoli nearby, and two others in close proximity: these were deemed sufficient until someone else began planning a new super cinema in the neighbourhood. This apparently spurred Gaumont into action and its cinema opened a little over a month before the new Mayfair on Aigburth Road.

The GB house had a powerful exterior with the slightly convex entrance section clad in wide horizontal bands of grey and cream faience tiles above the canopy and with bright blue faience tiles around the steps and columns below it. Above canopy height, six vertical ribs carrying neon tubing connected two sets of windows in the faience while the Gaumont sign was placed horizontally higher up. To the left of the entrance, the curve continued round a corner with brickwork in differently coloured bands that lined up with the bands in the faience and that concealed the bulk of the auditorium. To the right of the entrance (as faced), the bands of differently coloured brick formed a rectangular block which had a vertical name sign mounted on the slightly rounded corner.

There was a very wide auditorium with seating provided for 1,503 people — about the average size of a new circuit suburban hall. A square recess in the ceiling over the circle had concealed lighting in the rim on three sides, the back giving way to the apertures of the projection room. Other illumination came from a series of bowl-shaped fittings arranged around the recess: these were three-tier across the front, two-tier further back on each side, and single-tier at the rear. Towards the screen, the ceiling stepped down, the steps in line with vertical divisions of the splay walls across horizontal bands. The proscenium arch was emphasised by concealing lighting behind its rim. The dado was much plainer than in most earlier Gaumonts. The overall impression was of a slightly dull and airy auditorium but the broad curve of the circle combined satisfyingly with the inward curve of the splay walls.

The Gaumont was fitted with the new Western Electric Mirrophonic sound equipment and the company's own projectors. The throw was approximately 100 ft. Live show facilities were limited with a stage depth of 15 ft. and four dressing rooms. An organ console was placed in the usual position in the centre of the orchestra well.

Rose Hill (Carshalton)

When the London County Council started building the huge St. Helier housing estate near Wimbledon in South London, there was interest in operating a cinema there as early as 1932. In May 1937, a huge Gaumont was opened, designed by Harry Weston as part of a £100,000 scheme that included sixty flats and twenty-six shops on a V-shaped site along two main roads leading to a busy roundabout. Although originally the cinema entrance seems to have planed for the apex of the site, in the event the Gaumont sat across the rear far end of the development with an entrance on one street only, detached from the shopping parade and the flats with their streamlined balconies (these were designed by R. Jelink-Karl and followed later, opening in 1939/40). Whereas the Odeon circuit had been busy building cinemas in new areas of population, this was the only Gaumont opened in such a location. The circuit's other new cinemas were all based in town centres or well-established suburban locations. In fact, Gaumont already had a cinema in nearby Sutton, but this was one of a batch of projects in which

The Gaumont Rose Hill (Carshalton). Opening photographs from 1937. (Now Top Rank bingo club.)

architect - promoter Harry Weston had interested the company.

Known as the Gaumont Carshalton, later Rose Hill, this had a huge, well-handled front elevation with rounded corners and an advanced design of canopy with curved underside. At the rear was a car park, essential if patrons were to be drawn from a wide area.

The main foyer was eye-catching with circular windows to the payboxes set into the back wall and circular recesses in the ceiling carrying modern light fittings with matching circles in the floor pattern. In the back of a trough running across the foyer above the payboxes and entrance doors was a long freize on canvas depicting jungle foliage in bright colours, the first of several in the building by artist Henri Hague. Another was to be found in the balcony foyer, showing a tropical forest, while there were several on prominent display in the cafe located behind the tall windows of the frontage.

The auditorium was a breathtakingly simple but dramatic composition dominated by huge overlapping ribbed bands with concealed lighting at the front edge, set across the ceiling and sharply angled towards the screen. These bands extended down the side wall which was cut away diagonally.* The general impression was of the ceiling and side walls plunging towards the screen. This was reinforced by the pronounced angle of the completely plain circle front.

It has not been possible to discover the exact seating figure — 1,500 is the usual approximate total given, less than the size of the building suggests — but despite this comparatively modest total and a remote location, the Gaumont had full stage facilities with flytower and eight dressing rooms. The Compton organ was only to be expected.

Sheerness
Another cinema that became part of the Gaumont circuit at a late stage of construction was the Rio at Sheerness in Kent,

*The device of splitting the side walls at an angle was also seen at the Odeon Yeovil, opened a week before the Gaumont and at the Davenport Stockport, opened a month later, where in both instances the huge area of ceiling extending down the side walls was put to dramatic effect for coloured lighting displays using the Holophane moulded contour system. Later cinemas designed in the same way included the Apollo Ardwick, Manchester, opened in August 1938. As far as non-Holophane schemes are concerned, the Odeon North Watford, which opened in November 1937, had a somewhat similar auditorium scheme to the Gaumont Carshalton, but handled with less panache.

designed by George Coles for Kay Bros. with 1,546 seats, cafe and roof garden. Having sold their existing circuit to the early J. Arthur Rank company, General Cinema Finance, the Kays may have been reluctant to run this one on its own, especially as it was the third modern cinema to open in the town which as a consequence was hugely overseated. Gaumont seems to have found the problem insuperable. Within four years, the Rio had been leased to Lou Morris (who then controlled all four cinemas in the town) and it later passed to Essoldo, although it was still owned by Gaumont in 1957.

Finchley
In July, the Gaumont Finchley, North London, opened on an island site at Tally Ho Corner that had been part of land acquired for road improvements. The first scheme for a cinema was advanced around May 1934 by a specially formed company called Dominion (North Finchley) Ltd., which had plans for a 2,500 seater designed by J. Stanley Beard and Bennett. In July that year, the site was acquired at an auction by Gaumont for £30,000. Plans had been drawn up by October but it was nearly three years later that the cinema opened.

The combined work of W. E. Trent, W. Sydney Trent and R. C. H. Golding, this was one of the finest Gaumont cinemas and the last outstanding one to carry W. E. Trent's name. Externally, it had a projecting semi-circular tower at the corner, where there was a main road junction. The recessed top part of the tower carried the cinema name horizontally around the curve. This was a weak spot in the design as the entire name could only been seen from a very limited angle. Further down the tower was a bas-relief carving in Portland stone by Newbury A. Trent, perhaps his most elaborate work, depicting the shooting of a film with lights, camera, director and actors. As with several such freizes on Gaumont frontages, it was impossible to appreciate the detail because the panel was placed so high. Below this came the windows of the restaurant which seated 120 and extended one side above the main entrance. At ground level, there was waiting space for patrons.

Above the canopy and the extended window of the cafe was a wide expanse of brickwork on which the full cinema name should have been mounted: instead it merely carried the initials GB, no longer with the floral surround, although the name Gaumont was placed beneath the canopy in spaced out lettering, directly above the entrance doors. To the right of the en-

The Gaumont Finchley. All from opening in 1937, except for close-up of facade sculpture photographed just prior to demolition of the cinema in 1986-87 by Liz Heasman for the Museum of the Moving Image.

trance, the current attraction was mounted on bars in letters that lit up at night. The programme was also spelled out on the front of the long canopy. A rounded corner at this end complemented the curve of the tower feature and incorporated at ground level a single shopping unit, a rare feature in a Trent scheme.

The auditorium at Finchley was almost as wide at maximum (116 ft.) as it was long (120 ft.), giving excellent sightlines. The circle extended only slightly over the stalls. Total seating was on the large side, at 2,165. The discreet and tasteful decoration was in "the modern Swedish style", using various shades of peach with highlights in gold, silver and green. Nine elaborate light fittings suspended from the ceiling provided the main source of illumination: these had cone stems ending in a metal-bound glass ball with extended arms carrying glass cup fitments. Between the horizontal banding of cornice and dado, the wall decoration had a vertical emphasis, while to each side of the 88ft. wide proscenium was a cluster of thin columns painted silver with gold spirals.

The staff uniforms were mid-blue for men, trimmed with light blue and silver, while the usherettes wore royal blue with beige and silver lace, plus pill-box hats.

This was another of the Gaumonts equipped with organ and full facilities for live shows, with a stage 35 ft. deep and 70 ft. high, plus six large dressing rooms, two chorus rooms, and storage space for sets. The site permitted a substantial car park at the rear and the Gaumont name was spaced out across the back wall of the building in red neon.

Chichester

The Gaumont Chichester was a further contribution to the circuit by architect and promoter Harry Weston, who went into partnership with GBPC through a specially formed subsidiary, the Chichester Regional Theatre Company. The cinema had a curved entrance block in red brick and stone with a cafe at first floor level, and the main foyer, waiting space, and stairs to the cafe occupying the ground floor. The Gaumont name was rather awkwardly spread across the brickwork around the curve, although the result was more readable than at Finchley.

The auditorum seated 1,278 and was built on the stadium principle with a raised rear section of nine rows of seats serving as the balcony. There was an underwater decorative scheme with seaweed, air bubbles and ripples painted on the side walls

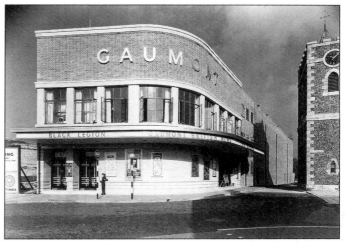

The Gaumont Chichester in 1937. (Courtesy of T. J. Braybon & Son and John Fernee.) (Auditorium demolished, frontage survives in other uses.)

The Picture House Salisbury in 1945 before opening time. (Converted to theatre.)

Gaumont Trowbridge:
1945 exterior and 1937 interior. (Demolished.)

and two floodlit canvas panels, 40ft. long and 6ft. 6ins. high, showing fish and plants. This scheme may have been partially influenced by the original plan (not carried out) to build a swimming pool at the rear of the site. A long cove in the ceiling was illuminated by indirect lighting, while further concealed lights picked out the grillework to either side of the proscenium arch and above its rim.

This pleasant cinema was situated on the edge of the town centre, less well placed than its two rivals. Limited stage facilities were provided, with a stage depth of 20 ft. and some dressing rooms. As at Sheerness, this was a town vastly overseated for its size and the Gaumont was never a big money spinner for the circuit.

Salisbury

Also in 1937, at Salisbury, Gaumont took the unusual step of opening a second new cinema in the same town centre. The Gaumont Palace remained the circuit's main outlet, but it was decided to replace the other cinema, a former chapel called the Picture House, with a modern one on an adjacent site. This was in response to the opening of ABC's Regal, which was bound to damage attendances at the old-fashioned hall.

As at Finchley, W. E. Trent teamed up with W. Sydney Trent and R. C. H. Golding to design the New Picture House. The recessed entrance had an interesting play of curves dominated by two flat-topped circular brick columns to either side. Reached through a long vestibule and foyer, the auditorium was another on stadium lines with a stepped rear section in place of a balcony, while the screen was framed by slender silver columns and three steppings of the ceiling to form a trio of canopies.

Gaumont Magnus projectors with installed with the customary British Acoustic Duosonic sound system.

Trowbridge

Out in the West Country, Albany Ward's Palace at Trowbridge gave way to a new Gaumont, designed by W. E. Trent and W. Sydney Trent to seat 1,200, almost double the number at the old cinema. The Gaumont had a very plain frontage in stone, while the auditorium was pleasant but unremarkable with horizontal bands on the side walls, one neatly blending into the front of the circle, and a vertical grille and illuminated fluting to each side of the proscenium. At first sight, this resembled a weaker effort by W. R. Glen for the ABC circuit.

1938

This year's new Gaumonts totalled a mere five (and the first of these was soon lost) whereas ABC expanded by another twenty-two new cinemas (the same number as in 1937) and Odeon added twenty-seven.

Two projects were abandoned during 1938. In October 1937, W. E. Trent was working on plans for a Gaumont at Chelmsford, Essex, on the Bell Hotel site in Tindel Street. But in July 1938, after preparatory work had been put in hand, the scheme was dropped.

In March 1938, Gaumont had begun reconstruction on the site of the Albert Hall, Sheffield, destroyed by a fire in July 1937 (the last film presentation having the apt title of *Splinters in the Air*). The plans were again by W. E. Trent. The Albert Hall was separated only by the width of a street from the much larger and more modern Regent, the key Gaumont house in the town. It is slightly surprising that Gaumont should have wanted to build a second cinema in Sheffield, although this would not have been totally unprecedented after the two cinemas built in Salisbury. The new Sheffield cinema would probably have been called Gaumont: but would it have become the circuit's leading hall in the town, or a second-string house?

Sheffield City Corporation had long expressed a strong interest in buying the site and in early August work stopped, with all but a few key workmen laid off, as negotiations resumed. Gaumont put a price of £70,000 on the site and later in the month accepted £50,000. (And what vital municipal edifice arose on the site? None. Instead, it became the home of another commercial enterprise, the Cole Bros. store, which presumably bought or leased the site from the Corporation.)

Dorking

Opened in February, the Gaumont Dorking was another scheme in which the circuit went into partnership with a company involving architect Harry Weston — Dorking Regional Theatre Ltd. In this instance, Gaumont and the local company each had three directors, but the Gaumont side had fifty-one per cent and appointed the managing director.

The cinema had a plain brick frontage with rounded corners. The auditorium was slickly designed with wide cove-lit bands across the ceiling that extended down the side, angled to lean towards the screen. The main decorative feature was a trough-lit decorative freize with Egyptian motifs, the work of

GAUMONT

DORKING

A GAUMONT · BRITISH THEATRE

Manager: PETER J. A. PESCHIER   Phone: Dorking 2423

SUNDAY, AUGUST 28th -	SUNDAY, SEPTEMBER 4th -
MADELEINE CARROLL in	IDA LUPINO in
IT'S ALL YOURS (U)	LET'S GET MARRIED (U)
Also - ROSALIND KEITH in	Also - DON TERRY in
FIGHT TO A FINISH (U)	A DANGEROUS ADVENTURE (U)
MONDAY, AUGUST 29th For 3 Days	THURSDAY, SEPT. 1st For 3 Days
RALPH RICHARDSON, EDNA BEST, EDMUND GWENN	DOLORES DEL RIO, GEORGE SANDERS, JUNE LANG
in	in
SOUTH RIDING	INTERNATIONAL SETTLEMENT
— Also — (A)	— Also — (A)
JUNE TRAVIS in	THE TEN-STAR FUN FROLIC:
OVER THE GOAL (U)	MERRY GO ROUND of 1938 (U)
MARCH OF TIME No. 3	

The last advertisement of the Gaumont Dorking in August 1939 before it became the Embassy, and a view of the auditorium on opening. (Demolished.)

Carshalton artist Frank Dickenson: this started in line with the balcony fascia and extended straight across the side walls to terminate behind the proscenium arch. There was also a cafe and a fully equipped stage.

Some undocumented disagreement broke out between the two groups of directors with the result that within a few months the local company arranged to break away from Gaumont and align itself with the Shipman and King circuit, the cinema becoming the Embassy, the name used by S&K for most of its best halls. Although the other Gaumonts associated with Harry Weston remained firmly part of the circuit, this ended the association and may explain why several other announced schemes never came to fruition.

Chepstow

In Chepstow, South Wales, the Albany Ward division of Gaumont operated the Palace Theatre, with a mere 424 seats. When plans were announced for a rival cinema in Beaufort Square (to be called the Beaufort), Gaumont first thought of rebuilding the Palace but then decided that two cinemas would be one too many in a town the size of Chepstow and arranged to take over the Beaufort while it was under construction. W. E. Trent made some alterations to the work of original architect Enoch Williams and it opened in May as the Gaumont, whereupon the Palace was closed. The main entrance was an adaptation of part of the former Beaufort Hotel while the old banqueting hall with round-headed windows on the first floor above the entrance hall was also retained.Seating 825, with a balcony as well as stalls, this was a unremarkable but agreeable addition to the circuit.

Birkenhead

Also opening in May, the Gaumont Birkenhead was a far more significant newcomer. Replacing an older cinema, this GTC property was built in a primarily residential area to the east of the centre, but of course could rely on the booking strength of the circuit to overcome this drawback.

In designing this Gaumont, W. E. Trent worked with Daniel Mackay. The central section of the front elevation was covered in cream faience tiles with blue bands across and a blue base. The main Gaumont sign was placed across the top and the central area was outlined in neon at night. As at Finchley and elsewhere, the name of the cinema also appeared under the canopy,

above the entrance doors, in spaced-out letters, mounted on the front of a trough and backlit. The wings of the front elevation were faced in tiles up to canopy level and in brick above that, with rounded corners where GB signs lit up in neon at the top between two parallel horizontal bands of tiles which carried neon strips extending to the main name sign. Between the main sign and a set of five tall windows above the canopy, three small medallions of clowns' heads, carved in stone in bas relief, were placed across the facade, the centre one looking straight ahead, the other two mounted on the brickwork to each side looking inwards. In an idea borrowed from Grauman's Chinese in Hollywood and previously carried out at the Granada Slough, which opened two months earlier, celebrity hand and footprints were recorded in cement to the right of the entrance — belonging to Nova Pilbeam, who was guest of honour at the opening ceremony.

Seating 1,694, the auditorium was very wide, like the Gaumont Dingle, with a short balcony, and similarly restrained in design. The principal illumination was from six large pendant fittings in the ceiling but these lacked the elegance of those at Finchley or Dingle. The ceiling was essentially flat apart from a recess lit by trough illumination over the centre block of seats at the back of the balcony. Vertical panels in blue and fawn were placed on the side walls, alternately plain and featuring abstract decorations, the latter also repeated in a freize along the side walls and across the proscenium arch. There was a very modest amount of grillework over the front side exits and in the lip above the proscenium arch. The stage was 18 ft. deep and there were seven dressing rooms.

Holloway

The last huge Gaumont to open was at Holloway, North London, on a corner site with an obvious cinema potential that had been explored by various chains. Back in 1930, it had been earmarked for another major Astoria to follow those at Brixton, Streatham, Old Kent Road and nearby Finsbury Park; then Paramount took over the circuit and dropped plans for further Astorias. In October 1936, plans were being drawn up for a Granada cinema on the site by the prominent American architect C. Howard Crane, who designed the Granadas built at Greenwich and Slough. By June 1938, Crane was working for new promoters, Hyams and Gale, and the cinema was to be known as the State, a sister cinema to the Gaumont State

The Gaumont Chepstow in 1938.
(Demolished.)

Right and below: the Gaumont
Birkenhead in 1938.
(Recently roller rink.)

The Gaumont Holloway in 1938. (New postwar auditorium now converted into multi-screen Odeon.)

Kilburn. It was then associated with Gaumont Super Cinemas but Major Gale, the financial brain behind the Hyams brothers, was worried by the likely advent of war and the damage that air raids might inflict on the big inner city cinemas they operated. Gale persuaded the Hyams to reduce their financial commitments by selling their interest in the half-completed Holloway cinema to their partners, so that it opened as a fully-owned Gaumont circuit house, seating just over 3,000.

The Gaumont Holloway had more impact at street level than any other cinema in the country, except perhaps the Odeon Leicester Square. This was in part due to the extreme width and straightness of the Holloway Road and the enhanced visibility of a corner site. But it also reflected an American bravura — its architect was, after all, the man who designed such colossi as the Fox theatres in Detroit and St. Louis. The massive square tower was equipped with broadcasting apparatus at the top (as was the Gaumont State Kilburn) but had no real purpose other than to dramatise the cinema and carry huge Gaumont signs on three sides (or perhaps all four?). It was broadly modern but with decorative panels and inset Corinthian columns that hinted at the design of the theatre within. One side of the auditorium block was on display along the Holloway Road above a line of single-storey shopping units. On this brick wall was mounted changeable lettering describing the week's current attraction on screen and on stage.

Patrons stepped into a magnificently decorated, wonderfully spacious main foyer lit by three massive chandeliers. This led, via a staircase that extended round the side wall, to a cafe on the mezzanine level above the entrance. The cafe seated 220 people and was to be extended in fine weather onto a loggia terrace above the line of shops for alfresco eating overlooking the Holloway Road (it had less traffic then). This, it was claimed, would be the first open-air cafe in a London cinema.

Alternatively, patrons could proceed to an auditorium that belonged more to an American movie cathedral of the Twenties than a modern British cinema in the Thirties. For this, one could thank Phil and Sid Hyams whose enthusiasm for neo-classical decoration had been seen at the Kilburn Gaumont State — but there the effect was much watered down compared to this latest venture in Italian Renaissance style. The proscenium surround was richly moulded in gold with blue highlights and flanked by Corinthian columns. A dome in the ceiling was surrounded by eight light fittings that gave the effect of a gigantic

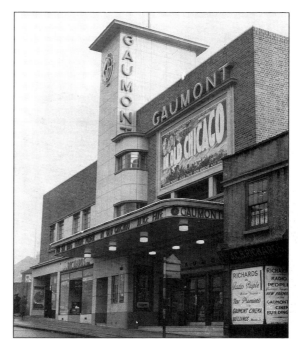

The Gaumont Wednesbury in 1939. (Now bingo club.)

The Coliseum Leeds gained a new auditorium (no photograph available) and took the Gaumont name but retained this exterior. 1945 photograph. (Now concert venue.)

ring of light. The illumination generally was intended to suggest a South of France sunshine amber. The side walls were richly decorated with pilasters, drapes and other fittings, while the seats were upholstered in rose pink. The cinema was so old-fashioned that ten panels of painted landscapes made an appearance on the walls underneath the balcony.

The stage was 54 ft. wide and over 30ft. deep, extending to 50 ft. when a lift rose to cover over the orchestra pit. The Wurlitzer organ was also on a lift that revolved. Besides several dressing rooms, there were two large rehearsal rooms, an organist's private rest room, and a fireproof music library. In the box, there were three Magnus projectors. With a large car park and waiting space to hold nearly an entire change of audience within the building (mostly under the shops), the last of the Gaumont palaces was an altogether special building.

Wednesbury

The Gaumont at Wednesbury in the West Midlands, a £45,000 replacement for the APPH's old Picture House, drew on the combined talents of W. E. Trent, W. Sydney Trent and H. L. Cherry in the architectural department. Externally, the Odeon influence seemed to be soaking in, with a centrally placed flat-topped 60ft. high tower that, together with the rest of the entrance area, was faced with cream faience tiles with some rounded corners and insert bands of thin blue (comparable to the red and green bands on Odeon frontages). There were even two shops to one side of the entrance — common enough with Odeons but exceptional for a Gaumont development.

Here was another wide auditorium, seating 1,594, the side walls carrying three vertical, concave, top-lit wide recesses, with horizontal bands, alternately carrying grillework, by the proscenium arch. Banded plasterwork across the ceiling plunged down behind a lip over the proscenium arch which carried concealed lighting. Principal illumination seems to have been from three chandeliers. There appear to have been minimal stage facilities.

Leeds

In Leeds, W. E. Trent, W. Sydney Trent and Daniel Mackay drew up the plans for reconstructing the interior of the old Coliseum, Cookridge Street. Dating from 1885, this former concert hall and music hall had been a cinema for over thirty years, the largest in Leeds, but the sound was admittedly dia-

The Gaumont Frome in 1939. (Frontage also shown on title page.) (Demolished.)

bolical and ground floor sightlines poor. Gaumont decided to gut the interior to create a completely new auditorium while retaining the exterior with its rather forbidding Gothic frontage with turrets and huge circular window, looking more like a church than a place of light entertainment. The work cost £30,000 and took almost six months. The building was renamed Gaumont when it re-opened in October with 1,750 seats.

The old gallery and supporting pillars had gone. The stalls floor, formerly level, was now raked. A completely new balcony had been inserted on stanchions clear of the old side walls and away from the original foundations. The new side walls had a horizontal emphasis in their decoration, primarily painted in pink, curving inwards toward the screen in a modern, streamlined way familiar from many earlier Gaumonts.

This Gaumont was not as well located as the circuit's other three halls in the centre of Leeds, nor now as large as the best of them (the Majestic), and it seems to have relegated to the second division from the start. It re-opened with the smash hit *Snow White and the Seven Dwarfs* in the fourth week of its run, after it had played the Majestic, Scala and Assembly Rooms.

Former Gaumont Alloa as a bingo club in 1955. (Photograph by John Duddy).

1939

Only two openings took place, both well before the declaration of war in September.

Frome

February brought the debut of the Gaumont at Frome, Somerset, replacing the Palace Theatre. This low-budget Albany Ward venture was credited to W. E. Trent, W. Sydney Trent and H. G. Payne. The front elevation was originally to have been in brick but Gaumont agreed to a local council request and dressed it in artificial stone, with shallow horizontal banding and a plain cornice. This stonework looked dirty and stained from the start. The banding served to separate the individual letters of the Gaumont sign mounted vertically on the side of the central block. The main name sign appeared across the front, outlined in neon.

The low auditorium seated 1,000 through a semi-stadium scheme by which the balcony seating did not overlap the stalls. Disc-shaped layered light fittings in art deco style were suspended from the ceiling while uplighters picked out the vertical decoration on the side walls and the grillework alongside the proscenium arch. The ceiling descended in shallow steps

The Electric Halifax with its modernised entrance dating from 1939. Photograph taken in 1945, showing measuring rods. (Snooker club in recent times.)

near the proscenium while horizontal bands over the grillework extended across the proscenium frame.

Alloa

The last pre-war new Gaumont was the only one ever built in Scotland. With its design credited to W. E. Trent, this was at Alloa, Central Scotland. Another modest small town cinema, it cost around £30,000, seated just over 1,000 people and replaced a smaller, older property. The auditorium was in a tiered or stadium arrangement without a balcony.

Externally, the Gaumont had a wide frontage covered in cream tiles with thin blue bands running horizontally between every second row, and a smaller number of more widely spaced vertical bands, also in blue. Built on a narrow street, the Gaumont Alloa had a modest canopy attached to a slightly recessed central section which was edged with three strips of vertical neon. The Gaumont name was mounted horizontally above a row of small windows in thin curved lettering of a new but unremarkable design. Like Wednesbury, this showed a distinct Odeon influence, being entirely clad in light-colour tiles, but it lacked the rounded corners and general flair of the rival circuit's work.

Halifax

Following the Alloa opening, there was the re-opening in May of the Halifax Electric after substantial modernisation under W. E. Trent. The exterior was refaced with shiney white and black vitrolite and included a small illuminated tower over the foyer with a 30ft. fin carrying the name of the cinema. Other areas had a sand-coloured finish in keeping with the colour of the local stone.

Abandoned schemes

When war broke out, Gaumont had no cinemas under construction, unlike its rivals ABC and Odeon, both of which had several.

There was one still active Gaumont scheme for a huge cinema at Brixton, South London, at 344-364 Brixton Road, on the site of Brixton Greyhound Stadium (or Dog Track). This was acquired by the London County Council for housing, but in July 1936 W. E. Trent had plans passed for a Gaumont cinema, after which the scheme lay dormant. In June 1939, a new Gaumont-associated company called H & B Cinemas was formed by Mark and Maurice Ostrer, George Black of GTC and Arthur Jarratt of PCT, to undertake the project, and Trent's revised plans were submitted the following month. Because of the war, this scheme never started and the site seems to have been transferred to Gaumont Super Cinemas.

And, at the end of July 1939, Gaumont announced its intention to replace the small Picture Theatre at Bellshill, near Motherwell, with a completely new 1,500-seater. This would have been a second new Gaumont for Scotland, close on the heels of Alloa, had it been able to proceed.

Over the years, many other Gaumont schemes had been announced but it is hard to determine which had been dropped, which were dormant, and which might have gone ahead but for Hitler. Harry Weston proposed many more cinemas than ever came to fruition. In 1936 alone, he worked on schemes for Gaumonts at Chertsey in Surrey (a 1,000 seater on London Road to be built by Rowlands Estates), Orpington in Kent, and Wokingham in Berkshire. Then, towards the end of 1937, Gaumont announced plans for a cinema to seat 1,350 at Old London Road, Patcham, a burgeoning suburb of Brighton, to be designed by W. E. Trent.

Another Weston scheme was for Danson Road and East Rochester Way at Bexley, Kent, originally to be called the Bexley and revised to seat 984. As previously surmised, the break-up of Weston and Gaumont's partnership at Dorking may have killed off any further collaborations.

Gaumont Organs

Tony Moss adds: "The organ at the Gaumont Manchester was a superb 14-rank Wurlitzer with 'phantom' grand piano attachment, playable from the organ console which had 4 manuals and Granada-style 'book-end' sides. Ordered by Granada and based on their excellent Wurlitzer at Tooting, this was a fine instrument made all the more powerful by installation in under-stage chambers. It was opened by Stanley Tudor from the Gaumont Palace Hammersmith, who began broadcasting it and continued to do so right up to 1953, apart from a break for war service.

"After Manchester, the Gaumont Worcester opened with a similar organ to Derby and Doncaster (see end of previous chapter), with broadcaster John Bee, who remained until 1950 (from 1942, as manager of the theatre). Worcester had the last of the illuminated consoles, as a year later the magnificent Bromley

Gaumont opened with a 10-rank Compton with the lift placed at the left-hand end of the pit to facilitate the installation of an orchestra lift. The console had a plain wooden end design similar to Compton's standard 'towers' of 1932, but turned through ninety degrees to allow for the small lift. An early visitor was Molly Forbes, only 24 years of age but later to find fame as resident broadcaster from the Warner Leicester Square. Bromley was opened by Terance Casey, who performed the same function a week later at the Palace Chatham, where there was no orchestra pit and a unique style of console arose through an art deco apron to the screen.

"Two interesting installations followed at the Gaumont Camden Town and the Gaumont Haymarket. Camden Town was provided with a magnificent 10-rank Compton with a 4-manual console that slid out from an alcove in the left-hand splay wall onto a dais and then revolved. The Compton at the Gaumont Haymarket dated from 1930 and was one rank smaller than Camden Town. In similar fashion, the console slid out on rails after the theatre was rebuilt, but from the right-hand side of the auditorium. Being post 1935 Comptons, those as Bromley and Camden Town were both equipped with the Compton patent Melotone (electronic) unit, producing beautiful mellifluous tones. In *Bagatelle*, my biography of Ena Baga, organist at Camden Town from 1937 to 1940, she recalls an incident when the apparatus that raised the festoon to allow the console to roll out on its rails failed and Ena had to leap off the console the avoid being knocked out by the falling curtain.

"At the end of March 1937, the Gaumont at Princes Park, Liverpool, opened — but not with a Compton. A 6-rank Wurlitzer of 1927 vintage was transferred from the Liverpool Trocadero and opened by William Whittle.

"The Rose Hill Gaumont had the standard 10-rank Compton, but with an ABC-style illumination. This reversal of the trend in console design may be explained by the fact that this was a scheme by architect Harry Weston, not originated by GB. Or perhaps this was just one in stock, a cancelled ABC order?

"A month later, the superb Gaumont Finchley opened with a very fine Compton of 9 ranks with Melotone, and with a plain console similar to Camden Town, finished in gold. The lift was at the left-hand end of the pit, alongside an orchestra lift."

The last organ opened in a Gaumont cinema was at Holloway and is described at the end of the next chapter on Gaumont Super Cinemas.

Above: Molly Forbes and the organ console of the Gaumont Bromley in 1938. Below: Edward O'Henry at the Gaumont Holloway where he was resident organist from 1942 to its closure in 1944. (Both from Tony Moss collection.)

7 : GAUMONT SUPER CINEMAS

In August 1935, Gaumont Super Cinemas was announced as a partnership with the Hyams brothers and Major Arthur J. Gale.

When Phil and Sid Hyams had sold their earlier circuit to Gaumont in 1928, the brothers had been retained as directors. Major Gale was also on salary as part of the deal under which he had disposed of the chain he ran with C. Repard. It was not long before, as part of a wider cost-cutting exercise, Will Evans sought to terminate their contracts.

Gale's son has recalled: "...it became apparent that Evans could not afford to buy the three of them out and their high salaries were becoming an embarrassment. Dad, whose financial position was very good and who with the Hyams brothers wanted to remain in the business, came up with a proposition that all three would resign and surrender their contracts in exchange for a vacant site owned by Gaumont British in the New Kent Road. This was agreed on condition that they would not open theatres in direct competition with the Gaumont-British Company if they decided to expand."*

And so the trio registered H. & G. Kinemas (H&G) in May 1929 and opened the Elephant and Castle Trocadero on the New Kent Road site in South London in December 1930. Subsequently, the Troxy Stepney was built and opened; a short distance from the Trocadero, the former Super Bermondsey was taken over and re-named the Troc-ette; the Regals at Edmonton and West Norwood were leased from A. E. Abrahams; and at least two sites were acquired, at Whitechapel and Kilburn.

*This quote is taken from the very beginning of extracts from an article by Gale's son filed in the CTA Archive. Regrettably, there is no indication of where or when this article appeared or even of the author's first name, so I have been unable to consult the complete piece, credit the author properly or obtain his formal permission to quote from the article.

At Whitechapel, the Pavilion, a former Jewish playhouse, was taken over for demolition around November 1933 (more than six years after Savoy Cinemas were reported to be converting it into a cinema); the Hyams' regular architect, George Coles, was appointed to draw up plans for a huge super cinema a few weeks later. For Kilburn, Coles had plans prepared by the end of 1935.

Early in 1935, difficulties had arisen. Major Gale's son tells the story: "Dad and the Hyams...became involved in attempting the flotation of H&G as a public company but unfortunately the country was going through one of its economic crises and Government measures had been taken to prevent new issues on the Stock Exchange. As H&G was unable to proceed, it was now faced with the problem of selling out or amalgamation. None of the big companies was prepared to buy because of the high value of H&G with its large theatre properties and because of the national financial situation and so the responsibility rested on Dad's shoulders to find somebody with whom he could amalgamate.

"Mr. Abrahams did not want to become involved in the exhibiting side of the industry but suggested that Dad should approach the Ostrer brothers who had taken over the Gaumont-British Picture Corporation. After long negotiation they were able to agree terms: Gaumont would concurrently book films for both organisations in return for a forty-nine per cent share in the H&G business. This arrangement lasted about a week! The American distribution companies stepped in, objected to the arrangement and said that they were prepared to deal only with a company which had a majority holding and this majority would have to be the Gaumont company. This had to be shown clearly on all documents and publicity.

"It was finally agreed that Gaumont would hold fifty-one per cent of the shares and the name of H&G would be replaced by a new company known as Gaumont Super Cinemas which sat-

The Gaumont Watford in late 1945

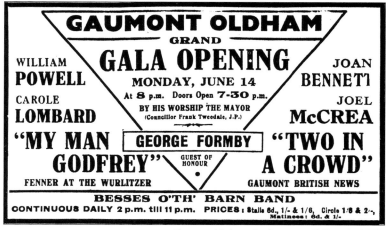

GAUMONT OLDHAM
GRAND
GALA OPENING
MONDAY, JUNE 14
At 8 p.m. Doors Open 7-30 p.m.
BY HIS WORSHIP THE MAYOR
(Councillor Frank Tweedale, J.P.)

WILLIAM **POWELL**
CAROLE **LOMBARD**
"MY MAN GODFREY"
FENNER AT THE WURLITZER

GEORGE FORMBY
GUEST OF HONOUR

JOAN **BENNETT**
JOEL **McCREA**
"TWO IN A CROWD"
GAUMONT BRITISH NEWS

BESSES O'TH' BARN BAND
CONTINUOUS DAILY 2 p.m. till 11 p.m.   PRICES: Stalls 6d., 1/- & 1/6.   Circle 1/6 & 2/-.
Matinees: 6d. & 1/-

Above and below: the Gaumont Oldham in 1937.

isfied the American distributors as it met all their requirements. In exchange for the concessions which H&G had been compelled to make, Gaumont agreed to transfer two of their large theatres at Lewisham and Hammersmith...to the new Gaumont Super Cinemas outfit. The new company operated independently of GBPC as it retained all its own personnel and departments; the only influence was in the film booking rights."

Gaumont's involvement in the new set-up, said to amount to £700,000, was channelled through the APPH subsidiary. And so the H&G properties became part of Gaumont Super Cinemas when the new company commenced operation in October 1935. Another Hyams brother, Mick, was theatre controller. (The Hyams also owned through separate companies the Metropole and Biograph cinemas at Victoria, on the fringe of the West End. These were never associated with Gaumont.)

Besides developing the Kilburn site into the largest and most spectacular of all the cinemas associated with the Gaumont circuit, GSS opened two other Gaumonts.

Watford

The first was the Gaumont at Watford in May 1937. This was a scheme taken over from Lou Morris, who had commissioned the architect, J. Owen Bond of Norwich. Bond provided an exceptionally dull frontage, perhaps because it had to be reduced in height to conform with adjacent buildings. There was a restaurant over the entrance. The auditorium which, according to the plans, seated exactly 2,000, was attractively simple in design, the highlight being the three sets of cove lighting around the proscenium arch and the honeycomb-like pattern of circular openings (outlets for the organ chamber and ventilation) on the side walls nearest the screen (the later Odeon Camberwell used the same idea).

Oldham

The next Gaumont to come from GSS was at Oldham, a reconstruction of an old theatre. It would be interesting to know how Hyams and Gale came to wander so far from their London base. Externally, only the corner entrance area was modernised with faience tiles and a plain dome from which strips of vertical neon descended to the canopy. The Gaumont name was mounted vertically in the centre.

The auditorium was entirely reconstructed with the main decorative feature being huge panels of grillework in repetitive squares, individually illuminated by concealed lights in front. The same side wall treatment had also appeared at the Embassy Chesham, Buckinghamshire, earlier in the year and would be used at the Embassy Esher, Surrey, and Embassy Waltham Cross, Hertfordshire, before the end of 1937.

Kilburn

The Whitechapel scheme never happened. The third and last new arrival was the enormous Gaumont State at Kilburn, North London. The words Gaumont State could be seen for miles around from the top of the 120 ft. skyscraper-style tower (which contained a radio broadcasting studio in the base). Built at a cost of £320,000, this was the third largest cinema in Great Britain and the largest in England, with 4,004 seats. It was said that huge holding areas or crush halls could accommodate another 4,000 patrons waiting to enter the auditorium. The restaurant had 400 seats. The architect of all this splendour was George Coles, who designed all the major cinemas initiated by the Hyams, including the Commercial Road (Stepney) Troxy, Elephant and Castle Trocadero and Stratford Broadway.

Coles' plans for the Gaumont State dated December 1935 show that it was then to be another Troxy. The State name was no doubt adopted to recall the Empire State building in New York and to suit the skyscraper tower, although it was already in British cinema use as at the State Shettleston, Glasgow. A modern looking secondary entrance on Willesden Lane would have been good enough in itself for most new cinemas. The impression of Thirties modernity continued in the outer lobby of the main entrance, with walls around the radiators and columns between the inner doors covered in green glass (plus a narrow horizontal band of thin cream tiles at cornice level) and a plain ceiling in three vaults.

However, one then stepped into the main entrance hall and was confronted by a breathtaking Italian Renaissance scheme with two gigantic crystal chandeliers holding 125 light bulbs (modelled on those in the banqueting hall at Buckingham Palace), towering black marble columns with Corinthian capitals, marble floors and walls, the latter broken up by pink mirrors. This led to an oval space with a central entrance to the stalls floor at the far end and marble staircases to each side, with art deco light fittings on the newels. The staircases curved to meet outside the circle lounge. In the lounge, square, plain art deco

*The Gaumont State Kilburn
at opening in 1937*

light fittings were suspended from a coffered ceiling. Adjacent to this area, presumably above the entrance hall to the subsidiary entrance on Willesden Lane, was the huge restaurant with a central dance floor.

The auditorium itself seemed enormous, especially in height, and continued the Italian Renaissance scheme, which had by then usually been discarded by cinema promoters and designers as too old-fashioned. But the Hyams wanted to impress the people of Kilburn with luxury and grandeur as they had done with their cinema palaces in other drab, working class districts of London (and as Sidney Bernstein and the Greens of Glasgow continued to do with their super cinemas).

A huge floodlit dome occupied the ceiling but the central light fitting seemed far too modest for the rich ornamentation of the surrounding plasterwork. The elaborate grillework over the side exits by the screen and the four-colour cove lighting that lit up the proscenium frame were impressive, yet the auditorium of the State Kilburn has always seemed to this writer rather plain and repetitive, and nowhere near as intoxicating as the auditorium Coles had created at the Elephant and Castle Trocadero, in similar style and of nearly the same size. The State is directly comparable to American movie cathedrals and its auditorium does not stand up in interest to the work of Thomas Lamb or Rapp and Rapp in the Twenties. Perhaps there were cost restrictions. Perhaps Coles was deliberately providing a simpler, less overwhelming scheme, in tune with the less ostentatious tastes of the later Thirties.

The Gaumont State had one of the largest stages in the country, over 100 ft. wide, 50 ft. deep and 60 ft. to the stage grid. It was provided with a cycloramic wall at the back for atmospheric effects using the stage lighting. The orchestra pit had a rising platform to bring it level with the stage. This was quite separate to the lift for the Wurlitzer organ console which had a revolve. There were twenty dressing rooms, a band room, and a workshop in a separate building for painting scenery. Cine-variety was very much the policy and continued even after the Second World War started.

As described in the previous chapter, the Gaumont Holloway was developed as a GSS enterprise but sold to GBPC during construction. The Hyams had plans by George Coles approved in March 1938 for a State cinema at Kingston upon Thames, Southwest London; this was also sold in the early stages of construction, to Granada, opening as part of its chain in November 1939. The scheme had no apparent connection with GSS.

The Wurlitzers

In Gaumont Super Cinemas, the favoured instrument was the Wurlitzer rather than the Compton, reflecting the preference of the Hyams brothers.

Tony Moss comments: "In May 1937, the Gaumont Watford opened with a Wurlitzer of 8 ranks and what was known as the French-style console on a large lift to the right of the orchestra pit. The reason for the large lift was that, although Hyams would have ordered the Wurlitzer, the original scheme was initiated by Lou Morris and provision would have been made for a Compton with illuminated surround. At Oldham, the organ opened in June was, again, an 8-rank Wurlitzer with French-style console.

"The giant Gaumont State Kilburn was equipped with a Wurlitzer twice the size of those at Watford and Oldham, with 16 ranks and a phantom grand piano. The organ was installed to the left of the stage with the console, specially designed by the theatre's architect George Coles, on a lift and turntable to the right. In such a vast theatre, this created a time-lag between the chambers and the organist, so that amplification to the console had to be installed. The great Sidney Torch returned to Hyams from a brief spell with Union Cinemas to preside at the State Wurlitzer but his stay there was cut short in 1940 by the Second World War.

"The last organ to be opened in a Gaumont theatre was a 12-rank Wurlitzer commissioned by the Hyams brothers for what opened as the Gaumont Holloway in September 1938. Like Kilburn, it was designed by Hyams/Gaumont organist Quentin Maclean, and the console was to a similar pattern but with only 3 manuals. Mac's specification included a tibia plena rank, one of only two such ranks in a British Wurlitzer, the other being at the Blackpool Opera House. The backbone of a theatre organ is the tibia clausa rank, a large stopped flute, preferably wooden, that produces a beautiful soft tone, rich in harmonics. The tibia plena, on the other hand, is an open wooden pipe giving a more fundamental tone (oomph!) than harmonic. The Holloway Wurlitzer was opened by Terance Casey."

8: CIRCUIT OPERATION BEFORE WORLD WAR TWO

Previous chapters have concentrated on the opening of new buildings, and Gaumont's progress in this area needs to be set in context.

Gaumont started the Thirties with 287 cinemas compared to ABC's ninety (Odeon was merely a gleam in the eyes of its founder, Oscar Deutsch). Gaumont ended the Thirties with 302 cinemas compared to 438 operated by ABC (include the Union circuit) and 263 controlled by Odeon (including the County and Paramount circuits). A lot of ground had been lost because Gaumont had constructed only fifty-one new cinemas compared to ABC's ninety-eight (including five opened in 1940) and Odeon's 136. Many other circuits and single operators had also built modern cinemas. These newer venues were likely to be more attractive to the public than older buildings, while Gaumont had a disproportionate number of outdated and small-sized halls which put it at a further disadvantage. Some idea of the impact comes from the drop in the ordinary dividend, breaking a nine-year run, at the Gaumont subsidiary, APPH, which was announced in November 1934. This was attributed to increased competition everywhere, while the case was cited of one city where a cinema had been operated for many years with very satisfactory results but since 1932 no less than four super cinemas had been erected. However, Gaumont's booking strength remained secure: despite its rows with particular distributors, it was able over the decade as a whole to gain a more than satisfactory share of the most popular pictures through circuit deals that protected many inferior halls.

In addition to their new builds, ABC and Odeon had purchased a number of existing cinemas, often very recently opened. Gaumont had stepped in and taken over several projects, opening them as part of its chain, but it had acquired comparatively few already functioning picture houses. Clearly, its severe financial problems from 1936 as a result of production losses had limited the money available to build new cine-mas just at the time when its rivals were expanding like mad, although there may have been a certain complacency over Gaumont's booking strength and sheer number of halls.

While it is comparatively easy to cover the opening of cinemas, it is impossible to be authoritative about the day-to-day operation of this vast circuit in the Thirties without further detailed research.

Live shows and talkies

Most of the purpose-built cinemas, and many of those taken over, had full stage facilities, as has been indicated previously. Some idea of the way the stage was used can be gleaned from the *Bristol Evening News'* report of the opening night at the Bristol Regent during PCT days: "There is a troupe of specially trained dancers, who are known as the 'Regent Girls', who go through a series of effective dances. There is also a special engagement of Graham and Douglas, a pair of simultaneous dancers, who give a display that is fascinating as well as unique. A beautiful soprano, Mlle. Rita Colère, who hails from Alsace Lorraine and who has obtained considerable fame for her singing...gives songs that win the utmost admiration. Other musical numbers are by an efficient orchestra, conducted by Mr. T. S. Clarke-Browne, who plays separate items in addition to the incidental music to the film plays. And if that were not enough there are solos by Mr. Frank Matthew on the Wurlitzer organ, an instrument of musical power and good quality of tone."

The first talking pictures to be widely shown drew huge audiences. The first to play the Regent Hanley in July 1929 was Warner Bros.' Al Jolson musical *The Singing Fool*. According to a *Kinematograph Weekly* report (July 25), the cinema's manager started a major advertising campaign two months ahead and gradually increased it until, in the week before its opening, the entire district was plastered with posters while

MAJOR CIRCUIT OPENINGS 1930-40

Omits reconstructions of existing cinemas

	Gaumont	ABC	Odeon
1930	4	3	– *
1931	7	4	–
1932	8	4	–
1933	2	2	5
1934	5	4	17
1935	4	7	13
1936	4	14	32
1937	10	22	35
1938	5	22	27
1939	2	11	7
1940	0	5	0
Total	**51**	**98**	**136**

* The Odeon Perry Barr, opened in 1930,
was an isolated venture, not the start
of the Odeon chain.

Queues outside the Regent in July 1929 for the first talkie to be shown in Hanley, The Singing Fool.

BRITAIN'S BIG COMPANIES—15

T HIS week our chart shows the interests of THE GAUMONT-BRITISH PICTURE CORPORATION, who have an issued share and loan capital of £11,187,496. Corporation control more than 330 theatres in London and the provinces and have studios at Shepherd's Bush.

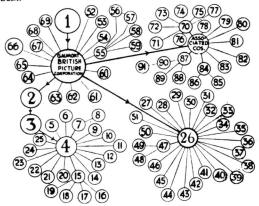

GAUMONT - BRITISH PIC-TURE CORPORATION — who are controlled by:—
1. Metropolis and Bradford Trust Company—themselves control :—
2. Standard Film Company, who control :—
3. New Standard Film Company, who in turn control :—
4. Provincial Cinematograph Theatres, who control :—
5. Birmingham West End Cinema.
6. Classic Cinemas.
7. Albany Ward Theatres, who control :—
   8. Jersey and Guernsey Amusements.
9. Tivoli Palace.
10. Leeds Picture Playhouse.
11. P.C.T. Construction Company.
12. Royal Hotel, Edinburgh.
13. Trocadero Super Cinema (Liverpool).
14. Doncaster Majestic Cinema.
15. Associated Provincial Picture Houses, who control :—
16. Scala, Ealing.
17. Scala, Maida Vale.
18. Scala, Kilburn.
19. Gaumont Super Cinemas.
20. City Cinema.
21. Hammersmith Cinemas.
22. York Cinemas.
23. Regent (Stamford Hill).
24. Granada (Manchester).
25. Dominion Theatre (1933).
26. Denman Picture Houses, who control :—
27. Alloa Picture Palace.
28. Ayrshire Cinematograph Theatres.
29. B.B. Pictures (1920).
30. Bellshill Hall Co.
31. Catwood Cinemas.
32. Denman (London) Cinemas.
33. Denman (Midlands) Cinemas.
34. Falkirk Picture House.
35. Glasgow Tivoli.
36. Grand Cinema.
37. Hamilton, La Scala.
38. Hendon Central Cinema.
39. Kirkcaldy Kinema.
40. Kirkintilloch Picture House.
41. Motherwell Picture House.
42. National Electric Theatres.
43. Newington Electric Theatres.
44. North of England Cinemas.
45. Parade Picture Houses.
46. Perth Alhambra.

47. New Century Pictures, who control :—
48. Holderness Hall (Hull).
49. Saltaire Picture House.
50. Scala (Leeds).
51. Wishaw Playhouse.
52. Gainsborough Pictures (1928).
53. Theatre, Grimsby.
54. Gaumont Construction Co.
55. Gaumont-British Distributors, controlling :—
56. Gaumont Co. (now incorporated in G.B.D.).
57. W. and F. Film Service (now incorporated in G.B.D.).
58. Ideal Films (now incorporated in G.B.D.).
59. Film Clearing Houses.
60. L.V.T. Syndicate.
61. Palmer Newbould and Co.
62. Celluloid Products.
63. Cinephonic Music Co.
64. Theatrical Publications (1930).
65. Gaumont-British Picture Corporation of America Inc.
66. Carshalton Regional Theatre.
67. Chichester Regional Theatre.
68. Palace (Chatham).
The following companies are associated with Gaumont-British:—
70. General Theatre Corporation, who control :—
71. Alhambra (Paris).
72. Haymarket Capitol.
73. Haymarket Estates.
74. Liverpool Hippodrome.
75. Portsmouth Hippodrome.
76. South of England Hippodrome.
77. Southend Hippodrome.
78. Moss' Empires.
79. United Picture Theatres.
80. Majestic (Rochester).
81. Regent (Stamford Hill).
82. Scala (Notting Hill).
83. Baird Television.
84. International Acoustic Films, in voluntary liquidation, who control :—
85. Bush Radio.
86. Electrical Fono-Films A/S.
87. British Acoustic Films, who control :—
88. G.-B. Instructional.
89. International Acoustic S.A.I.
90. G.-B. Equipment Co. who control :—
91. G.-B. Furnishers.

Gaumont-British made simple. From the City page of the News Chronicle, *Circa 1938. (The Projected Picture Trust magazine.)*

music stores gave window displays and Woolworth's prominently featured the book. Despite hot summer weather, all records were broken with an estimated near 50,000 admissions in the first week.

At the smaller Wolverhampton Agricultural Hall, the same film opened on 12 August 1929. Local historian Ned Williams has noted: "*The Singing Fool* broke all records at the Agri'. At the end of the week the manager, Mr. Adams, was able to report that 5,000 people a day had been in to see it. It was retained for a second week, and by the end of that week over 60,000 attendances had been recorded. (Previous record runs at this cinema had been 27,000 in one week to see Chaplin's *The Circus* and 26,000 in one week to see *Ben Hur*.) ... The Scala, PCT's third cinema in the town, was now given 'first run' status with double bills of the latest silent features and its orchestra was enlarged."

The musical side is recalled in *Tune Up the Hoover! Cinema Musicians Tell Their Stories* by Jon de Jonge: "The New Victoria in Bradford...opened in 1930 with a 30-piece orchestra led by Sydney Phasey. It was one of the supercinemas up and down the country combining talkies and bandshows. Stan [Anderson] and Billy [Stean] both worked [at] the New Victoria. When Stan joined it was a 12-piece band. They did three shows a day on the stage plus half an hour in the pit before the films while the audience filed in. They broadcast every Wednesday from the pit for half an hour and once a month the whole band was taken by coach to Leeds to do a broadcast."

Many cinemas were not licensed to open on Sundays and in *The Silver Screens of Wirral* by P. A. Carson and C. R. Garner, it is noted that the Gaumont Palace Wallasey put on concerts. A new manager, Henry Gurney, "introduced popular Sunday concerts at the Gaumont Palace for the winter season, commencing from 26 December 1937. The bands featured were usually local groups, as well as those employed at G.B.-operated ballrooms in the north of England, such as that of Bob Easson from the Rialto in Liverpool, but sometimes bands such as that of Larry Brennan from the Empress Ballroom in Blackpool appeared. The Sunday concerts were once nightly and were resumed again, after a break during the summer season, in September 1938, and then again from October 1939 when among the bands featured was one conducted by Henry Croudson, the organist from the Ritz Birkenhead. The introduction of Sunday cinemas to Wallasey brought an end to stage concerts

TO-DAY.   TO-DAY.

EDINBURGH'S BIG FIVE

THE NEW PICTURE HOUSE, 56, PRINCES STREET. Continuous from 12 noon.	A WM. FOX PRODUCTION. "MEN WITHOUT WOMEN," Featuring KENNETH M'KENNA and FARRELL MACDONALD. A GRIPPING, ALL-TALKING DRAMA. Also "MEDICINE MEN" and "LADIES' MAN" (Sound Comedies) CAFÉS OPEN ... ... 10 a.m. til 10.30 p.m.
ST. ANDREW SQUARE PICTURE HOUSE, CLYDE STREET. Continuous from 1 p.m. PRICES: Till 4.30 ... 6d & 1/-, After 4.30 ... 9d & 1/3.	TED LEWIS. The "High Hat Tragedian of Jazz," in "IS EVERYBODY HAPPY" ALSO "THE BLUE WALTZ," with ORCHESTRAL ACCOMPANIMENT by "SAM" and his POPULAR ORCHESTRA.
THE CAPITOL LEITH. Continuous from 2 p.m. Prices till 4 o'clock, 3d and 6d. After 4 p.m., 6d, 9d, and 1/-.	DOUBLE FEATURE PROGRAMME THE POWERFUL ALL-TALKING DRAMA, "WALL STREET," with RALPH INCE and EILEEN PRINGLE. ALSO "DIANE," with OLGA TSCHECHOWA and HENRY VICTOR.
"REGENT" PICTURE HOUSE, ABBEYMOUNT. Continuous from 2.30. Prices till 4.30, 3d and 6d. After 4.30, 4d, 6d, 8d and 1/-.	FOR THREE DAYS ONLY, ALL-TALKING COMEDY DRAMA, "SAILORS' HOLIDAY," Featuring ALLAN HALE and SALLY FILERS. RICHARD TELFER at the COMPTON ORCHESTRAL ORGAN.
THE RUTLAND, TORPHICHEN ST. Continuous from 2 p.m. Prices till 4.30, 6d, 8d, and 1/-. After 4.30, 8d, 1/-, 1/3, and 1/6.	A WM. FOX ALL-TALKING DRAMA, "MEN WITHOUT WOMEN," KENNETH M'KENNA, FRANK ALBERTSON. ALSO "THE BLUE WALTZ," Featuring LIANE HAID. NORMAN AUSTIN and the RUTLAND ORCHESTRA. LYNDON LAIRD at the MIGHTY UNIT ORGAN.

ALL SHOWING COMEDIES AND NEWS EVENTS IN SOUND

Note the special credit to "Wm. Fox" on Fox pictures, and the references to talking pictures. This 1930 advertisement predates the opening of the New Victoria. London also had its "Big Five" West End group in advertising at this time: the Tivoli, Capitol, New Gallery, Astoria and Marble Arch Pavilion.

at the Gaumont Palace..." How many others cinemas also featured such live shows on Sundays is not clear.

Take-overs

Besides the cinemas that were opened by Gaumont, there were a number of take-overs in the early years through the various associated circuits. In 1929, the large City Cinema in Leicester became a Gaumont theatre. In 1930, the circuit took over the Norwich Haymarket, Portsmouth Regent, Southsea Plaza, and Weston-Super-Mare Picture House, as well as gaining control of the United Picture Theatres circuit (see below). At the same time, a number of smaller cinemas were closed, without ever being equipped for sound, in towns where Gaumont had a surplus of properties because of the many circuits it had taken over.

In 1931, the Hull Holderness Hall, North Shields Princes, Notting Hill Coronet and Partick (Glasgow) Tivoli were added. But take-overs of operating cinemas then stopped almost completely. The next year did see the vast Tottenham Court Road Dominion join the circuit's stock of West End halls, but it would remain a difficult situation to programme for many years to come.

After this, circuit expansion was almost completely restricted to its own newly built cinemas and a few others acquired in the course of construction. The Florida at King's Park, Glasgow, was a rare take-over in the late Thirties.

United Picture Theatres

In April 1930, Gaumont outbid ABC to gain a five-year agreement to manage the United Pictures Theatres circuit, also taking a small financial stake.

UPT was more of a problem than a prize. Formed in January 1928 as the result of what the *Kine Weekly* described as "the most important kinema deal since the formation of the Gaumont-British circuit", it created a circuit of nine existing cinemas, mostly former music halls and theatres, all in the London suburbs. Then, in the last two months of 1928, with a new share issue, UPT added seven more properties, again in the London area. Its trading profit for the year was below the estimate in the prospectus, and in 1929 UPT showed a loss. It would never show a profit again.

The directors blamed the first loss on the cost of equipping UPT's properties for talkies and the higher cost of films under

Two 1930 additions to the circuit: the Plaza Southsea (seen in 1945 with Victory decorations) and the Regent Weston-Super-Mare circa June 1931.

the percentage deals that had replaced flat rate hire. In addition, they had built and opened the Southall Palace to replace an older cinema and contracted to buy the recently opened Leyton Savoy.

When Gaumont took over the management of UPT in July 1930, it effectively added UPT's cinemas to the circuit:

Camden Town Hippodrome
Charing Cross Road Super
Clapham Junction Shakespeare
Deptford Broadway
Kennington Theatre
Kilburn Picture Palace
Mile End Empire
Old Kent Road Picture House
Putney Hippodrome
Putney Palace
Southall Palace
Stamford Hill Cinema
Stepney (Commercial Road) Palaseum
Wandsworth Palace
Whitechapel Rivoli
Woolwich Hippodrome

Gaumont had to infuse capital to enable UPT to complete its purchase of the Leyton Savoy, even though Mark Ostrer declared the £100,000 agreed for the freehold to be "excessive". In fact, Gaumont were highly critical of the rents and other "prior charges" that had to be met for what were, for the most part, outmoded properties being badly hit by the opening of more modern rivals. When severe financial problems arose over the Charing Cross Road Super in 1930, Gaumont arranged to take the cinema off UPT's hands.

Despite Gaumont's involvement, UPT tumbled into receivership in January 1934. The Receiver sold off the six cinemas that were making a loss, taking the best offers he could get. This removed permanently from Gaumont management the Deptford Broadway, Kennington Theatre, Mile End Empire, Putney Hippodrome, Stepney Palaseum and Woolwich Hippodrome. The remaining ten profitable cinemas were put on the market but the offers were unsatisfactory and the Receiver decided not to sell them. In January 1935, the rival ABC chain approached the Receiver about taking over management at the end of the contract with Gaumont, but UPT was allowed to resume control of its activities and the existing agreement with

Gaumont was extended in July 1935. By 1937, Gaumont was managing the circuit for £10,000 per annum or five per cent of the net receipts (whichever was the greater) and the agreement had been extended to the end of December 1954, ensuring the cinemas would remain under the GBPC umbrella.

Specialised Theatres

One way of dealing with some of the more difficult, smaller capacity city centre properties, devised by Stuart Davis (of the Davis brothers), was to convert them to a repertory policy. The Avenue Pavilion in London's West End, Savoy Leeds and Liverpool's Mount Pleasant Picture Hall were selected for this scheme, introduced towards the end of 1928. The Mount Pleasant was even closed for a month's redecoration before re-opening as the Century Repertory Theatre, "the house of unusual films". The Savoy was renamed the Leeds Repertory Cinema and contacts were made with the University and arts groups to draw attention to the new policy. Although attendances did improve here in the short term, the repertory policy was abandoned after a year or so. The Century closed for good, citing the difficulties of continuing to find attractive silent films with the advent of sound and of popularising anything 'intellectual' in the way of film entertainment in Liverpool.

For most patrons, part of the appeal of going to the cinema was a chance to see on the newsreel moving images of the events that they could otherwise only hear about on the radio or read about in newspapers. Gaumont, of course, had long had its own newsreel. Then came the idea of the news theatre, imported from America, although a similar policy had been tried out, as previously indicated, with the very early Gaumont cinema, the Daily Bioscope.

To test the appeal of the idea in this country, the Avenue Pavilion in London's West End was throughly modernised and a Christie organ installed for it to re-open as the G.B. Movietone News Theatre on 18 August 1930, the first of its kind in this country. It was reported that 3,884 patrons packed the 510-seat hall on the first day, paying sixpence to enter the stalls and one shilling to sit in the circle. The policy succeeded here and was introduced at the Super Charing Cross Road as well on 16 February 1931, despite the two cinemas' proximity. The Super was renamed the Tatler and both cinemas continued with this policy for the rest of the decade, the Tatler also featuring documentary in its programmes and attracting school groups.

The Academy in Brighton was also turned over to a news theatre policy and renamed the Tatler but it failed within weeks and the cinema quickly reverted to feature films and soon after returned to its original name.

Booking

Gaumont-British was a major producer of films through its own studios at Shepherds Bush and an association with Gainsborough at Islington that led to full control from 1932. GBPC also had two distribution companies, Ideal and W&F, which also released other British pictures. Naturally, the company's own productions and releases played in its own cinemas to maximise returns. The circuit needed comparatively few Hollywood films because it made so many pictures itself. In 1932, the year that the Shepherds Bush studios were again enlarged to increase production, eighty per cent of the main features at Gaumont's top cinemas were British. What is more, they were doing very well, grossing twice as much as Hollywood fare — in fact, the British office of the American trade paper *Variety* went so far as to report that British pictures had a "complete stranglehold".

At the start of the decade, Gaumont tried to use the size of its chain to keep to fixed percentages but it lost Universal's *All Quiet on the Western Front* in 1930 when it would not offer more than twenty to twenty-five per cent of takings for a circuit release. Evidently regretting its obstinancy, the company offered better terms to make certain of obtaining *Raffles* from United Artists.

However, Gaumont showed an extraordinary knack for falling out with its suppliers. In 1931, it refused to play Paramount pictures because it resented the competition of the company's huge Astorias. It declined to play MGM product because that distributor insisted on a three-month gap after its films had opened at the Empire Leicester Square before they played at the New Victoria whereas Gaumont wanted them immediately after the Empire. (The Hyams brothers settled this one by accepting the MGM films on MGM's terms for their Metropole at Victoria.) Gaumont banned United Artists after that company dared to open its Eddie Cantor musical comedy *Palmy Days* at the Dominion (when it was being run by Moss Empires) instead of at a Gaumont West End outlet. Except for Fox, the other distributors at this time were aligned with the ABC circuit.*

Although the Fox company had a huge stake in the company from late spring 1929, the argument over control meant that Fox films were not shown on the circuit for two years — until *Daddy Long Legs* opened at the Tivoli in the Strand in July 1931 and then played the entire chain. The shortage of product from other sources led Gaumont to start taking Fox pictures in great numbers from October 1931 as its primary source of major Hollywood fare.

For the rest of the decade, the Ostrers kept the Fox company happy by booking its major productions to the circuit. This left a few other weeks in which chief booker Alfred Jarratt went after the most promising pictures from other sources.

Gaumont gained many of the smash hits of the Thirties and, as the largest circuit in Europe by 1932, distributors were anxious to do business with it. The Tivoli in the Strand seems to have been Gaumont's leading West End hall in the early and mid-Thirties. It was here that Universal's *Frankenstein* opened to huge business before going on to tour the Gaumont circuit with great success in 1932. In those days, managers competed to carry out promotional suggestions of live prologues, eye-catching displays and stunts. Unfortunately for the manager of the Classic Belfast, his advance efforts counted for little when *Frankenstein* was banned on the third day. In Newcastle, the film could only be shown after several meetings with the Chief Constable and a promise to refrain from sensational publicity, so that it was tamely if presciently announced as "the horror classic".

But in Scotland, for example, the managers went full out. A teaser prologue at the New Victoria Edinburgh, based on the storm scene in the film which culminates in the birth of the monster, recreated the same setting with storm effects and a device by which the monster's inert body was slowly raised until it was level with the top of the screen, at which moment there was a blackout and the film's trailer came on.

*The company was extraordinarily touchy in other ways. The souvenir opening programme for the New Victoria was scrapped after it was discovered that the agency responsible for its production had inadvertently accepted an advertisement from British International Pictures, part of the rival ABC empire. And when its 1931 production of *The Blue Danube* was panned by the critics and lasted only two weeks on its premiere run at the Tivoli in the Strand, Gaumont reacted by cancelling advertising in the national papers.

GAUMONT PALACE
JORDAN WELL   COVENTRY

SPECIAL ARRANGEMENTS FOR

NOEL COWARD'S

GLORIOUS   *MIGHTY*

Cavalcade
PICTURE OF THE GENERATION

Monday Oct. 16th to Sunday Oct. 23rd inclusive

Doors Open Monday to Saturday at 1-30.   Programme Begins at 2.
"   "   Sunday at 7.   Programme "   " 8.

No Increase in Prices of Admission.

USUAL BARGAIN MATINEES DAILY TO 2-30.

STALLS 7d.   CIRCLE 1/-.   Children Half-price.

PLEASE NOTE TIMES OF SCREENING AT

2-10, 4-25, 6-40 & 8-55.

So kindly be in your seats 10 minutes before above times.

Wherever "Cavalcade" has been presented thousands of people have been unable to obtain admission owing to the enormous queues that have formed to see this glorious and inspiring master-piece.

If you want to avoid these queues unprecedented in the history of Gaumont British Theatres be here at 4-0 o'clock, so that you may see this most moving pageant of our beloved country at the **4-25** performance.

Robertson & Sons, Three Spires Press, Coventry.

Fox's Cavalcade was a huge hit for the Gaumont circuit in 1933.
Left: Coventry flyer courtesy of Gil Robottom.
Above: eye-catching display at the Empire Southampton.

The foyer of the Regent Brighton
transformed into a station for the run of
The Ghost Train circa October 1931.

Promoting Dracula *in 1931. Above: spider's web display on the front of the Marlborough Holloway, North London. (The huge set-back frontage regularly featured eye-catching displays.) Below: lobby treatment of the Capitol Haymarket for its West End run.*

In Glasgow, the six-foot-tall foreman of the Picture House was made up as the film's monster and paraded the streets, cinema and café during the film's run, as well as visiting the Cinerama, another Gaumont house playing the attraction concurrently. The Picture House manager also turned his vestibule and lounges into a castle set with electric devices and a model of Frankenstein's monster resting on a table. The Marconi company helped by loaning two large coils which emitted a 6 in. spark.

Another film that was extravagantly promoted was Gaumont's own *The Ghost Train*, a Jack Hulbert comedy thriller. Cinemas went to considerable expense to convert their foyers into stations, with the payboxes dressed up as ticket windows, dummies of porters, and so on. Later in the year, a further Jack Hulbert comedy, *Jack's the Boy*, became the biggest hit of 1932, running ten weeks at the Tivoli before going on release.

Also in 1932, Gaumont distributed and gave a circuit release to *Congress Dances*, the English version of the German Ufa company's musical *Der Kongress tanzt* which enjoyed a six-week run at the Tivoli. This led to a co-production arrangement by which Gaumont supervised English versions of Ufa films for release in England.

In 1933, Gaumont booking chief Jarratt was again at odds with United Artists over an Eddie Cantor picture, *The Kid from Spain*, because UA insisted on tying it to two other less attractive releases. Both Gaumont and ABC stood resolute on rejecting any form of the block booking practised in the United States (except, of course, as far as their own films were concerned). Jarratt also refused to pay fifty-fifty terms (sharing the receipts equally) for RKO Radio's sensational *King Kong*, offering the distributor a mere one third. ABC stepped in and gained *King Kong* by going up to forty per cent.

However, Gaumont had a huge hit with Fox's *Cavalcade*, which clocked up half a million admissions at the Tivoli alone in a sixteen-week run. According to a 1973 interview with Victor Saville (quoted in Rachael Low's *Film Making in 1930s Britain*), *Cavalcade* was booked for circuit release on a fifty-fifty split, which may have been because of the special relationship with Fox as well as bowing to the obvious smash-hit potential of the film. Saville complained that his Gaumont-distributed production of *The Good Companions*, which he maintains surpassed the record attendances for *Cavalcade*, was booked at a mere twenty-five per cent.

President:
ISIDORE OSTRER.
Vice - President:
THE RT. HON. VISCOUNT LEE OF FAREHAM, P.C.
DIRECTORS:
MARK OSTRER, Chairman.   JOINT
C. M. WOOLF,   MANAGING
Deputy Chairman   DIRECTORS
MAURICE OSTRER.
    Assistant Managing Director.
COL. H.A. MICKLEM,   C.H. DADE.
    C.B.,C.M.G.,D.S.O.
S. R. KENT, (U.S.A.)   DIXON BOARDMAN, (U.S.A.)
IAN P. LITTLE.   O.H.C. BALFOUR, C.M.G.

PRIVATE & CONFIDENTIAL.

Gaumont-British
Picture Corporation Ltd.

Telephone
REGENT 8080 (27 Lines)
Telegrams
"PROCINTHE, PICCY, LONDON"
(New Gallery House)
Reg. Office
142-150. WARDOUR STREET,
LONDON, W.1.

New Gallery House,
Regent St. London, W.1.

DEPT. ....
REF. ....

HL/EM.

6th March, 1935.

To: All Managers.
        (Copies to Div. Supts. & Circuit Managers)

From: Mr. Lundy.

    I am conveying to you in this letter some information which is
of the utmost importance, and to obviate as far as possible an
incident of a similar nature occuring at your Theatre, it is
Mr. Ostrer's wish that you should be acquainted with the full facts.

    Quite recently at a London Theatre two ladies entered the
stalls, and as seats were not obtainable together, two single seats
were taken, one lady sitting directly in front of the other. After
some time had elapsed the lady in front turned round and found her
friend missing, and on going to the front of the house to make
enquiries, saw her friend, who appeared to be ill, being claimed by a
strange man as his wife.   The friend immediately confronted the man
who without further comment made good his escape.   It was evident
that this man, who had been seated near the lady, may have injected
into her arm some drug through the medium of a Hypodermic Syringe, and
but for the timely intervention of her friend would have been taken
away by this stranger.

    This, you will appreciate, might happen to anyone, patron or
staff, and with this in view, I am giving a definite instruction that
in all cases of illness, unless you are aware of the bona fides of
the person/s accompanying the party concerned, a doctor or a
policeman must be sent for, as a protective measure, and the matter
left for one or the other of them to deal with.

    Without imparting the above information to your staff, you
will instruct them to notify you immediately of any case of illness,
and you must deal with it personally.

    Mr. Ostrer is of the definite opinion that the public
generally will welcome the adoption of this procedure, and will
appreciate the endeavour on the part of the Corporation, of
safeguarding them from a similar happening.

                        H.H. LUNDY.

*Bizarre warning of the possible abduction of female patrons in 1935 from the
circuit's general manager. (Gaumont Palace Salisbury copy, courtesy of Alan
Richardson.)*

YOU
Shall
SEE and HEAR
THE CORONATION

For the millions of loyal subjects who have
not the privilege of a grand stand seat to
view the Coronation of our beloved
Majesties, we have arranged a most
comprehensive scheme to bring these
historic celebrations to you—as you sit in
comfort in your theatre seat.

THE ACTUAL BROADCAST!

By permission of the B.B.C. selected
high-lights of this broadcast will be
relayed to you direct. Our theatre sound
system will bring to you, WITH THE
PERFECT CLARITY of a SOUND PICTURE,
all the thrills of that historic day :

And, in the evening—
THE KING'S SPEECH TO HIS PEOPLE

COMPLETE NEWSREEL RECORD!

At hundreds of points along the route,
and in the Abbey itself, Newsreel cameras
will be turning—and, in a few hours, there
will unfold on your theatre screen a page
torn from history—a vivid, unforgettable
spectacle in sound and picture of the
events of this memorable day.

WATCH FOR THEATRE ANNOUNCEMENTS
OF EARLY OPENING TIMES !

5

*Bringing the Coronation of May 1937 to the picturegoer.
Above, page from a monthly programme (CTA Archive).
Below: arrangements at Gaumont Coventry.*

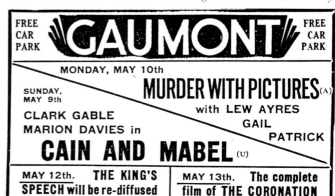

FREE CAR PARK

GAUMONT

FREE CAR PARK

MONDAY, MAY 10th

SUNDAY, MAY 9th

CLARK GABLE
MARION DAVIES in
CAIN AND MABEL (U)

MURDER WITH PICTURES (A)
with LEW AYRES
GAIL PATRICK

MAY 12th. THE KING'S
SPEECH will be re-diffused
to theatre patrons at 8 p.m.

MAY 13th. The complete
film of THE CORONATION
presented by G.B. News

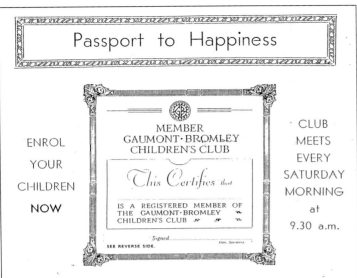

Passport to Happiness

MEMBER
GAUMONT·BROMLEY CHILDREN'S CLUB

This Certifies that

IS A REGISTERED MEMBER OF THE GAUMONT·BROMLEY CHILDREN'S CLUB

Signed.................... ....

SEE REVERSE SIDE.   Hon. Secretary.

ENROL YOUR CHILDREN NOW

CLUB MEETS EVERY SATURDAY MORNING at 9.30 a.m.

The purpose of the Gaumont, Bromley, Children's Club is to provide regular Saturday morning shows of films specially chosen to suit the youngsters at a reasonable price.

These shows are run in Club fashion and many surprises such as Competitions, Birthday Gifts, etc., are arranged for the children.

Parents will realise that such regular shows help to keep the children off the streets on Saturday mornings—an essential in these days of increasing traffic.

We recommend you to read the rules and regulations below and suggest that you obtain membership application forms for your own kiddies as well as your nieces and nephews.

RULES AND REGULATIONS

1. Badges to be worn at every Matinee.
2. Members to learn the essential Rules of Safety First in Public Place and Highways—to be repeated at all Meetings.
3. To take an intelligent interest in the Club and make every effort for its well being and improvement.
4. Club Meetings to be held each Saturday.

FIRST CLUB MEETING SATURDAY NEXT at 9.30
Programme Includes
RALPH LYNN
in
IN THE SOUP
DISTRIBUTION OF BADGES
FREE COMPETITIONS
MANY SURPRISES
ADMITTANCE
THREEPENCE & SIXPENCE

Gaumont cinemas ran children's clubs in the 1930s, as advertised here in the opening programme for the Gaumont Bromley. (Courtesy of Alan Scott.)

Gaumont were fond of promoting films in batches and these two titles formed part of a Gaumont-British Super Film Season running from October 1933 to February 1934 which included the company's own productions of *The Ghoul, Britannia of Billingsgate, I Was a Spy, Prince of Arcadia, Orders Is Orders, Falling for You* (the latest Jack Hulbert starring vehicle), *It's a Boy* and *Aunt Sally*. The few Hollywood films selected for the season included Fox's *Adorable, My Lips Betray* and *The Power and the Glory*, plus MGM's *Dinner at Eight*.

During 1934, Jack Hulbert's popularity made *Jack Ahoy!* into another huge hit while Jessie Matthews proved herself a major new star with the huge commercial success of *Evergreen.** George Arliss returned from Hollywood to make a series of films for Gaumont, beginning with *The Iron Duke*, that apparently scored well in this country. Alfred Hitchcock became an important contributor to the Gaumont output. Rachael Low's book makes the surprising allegation that Gaumont's "distribution pattern was not adjusted to help the company's own productions". Besides Victor Saville's complaint over the terms for *The Good Companions*, she offers this example: "at the behest of [C. M.] Woolf, notorious for his disparagement of Hitchcock films, *The Man Who Knew Too Much*, which was one of the most popular of them, was booked by the Gaumont-British cinemas at a modest fixed price as a second feature, instead of on a percentage of box-office takings". The list of circuit releases at the back of this book shows that it was double-billed with *Mrs. Wiggs of the Cabbage Patch*. The first picture Hitchcock made for Gaumont's producer Michael Balcon, *The Man Who Knew Too Much* would be followed by *The Thirty Nine Steps* (1935), *The Secret Agent* and *Sabotage* (both 1936).

It should be remembered that most of the biggest Gaumonts offered more than just films: there were live variety acts and organists included in the show. The chain was not the only one with a cine-variety policy by any means but, as has been seen, it did ensure that most of its new cinemas were particularly well provided with stage facilities including dressing rooms. A cine-variety policy was very expensive and the takings may have justified it, but it is worth noting that one competitor (Odeon, see below) preferred to show films only, except where forced to

*During this year, Gaumont contemplated starring Jessie Matthews in a film about the history of the Britannia Hoxton, a celebrated musical hall which was now one of the company's cinemas.

compete with rivals offering extras. As indicated elsewhere, many Gaumont cinemas such as the Birmingham West End, Brighton Regent, Leeds Majestic and Weymouth Regent, had dance halls. Virtually all the larger cinemas had café-restaurants.

West End changes

In 1937, the Gaumont Haymarket opened as the circuit's key West End house, even though it had a much smaller seating capacity than the Tivoli and others. Among the films to open at the Gaumont in its first year was the Will Hay comedy *Oh, Mr. Porter!*, one of a series of Gainsborough productions starring the comedian with Graham Moffatt and Moore Marriott. Some idea of the playing order of Gaumont's West End halls may be gleaned from the progress of *Oh, Mr. Porter!* It played at the Gaumont from 31 October (a Sunday) to 20 November. It then disappeared from the West End until 12 December when it opened for a week at the Dominion and New Victoria, after which it moved straight into the Marble Arch Pavilion until 1 January 1938.

Although the Tivoli would soon be supplanted by the Gaumont, it opened 1937's biggest hit, Columbia's *Lost Horizon*, where (according to an advertisement) it drew 258,193 paying customers in the first eight weeks of its run. The New Gallery also remained a first-run house, opening the Gaumont picture *Dr. Syn*, starring George Arliss, with a charity premiere on 10 November 1937. Like *Oh, Mr. Porter!*, this had a later run at the Marble Arch Pavilion.

Early in 1938 the New Gallery had the good fortune to open the first feature-length animated feature, Walt Disney's *Snow White and the Seven Dwarfs*, distributed by RKO Radio. This ran for a phenomenal nine months, drawing 819,000 admissions. The year's biggest moneymaker, it reportedly drew 43,000 people in its first two weeks of a run at the Birmingham Gaumont and was a goldmine on general release through the circuit. From August 1938, the Tivoli became a second-run house with weekly changes of programme, following the same policy as had already been inflicted on the Astoria Charing Cross Road and Dominion. (The New Victoria had always been a weekly change house.) Gaumont simply had too many West End halls for them all to play first-run.

Challenge of Odeon

In the later Thirties, Odeon established itself with its own circuit release. As indicated in the list of films at the back of this book, several films played both the Odeon and Gaumont cir-cuits at the same time, particularly major British films. There were few situations in which Odeon and Gaumont cinemas were head to head. Although United Artists was a partner in Odeon, the circuit did not have the spread of theatres to give the distributor's major releases a full showing, so it made sense to put them into the best cinemas of both circuits, particularly when they were popular, high quality British productions like *The Drum* or *The Four Feathers* that would help more cinemas achieve their British quota obligations and strengthen the British film industry. However, many of the Goldwyn and Selznick productions from Hollywood, like The *Hurricane* and *The Adventures of Tom Sawyer* also did double duty. In some situations where both Odeon and Gaumont had cinemas, they would both play the film, especially if they were some distance apart; otherwise there was, most weeks, a 'B' circuit release that could be played at one of the sites.

The 'B' circuit came about because in many areas Gaumont had two or more cinemas and only one could play the circuit release. On Lavender Hill at Clapham Junction, South London, for example, the Pavilion usually played the circuit programme while the Shakespeare took different films. Because of the large number of films available, the 'B' circuit often obtained quite attractive pictures. In 1938, for example, it gained MGM's *Three Comrades* with Margaret Sullavan and Robert Taylor. In 1939, it played three more MGM features: *Stand Up and Fight* with Wallace Beery, *Let Freedom Ring* with Nelson Eddy, and *Huckleberry Finn* with Mickey Rooney.

Some cinemas would play both the 'A' and 'B' circuit release on a split week. Other surplus cinemas like the Peckham Tower and Maida Vale Picture House in London tapped into the ABC release. The rival chains also had off-circuit cinemas: the Rayners Lane Odeon in North London almost invariably played the Gaumont release.

In ordinary weeks, until the early Forties, many of the bigger Gaumont cinemas not opposed by Odeon or ABC would combine the circuit's own top feature with the top feature of the rival circuit to make a giant double bill. Presumably any increase in rental costs was more than covered by a rise in attendances. Lesser halls would usually play the standard supporting feature with the Gaumont main picture.

Baird TV

In January 1932, Isidore Ostrer had taken a controlling interest in Baird TV for GBPC. However, it was not until 1936 that Gaumont began to explore the possibilities of television in the cinema. On 4 January, a specially prepared live programme was transmitted from a studio to the Dominion Tottenham Court Road, London, and shown on a screen 8ft. by 6ft. 6ins. It was pointed out that the same programme could have been received simultaneously by other cinemas in the London area.

There was a gap until 1938 when GBPC began experimenting with large screen television again. At the Dominion, Baird demonstrated two-colour television on a 12ft. by 9ft. screen. At the Tatler Charing Cross Road, the BBC's transmission of the Derby was shown on a 8ft. by 6ft. screen live as it happened. Two projectors were installed in case one failed. Subsequently, excerpts from BBC TV transmissions were included in the regular programme until a ban was imposed by the BBC later in the year. Large screen television was also installed for test purposes at the Tivoli in the Strand, and Marble Arch Pavilion as well as at the G.B. Movietone News Theatre. Other organisations were also active: Scophony, in which Oscar Deutsch of Odeon had a financial interest, also presented the Derby live.

The BBC ban was lifted to enable the Tatler and Marble Arch Pavilion to show a major boxing match on 23 February 1939. In May, the Derby was shown via the Baird system at the Tatler and Marble Arch Pavilion as well as the New Victoria, while it was also seen at the Odeon Leicester Square through the Scophony apparatus.

Large screen television was set for major expansion in 1939 at both Gaumont and Odeon cinemas. Twelve GB halls were to be equipped by the end of 1939 and the latest projection equipment had been installed at the Gaumont Haymarket and Gaumont Lewisham when war was declared, BBC Television closed down, and everything came to a halt. Isidore Ostrer had planned to have the Baird TV system installed at forty Gaumont cinemas by the end of 1940.

House style

As far as cinemas were concerned, the Gaumont name in the Thirties was confined to the new or reconstructed cinemas opened by the circuit and it therefore stood for the best and latest in cinema buildings. As previously made clear, the new cinemas opened as Gaumont Palaces until the autumn of 1935. Thereafter, they were called simply Gaumont. During 1937,

the Gaumont Palaces themselves were renamed Gaumonts in their press advertising, although the signs on the front of the buildings retained the full name until after the Second World War while some advertisements placed by film distributors listing cinemas showing a particular film would still refer to Gaumont Palaces as late as 1952.

The Gaumont colour seems to have been red. Certainly, many signs in red neon are remembered, including the GB sign with surrounding floral pattern. It appears that the widespread use of blue really dates from the postwar years. However, the staff uniform for both sexes in the Thirties was in royal blue trimmed with light blue and silver and the basic text of a surviving monthly programme is printed in blue.

The Gaumont name was known to all cinemagoers because of the large number of films which were produced and presented by the Gaumont-British Picture Corporation. In addition, the Gaumont British newsreel was shown in a large number of cinemas. In its advertising and promotion, Gaumont showed little flair or continuity. The blocks on press advertising kept changing in design. Although the marguerite or daisy design originally devised in France was retained, its use in press advertising was intermittent.

Technical

Most of the new Gaumonts were equipped with full or limited stage facilities, and with theatre organs, and most had cafes. The circuit preferred screens with rounded corners as opposed to ones masked off to provide a rectangle.

Gaumont had its own subsidary, G-B Equipments, which supplied its cinemas. The company installed the British Acoustic sound system, which gave way in 1937 to the Duosonic system that claimed a stereophonic effect. The Gaumont Eclipse projector was succeeded in the mid-Thirties by the Magnus and Magnus II projectors (with a smaller variation, the Magnette, for smaller halls). These were manufactured at Shepherds Bush.

As recalled by John Fernee in a note to the author, many Gaumonts had trailing dimmers that automatically faded the footlights as the screen tabs opened (and brought them on as the tabs closed). This seemed to be a special feature of Gaumonts, not found in Odeon or ABC cinemas. It is believed to have been a standard feature of installation (although it might possibly have been introduced during the War when staffing was reduced).

Cinema Organs

Tony Moss comments: "Many of the Gaumont-British theatres were built with full stage facilities and most of them were equipped with organs. Apart from transfers and take-over schemes, the company standardised on organs of Compton manufacture, generally medium-sized organs of from 10 to 12 ranks. Gaumont even installed organs in theatres they acquired, e.g. the 1903 Marlborough Theatre Holloway and the Coliseum Burslem, although these were slightly smaller, i.e. 8 ranks. The Dominion Tottenham Court Road, acquired in 1933, was equipped with a 14-rank Compton with under-stage chambers, opened by Fredric Bayco, who became the leading organist on the circuit.

"By the late Thirties, Gaumont had around seventy-five organists on their books. These included some regular broadcasters and famous names like Fredric Bayco, John Bee, George Blackmore, Ernest Broadbent, Terance Casey, the well-known composer Frederick Curzon, Con Docherty, Molly Forbes, Sydney Gustard, Vic Hammett, Peter Kilby, Rudy Lewis, Quentin Maclean, John Madin, Louis Mordish, Bobby Pagan, Felton Rapley, Sidney Torch and Stanley Tudor. The West End of London was the province of the famous Baga sisters, with Ena Baga at the Tivoli and Florence de Jong at the New Gallery. Both ladies toured the Gaumont circuit from time to time.

"Gaumont always showed a peculiar weakness where publicity for the organists was concerned. Although they plugged the films and stage shows, often in neon, the organist was always very much the 'also ran', with the name right at the end, almost like an after-thought. They had a strange habit of using the surname only, and one would see in small print 'Bayco at the Organ, 'Dando at the Organ' and 'Bevan at the Organ', etc."

Top: the Gaumont Eclipse with low intensity condenser arc lamp and British Acoustic type P sound head and disc turntable — found in early to mid-1930s in smaller Gaumonts. Lower picture: the Gaumont Magnus with British Acoustic G2 sound head and Brenkert "En-arc" high intensity arc lamp. In many Gaumonts from mid-1930s to the 1950s. (Both courtesy of Mike Taylor, Projected Picture Trust North West.)

9: WORLD WAR TWO AND J. ARTHUR RANK

Once war broke out, Gaumont-British News, in the voice of its commentator E. V. H. Emmett, proclaimed itself as "presenting the truth to the free peoples of the world" instead of simply "the world to the world". After a brief period when cinemas were closed as a safety precaution, Gaumonts and others carried on with the important task of taking the British people's minds off their worries. In fact, the morale boosting value of the cinema was considered so important that senior projection staff were placed in one of the "reserved" occupations exempt from the call-up although they often volunteered to join the forces. With as many as seven employed in the box, many shortages did occur and women trained to help fill some of the vacancies.

Bomb damage

The Gaumont circuit suffered far more long-term or final closures of its cinemas than rivals ABC and Odeon. In some cases, bomb damage could be repaired, and the Tivoli Strand and Gaumont Exeter re-opened after more than a year's gap. In France and the Channel Islands, Gaumont properties came under enemy occupation but were not otherwise harmed.

Nearly thirty cinemas closed permanently, mostly because of bomb damage, a few others because they were compulsorily taken over for other use or became no longer worth operating. (Because of the ban on reporting precise details of direct hits in case they aided the enemy, dates are often approximate.)

The first bombing raids occurred in August 1940, almost a year after the declaration of War. The London Blitz started on 7 September, followed by fifty-seven consecutive nights of air raids. The first Gaumont cinema to be destroyed seems to have been the Palladium at Balham, South London, during September. (The nearby Pavilion, which had been part of a "B" circuit, now became the outlet for the main Gaumont circuit release.) Other cinemas were closed simply as an economy measure once

audiences fell away. In the case of the Tower Annexe, Peckham, South London, and the Empire at Dudley in the West Midlands, Gaumont had other, better cinemas in both areas (the Peckham building was later hit by a bomb).

The first major casualty was the Regent Bristol, which was destroyed during the first air raid on the city on the Sunday evening of 24 November 1940. Fortunately, Bristol's cinemas were not then allowed to open on Sundays and the Regent was empty. A week later it would have been a different matter, as the licensing authorities had just decided to permit Sunday evening performances and the Regent had been scheduled to open its doors. There was some consolation for Gaumont in that it had a second substantial property in the city centre, the Palace.

In December 1940, the Gaumont News Theatre in Shaftesbury Avenue made news of its own when it was severely damaged. Also lost in the London area during the last four months of 1940 were the Whitechapel Rivoli, an early super close to the City, the Canning Town Grand and the Hoxton Britannia. Other casualties of the early years of the War were the Lion at Rotherhithe and the Shakespeare at Clapham Junction (although the latter's elaborate frontage remained standing). The Rivoli and Shakespeare were part of the UPT circuit, and five of its other eight cinemas, all of which were in areas of heavy bombing, closed by the end of 1940 to save money: the Camden Town Hippodrome, Kilburn Picture Palace, Old Kent Road Picture House, Putney Palace and Wandsworth Palace. Of the five, the Camden Town and Kilburn properties would never re-open as cinemas.

The Blitz was also the last straw where the Holloway Marlborough Theatre was concerned. Managed since 1925 by PCT for the lessees, a small company called Associated Cinematograph Theatres, this had been a profitable house until the huge new Gaumont had opened a short distance away. In

April 1939, PCT went to court seeking a declaration that half the losses on the theatre were payable by ACT. (This seems a little unfair since another Gaumont was the cause of the problem, but Gaumont might have argued that it was Hyams & Gale, not them, who started construction of the new cinema.) Once the Blitz started, the increased deficit forced the closure of the cinema until Odeon took over and re-opened it in 1942. The Hoxton Cinema was also closed during the Blitz for several months.

In Spring 1941, Gaumont's two lesser cinemas in Plymouth, the Palladium and Savoy, were destroyed by fire bombs a month apart, but here the circuit's key theatre, the Gaumont in Union Street, survived. At Coventry, the ballroom at the Gaumont Palace was totally destroyed by a bomb on 10 April but the cinema continued after a brief pause. In London that year, Ye Olde Varieties, another Gaumont cinema in Hoxton, and the Imperial Playhouse at Stratford both succumbed to enemy action, as did the Broadway at Bootle on Merseyside. The closure of the Blue Hall Annexe at Islington seemed to have been another economy move rather than the result of damage.

An important Gaumont house vanished on 10 May 1941 at Kennington, South London. More than forty years later, a local inhabitant, Suzanne Waite, interviewed in *Enter the Dream-House*, offered a vivid recollection: "I can remember the Princes Theatre being bombed out completely. We came out of the shelters one morning and there was the Princes no more. It was gone. That was sad. I can still see the smoking embers. That was a very nice cinema, very wide in the front — all steps so you had plenty of room to walk into the auditorium." It is a pity that not even photographs of the Princes appear to have survived.

In 1941 and 1942, the ranks of London Gaumonts were further depleted by bomb damage to the Clapton Rink, Crouch End Hippodrome, West Kensington Super and a once celebrated music hall, the Westminster Bridge Road Canterbury, near Waterloo.

Then, after a year of apparent respite, the circuit was dealt a heavy blow in the London area during 1944 when its two huge modern Gaumonts at Streatham and Holloway were closed by V1 bombs, and the older but very important Shepherds Bush Pavilion was also too badly damaged to continue (Gaumont must have regretted it no longer had the Marlborough in Holloway; the new operators of this difficult property, Odeon, can only

Above: the Gaumont Palace Guernsey in World War Two.

Below: war destroyed the Broadway Bootle.

Some London war-time closures. Clockwise from top left: Shakespeare Clapham Junction (seen late 1929); Hippodrome Crouch End (circa 1945); Rink Cinema Clapton (circa November 1930); Playhouse Stratford (closed and advertising films at the larger Broadway); and Blue Hall Annexe Islington.

have benefitted considerably.) Another late casualty was the Lavender Hill Pavilion, to add to the loss of the Shakespeare a short distance away.

Just when the worst seemed to be over, further V bombs delivered a final, nasty blow, closing the large Super at Ilford, Northeast London. At lunchtime one day early in February 1945, the opening time queue was being admitted. Several patrons had bought tickets and were on their way to the auditorium where four usherettes had taken up position to show them to their seats. At this moment a V bomb brought the roof crashing down, killing two of the usherettes and seriously injuring the other two. No patrons were badly hurt and two dozen diners in the Super's café escaped with superficial injuries. The most severe damage was inflicted on a clothing factory across the road where many more died.

A few properties were requisitioned by the Government for other uses: the Sydenham Rink in South London, the Bromley Palais de Luxe, Exeter Palladium, and the restaurant area of the Majestic Leeds.

Many London-area cinemas were briefly closed while bombing was at its most intense because it was hopelessly uneconomic to keep them open, or as a result of power cuts, or because of minor damage that could be mended. Major Gale's fears that World War Two would have a devastating effect on the business of Gaumont Super Cinemas proved well founded, and he must have been glad that he and the Hyams had sold their interest in the Holloway Gaumont now that it was out of action. The bombing was not as destructive as pre-war forecasts had predicted but the Blitz at its worst had a devastating effect on attendances as the population was scared to venture out. Gaumont Super Cinemas were forced to close the Elephant and Castle Trocadero and the Kilburn Gaumont State for more than two weeks from mid-October 1940, and then only reopened them at weekends for a while. At the Elephant, locals were queueing up every afternoon but not for the cinema: they wanted to be sure of places in the deep shelter at the Underground station that night. At some point during the War, another GSS site, the West Norwood Regal, was forced to close its ballroom through bomb damage.

There was an added problem in the West End when cinemas were forced to close in the evening during the height of the Blitz, then only allowed to open after dark on alternate weeks. Suburban picturegoers were in any case deterred from visiting

The Ilford Super "temporarily closed" in 1946, advertising the week's circuit release at other Gaumonts

the West End by the difficulties of travelling in the blackout and especially during bombing raids. The New Victoria, New Gallery, Dominion and others were all closed for a few weeks or months during the height of the Blitz.

Gaumont policy differed from that of Odeon and ABC. These two circuits continued to operate cinemas if at all possible as a matter of prestige and defiance, but it has to be remembered that Gaumont did have a higher number of awkward or surplus properties and greater financial problems. Every effort was made to keep top cinemas going and the Gaumont Peckham, South London, suffered a series of short closures during the worst of the bombing, always re-opening. In the *CTA Bulletin* (January-February 1975), George L. Frow recalled: "During the Blitz there was a tendency for cinemas to close earlier. One just had to rush in after business hours. I can recall being in the Gaumont Palace Peckham one evening when a particularly heavy bomb fell outside and all the lights went out in the auditorium. The audience was asked to leave when it was obvious there could be no further show. I never saw the end of the film, Alfred Hitchcock's *Foreign Correspondent*, until [it was] shown on television very many years later!"

In September 1940, audiences in London were at their lowest since the War started and all cinemas were losing money. In an attempt to improve the situation, within an area bounded by Finchley, Lewisham, Ilford and Ealing, the main feature was shown first at the evening performance followed by the B film before cinemas closed early at 9 pm. This enabled patrons to get safely home before the long night raids. The big attendances were at matinees, and some huge cinemas had less than twenty patrons at closing time. Main attractions like *Pinocchio* played only twice while the B feature could be screened three times daily.

There were various shortages. In common with others, Gaumonts were prohibited from selling ice cream from 26 September 1942 until 3 March 1945. As a result of confectionery rationing, sales of chocolates seem to have ceased from 20 March 1943 (not to be resumed until 30 August 1947). Because of cuts in the amount of film stock and a limit of forty-one prints of any new film from 9 May 1943 onwards, the London circuit release had to be spread from two to three areas: North and West, North and East, and South London. This was not popular with South London managers or audiences which had to wait a further week.

A side effect of the War was that various glass light fittings were removed for the ceilings of auditoria as a safety precaution. The eighteen 'stalactite' light fittings around the ceiling of the New Victoria in London were taken down, never to be restored.

Cinemas in areas far removed from bombing and evacuation saw huge increases in attendances, numbers often swelled by troops billeted nearby. And when there was a lull in air raids, audiences flocked back to cinemas they had temporarily deserted. Film exhibition was immensely profitable as a whole, despite price increases that resulted from the doubling of Entertainments Tax.

Film bookings

Despite the War, the Gaumont circuit continued to offer stage shows in support of films at many of its cinemas, including in London in August 1940 the Gaumonts at Camden Town, Hammersmith, Holloway and Lewisham, the Tottenham Court Road Dominion and the Islington Blue Hall. In addition Gaumont Super Cinemas offered cine-variety at the Kilburn State and Elephant and Castle Trocadero.

Gaumont's access to top pictures was becoming more limited now that ABC and Odeon were such powerful competitors. In particular, the Warner Bros. and MGM pictures that had often played the circuit now went to ABC entirely. Until 1942, certain films, including top British and some Hollywood attractions, continued to play both Odeon and Gaumont circuits at the same time.

The biggest special attraction of the war years was *Gone with the Wind*. This was first shown for extended runs in the big cities, often at independent cinemas. Then came the time for a general release. In March 1942, Gaumont arranged to show it on the entire circuit for a two-week minimum period during the summer but some hitch developed as it finally went to ABC instead.

Hit films of the later war years on the Gaumont circuit included *Hello, 'Frisco, Hello* and *The Man in Grey* in 1943; *Sweet Rosie O'Grady, This Happy Breed, Cover Girl, The Song of Bernadette* and *Fanny by Gaslight*, all in 1944; and *A Song to Remember, Since You Went Away, Tonight and Every Night* and *They Were Sisters* in 1945.

J. Arthur Rank Takes Over

October 1941 brought the expiry of the option purchased by

John Maxwell for the Associated British Picture Corporation on the Ostrers' controlling shares in Gaumont through the Metropolis and Bradford Trust. By this time, Maxwell had been dead for a year. Even before the expiry date, J. Arthur Rank had made approaches to purchase the shares for the General Cinema Finance Corporation, the company he ran with C. M. Woolf and Lord Portal. Isidore Ostrer was receptive to his proposals because he was now living in Arizona as a result of his wife's ill health. An agreement was reached, giving the Ostrers £750,000 for the shares, but no official announcement was made. At the end of October, Rank and his allies took over as directors of the M&BT and Rank was regarded in the film trade as the head of Gaumont. Although Mark Ostrer remained in high office, he now shared his position of managing director with C. M. Woolf until the latter's death on the last day of 1942, after which Ostrer was allowed to continue on his own again. Rank also retained the services of Maurice Ostrer as head of Gaumont film production. The continued presence of the two younger Ostrers was undoubtedly part of the deal with Rank.*

There were immediate fears among rival exhibitors that Gaumont would be merged with Odeon, of which Rank was a director, into one giant organisation and these were intensified by the death of Odeon's head, Oscar Deutsch, in December 1941, after which Rank took charge of that circuit as well as becoming chairman of GBPC. With the 350 cinemas of Gaumont and the 250 cinemas of Odeon, he now effectively controlled a circuit of 600 outlets.

Rather surprisingly, when Rank and his associates replaced the Ostrer side at M&BT, Rank had not obtained the consent

---

*Isidore Ostrer detached himself completely from the film industry. He used the money from Rank to gain control of the huge Bradford wool and cotton group, Illingworth Morris, in which he and Maurice already had a substantial shareholding. He returned to England from the United States, although he spent much of the year in Cannes in the South of France. In 1957, he published a book of poetry. He died in September 1975, aged 86. Isidore's daughter was the actress Pamela Kellino, who became Pamela Mason on marrying James Mason. She inherited control of Illingworth Morris and caused some boardroom ructions in what some might call a family tradition. Maurice Ostrer remained with Rank until 1946 and one argument too many. He tried independent film production, then became chairman of Illingworth Morris, although basing himself with Isidore at Cannes. He died in 1979, three months after Isidore, aged 79.

of 20th Century-Fox to any transfer of ownership in the controlling block of shares. Fox still held the right of approval or veto, and still retained this in January 1944 when the position became public knowledge. Rank noted that the position had been discussed in letters but he was waiting to take it up in person with the Chairman of 20th Century-Fox, and this had not been possible with the War raging. Consent was eventually forthcoming, partly because Rank changed GBPC's articles of association so that Fox could have representatives on the board. The outcome was that J. Arthur Rank, for an outlay of just £750,000 (although he also bought ABPC's non-voting M&BT shares for twenty-five per cent less than Maxwell paid for them), took over Gaumont, a company then worth approximately £13 million.

Gaumont Super Cinemas

Despite the War, J. Arthur Rank was eager to acquire more cinemas and many desperate owners were only too glad to sell. Most of those taken over were added to the Odeon chain but he was anxious to buy the forty-nine per cent share of Gaumont Super Cinemas owned by the Hyams brothers and Major Gale. According to Gale's son, "The working arrangement between Gaumont Super Cinemas and the Gaumont British company became increasingly strained because of Arthur Rank's endeavours to take overall control and meetings took place in an atmosphere of acrimony."

A deal was finally agreed, with a completion date of 29 February 1944, under which Gaumont (through APPH) bought out the minority partners to take complete control of the chain, consisting of the Kilburn Gaumont State, Elephant and Castle Trocadero, Stepney Troxy, Bermondsey Trocette, Edmonton Regal, West Norwood Regal, Oldham Gaumont and Watford Gaumont, as well as London area sites at Brixton and Whitechapel.

A single but notable addition to the Gaumont circuit through PCT in 1943 was the Ascot at Anniesland, Glasgow, a large and impressive cinema that had opened after the War had started.

Celebrating Peace: V E Day

When the end of the War was imminent, Gaumont made special arrangements to celebrate the arrival of peace. Here, as described by Coventry cinema historian Gil Robottom, is how it was handled at the town's Gaumont: "As the news came through by radio, the late afternoon screening of *Madonna and the Seven Moons* was halted by manager Hugh Deacon telephoning the projection box. Second projectionist George Smith put on a specially prepared record which had been received from the Gaumont head office a few days earlier. The audience heard E. V. H. Emmett, who for the previous five years had announced the Gaumont-British newsreel, telling them that the war in Europe was over and urging 'On this great occasion, let us voice our feelings in song.' He invited them to join in 'Land of Hope and Glory', spontaneously followed by 'Roll Out the Barrel' to which the audience enthusiastically joined in."

Throughout the circuit, cinema frontages were decorated with the flags of the Allies, pictures of the Western leaders and the King and Queen. Floodlights were turned on again to show the displays after dark. It was a time for rejoicing — and for relaxing at the pictures as never before.

An imposing addition to the circuit: the Gaumont (ex Ascot) Anniesland, Glasgow.

Victory displays from Gaumont British News & Views, *July 1945. (Courtesy of Andy Garner.)*

6. Manager Frank Bradley's display at Regent Sheffield. Set piece on canopy, 25' x 10'; canvas surround, 39' in length.

7. New Victoria, Bradford (Manager G. Ridler), on VE Day.

8. Gaumont Princes, North Shields (Manageress Phyllis Turnball).

9. Gaumont, Derby (Manager R. Todd).

10. The display at Gaumont Palace, Barnstaple (Manager A. M. Carpenter).

10: POSTWAR BOOM AND CMA

Postwar boom

The end of the War put people in a celebratory mood. As far as outside entertainment was concerned, the cinema was the most immediately available choice and attendances in 1946 soared to an all-time high of 1,635 million. Thanks in particular to the Gainsborough-Gaumont production of *The Wicked Lady* (with Margaret Lockwood and James Mason) and *The Bells of St. Mary's* (with Bing Crosby and Ingrid Bergman), the Gaumont circuit had its fair share of the windfall. Some films like *The Wicked Lady* were held over for as much as six weeks in locations like Sunderland, where weekly changes were normal.

Living standards did not improve for some years, and the very cold winter conditions of early 1947 led to fuel cuts. Cinemas were forced to delay opening until 3.30pm when they could be warm enough to admit patrons. There was a keen demand for ice creams, chocolates and cigarettes but problems frequently arose in obtaining supplies, especially of chocolates.

During the peak year of 1946, the Gaumont Portsmouth reached its highest-ever total of over 913,000 admissions and the Gaumont Derby admitted a record 46,000 patrons in one week to *The Bells of St. Mary's*, opening at 10am to accommodate the crowds. The all-time record weekly figure at the Gaumont Sheffield was 47,846 — but the title of the attraction is not clear. However, the film which came only 106 admissions short of beating that total in February 1948 is a surprise: *The Birth of a Baby*. Wednesday's total attendance of 8,499 was an all-time record for the cinema. The film played a second week to 21,944 paying patrons, with snow hurting attendances.

The Birth of a Baby was a 1937 independent American educational production which used little-known players to tell a story of pregnancy and show an actual childbirth. It was banned in many American states and reputedly caused some members of the audience to faint. Although sponsored by the National Baby Welfare Council, it was refused a certificate by the British Board of Film Censors but approved for adult only screenings by the London County Council. It had played a week of matinees at the huge Gaumont Hammersmith in February 1940, with showings for women only on Monday, Wednesday, Friday and Saturday at 11.30am and 2.50pm, and men only admitted on Tuesday and Saturday at 1pm and 4.30pm. At Sheffield, it carried a local A certificate but no-one under 18 was admitted to witness "Dame Nature's Great Miracle SINCERELY PORTRAYED". There wasn't even a second feature, only *Antarctic Whale* in the series "This Modern Age", so that the main attraction could be shown four times. The column by Showman in the local press declared that sensation seekers would be disappointed: "It may be criticised as a film but its value as a social document cannot be over-estimated. A difficult subject is handled with great delicacy, with the result that there is nothing to offend good taste."

A very successful American re-issue of *The Birth of a Baby* in 1947, plus a shortage of new Hollywood product, seems to have stimulated Gaumont to give it a circuit release wherever local authorities would permit it to be screened.

The lack of American pictures followed the decision of the Labour government, attempting to stem the flow of sterling across the Atlantic, to impose a staggering seventy-five per cent ad valorem tax on films imported into Britain. The major studios responded by refusing to send any more productions to Britain. This left a substantial backlog of sixty first features already in the country but these were eked out and each of the major chains started playing a number of reissues of hit films that had previously played a rival circuit.

At Gaumonts, a top 1946 ABC release *Piccadilly Incident* reappeared as early as November 1947, but the glut of re-runs became so pronounced by April 1948, with such double bills as *Up in Arms* plus *Bambi* and *The Return of Frank James* paired with *Where There's Life*, that a rare exception, *The Lady from Shang-*

hai, was actually advertised as "It's New!". Audiences were fed up with re-issues and attendances suffered as a result.

The booking crisis seems to have prompted an increase in the use of the largest cinemas for live shows. From Boxing Day 1947, the State Kilburn presented Billy Smart's Circus live on stage for four weeks while four more of the London supers switched from the circuit release to start a month of pantomimes. The Edmonton Regal offered *Cinderella*; the Elephant and Castle Trocadero staged *Mother Goose*; the Stepney Troxy presented *Dick Whittington*; and the Hammersmith Gaumont paraded *Snow White and the Seven Dwarfs*. Each pantomime played one week at each of the four cinemas.

The British market was so valuable to Hollywood that its loss had serious repercussions, with some expensive films being postponed or made in black and white rather than colour. J. Arthur Rank responded to what seemed like a permanent situation by stepping up the production of British films to fill the gap. At this point, the British government suddenly caved in and withdrew the tax with effect from 3 May 1948, unleashing a flood of Hollywood movies. The British films that Rank had rushed into production were no match for the American product. By the end of 1949, Rank had to admit to losses on film production of £3,350,000 and the company came perilously close to collapse.

Saturday morning pictures

We come along on Saturday morning
Greeting everybody with a smile
We come along on Saturday morning
Knowing it's well worthwhile
As members of the G.B. [later *Gaumont*] *Club,*
We all intend to be
Good citizens when we grow up
And champions of the free
We come along on Saturday morning
Greeting everybody with a smile — smile — smile
Greeting everybody with a smile.

This song for the Gaumont British Junior Club was written by organist Con Docherty who made the recorded accompaniment on the organ at the Newcastle Odeon. This was later adopted by Odeon as its club song as well, with the appropriate change in name.

The clubs had continued at many cinemas during the War —

Two incidents from 1947. Cinemas had to campaign to operate on Sundays. Above, the war-battered Hippodrome Nottingham urges electors to support a new vote on Sunday opening. Below, it's "swimming room only" at the flooded Picture House York in July 1947 (courtesy of Andy Garner). Note the rounded corners favoured for Gaumont screens.

Coventry's had even gained 500 Dutch refugee children as honorary temporary members — and the London clubs, which had been closed, re-opened in June 1945.

In *Bradford's Rock 'n' Roll: The Golden Years (1959-1965)*, Derek A. J. Lister recalled: "In 1945, I had joined the Gaumont Saturday Morning Club, consisting of a sing-along — the one with the bouncing ball moving over the words on the screen. This was accompanied by the giant Wurlitzer organ which had previously risen from the depths of the cinema. After the songs Uncle Phil (Ridler), the manager, would find his way down from the top of the stalls to a microphone on the stage, All the way down he would be dodging the many missiles that were aimed at him from all corners. This was also accompanied by a loud booing and stamping of feet. Arriving at the microphone he would give us a little message, though no-one could hear it. Then we sang the National Anthem, followed by a cartoon, serial, and picture. [...] A few years later ... I met Mr. Ridler (Uncle Phil) and asked him 'Why the National Anthem *before* the films?', to which his logical answer was 'Did you wait to the very end of the picture?' Looking back, nearly everyone seemed to be edging up the aisles to the doors to rush out while still watching the film. You were not allowed to sit in the back stalls, only the front stalls. The only time this did not apply was after the 1946 flood. The Gaumont had been under water, just like the rest of Bradford, but it had only affected the lower front stalls. The back stalls, being at a higher level, had not been hit. For weeks after you could see the tide mark where the water had reached."

Besides the selection of films and singing, there was an educational aspect to the shows. A local policeman, usually called Uncle Bob, would often appear to issue road safety tips like looking to left and right before crossing the road.

Regrettably, insufficient information has come to light to provide a proper account of Saturday morning pictures, although it seems there were 156 clubs established at Gaumonts by 1953.

One large family: CMA

J. Arthur Rank was not allowed by the Labour government to amalgamate the two circuits he now controlled, although in late 1947, to raise money for film production, he had arranged for Odeon to take over GCFC. As it was through GCFC that he controlled Gaumont, Odeon now became top dog.

The two circuits had to have separate circuit releases and re-

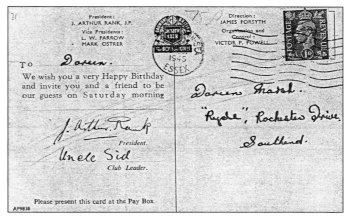

Gaumont British Junior Clubs sent greetings to members on their birthdays. Not all the postcards offered free admission. (Courtesy of Ken George.)

tain their separate identities with two separate bookers. However, consent from the Board of Trade (headed by Harold Wilson) was forthcoming for a scheme to make some substantial operating economies by creating a new company to service the two circuits. This was formed with the prosaic name of Circuits Management Association (CMA) in an agreement dated 15 June 1948 and approved by shareholders on the 23rd of the month. J. Arthur Rank was chairman and John Davis managing director with the other directors being J. A. Callum, L. W. Farrow, L. Kent, and Mark Ostrer. Until this point, Ostrer had been chairman and managing director of GBPC and this marked the end of his control over day to day operations, although he remained a director of GBPC and various subsidiaries until his death in 1958.

A letter dated 24 June 1948 and addressed to employees read: "A new company known as Circuits Management Association Limited (CMA) has been formed for the purpose of operating all theatres at present forming part of the Odeon and Gaumont circuits. The scheme will come into operation on Sunday, 27th June, 1948, and on that date all persons employed in the Gaumont circuit will be automatically transferred to the employment of CMA.

"This transfer will in no way alter the obligations, rights and privileges attached to your present employment. The new arrangement permits complete co-operation between all theatres now operated by Odeon and Gaumont and will enable the house staffs to feel they are now — as never before — part of one large family."

Most of the rest of the two-sided letter discussed the effect on company pension schemes. Elsewhere, it was estimated that CMA would take a whole year to come fully into operation and 400 jobs might be axed.

Covering 564 operating cinemas, plus various sites, closed cinemas and other property interests, CMA immediately put Gaumont in an inferior position to Odeon, as Odeon had a $58^1/_2\%$ interest in the new company compared to $41^1/_2\%$ for Gaumont. No doubt this accurately reflected the value and earnings potential of the two circuits (Gaumont had approximately 250 cinemas to Odeon's 310), but nevertheless it did little for Gaumont staff's morale. Nor did the rapid departure of the Gaumont booking chief Arthur Brown (who had succeeded Arthur Jarratt in 1943) to programme a minor circuit in Wales. Odeon's Richard Hamer becoming booking controller of CMA

in October. New CMA Weekly Return forms had to be filled in by managers from 3 October.

New policies were applied to both circuits with a sharp reduction in the number of live shows, reversing Gaumont's position of favouring them as an occasional novelty. It was argued that there was an excess supply of films and no need for the additional expense involved in presenting live entertainment.

The Gaumont name had previously been reserved for the cinemas that the circuit had built for itself, or older buildings that had been entirely reconstructed, plus one or two very new cinemas taken over like the Embassy Chadwell Heath. Shortly after the War, the newly acquired Savoy Chorlton-cum-Hardy took the Gaumont name, as did the Regent Sheffield, Picture House Saltaire and Borough Theatre Wallsend.

Then, beginning in late 1949 and extending through 1950, a vast number of the other cinemas on the circuit were renamed Gaumont. These were not only the bigger cinemas, like most of the PCT Regents, but also some humbler properties like the Pavilion at Balham. And so it was from this point onwards that the Gaumont name achieved its greatest prominence and impact, rivalling Odeon as a High Street name, even though its name no longer applied to the cream of the circuit. The other major chain, ABC, still called its cinemas by various names — primarily Regal, Savoy and Rex.

Under CMA, blue was emphasised as the circuit colour. Monthly programmes were printed in blue. Gaumont signs were usually in blue reinforced by blue outline neon, although those on the back walls at Finchley and Bromley remained red, while many cinemas in the West Country, especially from the former Albany Ward division, continued to carry the Gaumont name in red, with red neon. In Edinburgh, when the Rutland was renamed, the Gaumont sign was, for no apparent reason, in a scroll design like that of the first Gaumont Palace in Birmingham. Press advertising took longer to sort out, but by the early Fifties the Gaumont name was usually printed in a thick, italic sans serif typeface, later to be given a three-dimensional look.

A handful of Odeon cinemas were renamed Gaumont. This applied in situations where the Odeon circuit had two cinemas in close proximity and one of them customarily played the Gaumont circuit release. The change, of course, made it much easier for picturegoers to link advertising for the Gaumont circuit release with the cinemas that were playing it. Thus the

Odeons at Eltham Hill and Kingsbury, the Heathway Dagenham and Regal Wimbledon were among those renamed and then listed as part of the Gaumont circuit, although they were never in fact owned by Gaumont. But Odeon cinemas at Sudbury and Weybridge as well as (among others) the Bethnal Green Foresters, Guildford Playhouse and Hounslow Dominion were attached to the Gaumont circuit in programming without a change of name.

There seem to have been just two examples of a change in the reverse direction, of a Gaumont theatre being attached to its former rival. One took place in Salisbury where Gaumont had two cinemas and the Picture House was renamed Odeon as it took the Odeon release. The other was in Islington, North London, where the Angel and the Blue Hall/Gaumont were in close proximity. The Angel took the Odeon release concurrently with the actual Odeon Islington which was far enough away in Upper Street to make this practicable, although they retained their different names to avoid confusion.

As far as film bookings were concerned, a joint booking department negotiated circuit releases with the same distributors for both circuits. There was no difference at all in the sources of product. New Paramount films had stopped playing the Gaumont circuit after *I Wanted Wings* went out in August 1941 (with the exception of a B feature, *Henry Gets Glamour*, in November 1943). *Blue Skies* had been revived in May 1948 during the shortage of new films. Under CMA, Paramount pictures played both circuits and in November 1948 *A Foreign Affair* became the first new main feature from the studio to play the Gaumont circuit in seven years.

MGM and Warner Bros. films even made a return to Gaumont and Odeon screens under CMA. *The Duchess of Idaho* in September 1950 was the first Metro picture to obtain a Gaumont release since 1943. However, the MGM output soon reverted solidly to the ABC circuit for several years, although Warner Bros. double bills featured occasionally on the Rank chains for some time.

Despite the separation of the two circuits for booking purposes, there were occasions when major films would play on one circuit and at as many non-competing cinemas on the other circuit as possible. For Odeon releases, Rank's hugely expensive *Caesar and Cleopatra* was a case in point in 1946 with later examples including *The Best Years of Our Lives* and *Oliver Twist*. *XIVth Olympiad* was a Gaumont circuit release that many Odeons took.

Competing Gaumont and Odeon cinemas stuck rigidly to their own circuit release, even when there was a marked discrepancy in seating capacities which resulted in insufficient seats being available for hit films at the smaller of the two: queues quickly formed outside a small cinema like the Gaumont at Balham, South London, especially for the cheaper prices, while there were often seats to spare up the road at the much larger Odeon. However, when the same circuit had two or more cinemas it could favour the larger of the two with the better programme of the week. This happened in Kilburn where the vast Gaumont State with its 4,004 seats took all the really strong releases, whether Odeon or Gaumont, and the Grange across the road, with a far from negligible 2,028 seats to fill, played the other programme. In the many weeks when there was little to choose between the two circuits' offerings, the Gaumont State would take the Gaumont release.

Then there were situations in which an Odeon or Gaumont cinema operated on its own. While normally taking its own circuit's release, it would defect to pick up an exceptional picture going through the other, especially when this was a hit British film from the Rank organisation. Gaumont cinemas in this position included the Regal West Norwood and Gaumont Clapham in South London. Odeon releases of the early 1950s that played a substantial number of Gaumont halls in place of the weaker Gaumont programme for the week included *The Card* and *Son of Paleface*.

In a town like Sheffield, where (until the Odeon opened in 1956) Rank had only the large Gaumont but there were competing independent cinemas, the situation was also somewhat flexible. Until the Odeon arrived, all the city centre opposition cinemas were older than the Gaumont and all independently run from 1948: the huge Hippodrome played the ABC release most weeks but also took many of the best Odeon releases. The other two regular first-run outlets were Cinema House (763 seats, run by a small local circuit) and the Union Street Palace (985 seats). The Gaumont would regularly play four or five of the best Odeon programmes each year and even nabbed the ABC hit *Spring in Park Lane* for a two-week run in 1948, resulting in attendances bettered only by *Forever Amber* that year. The Odeon circuit's *Jolson Sings Again* in 1950 and *Samson and Delilah* in 1951 were the top attractions to play the Gaumont in these years. Occasionally, when independents seemingly balked at playing difficult Rank films on Odeon release such as *Corridor of Mirrors* (1948), *Romeo and Juliet* (1954) and *Richard III* (1955), the Gaumont would oblige.

Curse of the Quota

The Films Act of 1948 set a quota of forty-five per cent for British main features and twenty-five per cent for supporting features (the latter based on footage). The main feature requirement dropped to forty per cent a year later and to thirty per cent from 1950 onwards. The trade was continually irked that, solely in order to fulfill this legal requirement, films had to be played that were likely or certain to annoy audiences rather than entertain them. To take some 1952 comments from the Gaumont Sheffield Weekly Returns: the manager reported that *Old Mother Riley Meets the Vampire* was generally considered "an insult to people's intelligence", to which he added: "There is no doubt this film had a very bad effect on the box-office". And of *Distant Trumpet*: "This type of film does untold harm to the British film industry — general opinion, 'a real stinker'".

Often, poor British main films were paired with more attractive Hollywood features that usually played second on the double bill. When the British comedy *Treasure Hunt* played with the American thriller *The Captive City*, Sheffield's manager reported: "Everyone agrees (even the complimentaries complained) that *Treasure Hunt* was one of the worst films ever shown in this theatre. I am positive that if we had shown *The Captive City* last as requested, we should have done a little better. This type of programme is partly responsible for driving patrons away from this theatre."

In addition, many popular British features of the recent past, which still counted for quota purposes, were revived as supporting features, usually abridged. These repeats did not always please audiences either. When *The Fallen Idol* reappeared in support of *This Woman is Dangerous* at Sheffield, the manager noted: "Enjoyed by most patrons, but many patrons when looking at the stills on the front went away when they knew it was a re-issue." And when *Passport to Pimlico* returned with *Mandy*: "*Mandy* received as a wonderful film — I am convinced we would have done better business if the second feature had not been a re-issue. Many patrons are asking why we are showing old films."

The postwar popularity of foreign-language films, both subtitled and dubbed, did not at this time gain such pictures a Gaumont circuit release but at some situations (not Sheffield) they were booked as second features in place of Hollywood fillers. Thus audiences at the Chelsea and Finchley Gaumonts and West Norwood Regal seeing *Phone Call from a Stranger* in 1952 were spared the Hollywood B picture and shown various sophisticated French films instead, such as *Edward and Caroline* at West Norwood.

Technical

Among many other manoeuvrings of the early Forties, J. Arthur Rank had amalgamated G-B Equipment and its rival Kalee into G.B.-Kalee. The Gaumont-Kalee 21 projector appeared in 1946, manufactured by Kershaws of Leeds. This encased the projector, soundhead, arc lamp, spool boxes, motors and rest in a streamlined protective housing of beige colour with white control panels. Although totally enclosed, the film path remained fully visible and all the parts remained readily accessible for inspection and servicing. The soundhead was re-designed Duosonic. This new design of projector was widely exported as well as being installed not only in Gaumonts but in many Odeons which had previously relied on B.T.H. This was supplemented in 1948 by the G-K 20 of much simpler design and less massive stand, with a substantially lower price. This was best suited to cinemas seating up to 1,400. The Kalee 21s and 20s would stay in service for the remaining life of many cinemas and be replaced at the long-term Gaumont and Odeon survivors by imported Italian Cinemeccanica equipment.

The former Rank top executive Stan Fishman recalls that G.B.-Kalee also manufactured a perfume that was sprayed by ushers to give cinemas an opulent aroma. The same essence was introduced into the washed air in the plenum room, further spreading a nice smell around the auditorium.

Decline of the Cinema Organ

Tony Moss comments: "By 1946, the number of organists had been reduced to about sixty and, after the merger with Odeon under CMA, all but five of the contracts came to an end between 1947 and 1951.

"There were two well-known theatre and broadcast organists who began or developed their careers at Gaumont during this period. On release from war service with the R.A.F., William Davies joined Gaumont at Wolverhampton in 1946 and impressed the circuit's musical director, Felton Rapley. The following year, he was transferred to the Gaumont Finchley. In 1949/50, when Rapley left to joint Chappell of Bond Street, he

The Gaumont-Kalee 21 with "elephant's foot", streamlined with G.-K. type 83 sound head and G.-K. Lightmaster arc lamp — seen here at the Gaumont Dingle. (Courtesy of Mike Taylor, Projected Picture Trust North West.)

The Court Darlington, seen here celebrating the peace in 1945, was burned down in a fire in August 1947.

was succeeded by William Davies at the Dominion Tottenham Court Road. In the same year, Davies joined the Jack Hylton Organisation as organist and musical director for artists such as Arthur Askey and the Crazy Gang.

"Charles Smitton began his theatre organ career at the Curzon Old Swan, Liverpool, joining GBPC at the Gaumont Manchester in 1944 for a very short time before being called up for military service. On demob in 1945, he gave one performance at the Tivoli in London's Strand before returning to the Gaumont Manchester. In 1946, he transferred to the Gaumont Worcester and in 1947 to the Gaumont Wood Green, followed by a year at the Dominion Tottenham Court Road. From both Wood Green and Tottenham Court Road, he toured the Gaumont circuit as guest organist. With the merger of Gaumont and Odeon under the CMA banner, he became resident at the Odeon Manchester, followed in 1950 by two years at the Odeon Birmingham. In 1950, he returned to Worcester to open the new Odeon in concert with two other CMA organists, Stanley Tudor and Bobby Pagan.

"Many of the organists whose contracts ran out transferred to theatre management. Besides Bobby Pagan, who was at the Odeon Blackpool until 1953 and Stanley Tudor, who remained at the Gaumont Manchester until 1953. the other three from Gaumont who remained with CMA were Tommy Dando, who in 1949 went from the Gaumont Watford to Rank's new cinema in Cairo, the Rivoli, returning to Odeon (Ireland) from 1951 to 1956; Louis Mordish, who was at the Gaumont State Kilburn until 1953 and the Leicester Square Theatre until 1958; and Terance Casey, who left the Gaumont Hammersmith to freelance in 1949, but returned to the Gaumont Haymarket from 1956 to 1958."

War and other damage

For nine frustrating years, postwar restrictions on "luxury" building prevented Gaumont constructing new cinemas on its pre-war sites and re-constructing those that had been severely damaged by bombing. During this time further cinemas would be lost in fires: the Court at Darlington in 1947 (hardly lamented, because the circuit had two other properties in the town), the St. Andrew's Square Picture House in Edinburgh in November 1952, and the Empire Barnsley at the beginning of 1954.

Gaumont was keen to purchase sites for future expansion. At

the start of 1947, exhibitors in Northern Ireland must have been shocked when the circuit announced that it would acquire a number of sites as soon as building restrictions were lifted, starting with one on the Antrim Road, Belfast. Until then, the chain had seemed content to operate just one large cinema, the Classic, in the centre of Belfast.

A property list of circa February 1952 date includes a number of cinema sites. Even though no Gaumonts ever appeared on them and many may have been dismissed on further consideration before the War, some may indicate the way the circuit would have eventually expanded but for the war. In any case, these sites are part of the circuit's history and a list of them may be of some interest to local historians. Sometimes, an address is given in the records, sometimes the location is based on other sources.

Banstead, Surrey (believed to have been on the site of the Vicarage where Odeon had planned to build in 1937)

Belfast, Antrim (a house in Antrim Road, the start of Gaumont's proposed Northern Ireland expansion – probably the cinema site for which an office block application was made in January 1958)

Bexley, on Rochester Way (believed to have been at the junction of Danson Road — the pre-war Harry Weston scheme)

Bexleyheath, Southeast London (on Broadway)

Bristol, Avon (at Hanham, part of the Kingswood district to the east of the city)

Brixton, South London (the previously mentioned Greyhound Stadium site at 344/364 Brixton Road, associated with Gaumont Super Cinemas and, in July 1939, with GTC and plans by W. E. Trent)

Buckhurst Hill, Essex

Burton-on-Trent, Staffordshire

Canning Town, Northeast London (on the site of the Grand, destroyed in the War)

Chertsey (from the 1936 Harry Weston scheme in London Road)

Clapham, South London (at 75/87 High Street, despite the presence of the circuit's large Majestic on the other side of the road)

Clapham Junction, South London (the bombed Pavilion site, and another at the corner of Dorothy Road)

Dublin, Ireland

Durham, Co. Durham

Falkirk, Central Scotland (a cinema on this, or another site, was promised in 1957 and again in 1958)

Guernsey, Channel Islands (two sites described as "Esplanade" and "Mouettes")

Hayes, Middlesex (believed to have been at the corner of Derwent Drive and Uxbridge Road)

Leicester, Leicestershire

Lincoln, Lincolnshire (two sites, High Street and Queen Street)

Liverpool, Merseyside (on Aigburth Road)

Plymouth, Devon (the sites of the war-destroyed Savoy and Palladium)

Poole, Dorset (two sites, one in Commercial Road, one at Wallisdown)

Portsmouth, Hampshire (in Commercial Road)

St. Helens, Merseyside (this site was auctioned off in September 1957)

Scunthorpe, Humberside (at the junction of Exeter and Doncaster Roads — plans were withdrawn in March 1948)

Southbourne, Dorset (this would have been a suburban Bournemouth cinema)

Westcliffe-on-Sea, Essex

West Hartlepool, Cleveland (two sites — one at 16 Lynn Street, originally purchased by PCT on 21 September 1920, eventually sold following a Compulsory Purchase Order on 19 November 1969)

West Worthing, West Sussex

Whitechapel, East London (the site of the former Pavilion associated with Gaumont Super Cinemas, not that of the bombed Rivoli)

York, Yorkshire (two sites, one being the long-closed Scala, the other at Castle Gate)

Gaumont had been interested in rebuilding where the remains of the Shakespeare stood at Lavender Hill, Clapham Junction, but seems to have disposed of the site after planning permission was refused in 1950. It had definitely decided against returning several other war-damaged sites to film use, including the West Kensington Super in London where the freehold was put up for sale in August 1949.

Although major work was excluded by the regulations, it became possible to make substantial improvements to some of the more battered properties that had survived the War, taking the opportunity to rename them Gaumonts when they didn't already have the name. The Gaumont Peckham, South London, was closed for nearly four months in 1948 while the auditorium was "torn out" and new fittings and equipment installed. This had a gala re-opening with a personal appearance by Anne Crawford. The Halifax Picture House was closed for nearly nine months after a fire in 1948 and re-opened as the Gaumont in early 1949. The Morecambe Tower was closed for a couple of months before re-opening for the 1949 summer season, much improved. The King's Cross Cinema in London also closed for improvements in 1949, but here it took nearly three years to create a more modern auditorium and to resume activities. By contrast, the heavily battered Coventry Gaumont was restored and redecorated without closing during 1949. The Stoke-on-Trent Hippodrome underwent seven months of modernisation while the Northampton Exchange closed more briefly for a flat ceiling to be installed under the barrel-vaulted timber roof. Such work continued into the early Fifties with the Kettering Pavilion closing for several weeks for refurbishment and re-opening as the town's Gaumont.

At the end of 1946, the GTC division of Gaumont purchased from Moss Empires the two Empires at Cardiff and Southampton which had been on films, functioning as part of the Gaumont circuit, for many years. The price paid was £261,000. At the same time, GTC sold to Moss Empires for £1,112,000 six of its music halls (the Prince of Wales and Palladium in London's West End, the Empires at Holborn and Penge, the Hippodromes at Brighton and Wolverhampton). Two others, the Hippodromes at Birmingham and Portsmouth, owned by a GTC subsidiary, soon followed.

At the end of the Forties, a big effort began to liquidate the many Gaumont and Odeon subsidiaries and transfer their assets to a parent company. At this time, APPH, for example, was absorbed into GBPC, following an offer to the subsidiary's shareholders in 1947. This was the beginning of a long process that would lead to them being absorbed into one company, the Rank Organisation.

And so we say farewell...
A number of very old-fashioned, completely unwanted cinemas were quietly shed, beginning with the St. George's Hall Bradford and Queens Birkenhead in the spring of 1949. In October of that year, the impending closure of the Edinburgh Picture House was announced. This was one of the two first-run Rank cinemas in the town and occupied the former banqueting hall of the Royal Hotel. PCT had bought a controlling interest in the hotel in 1918 and Rank sold all or part of the site including the cinema for £750,000. However, it did not actually close for redevelopment until May 1951 (Marks and Spencer opened a new store in June 1957 with a new Mount Royal Hotel above). At that time, there was a surplus of Gaumont halls in the town and the nearby St. Andrew's Picture House more than replaced it, but that would soon be destroyed by fire. Elsewhere, the rather striking Corona Gorton (Manchester) left the Gaumont empire to join the Snape cinema circuit. The venerable Electrics at Chatham, Sowerby Bridge and York were shed, the last two of these being taken over by an independent operator.

In 1953, the West End scene was shaken up when both the Marble Arch Pavilion and Regent Street New Gallery were leased to foreign film distributors. Now that CMA combined the West End Odeon and Gaumont properties for booking purposes and West End business generally was in the doldrums, neither of these cinemas was as valuable as it had previously been. The Pavilion had been linked with the Gaumont Haymarket in opening new films. After Archway Film Distributors had presented four dubbed Italian films at the Pavilion, the company leased the cinema for further presentations in a similar vein from October 1952. Rank sold the freehold a few months later but the cinema continued as a foreign-language venue for a few years. The New Galley had become a huge lossmaker and Rank were glad to lease it to Regent Film Distributors which premiered its new releases there along with occasional second runs of English-language attractions. Again Rank soon sold the freehold, this time to the Seventh Day Adventist Church which soon ended Regent's lease and put the building to religious use with few alterations, often showing Christian films.

11: THE AGE OF CINEMASCOPE

Hollywood's response to declining attendances figures at American movie theatres was to make more productions in colour and to re-introduce 3-D and wide screen — all ways of giving the cinema image more impact than the black-and-white television picture.

In Britain, admissions were steadily falling but far less dramatically — from the 1946 peak of 1,635 million down to 1,285 million in 1953. One innovation by CMA from November 1953 was Cinetokens, the equivalent of book tokens that could be exchanged at Odeons or Gaumonts for cinema tickets. Whether they ever caught on to a significant degree is doubtful.

Colour
Colour was increasingly used in both American and British pictures. There is no doubt that Technicolor and Eastman Color went down well with audiences. However, many cheaper processes became available and these may have been counter-productive, at least on the prints made available in this country. Returning to the report sheets of the Gaumont Sheffield, one finds that, when the Jane Russell western *Montana Belle* played, there were complaints about the Trucolor process, while the Pathécolor of the Errol Flynn adventure *Crossed Swords* was described by the manager as "atrocious". To be fair to Trucolor, the same system was praised when *Jubilee Trail* was shown. In the case of the British film *Conflict of Wings*, its use of Eastman Colour went on record as the sole aspect of the film to receive praise from patrons.

3-D: "A lion in your lap"
3-D had been around in the Thirties but was relaunched with the African adventure picture *Bwana Devil*, which opened at the Odeon Marble Arch in London on 20 March 1953 and soon after at three Gaumont theatres: the West End Birmingham and Gaumonts Leeds and Glasgow, playing from 11am daily.

This required the installation of a metallised screen and a linking system between the two projectors to show forty-minute reels of the same film simultaneously with an interval for re-loading. Audiences had to wear special glasses so that the two overlapping images on the screen merged into a three-dimensional picture.

A few other Gaumonts, like the second-run Rialto Liverpool played some later 3-D films like *Sangaree*, but no 3-D film was ever given a full release on the Gaumont (or Odeon) circuit, and ABC was the only national chain to embrace 3-D on a big scale. Once the novelty aspect of 3-D had been absorbed, it seemed clear to Hollywood that the system had no lasting power to boost attendances — indeed, it was unpopular with those who already wore glasses and there were complaints of eye strain and headaches. Many cinemas were too wide for it to be seen properly from the side seats. It was quietly dropped with several later 3-D productions being shown only 'flat' in this country.

CinemaScope: "You see it without the use of glasses"
What helped finish off 3-D was the launch in 1953 by 20th Century-Fox of CinemaScope, the wide screen process that was in part a revival of the Fox Grandeur system which had failed to take off in 1929-30. CinemaScope even claimed to have an increased sense of depth. (This had been preceded by larger panoramic screens that created a wider picture in 1.75:1 ratio using regular prints but cutting off the top and bottom.)

Because of its ties with Rank, Fox expected to show its line-up of CinemaScope pictures in Odeon and Gaumont cinemas. The first CinemaScope feature, the religious epic *The Robe*, opened at several key Odeon theatres while the second, a conventional comedy called *How to Marry a Millionaire*, also made its debut at an Odeon cinema in London — the Odeon Marble Arch — but was otherwise set for a Gaumont release. Most of

THIS COPY TO....File....................................

Theatre No. 14

C.M.A. LTD. WEEKLY RETURN [GAUMONT RELEASE]

Week No.....5.... Week Ending....8th AUGUST........................ 1953.

Theatre....GAUMONT.... Town....SHEFFIELD....

	(1) ATTENDANCES EXCLUDING C.C.C.	(2) NET HOUSE RECEIPTS EXCLUDING HIRE FEES	THEATRE SALES					
			(3) CON-FECTIONERY	(4) CIGAR-ETTES	(5) ICES	(6) DRINKS	(7) NUTS	(8) TOTAL SALES
			ALL FIGURES TO NEAREST £					
WEEK'S RESULTS : This Year	23329	1522	185	161	117	76	27	566
Attgs.118/94 Last Year	20411	1363	60	119	161	51	57	448
CUMULATIVE This Year	118714	8050	966	802	512	336	119	2725
RESULTS: Last Year	104781	6606	491	573	692	266	147	2169
CUM. INCREASE : This Year	13933	1444	465	229	-	70	-	556
CUM. DECREASE This Year	-	-	-	-	180	-	28	-
PENCE PER PERSON This Week			2.03	1.76	1.27	.83	.30	6.19
CLOSING STOCK (to nearest £)			206	412			45	

THIS YEAR FILMS SHOWN	LAST YEAR	DAILY RECEIPTS		
		NET HOUSE RECEIPTS		
		DAILY RECEIPTS £	SUB-TOTALS £	
SUN. Prog. length.....2.....hrs.0....mins.	SUN.			
ABBOTT & COSTELLO IN HOLLYWOOD.	VARIETY GIRL.	153	153	Sun
MON. Prog. length.....3.....hrs.7....mins.	MON.	163		Mon
GENEVIEVE.	LITTLE BIG SHOT.			
MURDER AT 3.a.m.	CHILTERN HUNDREDS.	313		Tues
THURS. Prog. length.....hrs.....mins.	THUR.	306		Wed
as above.	as above.	248		Thur
		170		Fri.
OPPOSITION FULL PROGRAMME.	This Year Only.	169	1369	Sat
Cinema House.	"HANS CHRISTIAN ANDERSEN (2nd week)			As per sub-total on Weekly Price Category Summary
Hippodrome.	TIME BOMB CONFIDENTIALLY CONNIE		1522	C.C.C.
				Sunday Concerts
Union St.P.P.	TOP OF THE FORM REDHEAD FROM WYOMING		1522	As per Col. (2)
				Hire Fees
AUDIENCE REACTION			1522	Total

"GENEVIEVE" This film has delighted our Patrons thoroughly. There has been no doubt about the most favourable impression created by GENEVIEVE. 'The best British comedy ever seen''A really great film' 'The best film for a long time' are a few of the comments passed.
"MURDER AT THREE A.M." One comment only on this film...Shocking.

SOUND PROJECTION AND SCREEN
*SATISFACTORY
*SEE REPORT ATTACHED
*Delete where necessary.

R.MAISTRICK.
Manager.

TOLL AND TRUNK CALLS

Date	Exchange	No.	Caller	Called	Subject	Charge
3/8	Telegram.	Nascreno. London.		N.S.S.	Trailers.	1/6d.
4/8	"	"		"	"	1/6d.
5/8	Leeds.	23136.		D/Manager.	Nett Figs.	1/6d.
7/8	"	"	A/Manager	"	Emergency Repair	2/0d

Cw. £1341.66.

FORM A6   A6/4428

Carbon copy (filed at cinema) of a typical weekly return to head office from the Gaumont Sheffield, recording audience appreciation of the vintage car comedy Genevieve in August 1953 and a savage comment on the British B feature. (Courtesy of the late Paul Archer.)

3-D in Glasgow during March 1953 and the second Fox CinemaScope release in Manchester during February 1954. (Poor quality images from microfilm.)

the Gaumonts in the key cities received a CinemaScope installation with full stereophonic sound, and the Fox comedy opened on 31 January 1954 at the Gaumonts Birmingham, Liverpool and Manchester, plus Majestic Leeds; then a day later at the Gaumonts Bradford, Glasgow, Newcastle and Sheffield, plus the New Victoria Edinburgh; and on 8 February 1954 at the Gaumonts Bournemouth, Bristol and Plymouth. (In Cardiff, the film opened at the Odeon after *The Robe* had made its bow at Rank's Capitol. The Gaumont remained on regular releases.)

At Sheffield, there were queues outside the Gaumont at opening time, and *How to Marry a Millionaire* ran two weeks, achieving in its first week the second highest admissions figure of the year (33,631), and in its second week still registering way-above-average attendances (23,224). (Only Doct*or in the House* did better in its one week booking, drawing 37,944.) Manager Roy Raistrick noted that "patrons are most enthusiastic in their praise for CinemaScope presentation, but are of the opinion that the subject chosen could have been more impressive." This turned out to be the last Fox picture to play the Gaumont Sheffield or any other Gaumont on general release for five years. It is clear that the Odeon circuit had gained a much stronger attraction with *The Robe*, which was publicised as the first CinemaScope picture and enjoyed longer runs than *How to Marry a Millionaire*. (In Sheffield, for example, *The Robe* played eight weeks, although at a smallish independent hall, the Palace Union Street.)

The installation of CinemaScope was an expensive business: it cost about £5,000 for a one thousand seat cinema and about £6,500 for a hall twice as large, half the cost going on the installation of stereophonic sound with speakers behind the screen and around the auditorium. Old wooden frames had to be torn out and new tubular frames installed with motorised masking to change the size of the screen between wide screen and 'scope ratios, with new wiring through to the projection box to allow this to be controlled from there.

Though Rank installed CinemaScope at seventy cinemas, it objected to putting in stereophonic sound at the others. Fox was not as unyielding as has subsequently been maintained, but it did expect full installations on the Gaumont circuit because of its sizeable shareholding. What proved to be the real stumbling block between Fox and Rank was Fox's demand that its films should receive extended runs throughout the two circuits. Rank gave extended runs in London's West End and the

Trade advertisement for the Gaumont equipment subsidiary in the wide screen era. (Courtesy of Mike Taylor, Projected Picture Trust North West.)

other big city centres but it did not want to change the single week run at suburban cinemas for fear of breaking the weekly attendance habit that was considered responsible for an appreciable part of its business. Fox maintained that Britain was the only country in the world where bookings were regularly limited to a maximum of a week at all but a handful of cinemas.

Fox promptly decided not to release its CinemaScope films through Rank at all but to make them available to other circuits. This led to the Granada and Essoldo chains becoming the primary outlets for the pictures with effect from August 1954, and the backbone of what was called the Fox or fourth circuit. The new grouping offered nowhere near as thorough a release as the Odeon or Gaumont circuits and included many cinemas that were distinctly inferior to the competing Rank halls. In Sheffield, for example, Fox product played at the Palace Union Street but undoubtedly drew audiences away from the Gaumont, especially while the novelty element of the CinemaScope screen and stereophonic sound lasted.

The new set-up had a further devastating impact on the Gaumont circuit when many of the cinemas that had traditionally taken the Gaumont release, including some of the largest Granadas, defected to Fox as its new CinemaScope pictures, like *The Robe, How to Marry a Millionaire* and *Beneath the Twelve Mile Reef* were generally released. While the Granada circuit had for many years dropped films to stage Christmas pantomimes at its biggest halls and had selected its own release on occasion in preference to a Gaumont programme, this was a minor problem compared to the way it was now tied up with Fox pictures which were played even when they were duff offerings and the Gaumont release would have done the better business.

CinemaScope was installed at all the remaining Odeon and Gaumont theatres, usually without full stereophonic sound. The norm, as at Coventry, seems to have been to restrict stereophonic sound to three speakers behind the screen with none in the auditorium. Screens generally had to be installed further forward than before so that the ends were visible from the side seats, and often screen tabs were discarded, keeping only the front set of curtains. Front rows of stalls seating often had to be removed as they were too close to the screen for comfort.

The essence of the process was, of course, to provide a larger, more overwhelming picture than the normal one, but in many cinemas, especially the older type of building, the proscenium arch was very narrow. Sometimes, a new screen and tabs could be erected in front of the old proscenium frame, as at the Gaumont Richmond, but in other instances the only way to achieve an image of correct CinemaScope proportions was to lower the masking on the screen so that the picture was smaller than for films not using the process. Dan Ford was chief projectionist at the huge Stratford Gaumont in northeast London: "While CinemaScope was supposed to be bigger, it was in fact a lot smaller: we had to fetch in the top masking by 4 ft. 6 ins. and open the side by 5 ft. 6 ins. It looked appalling. I complained like hell but it was a total waste of time."

One of the worst installations of CinemaScope was at the Picture House Leicester, an important city-centre Gaumont cinema. Here patrons for both stalls and balcony entered the auditorium at the screen end alongside a tall, very narrow proscenium arch that could not be widened. The much smaller CinemaScope picture did indeed give a "letterbox" effect unless one was very close to the screen. Another 'scope installation that was notoriously bad was at the Gaumont Ashton-under-Lyne. Even so, it did not prevent both these cinemas outlasting many that had a perfect 'scope picture.

In Brighton, a different installation problem affected the huge Regent. As noted by John Fernee (Letters to the Editor, *Picture House* no. 11, Winter 1987/8), the deep bow of the circle obstructed the projection of a CinemaScope image. The cinema had to be closed for five weeks in April/May 1955 for the circle to be shortened.

Despite the row with Fox, CinemaScope had to be installed because the other studios which supplied Rank were using the process. The first CinemaScope film to play the full Gaumont circuit was Universal's *The Black Shield of Falworth*, released through Rank's distribution arm, General Film Distributors. At many theatres that could not be equipped in time, an alternative standard wide screen version was used. In fact, when *Falworth* started out on its London release on 8 November 1954, there was no mention of CinemaScope in general advertising because most Gaumonts had not received it. In the North West London first week area, the major Gaumonts at Camden Town, Chelsea, Finchley and Hammersmith and the State Kilburn had, not unexpectedly, been given preference and outfitted to play the 'scope version, but of the other Gaumonts only Acton and Hendon had also been equipped in time. Non-'scope versions were only made for a few early productions.

The Gaumont Bootle (above and below) opened in 1956 as a low-cost replacement for the war-destroyed Broadway (see page 119). (Snooker centre in recent years.)

The Shepherds Bush Gaumont with its award-winning 1923 exterior intact and (below) its completely new 1955 interior. (Now Top Rank bingo club downstairs, disused cinema upstairs.)

While Fox's CinemaScope films continued to appear almost every other week at Granadas and Essoldos (though rarely for more than a week), no further CinemaScope film had a Gaumont release until Columbia's first venture, the Western *Rough Company*, went out on 14 February 1955, followed two weeks later by United Artists' *Sitting Bull*. Only two more CinemaScope features played the circuit during the rest of the year, although some other big films in SuperScope and the non-anamorphic VistaVision system were booked. When Sitting Bull played the Gaumont Sheffield, manager Roy Raistrick commented: "This film has not met with the enthusiasm expected. The main comment has been that the sound is not what is expected on CinemaScope films. It has been most noticeable the number of patrons noticing the absence of stereophonic sound."

Another difficulty that the Gaumont and Odeon circuits faced was the increasing number of major films that were being given an X certificate, preventing those under the age of 16 being admitted to any part of the programme that included them. For several years, following early experiments on the Odeon circuit, it was Rank policy not to show X films on its two circuits (off-circuit halls did play them) for fear of alienating the family audience. The company's attitude was probably also influenced by the Methodist beliefs of J. Arthur Rank, and the fact that a religious trust was the ultimate holding company, as X films had a bad reputation. However, their rejection was not too popular at managerial level, to judge by the comments of R. G. Mason, the Gaumont Sheffield manager in February 1952, when he was stuck with *Anne of the Indies* plus a reissue of *The Small Back Room* and noted: "Opposition doing wonderful business with *Murder Incorporated*" [a Humphrey Bogart X-certificate crime drama that received an ABC circuit release].

Rank was forced to give in eventually, and the first X films to play the Gaumont circuit were the double bill of *The Bachelor Party* and *Monkey on My Back* which went out in July 1957. By this time X certificate films were commonplace and this programme aroused no comment. Rank avoided horror and science-fiction X films, leaving them to the less fastidious ABC circuit, but it did eventually succumb with a full Gaumont booking of the Hammer remake of *Dracula*, which proved very successful. At the Sheffield Gaumont it did the biggest business since *Doctor at Large* fourteen months earlier (then manager Harry Murray wrote: "The reaction of a typical thrill-seeking audience — they had a wonderful time. Even those who fainted!

Lost one to the hospital Thursday. We missed the family trade. By this we mean the children — their parents were here in force").

The Gaumont programmes that went on release at the same time as new Fox CinemaScope pictures inevitably suffered, not just from fewer bookings but from the greater competition with four major new programmes competing for a share of the diminishing audience instead of three. Distributors became reluctant to have their films shown on the Gaumont circuit. One telling indication of the decline in release quality came from the Regal Sidcup. This ABC hall played the Gaumont release but the manager told head office that he would rather take his own circuit's release, even though so many other ABC cinemas were showing it in his area, than play Gaumont's programmes.

Green light for reconstruction

In the summer of 1954, the go-ahead was given for major repairs to war damaged cinemas, and it was announced that in the London area the Gaumonts at Shepherds Bush and Streatham plus the Super Ilford would be re-opened, while elsewhere the properties at Barnsley and Bootle would be rebuilt. Rank's architect for most of its schemes of this period was T. P. Bennett & Son. No mention was made of other closed cinemas and these evidently had no prospect of re-opening.

The Shepherds Bush Pavilion received an entirely new auditorium within the old shell, designed by Sam Beverley, former partner of the original architect, Frank T. Verity, whose award-winning exterior was renovated. Renamed the Gaumont, it re-opened in July 1955 with a reduced but still huge seating figure of 2,036. Also returning to business on the same day was the Gaumont Streatham, where another modern auditorium had been created by T. P. Bennett & Son within the original walls. This had a much lower ceiling and a much reduced circle, blocking off the rear section, giving 1873 seats in a superbly proportioned viewing space. It was by far the most successful of T. P. Bennett's undertakings of this period.

At Ilford, T. P. Bennett & Son gained planning permission for work at the Super in May 1955, but the site was then sold to C&A Modes for a department store, even though the re-opened cinema would have been certain of success in the middle of this large town.

Early in 1956, a completely new Gaumont arose at Bootle on the site of the Broadway. This was a low cost (£120,000), very

Left and above: the Gaumont Barnsley opened in 1955 to replace the burned-down Empire.

August 1944: the Gaumont Holloway after being hit by a flying bomb . . .

. . . and the Gaumont Holloway in 1958 with the exterior and foyer reinstated but a completely modern auditorium (compare with page 94). (Now multi-screen Odeon cinema.) (Below left, courtesy of Graham Rumble.)

The restored Gaumont Holloway on its re-opening night, July 21 1958.

The formerly independent Wembley Hall Cinema was smartened up to become a Gaumont in 1955. (Demolished.)

plain and simple hangar-like structure designed as a prototype for similar locations elsewhere and evidently inspired by a quick-build movie theatre developed by the Skouras chain in the United States some years earlier. Seating was on the stadium principle below a plain curved ceiling. Thankfully, no others followed.

Another new Gaumont appeared at Barnsley to replace the Empire. The front elevation resembled an office block as much as a cinema but the auditorium was spacious and welcoming.

The last restoration of a war-time casualty was at Holloway where the Gaumont received a smaller 1,987-seat auditorium, designed in a modern idiom by T. P. Bennett & Son, within the shell of the old building, with much of the old circle blocked off as at Streatham because it was no longer needed.

Foyers were also reconstructed elsewhere but here the neo-classical foyer, which matched the original auditorium scheme, was retained in an awkward clash of styles. (The ideal answer here, of course, would have been to reinstate the pre-war auditorium scheme.) The opening of the Gaumont Holloway had a knock-on effect as the nearby Finsbury Park Gaumont was purposely closed just before its re-opening.

These additions considerably strengthened the Gaumont circuit, while many older cinemas were modernised. The Gaumonts at Clapham and Sutton and the Tower at Peckham in the South London area were among many that had their entrances remodelled to create a more up-to-date look. Elsewhere, more extensive modernisation took place, as when the auditorium of the Grand Gainsborough was given a lower false ceiling during a four week closure.

And takeovers, too

Postwar reconstructions were not the only source of additional cinemas. During the mid-Fifties, Rank went on a buying spree and a number of cinemas came under CMA control. None of the seven taken over in Glasgow (the Astor, Astoria, Avon, Carlton, Roxy, Seamore and Standard) were ever renamed Odeon or Gaumont, and a sample check on booking does not suggest that any of them were dedicated to the Gaumont release in particular.

However, in Burton-on-Trent, Carlisle, Chesterfield, Crewe, Gloucester, Greenock and Wembley, newly acquired cinemas took the Gaumont circuit release and, sooner or later, the Gaumont name. In 1956, Rank gained the jointly-owned Ritz and Astoria in Lincoln. The latter had been a Gaumont hall briefly in the early Thirties and was no more wanted now than it had been then, closing a few months later while Rank turned the more modern Ritz into an Odeon.

The great rock 'n' roll furore

The major studios were producing fewer pictures and many poor films were given a Gaumont circuit release because there was nothing better available, while the number of weeks in which recent hits had return runs was a further indication of the product famine. It is very unlikely that an exploitation film like Columbia's *Rock Around the Clock*, starring Bill Haley and the Comets, would have gained a Gaumont circuit release a few years earlier, and quite probable that it would have been withdrawn after disturbances became commonplace. (The title number had been played in a drama, *Blackboard Jungle*, that had gone around the ABC circuit, and had become a hit, building up interest in the Haley film.) Teenagers everywhere were leaving their seats to jive in the aisles and on the stage and police were called to restore order. In fact, the film became a challenge to local Teddy Boys to stir things up, but Rank and other cinema owners thought any property damage and adverse publicity worth enduring to have a film that drew in such large audiences.

By this time, in the autumn of 1956, Gaumont suburban cinemas were gradually switching over to seven day runs from the Sunday rather than opening a new programme on Mondays and showing revivals on the Sabbath. Rank banned Sunday showings of *Rock Around the Clock* after it proved the most troublesome evening. This shifted disturbances to Monday evenings as eager teenagers crowded in at the first opportunity. They were aggravated by the "square" supporting programme, revivals of the Rank comedies *One Good Turn* (with Norman Wisdom) or *Doctor at Sea*, evidently chosen in the hope of widening the audience beyond rock 'n' roll fans.

At the Trocadero in the notoriously rough Elephant and Castle area of South London, ace former manager Maurice Cheepen was brought back to take charge. Over thirty police were in attendance every night and rowdies were forced to dance outside. Nearly 800 youths marched down the New Kent Road jiving on the pavements and holding up traffic.

The film's lively reception in the London suburbs made national headlines, suggesting riots were taking place rather than teenage high spirits. Many towns like Gateshead, South Shields, Tynemouth and Wigan banned the film to be on the safe side while Birmingham and Brighton outlawed further screenings after it had already been shown for a trouble-free week. Bootle also banned additional bookings after the licensing committee declared that it was wrong for an understaffed police force to have to concentrate its resources on ensuring public order at a cinema.

Here is a reminiscence from the book *Talking Pictures: The Popular Experience of the Cinema*, of the film playing at the Gaumont Saltaire, near Shipley in Yorkshire, a year before the cinema closed from poor attendances: "The performance I attended was full to capacity with a fair sprinkling of Teddy Boys in the audience. A row of policemen were standing along the way at the back of the stalls. The patrons were clearly present for the music only and made this apparent by a collective groan whenever the film cut away from it to concentrate on some fatuous piece of dialogue. Occasionally one of the bolder Teddy Boys would entertain the rest of us with a spot of jiving in the aisle while the floor beneath us reverberated to the massed tapping of feet. The atmosphere was entirely good-humoured and, as far I could tell, the policemen were not called upon to arrest anyone. Since they were all young, perhaps they were too absorbed in the music themselves."

Rock Around the Clock was the extreme example of the kind of film which did great business in the stalls while ticket sales for the circle suffered: the teenagers wanted the ground floor because it was cheaper and they could move around more easily.

When the Bill Haley follow-up, *Don't Knock the Rock*, was booked to the circuit a few months later, it did the rounds without making such a splash. Bill Haley and the Comets arrived in person in February 1957 to perform to a full house at the Dominion Tottenham Court Road. Twelve dates were quickly arranged, beginning with the Coventry Gaumont and including the Edmonton Regal on Sunday 3 March.

The big shutdown

At the same time as *Rock Around the Clock* was making headlines in the autumn of 1956, a further news splash in two waves announced first that forty Odeon and Gaumont cinemas were to close, then that a further thirty-nine would join them. The *Daily Mail* headline read "The lure of ITV empties cinemas." J. Arthur Rank declared that the introduction of ITV had led

Time ran out for the Old Kent Road Picture House in October 1956. Photograph from circa 1945.

The Gaumont West Wickham shortly after closure, up for sale as "valuable premises" with its original name of Plaza again revealed. (Demolished.) (Early photograph by author.)

to a ten per cent fall in attendances in the areas it covered compared to the rest of the country. Part of the reason for dramatising the closures was to campaign against entertainments tax. Rank said, "We have in our circuits at this time 184 theatres which, after taking all revenue into consideration, are losing money at the rate of £440,000 per annum." Most of the cinemas would have been profitable if they were not paying the tax. Figures released in the case of the West Wickham Gaumont indicated that, in the year ending in June 1956, the cinema had taken £18,500, paid £6,200 in tax and lost £5,400.

Over the previous few years, there had been isolated closures of surplus cinemas, like the Picture House in York and Arcade in Darlington, but both towns retained other, better Gaumont halls. And Rank had attempted to resolve the problem of the Trocette Bermondsey and Old Kent Road Picture House, both huge cinemas in close proximity in South London. At different times in the past, one or the other had been paired with the Elephant and Castle Trocadero for first-run releases but now both were playing second-run and off-circuit programmes, usually in split weeks. Originally it was planned to close the Picture House first but this was delayed and the Trocette shuttered instead.

Between 29 September 1956 and 5 January 1957, Rank brought down the final curtain at fifty-nine cinemas, most of which were old-fashioned, off-circuit properties that clearly had no future. (Making certain of this, there were restrictive covenants to prevent anyone else running the buildings as cinemas. However, one Odeon, at Colwyn Bay, did re-open as an independent cinema ten years later.) The doomed properties were fairly evenly split between Odeon and Gaumont, and few of the Gaumont halls were of sufficient importance to have been given the circuit name.

The biggest shock on the Gaumont side was the termination of the Tivoli in the Strand. A surplus of Rank West End halls had been resolved some years earlier by making six cinemas into weekly-change sites, paired to show the three main circuit releases a week before they appeared in Northwest London on the first leg of their suburban release. The Tivoli had been linked with the Astoria Charing Cross Road to play the rival ABC release, although it was occasionally recalled for special presentations, including a festival of Italian films (attended on openng night by Princess Margaret) and a run of a puppet version of *Hansel and Gretel* that never received a circuit release.

The Tivoli was the first huge West End cinema to disappear, its valuable site being redeveloped for a department store.

The departure of the Southend Gaumont is explained by the fact that Rank had two much larger and more modern properties, the Odeon and Ritz, with the latter more suited to taking the Gaumont release. Rank wanted £50,000 for the Gaumont and reputedly barred not only film use but dancing. Although a councillor suggested that the town should take it over for theatrical performances or conferences, the idea was rejected and so this 1909 Bertie Crewe theatre was demolished.

The shutting of the Twickenham Gaumont, actually an Odeon property, seems to have reflected an excess number of seats in the town or an exceptional apathy to films as the early closure of ABC's Regal soon left only an Odeon. However, the manager up to three months before the Gaumont's closure insisted that it had been a very profitable theatre, so perhaps there was a high offer for the site or lease renewal problems.

The Gaumont West Wickham's closure provoked a considerable uproar. It came just two years after the cinema had celebrated its twenty-first birthday with rising star Adrienne Corri cutting the cake. For the past few months, the 896-seat cinema (another Odeon property carrying the Gaumont name) had been exchanging programmes midweek with the Elmers End Odeon (which was also to close) and the local Chamber of Commerce wanted a postponement of three to six months to see if attendances increased once this Odeon and another Odeon nearby at Hayes, Kent, had gone. A petition with 2,000 signatures was collected in two days. The last children's show drew 750 and a headline quote in the local press from a spastic boy ("I Am Sorry You Are Going") while the last evening show (the Martin and Lewis comedy *Hollywood Or Bust* plus *Breakaway*) had a capacity house with the audience singing "Auld Lang Syne" and longtime manager Percy Farmer making a speech. Rank hoped to concentrate business on its cinemas in Penge and Bromley but left the area of 75,000 people served only by the ABC Regal Beckenham, which is still operating in 1995 — so perhaps Rank did cut too deep in its closures here. But the figures quoted earlier indicated that, even with tax completely abolished, the Gaumont would only have made £800 profit.

Also in South London, the time was finally up for the Old Kent Road Picture House, while many were particularly saddened by the end of the large Tower in Rye Lane, Peckham. This played the ABC release because Rank was in an unusual

The Cameo Liverpool, photographed circa 1945, lasted just into 1957. (Became warehouse.)

The tiny Belle Vue cinema in Weymouth, seen here circa 1945, closed in 1956. (Survives largely intact as a church.)

situation — though paralleled at Finchley in North London — of operating three first-run cinemas and being able to take the ABC release as well as the Gaumont and Odeon programmes. The ABC line-up had appeared quite faithfully at the Tower, with only the most dubious programmes being replaced, and it should have been profitable, but clearly Rank had less commitment to this than to the Odeon and Gaumont Peckham which were showing its own releases and may well have felt these would do better if the Tower was removed. Its last manager told this author that it was a successful cinema, but, being on the Golden Mile (as that part of Rye Lane was then known), it paid very high rates.

The removal of the former Cirencester Picture House is a little surprising as there had been enough enthusiasm to give it the Gaumont name earlier in the Fifties. However, at Burton-on-Trent, the ancient Gaumont's number was up because Rank had just acquired the more modern Ritz, which was lying in wait to take over the Gaumont name.

The remaining casualties of this purge were: the Aigburth (Liverpool) Rivoli; Barnsley Princess; Birkenhead Super; Bradford's Morley Street Picture House; Chester Majestic; Coatbridge Picture House; Crosby (Merseyside) Corona; Dingle (Liverpool) Beresford; Dudley Criterion; Gateshead Scala; Halifax Electric; Hanley Empire; Hoxton (North London) Cinema; Hunslet (Leeds) Pavilion; Hyson Green (Nottingham) Grand; Liverpool Savoy; Mansfield Rock; Middlesbrough Hippodrome; New Brighton Trocadero; Partick (Glasgow) Standard; Seacombe Marina; Sefton Park (Liverpool) Cameo and Grand; Smethwick (Cape Hill) Electric; Sunderland Palace; Wakefield Carlton; Weymouth Belle Vue; and Wolverhampton Scala.

Space and knowledge limitations prevent detailed comment on all of these. But it is worth noting that the Belle Vue Weymouth had only 314 seats, which had made it one of the smallest properties on the circuit. The Cameo Liverpool was a former church and a particularly miserable-looking property that had been closed for several years in the 1930s and gained notoriety when its manager was murdered during a robbery in 1949. This was one of the Rank cinemas that played split-week late runs after films had been seen at other cinemas in the area. The other four Liverpool halls in this category also closed — the Beresford, Grand, Rivoli and Savoy. Of the nine fortunate Gaumont cinemas that played first suburban run, only the Corona Crosby was closed at this time.

In many instances, one part of the Rank organisation had no inkling of what the other part was planning as the Twickenham Gaumont had just been redecorated throughout and a new heating system installed while the Seacombe Marina had been redecorated only six months earlier and, as previously mentioned, the Peckham Tower's entrance had been very recently modernised.

In mid-February 1957, a special anti-tax trailer was screened throughout the circuit, warning that more cinemas were threatened and showing the closed West Wickham Gaumont among others. The newsreel ended with the message: "These Lights Must Not Go Out!"

Just two months later, further Gaumont (and Odeon) halls began to be chopped in a steady, discreet trickle. The Canning Town (North London) Cinema and Harborne (Birmingham) Picture House went in April 1957, the Dorchester Palace followed in May, then the Leigh Palace in June, the Holloway (North London) Marlborough and the Leeds Scala in August (the latter a notable building in its time, but Rank had three other city centre cinemas), the North Shields Boro in September, the Saltaire Gaumont in October, the Reading Gaumont in November (with the neon name sign being carefully stashed down the side of the Pavilion as the new Gaumont-in-waiting), then nothing in December.

1958 started on a glum note when CMA announced that up to twenty Odeon and Gaumont cinemas would soon be cutting out matinees, except in school holidays, and opening between 5pm and 5.30pm to save money. These included the Highbury Picture House in North London, where the cutback received prominent press coverage which hardly encouraged patronage. Over the circuit as a whole, three hundred jobs were to be shed while four film Rank film productions were postponed. All this was a reaction to a dramatic slump in attendances in late 1957, bringing figures for the year down twenty per cent, with smog as a contributing factor.

However, there was better news regarding the Chepstow Gaumont, Cinderford Palace, Lydney Picture House and Monmouth Picture House which were all taken over by a syndicate in January 1958 to continue operation as independent cinemas (changing the Gaumont name at Chepstow to Regal). But the Ealing Palladium closed for good in February, the Leeds Assembly Rooms in April, and the Finsbury Park Gaumont in July (as previously mentioned, this was linked to the re-opening of the Holloway Gaumont).

The end of weekday matinees at the Highbury Picture House in North London (shown here circa 1945) was soon followed by complete closure. (Demolished.)

These figures, drawn from totals in surviving weekly returns, show how the inexorable decline in film exhibition affected one Gaumont cinema. This particular property also suffered from the opening of a new Odeon in July 1956.

```
GAUMONT SHEFFIELD

Year ending    Admissions (rise/fall)   Receipts (rise/fall)
-- June 1948   1,340,203                 £83,936
26 June 1949   1,286,397   (-53,806)     £79,219   (-£4,717)
24 June 1950   1,178,911   (-107,480)    £72,494   (-£6,725)
23 June 1951   1,200,228   (+11,339)     £74,630   (+£2,136)
21 June 1952   1,154,875   (-45,443)     £74,483   (-£147)
27 June 1953   1,138,564   (-16,311)     £78,157   (+£3,674)
26 June 1954   1,159,051   (+20,487)     £80,419   (+£2,262)
25 June 1955   1,049,863   (-109,188)    £81,083   (+£664)
25 June 1956     960,305   (-89,578)     £74,817   (-£6,286)
22 June 1957     814.663   (-146,232)    £69,017   (-£5,800)
28 June 1958     658,061   (-156,602)    £63,215   (-£5,802)

Notes: Total admissions exclude children's club shows and
any hire income, and may have been slightly revised after
auditing. Receipts relate only to ticket sales and exclude
concessions sales (which were £15,318 in 1947/48 and there-
after remained in the range £18,472 to £26,190, generally
rising in later years) and further exclude café takings.
```

By this time, however, there was a change in approach to the disposal of properties. Previously, cinemas had been closed as money losers and put up for sale through estate agents Goddard and Smith, many becoming derelict eyesores for several years like the Bermondsey Trocette. Now cinemas were increasingly been sought by developers and some were closed in response to offers being made. Others were put up for auction while still open, to see if anyone was interested in purchasing them. But, even more significantly, alternative leisure uses were becoming apparent.

Large-screen TV

Large-screen television in cinemas made its first post-war impact in presenting the Coronation of Queen Elizabeth II on 2 June 1953 to packed audiences. Cinema-Television, the company formed by Rank after its take-over of Baird Television, equipped various cinemas to show the great event as it happened in black-and-white. The Gaumont cinemas participating in this occasion were the Gaumont Haymarket, Marble Arch Pavilion and New Gallery in London's West End, and the Gaumonts at Doncaster and Manchester in the regions. Millions more clustered around the nation's television sets and many were encouraged to buy sets of their own. In fact, the cinema's greatest triumph was in showing edited full colour documentaries shortly after the event.

Another major experiment with large-screen television took place in early December 1954 when BBC coverage of the England versus Germany soccer match at Wembley was watched by 13,000 people in eight cinemas ranging from large houses to small newsreel theatres. The Doncaster and Manchester Gaumonts were among the five venues outside London, where attendances overall were said to about seventy-five per cent of capacity, less than in London but still encouraging. This does not seem to have led to many further such presentations. There were serious problems in persuading the BBC to participate in reducing its own audience and in sharing the receipts with the BBC and organisers of events.

The threat of ITV

Television was regarded as an aid to cinema attendance in as much it had programmes featuring new cinema releases. When *The Proud and Profane* played the Gaumont Sheffield for the week ending 20 October 1956, manager Roy Raistrick commented:

"TV excerpts have given considerable help to the feature. Many patrons have remarked [that] their desire to see this film had been whetted by this excerpt." And, the following week, when *Beyond Mombasa* was shown, "TV excerpts have again assisted the feature offering. Very many comments have been heard on the fact that this has been seen."

However, the arrival of ITV in 1956 posed a threat as it was feared that the choice of two channels would tempt more people to stay at home and also that the new stations would be less sober and more appealing than the BBC. At the Gaumont, the situation was monitored from the start of ITV in the Sheffield area, with this comment for the week that *A Hill in Korea* was showing: "The opening of ITV at the local station of Emley Moor, on Saturday 3 November, has had no effect whatsoever on our business this week. It will be noted that on Saturday we have well overtaken the box-office figure for the previous Saturday." A week later, when *Beyond a Reasonable Doubt* and *A Touch of the Sun* were on offer as a double bill, some effect was acknowledged: "The takings reflect, to a small degree, the impact of ITV, but more the forthcoming Christmas season and the urge to save... ITV to my mind has not affected us as much as was first anticipated. This may be due to the fact that ITV reception in this city centre is not as good as was thought. Not many sets can received a good clear signal for any length of time and this may prove disconcerting to ITV programme planners." Mr. Raistrick concluded: "In this situation, ITV offers no competition to first class screen material." Two weeks later, *The Great Locomotive Chase* and the Bardot comedy *Mam'zelle Pigalle* were on offer: "ITV effect – this is still difficult to assess correctly. This particular week, we have had very adverse weather conditions – fog, frost, very cold and showery weather, which does not in any way help our business. ITV reports are not good – we have plenty of comment on quality of material put out by ITV and none of the comment very flattering. Against this, however, we had not had a good strong programme to combat any ITV opposition."

A week later, attendances plummeted for *Nightfall* and *Bermuda Affair* and Mr. Raistrick observed, "I am at a loss for a reason", while insisting "as far as ITV in Sheffield is concerned, no enthusiasm has been registered." On the week before Christmas, when a double-bill of *Death of a Scoundrel* and *Tension at Table Rock* was showing, his views began to waver: "It is reported that the reception of ITV has considerably improved in this area, although there are still some districts unable to receive ITV. This week we find that a possible cause of absenteeism among patrons is ITV, although the main cause will be seasonal shopping etc. In addition to the above, the weather has been most atrocious." One has the feeling of a manager reluctantly acknowledging the film industry's worst fears.

A market survey made for Rank in 1958 noted: "It appears that the introduction of television to an area has a major effect on cinema attendances after the station has been established for about a year. As yet there are no signs of any halt in the decline in areas where television is no longer a novelty. It is clear that the decline in cinema-going is not attributable to any one group although the extent of the changes in habit does vary considerably with age and social grade. The groups which show the most serious relative drop are the high socio-economic groups and the age groups above thirty-five, particularly the thirty-five to forty-four group. From this it can be seen that, contrary to what might be expected, in television households many out-of-the-home activities seem to have been affected hardly at all and in fact one activity, dancing, seems to be more popular in television households than others. Theatre going has only suffered slightly from television. The coffee bar and the public house also seem to draw people out of their homes. It seems then that the cinema is more vulnerable to the counter-claims of television than other forms of entertainment."

Of course, it should be added that the film industry had a big foot in the other camp. Rank were involved in Southern Television, while ABC and Granada had similar interests. And this market report does explain Rank's enthusiasm for turning cinemas into dance halls.

Live shows

The very largest Gaumont theatres continued to offer live shows from time to time. In June-July 1953, while appearing during the week at the London Palladium, Frank Sinatra gave concerts on successive Sundays at the State Kilburn, Regal Edmonton and Trocadero Elephant and Castle (being poorly attended at Edmonton, at least).

In response to declining film attendances, more and more cinemas returned to live shows, including several of the well-equipped Gaumonts. This was not just a Sunday event but spread to weekdays interrupting the run of the film programme. Artists would even perform on Saturday nights despite tough resistance by film distributors loathe to forfeit their share of the takings on the best night of the week.

Pop stars made national tours of fifty or more large cinemas from all the major circuits. The Beatles did a sensational live tour that brought them to the Gaumonts at Lewisham (29 March 1963), Bournemouth and Wolverhampton among others.

In the West End, the Dominion Tottenham Court Road, which had started life as a live theatre, was reviewed in December 1956 as a base for live shows and internal estimates were made of the costs involved in rewiring and refurbishing the stage facilities. Its first major re-use as a live venue came when Judy Garland appeared in her own show from Wednesday 16 October to Saturday 16 November 1957. Other shows included Tommy Steele, Sophie Tucker, and the Bernard Buffet ballet *Le Rendezvous Manqué*. However, the Dominion would remain firmly a cinema for some years to come.

Roadshows

Throughout the history of film exhibition, certain productions had been presented as special attractions and given extended runs at higher prices, usually with separate performances, before being generally released. These were usually big-budget pictures like *Gone with the Wind* and *Quo Vadis* that had to be presented in this way if they were to recoup their huge budgets. In the wide-screen era, various films shot in Todd A-0 and 70mm were made available to cinemas that installed the necessary equipment and giant screens. In July 1957, Michael Todd's *Around the World in 80 Days* launched the Astoria Charing Cross Road in London's West End on a new career as a roadshow house. Later attractions here included *Solomon and Sheba* and *The Alamo*.

The most outstanding of these attractions was the musical *South Pacific* in Todd A-0, released by 20th Century-Fox. For this one film at least, the rift between Rank and Fox did not count, and it played extended runs at a number of Odeon and Gaumont theatres. It had its British premiere at the Dominion Tottenham Court Road. Two Philips 70mm/35mm projectors were installed in a new projection box at the back of the stalls, providing a 78 ft. level throw to the screen, erected in the 54 ft. wide proscenium opening with a 5 ft. deep curvature. Stereophonic sound was provided and seating was reduced to 1,654 with the upper gallery being curtained off. Opening on 21 April 1958, *South Pacific* racked up the longest-ever run in a British

The new downstairs projection box at the Majestic Leeds, installed to provide a more direct throw when a large new screen was fitted for roadshow presentations. Note "GB" monogram on seat standards and (barely visible) part of the huge freize of galloping horsemen on the rim of the dome. (Now Top Rank bingo club.).

The Gaumont Manchester gained a new advance booking office for its roadshow presentations. It is seen here circa 1960 with Can-Can *running and* The Alamo *imminent.*

cinema, four years and twenty-two weeks, closing on 30 September 1962. One print was shown no less than 1,382 times before being replaced.

Other Gaumont cinemas that played the Rodgers and Hammerstein musical were the West End Birmingham. New Victoria Edinburgh, Gaumont Glasgow, Majestic Leeds and Queens Newcastle. At the Majestic Leeds, a vast screen was erected in front of the old one and a new projection box was set up beneath the circle to give a direct throw onto the gigantic screen, minimising distortion. Six-track magnetic sound was installed.

South Pacific was not restricted to Rank outlets. In Brighton, for example, the film played at ABC's second cinema, the Astoria, as this was the only one equipped to show it, even though Rank had three halls in the town. Elsewhere it played at many independent halls.

Dance halls

To some extent, dance halls had long been run in association with cinemas. Some of the big PCT theatres like the Regent at Brighton and the New Victoria in Bradford had huge dance halls. The Tower/Gaumont Morecambe was very much a cinema and ballroom while the New Cross Gaumont in Southeast London had a huge dance hall over the entrance.

However, it was a new development when Rank partnered band leader Victor Silvester to launch a chain of Victor Silvester Dance Studios, usually in former restaurant areas (cinema catering was on the decline). One opened 26 February 1957 at the Gaumont Lewisham where the cafe had closed three months before, and lasted until 9 October 1965. Other appeared at such Gaumonts as Bromley, Chelsea, Kilburn (State) and Wimbledon, as well as at the Regent Brighton (using the North Street entrance).

And then entire cinemas were converted by Rank into a small chain of Majestic Ballrooms, with the stalls being levelled and a dance floor put in. The Gaumont Newcastle closed in December 1958 to re-open as a Majestic in February 1959. The already shut Gaumont Finsbury Park, North London, followed a few months later. The Gaumont at Witham, Hull, the closed Arcade at Darlington, and the Gaumont Crewe were later conversions. Though these dance halls would not succeed for long, they were the first examples of cinemas being turned over to other leisure uses by Rank rather than being sold off.

Ending the Fox row

The dispute with Fox went so far that the Hollywood company started to build a new cinema to show its own films in Plymouth. However by the time the Drake opened in June 1958, Fox and Rank had buried the hatchet. There were nowhere near enough good films being made to support an Odeon, Gaumont, ABC and Fox release (December was the most desperate month when no distributors wanted to release a good film before Christmas as cinemagoers were pre-occupied with shopping: dud programmes abounded, including many deferred British pictures shown largely to fulfill quota obligations).

It seems likely that the impending release of the smash hit *Peyton Place* focussed minds at Fox and Rank: Fox wanted to realise the film's full box-office potential, and Rank were keen to play it. However, this did not mean the end of the Fox release just yet. In January 1958, Fox agreed to allocate half its output to the Gaumont and Odeon circuits while promising its regular outlets the other half which would be qualitatively equal and include all Fox's British productions to help those cinemas meet their quota obligations.

Fox split the Rank half fairly evenly between the two circuits as far as numbers were concerned. However, *Peyton Place* was given an Odeon circuit release. The Gaumont circuit received as its first Fox titles in five years a romantic drama called *The Gift of Love*, then *Fraulein*, then a double bill of *Sierra Baron* plus *How To Rob a Bank*. None of these had remotely the drawing power of *Peyton Place*. Once again Gaumont took second place to Odeon.

Decline and fall of the Gaumont release

An indication of the ultimate weakness of the Gaumont release is the small proportion of each year's top box-office attractions that played the circuit. In 1954, it had a decent share with three of the top ten: the Norman Wisdom comedy *Trouble in Store* (which started its general release in the last week of 1953), the American drama *From Here to Eternity*, and the year's number one hit, the British comedy *Doctor in the House*. In 1955, it gained only *Above Us the Waves*. In 1956, it had not one of the year's hits while Odeon gained three of the top four. In 1957, Gaumont rebounded somewhat with the year's second biggest hit, *Doctor at Large*, and one other major success, *Ill Met by Moonlight*, from the top fifteen. In 1958, it had none of the top fourteen while Odeon played seven. In its last three releases at

CINEMAS IN RANK 'A' CIRCUIT

ODEON

London Area

Acton, Odeon.
Barnet, Odeon.
Ealing, Odeon.
Edgware Road, Odeon.
Finsbury Park, Astoria.
Harlesden, Odeon.
Hendon, Odeon.
Kensal Rise, Odeon.
Muswell Hill, Odeon.
Southgate, Odeon.
South Harrow, Odeon.
St. Albans, Odeon.
Swiss Cottage, Odeon.
Temple Fortune, Odeon.
Watford, Odeon.
Wealdstone, Odeon.
Wembley, Odeon.
Westbourne Grove, Odeon.
Kensington, Odeon.
Highgate, Odeon.
Shepherds Bush, Gaumont.
Islington, Angel.
Barking, Odeon.
Brick Lane, Odeon.
Chingford, Odeon.
Dalston, Odeon.
East Ham, Odeon.
Forest Gate, Odeon.
Hackney Road, Odeon.
Hornchurch, Odeon.
Hounslow, Odeon.
Ilford, Odeon.
Kingston, Odeon.
Mile End, Odeon.
Richmond, Odeon.
Romford, Odeon.
Shannon Corner, Odeon.
Southall, Odeon.
Surbiton, Odeon.
Twickenham, Odeon.
Uxbridge, Odeon.
Walton, Odeon.
Balham, Odeon.
Brixton, Astoria.
Bromley, Odeon.
Camberwell, Odeon.
Croydon, Odeon.
East Dulwich, Odeon.
Deptford, Odeon.
Epsom, Odeon.
Guildford, Odeon.
Morden, Odeon.
Peckham, Odeon.
Penge, Odeon.
Redhill, Odeon.
South Norwood, Odeon.
Streatham, Astoria.
Well Hall, Odeon.
Welling, Odeon.
Woking, Odeon.
Woolwich, Odeon.

Provincial

Aberdeen, Odeon.
Accrington, Odeon.
Airdrie, Pavilion.
Aldershot, Empire.
Alfreton, Odeon.
Andover, Odeon.
Ashford, Odeon.
Aylesbury, Odeon.
Ayr, Odeon.
Barrow, Odeon.
Bath, Odeon.
Bedminster, Odeon.

Bilston, Odeon.
Birmingham, Odeon.
Bishop Auckland, Odeon
Blackburn, Rialto.
Blackpool, Odeon.
Bognor, Odeon.
Bolton, Odeon.
Boston, Odeon.
Bradford, Odeon.
Brentwood, Odeon.
Bridgwater, Odeon.
Brighton, Odeon.
Bristol, Odeon.
Burnage, Odeon.
Burnley, Odeon.
Burton, Odeon.
Bury, Odeon.
Bury St. Edmunds, Odeon.
Byker, Odeon.
Camberley, Odeon.
Canterbury, Odeon.
Cardiff, Capitol.
Cheetham Hill, Odeon.
Chelmsford, Odeon.
Chester, Odeon.
Chesterfield, Odeon.
Chorley, Odeon.
Clacton, Odeon.
Cleveleys, Odeon.
Coatbridge, Odeon.
Colchester, Regal.
Corby, Odeon.
Costam, Odeon.
Coventry, Regal.
Crewe, Odeon.
Crosby, Odeon.
Cowcaddens, Astoria.
Darlington, Odeon.
Deal, Odeon.
Dover, Odeon.
Dudley, Odeon.
Dundee, Odeon.
Erith, Odeon.
Exeter, Odeon.
Falmouth, Odeon.
Farnborough, Rex.
Farnham, Regal.
Folkestone, Odeon.
Gateshead, Odeon.
Gillingham, Odeon.
Glasgow, Odeon.
Gloucester, Odeon.
Guide Bridge, Odeon.
Halifax, Odeon.
Hamilton, Odeon.
Harrogate, Odeon.
Hawick, Odeon.
Hereford, Odeon.
Herne Bay, Odeon.
High Wycombe, Odeon.
Horsham, Odeon.
Hove, Odeon.
Harlow, Regal.
Ipswich, Odeon.
Kettering, Odeon.
Kingstanding, Odeon.
Kingswood, Odeon.
Leigh, Odeon.
Lancaster, Odeon.
Leeds, Odeon.
Leicester, Odeon.
Liverpool, Odeon.
Llanelly, Odeon.
Llandudno, Odeon.
Lincoln, Odeon.
Loughborough, Odeon.
Lowestoft, Odeon.
Luton, Odeon.
Maryhill, Roxy.
Manchester, Odeon.

Middlesbrough, Odeon.
Morecambe, Odeon.
Motherwell, Odeon.
Newcastle, Odeon.
Newport, IoW, Odeon.
Newport, Mon., Odeon.
Newton Abbot, Odeon.
Norwich, Odeon.
Nottingham, Odeon.
Oldham, Odeon.
Paignton, Odeon.
Perry Barr, Odeon.
Peterborough, Odeon.
Plymouth, Odeon.
Port Talbot, Odeon.
Ramsgate, Odeon.
Reading, Odeon.
Rhyl, Odeon.
Rotherham, Odeon.
Rutherglen, Odeon.
Salisbury, Odeon.
Sheffield, Odeon.
Sale, Odeon.
Scarborough, Odeon.
Scotstoun, Odeon
Shettleston, Odeon
Shirley, Odeon.
Sittingbourne, Odeon.
Southampton, Rialto.
Southend, Odeon.
Southsea, Odeon.
Sunderland, Astor.
Springburn, Astor.
South Shields, Odeon.
Stafford, Odeon.
Staines, Odeon.
St. Austell, Odeon.
Stockton, Odeon.
Stourbridge, Odeon.
Sutton Coldfield, Odeon.
Torquay, Odeon.
Warley, Odeon.
Warrington, Odeon.
Weston-super-Mare, Odeon.
West Hartlepool, Odeon.
Winchester, Odeon.
Wolverhampton, Odeon.
Worthing, Odeon.
Wrexham, Odeon.
Yeovil, Odeon.
York, Odeon.
Guernsey, Odeon.
Hatfield, Odeon.
Jersey, Odeon.

GAUMONT

London Area

Camden Town, Gaumont.
Chelsea, Gaumont.
Cricklewood, Gaumont.
Finchley, Gaumont.
Hammersmith, Gaumont.
Kings Cross, Gaumont.
Palmers Green, Gaumont.
Stamford Hill, Regent.
Walham Green, Gaumont.
Wood Green, Gaumont.
Holloway, Gaumont.
Burnt Oak, Gaumont.
Kingsbury, Gaumont.
Rayners Lane, Gaumont.
Chadwell Heath, Gaumont.
Hackney, Pavilion.
Leyton, Gaumont.
Stratford, Gaumont.
Dagenham, Gaumont.

Weybridge, Odeon.
Lewisham, Gaumont.
Putney, Gaumont.
Rushey Green, Gaumont.
Sutton, Gaumont.
Wandsworth, Gaumont.
Wimbledon, Gaumont.
Edmonton, Regal.
Elephant and Castle,
Trocadero.
Kilburn, State.
Stepney, Troxy.

Provincial

Allerton, Gaumont.
Anoa, Gaumont.
Anniesland, Gaumont.
Barnsley, Gaumont.
Bellshill, Gaumont.
Birkenhead, Gaumont.
Bootle, Gaumont.
Bournemouth, Gaumont.
Burslem, Gaumont.
Carlisle, Gaumont.
Chatham, Gaumont.
Chichester, Gaumont.
Coventry, Gaumont.
Dennistoun, Gaumont.
Derby, Gaumont.
Doncaster, Gaumont.
Dundee, Gaumont.
Edinburgh, New Vic.
Edinburgh, Regent.
Falkirk, Gaumont.
Glasgow, Cinerama.
Belfast, Odeon.
Glossop, Empire.
Greenock, Gaumont.
Grimsby, Gaumont.
Handsworth, V. Cross.
Hanley, Gaumont.
Hull, Gaumont.
Hinckley, Gaumont.
Ibrox, Gaumont.
Kensington (L'pool),
Casino.
Kirkcaldy, Gaumont.
Leith, Capitol.
Liverpool, Rialto.
Northampton, Gaumont.
North Shields, Gaumont.
Partick, Tivoli.
Perth, Gaumont.
Portsmouth, Gaumont.
Preston, Gaumont.
Princes Park, Gaumont.
Redditch, Gaumont.
Rochdale, Rialto.
Rochester, Gaumont.
Smethwick, Gaumont.
Southampton, Gaumont.
Southport, Gaumont.
Townhead, Carlton.
Wakefield, Gaumont.
Walsall, Gaumont.
Wednesbury, Gaumont.
Whitley Bay, Gaumont.
Wishaw, Gaumont.
Barnstaple, Gaumont.
Cheltenham, Gaumont.
Chippenham, Gaumont.
Stroud, Gaumont.
Taunton, Gaumont.
Swindon, Gaumont.
Trowbridge, Gaumont.
Weymouth, Gaumont.

This list, published in a trade paper in October 1958, was the first indication of which cinemas would make up the new Rank circuit. Some adjustments were later made but Odeons are listed first and heavily outnumber the Gaumonts.

the start of 1959, Gaumont gained one final hit that proved to be the seventh top attraction of the year, the Norman Wisdom comedy *The Square Peg*.

In most cases, the very top films were assured of becoming box-office champions in advance. So it cannot be said that Gaumont was simply unlucky when the Odeon circuit gained the biggest draw of the year three times — *The Greatest Show On Earth* (1952), *Reach for the Sky* (1956) and *The Bridge on the River Kwai* (1958). Perhaps under pressure from the distribution side which demanded an Odeon release, CMA's bookers were clearly favouring the Odeon circuit while no doubt trying to throw the occasional plum to Gaumont.

The most serious problem facing Rank was how to improve business at the biggest and best Gaumont cinemas, which were not realising their potential. Taking into account the shortage of product, the obvious if controversial answer was to combine them with the best Odeons to create a new circuit. This would also offer a bigger return to producers and distributors. Of course, Rank as a producer and distributor would be a major beneficiary, no longer having to accept reduced returns from sending some of its output through the Gaumont circuit. Fortunately for Rank, the government recognised the problem and was willing to relax its restrictions, dating from the 1940s, on the two circuits being combined.

Rank chief John Davis addressed a meeting of exhibitors on 9 October 1958. He said in part: "We have had two circuits, with the Gaumont the weaker booking proposition in the eyes of distributors and producers. The falling supply of product has put the producer ... in the position that he could dictate to which theatre or group of theatres an important film should go. You know that up to about two and a half years ago we were able, under the then existing conditions, to keep the supply of product in balance between the Odeon and Gaumont circuits. We have slowly lost ground since then as under changed conditions, it being a suppliers' market, the distributor has been able to dictate his terms as to where his product would play, often with the threat that if we did not agree his proposition he would take it to ABC. In addition to which, to find 104 programmes a year, many of them double features, which would appeal to the public, was an impossible task under present conditions. Do you realise that we played last year six reissue features, and fifteen supporting reissues on the two circuits, at a time when we should be competing with television with top

The New London Release Pattern for Odeon and Gaumont Theatres

Check from this leaflet

which of your favourite Odeon

and Gaumont theatres will

play Rank Release Programmes

and which will play

National Release Programmes

NORTH-WEST LONDON starting February 1
NORTH-EAST LONDON starting February 8
SOUTH LONDON starting February 15
. . . there will no longer be an ' Odeon ' release or a ' Gaumont ' release for the week.

Instead, selected Odeon **and** Gaumont theatres will play films advertised as **THE RANK RELEASE PROGRAMME** while other Odeon **and** Gaumont theatres will play films advertised as **THE NATIONAL RELEASE PROGRAMME.**

Why is the change being made? So that really big and important films can be shown as widely as possible to the greatest number of people throughout the Odeon and Gaumont circuits quite regardless of the names of theatres. It really will mean that bigger and better entertainment comes to Londoners at their favourite theatres.

How do I know what is on at my local theatre? From the lists given in this leaflet, check whether your favourite Odeon or Gaumont theatres will show **Rank Release Programmes** or **National Release Programmes.** Then refer to the amusement guides in the three London evening newspapers. **Rank Release Programmes** will be shown at all the theatres so listed no matter whether they are named Odeon or Gaumont. **National Release Programmes** will also play at all the theatres so listed no matter whether the theatre name. (Some theatres which are listed separately will have a flexible policy of playing either Rank Release or National Release programmes or sometimes other alternatives.)

All Odeon and Gaumont theatres will continue their existing advertising in the local newspapers, by posters, and by programme cards where applicable. This advertising will clearly show whether the theatre concerned plays **Rank Release Programmes** or **National Release Programmes.**

But if you are in any doubt or difficulty, telephone to the Odeon and Gaumont **INFORMATION CENTRE** at TRAfalgar 5471 who will be pleased to give you any facts you require.

ODEON AND GAUMONT THEATRES WHICH WILL PLAY RANK RELEASE PROGRAMMES

NORTH-WEST

Acton Odeon	Kensal Rise Odeon
Barnet Odeon	Kensington Odeon
Burnt Oak Gaumont	Kilburn State
Camden Town Gaumont	Kingsbury Gaumont
Chelsea Gaumont	King's Cross Gaumont
Cricklewood Gaumont	Muswell Hill Odeon
Ealing Odeon	Palmers Green Gaumont
Edgware Road Odeon	Shepherds Bush Gaumont
Edmonton Regal	Southgate Odeon
Finchley Gaumont	South Harrow Odeon
Finsbury Park Astoria	St. Albans Odeon
Hammersmith Gaumont	Stamford Hill Regent
Harlesden Odeon	Swiss Cottage Odeon
Hendon Odeon	Temple Fortune Odeon
Highgate Odeon	Watford Odeon
Holloway Gaumont	Wembley Odeon
Islington Angel	Westbourne Grove Odeon
Islington Odeon	Wood Green Gaumont

NORTH-EAST

Barking Odeon	Ilford Odeon
Chadwell Heath Gaumont	Leyton Gaumont
Chingford Odeon	Mile End Road Odeon
Commercial Rd. Troxy	Richmond Odeon
Dagenham Gaumont	Romford Odeon
Dalston Odeon	Shannon Corner Odeon
East Ham Odeon	Southall Odeon
Forest Gate Odeon	Stratford Gaumont
Hackney Road Odeon	Surbiton Odeon
Hackney Pavilion	Twickenham Odeon
Hayes Ambassador	Uxbridge Odeon
Hornchurch Odeon	Walton Odeon
Hounslow Odeon	Weybridge Odeon

SOUTH

Balham Odeon	Putney Gaumont
Brixton Astoria	Redhill Odeon
Bromley Gaumont	Rushey Green Gaumont
Camberwell Odeon	Sidcup Odeon
Croydon Odeon	South Norwood Odeon
Deptford Odeon	Staines Majestic
East Dulwich Odeon	Streatham Astoria
Elephant & Castle Troc.	Wandsworth Gaumont
Epsom Odeon	Well Hall Odeon
Guildford Odeon	Welling Odeon
Lewisham Gaumont	Wimbledon Gaumont
Morden Odeon	Woking Odeon
Peckham Gaumont	Woolwich Odeon
Penge Odeon	

ODEON AND GAUMONT THEATRES WHICH WILL PLAY NATIONAL RELEASE PROGRAMMES

NORTH-WEST

Camden Town Plaza	Rayners Lane Gaumont
Colindale Odeon	St. Albans Gaumont
Edgware Road Gaumont	Tottenham Palace
Finchley Odeon	Walham Green Gaumont
Hendon Gaumont	Wealdstone Odeon
Kentish Town Gaumont	Wembley Gaumont
Kenton Odeon	

NORTH-EAST

Dagenham Grange	Romford Gaumont
Dalston Gaumont	Southall Gaumont
Kingston Odeon	Whalebone Lane Odeon
Richmond Gaumont	

SOUTH

Bromley Odeon	Putney Hippodrome
Clapham Gaumont	Streatham Gaumont
Eltham Hill Gaumont	Sutton Gaumont
Guildford Playhouse	Wimbledon Odeon
New Cross Gaumont	Woking Gaumont
Peckham Odeon	

ODEON AND GAUMONT THEATRES WHOSE PROGRAMMES WILL VARY
(please see theatre advertisements for programme details)

NORTH-WEST

Acton Gaumont	Kentish Town Gaisford
Barnet Gaumont	Kilburn Grange
Ealing Walpole	North Watford Odeon
Finchley New Bohemia	Notting Hill Gaumont
Haverstock Hill Odeon	Park Royal Odeon
Highbury Picture House	Watford Gaumont
Islington Gaumont	

NORTH-EAST

Becontree Odeon	Hounslow Dominion
Bethnal Green Foresters	Stepney Odeon
Brentwood Odeon	Upminster Gaumont
East Ham Gaumont	Whitton Odeon
East Sheen Odeon	

SOUTH

Balham Gaumont	Rosehill Gaumont
Erith Odeon	(Carshalton)
Greenwich Odeon	Tolworth Odeon
Old Kent Road Astoria	West Norwood Regal

At all theatres programmes may occasionally vary

From a leaflet issued in January 1959 to explain the two new releases which replaced the Odeon and Gaumont ones. The feeble position of the National circuit is evident. The new release pattern started a week earlier than is indicated here.

new product? At the moment we have no less than seven unbooked dates before Christmas...

"Consequently, we are creating a Rank releasing circuit of approximately 300 theatres which will have a booking strength of approximately that of the Odeon release at its peak. [...] We have had a look at the split between Odeon and Gaumont last year. This may surprise you. It is our considered opinion that not more than half a dozen of the Gaumont releases last year would have played on the new Rank circuit."

This was presented as a fait accompli, with films already being booked for the new super-circuit which comprised, on the initial list released to the press, 207 Odeon cinemas and only ninety-one Gaumonts. Though this would be subsequently revised, the basic imbalance remained. Looking at the list, it is clear that it did gather together the best and biggest cinemas on the circuit, although in some competing situations there was little to choose between cinemas. At this point, Rank maintained that its surplus cinemas, combined with those of the Fox circuit, would provide a third release grouping of perhaps 306 cinemas, comparable to ABC's 272 and Rank's 300 outlets.

By January 1959, this third circuit had been given the name of the National release and it fell to Rank to choose its programmes, which other cinemas not able to obtain the Rank or ABC release were likely to book as well. Rank's Kenneth Winckles said, "The National circuit is basically a merger of Gaumont and what was known as the Fox circuit." This was not the case, as most of the biggest Gaumonts were now attached to the Rank circuit.

The very last Gaumont circuit release started the rounds on 19 January. It was a Columbia programme, *The Seventh Voyage of Sinbad* and *The Hard Man*.

It was time for another major change. Gaumont-British News closed down on 29 January 1959 along with Universal News, the pair being replaced by a new topical "interest" series produced by Rank in colour, *Look at Life*.

And endings in the West End
The Gaumont circuit had long been in a weak position in the West End of London, especially after the CMA amalgamation meant that its central cinemas were pooled with those of Odeon. In the Fifties, the Dominion and the Astoria were elevated from second-run status to become valuable road-show houses, the New Gallery, Marble Arch Pavilion and Tivoli had all vanished, while the one West End premiere run cinema to carry the circuit name, the Gaumont Haymarket, fell on hard times. The days when it could open the year's top attraction, as in the case of *The Wicked Lady*, were past. The Gaumont was inferior to the Odeon in Leicester Square and the Leicester Square Theatre in location and seating capacity while the Marble Arch Odeon also took priority because of its size. The Gaumont seated a somewhat modest 1,328, which put it at a disadvantage, and it had been paired with the Marble Arch Pavilion to raise the number of seats available for new films. After the Pavilion was leased out in 1952, the Gaumont opened new films on its own. In the wide screen era, its seating seems to have been slightly reduced to around 1,300. Under CMA, the cinema lost money every year from 1949 to 1956, the deficit totalling around £100,000, except for 1955 when it made a small profit while paying more for film hire (suggesting that it had been allocated better films). This financial loss was revealed in 1957 when Rank stated than an average of only 400 were attending performances as it sought planning permission to replace the Gaumont with offices and a new basement luxury cinema. Approval was first refused, then won on appeal, and the cinema closed in June 1959. The Gaumont name vanished from the West End — never to return. The new cinema on the site, when it opened three years later, was named Odeon.

The cinema organ
Tony Moss notes: "In 1958, Rank terminated the contracts of all its organists, apart from Gerald Shaw who transferred from the Odeon Marble Arch to the flagship Odeon Leicester Square until his untimely death in 1974.

"The theatre organ in the U.K. enjoyed a brief renaissance in the late Fifties as a prelude to long-run films like *South Pacific*, but this ended in 1960 when the Entertainments Tax on cinema seats was removed and there was no longer any advantage in advertised live music." (The Tax could be avoided if one third of a programme was live and advertised.)

12: THE SIXTIES

Cinema admissions during the Fifties had dropped from 1,396 million admissions in 1950 to 581 million in 1959. The decline had been slight in the first five years but had accelerated dramatically with 160 million or more admissions being lost annually from 1957 onwards. In the Sixties, the fall would continue but at a lesser rate. The figures were still startling: an attendance of 501 million in 1960 had sunk to only 193 million ten years later.

Farewell to Fox

At the end of 1960, 20th Century-Fox finally sold its interest in the Metropolis and Bradford Trust, controlling Gaumont, to the Rank Organisation for £4 million. Gaumont-British was now one hundred per cent British. And, in 1962, Circuits Management Association had a change of name to the Rank Theatre Division.

Rank versus National release

The future of those Gaumont cinemas which had been selected to take the Rank release was bright. But it was obvious at a glance that the remaining cinemas that made up the National circuit were mostly older and inferior properties with a patchy and limited geographical spread, ridiculing its very name. On top of this, Rank had admitted from the first that half were destined for closure when they could be disposed of at a fair price, so its own commitment to the National release seemed half-hearted. Then Paramount — which, as one of the main suppliers to the old Odeon and Gaumont circuits, had continued to place its films with the Rank and National groupings — became unhappy when its Dean Martin/Shirley MacLaine comedy *All in a Night's Work* was only offered a National release instead of a Rank release, and switched to the rival ABC circuit for this and all its subsequent offerings. In effect, this meant that only half the output of the Hollywood majors was now available to provide both the Rank and National releases.

Those Gaumont cinemas in very large cities seemed safe, even if associated with the National release, as most had opportunities to indulge in 70mm roadshow presentations. However, in Birmingham, the Gaumont initially became the National release outlet full time while roadshows played at the West End. In Bristol, the Gaumont was in the happier position of taking the Rank release full time. In Cardiff, the Gaumont took the National programme but switched to the Rank release whenever the huge Capitol, its proper home, had a special 70mm presentation (the National release then went to the Odeon, placed last among Rank's three city centre properties). In Glasgow, the Gaumont played the National release whenever it wasn't tied up with a 70mm extended run. In Leeds, the Majestic likewise combined National release programmes with roadshow presentations, and the Gaumont, normally a second run house, often gained the National release when the Majestic wasn't available. In Liverpool, the Gaumont took the National programme but switched to the Rank release when the Odeon dropped it for a roadshow run; then the Rialto and Hippodrome moved up from second runs to play the National release concurrently. In Manchester, the Gaumont, although originally scheduled to take National programmes, went in for roadshows. In Newcastle, the Queen's and Pavilion both concentrated on roadshows but took some National releases during gaps. Lastly, in Sheffield, the Gaumont took the Rank release.

For Gaumonts allocated the National release in the suburbs and smaller towns, the future looked very uncertain, if not bleak. Some adjustments had been made to the original selection. In the London area, the National release was bolstered slightly by the transfer of the Commercial Road (Stepney) Troxy, Finsbury Park Astoria and the Stratford Gaumont from the original Rank release list but, as it turned out, this merely hastened their demise.

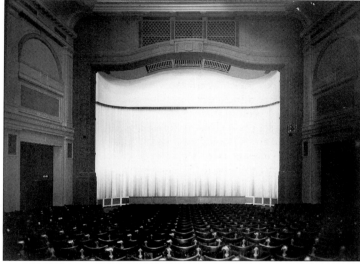

Cinema fires occasionally added to the list of closures. The Gaumont Edinburgh burned down in May 1962 (below left). It is seen (above left) as the Rutland when it opened in 1930 and (above) as modernised by the early 1960s. The site was cleared. (P.S. There is a thesis to be written on the disproportionate number of cinema fires in Scotland.)

In an attempt to make the National release work, it was booked rigorously into the Rank cinemas that had been designated as outlets, except when they were tied up with roadshow presentations. Initially, National outlets gained some acceptable product like the Steve Reeves epics *The Last Days of Pompeii* and *The Giant of Marathon* and even an occasonal plum such as 20th Century-Fox's John Wayne action comedy *North to Alaska*, making it occasionally more attractive than the Rank release. But the other circuits and independent cinema operators which were expected to lend support proved very choosey about which National releases they took. And Rank's own closures continually reduced the number of National release cinemas: the Acton, Sutton and Kentish Town Gaumonts and the Highbury Picture House were gone within three months of the National release beginning, the start of a steady trickle.

The very large suburban cinemas taking the National release had no hope of surviving. In Wimbledon, the Gaumont was saved by inheriting the Rank release when the Odeon was sold off for redevelopment. At Rose Hill, a curious and shortlived attempt was made to keep the large Gaumont afloat by showing the National release only half the week or not at all, filling in with three day runs of reissues. This and many other large cinemas like the Hounslow Dominion, East Ham Gaumont and Exeter Gaumont were soon put to profitable use as bingo halls.

By the autumn of 1961, there was insufficient new product to provide a National release every week and re-runs were scheduled; a year later, it was struggling to keep going, and it reached its last legs in June 1963. In the key cities, the Birmingham Gaumont and Newcastle Queen's were expensively remodelled to concentrate solely on roadshow presentations (see next section). The Gaumont Cardiff (which, as a former theatre, also offered many live shows) had been sold and demolished, leaving the Odeon and Capitol sharing the Rank split of new releases and special presentations. The Glasgow Gaumont and Leeds Majestic continued with roadshows, while the Leeds Gaumont had gone over to bingo. The Liverpool Gaumont and Hippodrome carried on, as did the Odeon, while the Rialto soon closed for bingo. In Manchester, the Gaumont shared in the Rank allocation of films with the Odeon and New Oxford between roadshows. In Sheffield, the Gaumont continued to play the best Rank product.

After the complete collapse of the National release, a very

small rump of Gaumont cinemas in the London area hung on as best they could. The Eltham Hill Gaumont and the Tottenham Palace (one of the very few cinemas to still have back projection) did very well to last until the late Sixties before being turned over to bingo. In some towns like Weston-Super-Mare and St. Albans where there were no other cinemas apart from an Odeon, the Gaumont was able to survive as well as it could draw on the ABC releases, but here they became redundant once it was decided to triple the Odeons (although some enterprising off-beat programming staved off the end at St. Albans for a while). And, even after the tripling of the Richmond Odeon, the town's Gaumont went on until 1980, becoming a semi-art house but lacking a sufficiently consistent policy to ensure total success.

Even the Rank release had not been safe from a early reduction in numbers, if slight by comparison. The small though attractive Rushey Green Gaumont was expendable as it stood in the catchment area of the huge Lewisham Gaumont. The Cricklewood Gaumont was large and in an unopposed location, but old-fashioned and Kilburn was in easy reach, so that was inessential. The Chichester Gaumont closed as part of a deal with Granada to eliminate competition in a few locations where they were competing: this left Chichester with just a Granada to cherrypick all the new films. The Bromley Gaumont was sold for redevelopment, enabling the large if less prominent Odeon to move over to the better release.

It was decided to sell off the Elephant and Castle Trocadero which, with 3,329 seats, was too large to make economic sense, even with the Rank release and popular live shows (which, at most, counted for perhaps two nights a month). Rank had always been interested in retaining a cinema presence on a smaller scale and plans by T. P. Bennett and Son were drawn up for a two-level 1,050- seat cinema, coffee bar, underground car park and eight-floor office building. These was rejected. Some two years later, in October 1963, the Troc closed — having been sold to developers who contracted to lease back a new cinema (which opened as an Odeon in December 1966).

Roadshows

In city centres, the position of secondary theatres was far stronger because of the number of films being given roadshow presentations. In the Sixties, *The Sound of Music* was by far the most successful, overtaking the amazing appeal of *South Pacific*

The Queens Newcastle was modernised for Cinerama. The photograph showing the roof off is dated 12 July 1963. Below right is the final result. At this time the process required an additional projector at each side: the corner of one juts out at the top right, the porthole of the other is just visible on the far side. The Queens had a balcony. (Demolished.)

The old above, the new below. Again in Newcastle, the Pavilion was modernised in 1961 as a second roadshow house. In 1968, a false ceiling was built across, concealing the evidence of its 1903 theatre design. (Demolished.)

in the Fifties. Another Rodgers and Hammerstein musical released by 20th Century-Fox, it tended to play the same theatres as these had demonstrated their ability to draw audiences to this kind of film.

At the Dominion Tottenham Court Road in London's West End, *The Sound of Music* played for three years and three months — from 29 March 1965 to 31 June 1968. At the Majestic Leeds, *The Sound of Music* ran for more than two and a half years, being so carefully handled by the projection staff that it required only one change of print.

Roadshows had become a fixed part of the business and Rank set about remodelling cinemas or building new ones to show them. When the Majestic Leeds was supplanted by the new Odeon Merrion Centre, this opened with *The Fall of the Roman Empire*. Ironically, it would have been an ideal attraction for the Majestic, complementing the classical freize of charioteers around the dome. Bingo had already taken root in the Majestic's former ballroom, served by a separate entrance, and now Rank closed its bingo operation at the town's Gaumont and turned the huge main auditorium of the Majestic over to the number watchers. (Since then, alas, a false ceiling has been introduced hiding the ornate dome and, while the changes are reversible, the recent listing of the building has come too late to keep the splendour of the auditorium on view.)

In London, the Astoria Charing Cross Road hosted the world premiere of *The Fall of the Roman Empire* and the cinema was redecorated to accent the classical motifs in the auditorium's freize, columns and ceiling. The circle lounge was covered in a wallpaper of classical design and the main foyer given extensive Roman trimmings. Others films such as *Those Magnificent Men in Their Flying Machines* and *The Agony and the Ecstasy* opened in 70mm prints for extended runs on the Astoria's huge screen.

Some alterations were carried out to introduce Cinerama to the regions. This had been a London attraction since 1954 and now that features were appearing in the process, cinemas began to be adapted to present them, initially using three projectors, then the single projector system which could play 70mm prints.

In Newcastle, the Queen's closed for five months in 1963 to have the roof removed and a completely new auditorium built for Cinerama, with three projectors, modern drapes over the side wall and a very plain ceiling, seating reduced to 963. When Cinerama productions dried up, it carried on with 70mm pres-

The Gaumont Birmingham was another Cinerama conversion, in 1963. The Cinerama sign blocks out the windows of the old projection box. An advance booking office was established in the base of the tower next to the entrance. The old foyer (top) was modernised (as seen above) although the triangular stand with the cinema's opening time amazingly survived. The new auditorium, very similar to the one installed at the Queens Newcastle, is seen at left (the original one is shown on page 43).

entations. This was another cinema that did spectacularly well with *The Sound of Music*, holding it for 140 weeks.

During the same year, the Birmingham Gaumont underwent a similar transformation, keeping its roof but closing for fourteen weeks that obliterated or concealed every trace of the auditorium's original decor, moved the projection room to the back of the stalls floor, and provided the biggest screen in Europe (84 ft. by 33 ft.), a point advertised for years on the canopy. Seating was reduced to 1,212 seats. Fawn drapes extended outwards from each side of the screen to cover the side walls. The word Cinerama in trademark lettering obscured the windows of the projection box high on the facade. When *The Sound of Music* played here from 18 April 1965 to 6 July 1968, its 168 week run was second only to that of the Dominion in London, with two million admissions from all over the Midlands, including 600 visits by a single patron, Miss Alice Jackson.

Another roadshow conversion in 1964 transformed the vast Gaumont Leicester into a 822-seat Odeon at a cost of £130,000. The building seems to have been demolished except for its front. The cinema was placed above a ground-floor Odeon Arcade of shops and had an entrance of miserly proportions which led to an attractive venue, equipped with 70mm, for extended runs of films like *A Man for All Seasons*. This still left Rank with an Odeon and Picture House for regular runs. (For 70mm presentations, key Rank cinemas installed the Philips D.P. 70 multipurpose projector for both 35mm and 70mm prints.)

Elsewhere on the circuit, alterations were less drastic. At the Coventry Gaumont, for instance, the projection box at the back of the dome was closed and a new one built in the rear circle. This enabled a 62 ft. wide screen to be installed (9 ft. wider than before) but it could no longer be flown, so live shows came to an end. The Compton organ was removed. A plain proscenium arch was introduced and the orchestra pit covered over. In 1967, further modernisation took place and the dome and surrounding decorations were concealed by a flat ceiling. A plain false ceiling reduced the height of the main foyer. The result was a sad mess.

The roadshow era went into decline in the late Sixties as suitable product dried up. Many cinemas that had survived on extended runs now found themselves forced back to routine programming with frequent changes of films.

Alternative uses: more dance halls

It is not always remembered that the potential profits from dancing stimulated the very first subdivisions of British cinemas. As early as August 1957, T. P. Bennett and Son were commissioned to draw up plans for the New Victoria, London, using the stalls floor for a ballroom and the stage area for shops, keeping an 800-seat cinema in the circle. Various alternative conversion proposals were examined before the idea was dropped.

However, at the Gaumont State Kilburn, the area under the balcony was sealed off in 1960 to become the New State Ballroom, leaving the rest of the auditorium intact, still with over 2,000 seats. Then the Gaumont Plymouth closed for nine months in December 1961, followed by the Gaumont Preston for a similar period in the middle of 1962. In both buildings, the old circle was extended to form a smaller cinema with a new screen and proscenium arch, while the ground floor was levelled to form a substantial ballroom.

Alternative uses: bowling alleys

In the late Fifties, American-style bowling alleys suggested themselves as profitable alternative uses for large cinemas of suitable shape. The ABC circuit was first in the field, and the initial response was highly encouraging. Late in 1960, Rank decided to convert six cinemas, of which two were Gaumonts: the Gaumont Chatham closed in February 1961 and the Gaumont Streatham followed a month later. Streatham was to become the largest bowl in the country with forty lanes. Other cinemas were surveyed for conversion: the Tivoli at Partick, Glasgow, was rejected but the Gaumonts at Chester and Oldham measured up and closed in December 1961. After initial success, none of these bowls performed well, and only the Streatham one has staggered through changes of ownership and periods of closure to remain in operation in 1995.

Alternative uses: bingo halls

Bingo proved by far the most successful and enduring means of turning cinemas to more profitable use. It also provided the answer for many cinemas that had become unprofitable dance halls and bowling alleys.

The Gaumont Peckham was the first big Rank cinema to be turned over to the eyes down brigade, closing in January 1961. At first, bingo sessions took place only on Wednesdays, Fridays, Saturdays and Sundays. On Tuesdays, many wrestling matches were staged. Still operating as a bingo hall in 1995, it has now

ODEON
HAMMERSMITH Tel: RIV 4081

ON THE STAGE

BRIAN EPSTEIN Presents

ANOTHER 'BEATLES' CHRISTMAS SHOW

THE BEATLES

FREDDIE and the DREAMERS

JIMMY SAVILE · SOUNDS INCORPORATED

ELKIE BROOKS · THE YARDBIRDS · MICHAEL HASLAM
THE MIKE COTTON SOUND · RAY FELL

OPENS 24th DECEMBER to 16th JANUARY 1965
(EXCEPT SUNDAYS)

BOX OFFICE NOW OPEN
Performances at 6.15 pm & 8.45 pm
One performance Christmas Eve at 7.30 pm
One performance 29th Dec at 6.15

| STALLS : | 20/- | : | 15/- | : | 10/- | | |
| CIRCLE : | 20/- | : | 15/- | : | 10/- | : | 7/6 |

SEND NOW TO THE
ODEON THEATRE
HAMMERSMITH
Tel: RIV 4081

ENCLOSE A
STAMPED/
ADDRESSED
ENVELOPE

Please send .... Stalls tickets (a) .... each for 6.15 or 8.45
performance on alternative date(s) .... Circle
Cheque/P.O. Number .... enclosed
Name ....
Address ....

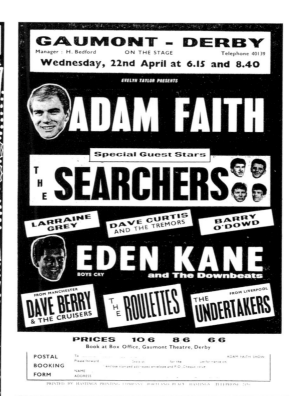

GAUMONT - DERBY
Manager : H. Bedford **ON THE STAGE** Telephone 40139
Wednesday, 22nd April at 6.15 and 8.40

EVELYN TAYLOR PRESENTS

ADAM FAITH

Special Guest Stars

THE SEARCHERS

LARRAINE GREY DAVE CURTIS AND THE TREMORS BARRY O'DOWD

EDEN KANE
BOYS CRY and The Downbeats

FROM MANCHESTER **DAVE BERRY & THE CRUISERS** THE **ROULETTES** **THE UNDERTAKERS** FROM LIVERPOOL

PRICES 10 6 8 6 6 6
Book at Box Office, Gaumont Theatre, Derby

POSTAL BOOKING FORM
To ....
Please forward .... Seats at .... for the .... performance on .... ADAM FAITH SHOW
enclose stamped addressed envelope and P.O./Cheque value
NAME ....
ADDRESS ....

PRINTED BY HASTINGS PRINTING COMPANY, PORTLAND PLACE, HASTINGS · TELEPHONE 2696

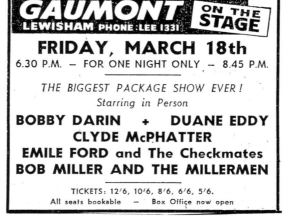

GAUMONT
LEWISHAM PHONE : LEE 1331 **ON THE STAGE**

FRIDAY, MARCH 18th
6.30 P.M. — FOR ONE NIGHT ONLY — 8.45 P.M.

THE BIGGEST PACKAGE SHOW EVER!
Starring in Person

BOBBY DARIN + DUANE EDDY
CLYDE McPHATTER
EMILE FORD and The Checkmates
BOB MILLER AND THE MILLERMEN

TICKETS: 12/6, 10/6, 8/6, 6/6, 5/6.
All seats bookable — Box Office now open

Live shows continued to be featured at many Gaumonts in the 1960s, although the huge Hammersmith theatre became an Odeon. The Lewisham concert was in 1960. (Hammersmith advertisement courtesy of Stan Fishman. Derby flyer courtesy of Ken Roe. Lewisham advertisement courtesy of Alan Scott.)

spent more years at this than it did screening films, and in the process has changed internally beyond all recognition. Besides the cinemas which were soon switched to full-time bingo, the game was also introduced for a while on Sunday afternoons at many halls including, in the London area, the Gaumonts Camden Town, Hammersmith, Shepherds Bush and Watford, plus the Edmonton Regal and Elephant and Castle Trocadero. At Shepherds Bush, there were also sessions on Saturday mornings.

Hotel incentive

In 1964, the British government offered, for a very limited period, a twenty-five per cent hotel grant to encourage the construction of more hotels as a boost to the tourist industry. This led to the closure and rapid demolition of the Gaumont Middlesbrough with a Gaumont hotel planned (but not built) as its replacement.

Goodbye "Gaumont"

With the end of the Gaumont circuit release, there was no longer a powerful reason to keep the Gaumont name. But it was still being introduced at one or two sites early in the decade. The last cinema to be branded Gaumont was the Broadway in Peterborough in November 1961 but the name was shortlived as it closed two years later for bingo. Almost as brief was the change of name at the Regent Stamford Hill, North London. The Regent was renamed Gaumont in January 1960 but within three years it had become an Odeon.*

A little over a month after the Gaumont name appeared at Peterborough, two comparatively unimportant Gaumonts, at Southall and Wembley, were renamed Odeon. In both locations, Odeon theatres had been closed and the name was therefore available to be transferred to the former rival.

In July 1962, the fire-damaged Gaumont Lewisham, Southeast London, re-opened after extensive modernisation (in particular, the huge old foyer had been boxed in to much smaller size) and this was now called the Odeon.

When the new upstairs cinema opened above a dance hall at the former Gaumont Plymouth in September 1962, it was

*The Regent Brighton was the only PCT Regent never to change its name, probably because of the local significance of the name and the resentment that any change to Gaumont might have induced.

The Hackney Pavilion survived nearly sixty years without changing its name or being heavily modernised. Exterior from 1969 (photographer unknown), interior from 1972 when it closed (courtesy of former GLC Department of Architecture and Design). (Demolished, and replaced by a bank.)

named Odeon. The Gaumont name was discarded in identical circumstances at Preston, giving that town an Odeon for the first time ever in January 1963.

A major wave of name changing to Odeon took place in October and November 1962 and it was clear that the Gaumont name was being phased out. It was during this period that the Stamford Hill cinema changed its name again.

Once the key Gaumont cinemas at Hammersmith, Holloway, Lewisham and Wood Green in London had all been branded Odeons, the Gaumont name had been mortally wounded. Yet even Gaumont veterans could accept that the Odeon name carried equal if not greater prestige and recognised that the change of name represented a gesture of confidence in the future of the buildings concerned.

In 1968, there were twenty-five situations in which an Odeon and Gaumont still competed, ruling out any switch of name. In four other places — Finchley, Kilburn and Notting Hill Gate in London, South Shields — there were Gaumont cinemas that could have been renamed Odeon, although the Kilburn theatre was too well-known as the State or Gaumont State for any alteration to be contemplated. At Weymouth, the Odeon name had only just disappeared but would in time be reintroduced at the Gaumont (see next section). There were still a number of other cinemas like the Hackney Pavilion and London New Victoria that had not changed their names at all.

Sold as going concerns

In December 1967, a number of ailing Rank cinemas were sold to the Classic circuit and immediately took the Classic name. These included the Gaumonts or former Gaumont cinemas in Chippenham, Frome, Hendon, Hinckley, Redditch, Stroud, Wallasey (Egremont) and Yeovil. Few of these properties survived for any length of time as Classics, being switched to bingo or sold off for redevelopment, but the Gaumont Hendon did manage an amazing comeback from its deadly period as a Northwest London frontline National release outlet when it played some programmes like *Stork Talk* that did such diabolical business their further release was virtually terminated. As the Classic, it inherited the Rank release when the Odeon Hendon closed, and is apparently flourishing in 1995 as a three-screen MGM operation. The Gaumont Wallasey still stands, but the interior has been subdivided into six cinemas, removing all trace of its interesting original interior.

It was the Classic deal, with its take-over of the Odeons at Taunton and Weymouth, that paved the way for those towns' Gaumonts (the better cinemas in both cases) to inherit the Odeon name after a decent interval.

The twinning of the Gaumont Sheffield in 1968/69. "What we had here was one of W. E. Trent's famous Regents, now hopelessly elaborate and out-dated", declared Trevor and Mavis Stone, interior designers for the conversion. See page 25 for the original interior. At top right is the new Gaumont 1, with Cinerama and 737 seats. Right, the 1,150-seat Gaumont 2 with transparent curtain. (Demolished.)

13: TWINS AND TRIPLES

In the late Sixties, it became obvious that most cinemas were far too large. The initial response was to elaborately divide some of them into twin cinemas by extending the circle forward to create one still large auditorium above another. This was a variation on the previous subdivisions at Plymouth and Preston where the lower space had been used for dance halls. Creating two cinemas in one building introduced booking flexibility by which films could be retained longer. As early as 1963, a preliminary scheme had been drawn up to show how the New Victoria, London, could be split horizontally into two cinemas, leaving the stage free for other uses. In fact, Rank carried out its first twinning scheme in 1965 at the Odeon Nottingham. In late 1968, the Odeons at Leeds and Liverpool and the Gaumonts at Bradford, Bournemouth and Sheffield closed for similar treatment, the conversions in each case removing all trace of the original auditorium's decor.

In Bradford, Rank had decided to retain the Gaumont rather than the Odeon, even though the latter had been modernised seven years earlier. The Gaumont building was so huge that it could be remodelled into twin cinemas and also accommodate a 2,000 seat bingo hall in the former stalls. While the Gaumont was shut for nine months of reconstruction, the Odeon also closed permanently, clearing the way for the new twin cinemas to take over the Odeon name when they opened.

In Bournemouth and Sheffield, Rank kept its Odeons open for a while, and the name Gaumont was retained for the new twin cinemas, each said to have cost £320,000. In both cases, Gaumont 1 was outfitted for roadshow presentations in 70mm/Cinerama. At Bournemouth, the auditorium was rounded to suit the giant curved screen. Gaumont 2 here was mostly used for 35mm films but could show 70mm prints. At Sheffield, the roof of the building had to be raised more than 15 ft. to house the giant 29 ft.-high screen in Gaumont 1.

At other locations, very large Rank cinemas were divided horizontally to provide a smaller cinema upstairs and bingo accomodation downstairs. This involved several months of closure and affected the former Gaumonts at Camden Town (in 1967/68) and Shepherds Bush (1969/70). At the former Gaumont Chelsea, an eighteen-month period of closure in 1972/73 produced a new cinema in the former circle, reached by a former side exit, while the foyer and stalls space became a Habitat store and the fly tower was converted into flats.

In 1970, Rank opened its first mini-cinema, a 105-seater in the former restaurant space at Preston.

In another doomed attempt to crash the dance market, a few large cinemas, including the Edmonton Regal, were converted to a new chain of Sundown discotheques in the early Seventies.

Sometimes leases would run out and throw up the question of whether renewal was worthwhile. On 24 June 1973, the fifty-year lease on the Leicester Picture House (which had cost £1,250 per year until 1931 and £2,000 since) expired and Rank decided against seeking an extension as it had two cinemas in the town.

Another approach that removed at least three cinemas was the arrival of Rank City Wall, a new property development subsidiary. This seized on the Islington Angel (by now Odeon) and demolished the auditorium for an office block entered on a side street, stranding the tower entrance as a North London landmark signifying nothing. (This remnant was made a listed building in 1991, nearly twenty years too late to save a fascinating auditorium which Rank had modernised after a fashion, suspending powerful down lights making it almost impossible to see the lofty, old-fashioned barrel-vault ceiling.)

Another imposing victim of Rank City Wall was the Gaumont Wolverhampton, which was no longer needed after the town's Odeon had become a three-screen operation (see below). It went with some style, closing in November 1973 with a revival of two MGM musicals, *The Great Caruso* and *Singin' in the Rain*, plus

The new Odeon Chelsea in the old balcony used a former exit staircase as its entrance, with the original entrance taken over by Habitat. (Circa 1978 photograph by Allen Eyles.) (Now Chelsea Cinema.)

One of the two minis beneath the balcony in the former Gaumont (now Odeon) Watford. Note some double seats in the back row. (Adapted from a colour transparency by Allen Eyles.) (Demolished.)

Graeme Hawkins at the specially imported Rodgers Theatre organ, to a final audience of six hundred. It had remained active with live shows almost to the end: the last one, a Morecambe and Wise show a few months before its demise, reportedly achieved a record level of bookings, ahead even of Bill Haley and the Beatles on their respective hysterical appearances. The replacement for the Gaumont was a typically drab showroom and office complex.

The Odeon Burnt Oak, North London, which had at one time been renamed Gaumont, provided another site for redevelopment by Rank City Wall.

"Drop wall" conversions

In time, Rank hit on a less expensive way of converting most of its cinemas to smaller units. Three screens were created by blocking off the space beneath the circle and dividing it down the middle to create two small cinemas, leaving the rest of the building to become the largest cinema, using the old screen and circle seating, occasionally supplemented by the front stalls seats. These conversions had the advantage that the cinema could stay open for evening performances throughout the work period, or close only for the final week, retaining its regular patrons and earning some money. The development of the single projector, using the platter or "cakestand" to hold a complete programme on one large horizontal reel, helped make this possible, requiring smaller new projection booths downstairs with single portholes: equipment was reliable enough to be left unmanned for substantial periods, reducing staff costs.

Over a two-year period beginning in November 1972, the Gaumonts or former Gaumont cinemas at Salisbury, Wimbledon, Cheltenham, Doncaster, Wood Green, Holloway, Rochester, Hanley, Watford and Derby all opened as three-screen film centres, to be followed a year later by Coventry. The same work was, course, carried out at many Odeons, including Wolverhampton. The older Gaumonts had an advantage in that their larger auditoria enabled the minis under the circle to seat as many as 150. The more compact Odeons tended to allow around 110 seats with lower ceilings. However, only rarely, as at Hanley, did Rank have a choice of buildings.

These drop wall conversions required no major alterations to the cinema except underneath the balcony. The view for patrons seated in the old circle remained essentially unaltered. At Doncaster and Hanley, seating was even retained in the front stalls and brought into use when required, especially for the live shows that continued to be presented on occasion at the former venue. In other cinemas, the front stalls area was just left empty, and even though sound-absorbent material faced the speakers under the balcony, the results acoustically for those sitting in the former circle were sometimes less than ideal.

There were also some severe drawbacks to these mini-cinemas. The original side walls did not match, in either decoration or angle, the plain new walls inserted down the middle; the ceilings often retained prominent but awkwardly truncated ornamentation such as coves for now-disused lighting; and the screens often had to be off centre to allow for a front side exit and to face more directly the projection box that was built at the back inner corner to serve both new auditoria. In terms of appearance, the best effort was made at Watford where carpeting extended from the floor up the side walls — rumour had it this was because so many directors of the Rank Organisation lived in the area.

Sightlines in the minis tended to be poor and screens had to be small because of the low height and the slight rake. Audiences were often unimpressed, referring to 'broom cupboards' and 'postage-stamp screens'. Tickets sold with numbered seats removed the advantage of choosing where to sit, as was usually possible upstairs. From a film booking point of view, a big problem was that the mini-cinemas were often far too small to meet demand, even though many could be cross-linked to show the same print of a film seconds apart. In some instances, as at Wimbledon, it was possible to enlarge the mini-cinemas, although this could mean their roofs extending visibly in front of the circle.

In contrast, the ABC circuit usually went to much greater expense in tripling its cinemas by closing for several months to create much larger auditoria, doing away with the original proscenium arch and screen. The period of closure and degree of alteration enabled the cinemas to be launched more convincingly as a completely new development.

Once a twin or triple cinema had been created, Rank's emphasis naturally lay in concentrating business on that and recovering its investment, so that the future for any other cinema still operated in the locality became bleak as major attractions tended to be confined to the new facility. Thus in Manchester the Gaumont closed when the new Odeon twins were launched. At Wolverhampton, the Gaumont closed just over a month after the Odeon re-opened with its three screens. In Hanley, the Odeon survived the tripling of the Gaumont with extended runs of new films but only for eighteen months. Bingo was rarely an option as, if these cinemas were suitable, they would probably have been converted earlier.

An unfortunate drawback to these conversions was that it usually ended live shows. As previously recorded, many of the Gaumonts had been designed for full stage use and from the late Fifties there had been a substantial resurgence in their use for this purpose, particularly for one night stage shows with pop stars. Such shows were still profitable and took place until the last possible moment: Jimmy Tarbuck, for example, starred at Cheltenham only two weeks before the stalls closed for sub-division.

In general terms the Rank chain had been reshaped to face the future with its better cinemas mostly converted to two or three screens. Unfortunately, this would not be enough.

Closures of '75

Although isolated closures continued to take place, late in 1975 Rank cleared out a further dozen unprofitable theatres in one batch. Most were announced in advance, but the New Victoria in London was an unexpected addition, having been leased to a pop music impresario. This sweep also spelled the end for the former Gaumont at Anniesland in a northwestern suburb of Glasgow, for the postwar cinema at Bootle and for the Newcastle Pavilion (which had been a second Rank roadshow house for many years) — but not for the the former Gaumonts, now Odeons, at Southport, which had been scheduled for the chop on 22 November 1975, and at Perth, which should have followed a week later.

The Southport cinema was reprieved following a recent surge in cinema attendances. It was not amenable to subdivision by the comparatively inexpensive drop wall method because it had a shallow balcony with insufficient space beneath to accommodate mini-cinemas, and so it soldiered on as an oversize single screen cinema for another four years until Sainsbury's moved in and demolished it for a new supermarket.

The Perth property was saved on the intervention of the circuit's booking controller, George Pinches, who believed it could be made to pay. This survived for another five years on a peculiar diet of sex films in the afternoon and regular programmes in the evenings which eventually gave way to "adult" entertainment almost entirely. Although sex films were played on occasion throughout the Rank circuit during this period, the Perth cinema was unique in being so dependent on them.

Other Gaumonts halls at Grimsby and South Shields were sold to Brent Walker and became Focus cinemas. On a brighter note, the Gaumont Notting Hill Gate was redecorated: the nearby Westbourne Grove Odeon prevented it from obtaining major releases but, like the Richmond Gaumont, this was in just the right area to survive on specialised, up-market programming.

One screen was even added to the circuit, although it proved to be short-lived: this was the conversion of the former restaurant at the Gaumont State Kilburn to provide a 200-seat second auditorium. It had its own separate entrance and paybox on Willesden Lane.

Super Saturday Shows

Saturday morning pictures were not quite dead. Indeed, they were fighting back in 1976 under the new name of Super Saturday Shows. At Shepherds Bush, admissions went up from 238 to 500-600 in six months. Rank's Barry Goodwin exhorted other managers to follow the example set by manager Dave Watts: "TV competition is just as much a problem in Shepherds Bush as anywhere else in the country. But nevertheless Dave Watts keeps packing 'em in. How? Because his Super Saturday Show is not just films but above all a great deal of 'other than film fun' which instills a 'belonging to a club' atmosphere rather than 'just going to the pictures'. Dave Watts has hit upon the key to SucceSS by giving the youngsters of today just what they want — POP MUSIC and LOTS OF IT, fast and loud so they can get up and *dance*. It's not really surprising when you consider that most of today's 'teenybopping' groups are at the top because youngsters in the age range of *our* members buy their records....if that's not proof enough then come along to Shepherds Bush and see over 300 youngsters bopping away to 'Jungle Rock' (quite a sight and what's more they're very good!).

"You don't need a complete Disco Unit (Dave Watts hasn't) — you can use the record player in the box, but give it to 'em loud and fast, not just the odd one or two records but a full half hour's worth before your programme starts and more later during the break, in between a couple of competitions. I bet there isn't anywhere in your town that gives youngsters somewhere to let their hair down dancing and believe me that's what they want. They'll still enjoy the film, cartoons, serial, competitions, etc., but we've still got to get 'em in first!"

At Lewisham, a bus conductor called Andy Mellish who regaled passengers with jokes, songs and acrobatics was recruited by deputy manager Harry Royle to entertain the kids after the Saturday morning film shows. At Wood Green, a pop group called the Jarvis Brothers from nearby Tottenham were engaged to perform a song from their latest record.

At the same time, 1976 was the twenty-fifth anniversary of the Children's Film Foundation and five new films made for children were premiered at ten cinemas during May.

Quite how long these Super Saturday Clubs survived is unclear, although the children's clubs at the rival ABC chain ended in 1980.

14: LAST OF THE GAUMONTS

As cinema attendances continued their downhill plunge, the position became untenable for the last few single screens. The former Gaumont Hammersmith, by now the largest cinema in the country with 3,485 seats, was essentially devoted to live shows by the early Eighties with films as filler material, and by 1984 its projectors whirred into life for, at most, a couple of weeks a year, usually to minimal audiences. There was, however, a brief reminder of former glory when on Saturday 30 July 1983, the hottest day of the year, it revived the trilogy of *Star Wars, Return of the Jedi* and *The Empire Strikes Back* in one giant show running from 2.30pm to 9.40pm. All 3,485 seats were snapped up by the fans and 600 were turned away. More than £3,000 worth of refreshments were sold.

As for the other former giant of the circuit, the Kilburn State, the seating in the original auditorium had been reduced to 1,354 seats in circle and front stalls but this left a huge space that had become too prohibitively expensive to heat and it shut in the autumn of 1980, leaving the mini-cinema in the former restaurant to linger on a while. The closure did at least prompt the listing of the building within a few weeks, thwarting a proposal to erect a supermarket on the site. Bingo subsequently spread from its berth beneath the circle to occupy the whole auditorium so, as a building if not as a cinema, this can be numbered among the survivors (see next chapter).

A less conspicuous closure was that of the Gaumont Finchley five weeks later. This cinema was exceptional not only its own right as a piece of cinema architecture but also in that it had sailed through more than fifty years with no substantial alterations at all, not even changing its name. The exterior signage and the elaborate stone mural depicting the shooting of a film, the entrance foyer with its walnut panelling, and the light fittings in the auditorium all remained unaltered. As it was not only a prominent and well-designed landmark externally but also represented an intact super-cinema of W. E. Trent's later

period, its failure to become a listed building is regrettable. The auditorium had survived intact because it was very wide and the circle only extended over the rear stalls for a few rows. This ruled out an inexpensive dropwall conversion to create mini-cinemas downstairs. In its later years, the balcony was closed and side sections of the stalls curtained off to reduce its capacity to 831 seats. The Gaumont exhibited a certain sense of style with a final late night performance, booking *The Last Picture Show* as its last picture show. When the property was sold, Rank's original intention was to lease back two new small cinemas that were proposed in its redevelopment and reinstate the mural sculpture somewhere. The cinema was demolished but plans for offices plus the two cinemas were repeatedly rejected by Barnet Borough Council. Apart from a new block of flats occupying the old car park at the rear, the site has remained vacant and unused except as a market on one day a week.

The only other cinema still carrying the Gaumont name in the London area, the Gaumont Richmond, closed on the same day as Finchley. It had done well to survive for more than six years after the nearby Odeon had been tripled but the up-market nature of the area and some astute programming of revivals and foreign films, often at the prompting of its manager, had enabled it to continue operating profitably before Rank decided to concentrate business on the Odeon. Planning permission required a smaller replacement cinema which took many years to materialise as an independent art house with its entrance hidden away down a side street.

The demise of the Odeon (ex-Gaumont) Lewisham in early 1981 remains a bit of a puzzle. Although it was readily suited to a simple dropwall scheme for three screen operation, it missed conversion in the early 1970s, probably because it was still in heavy demand for pop concerts (the Bay City Rollers, in particular, brought out crowds in 1974 reminiscent of the siege conditions when the Beatles had appeared in 1963). Another useful source of revenue had been live television specials by satellite, such as the Muhammed Ali/Joe Frazier fight beamed to the cinema in 1975. For film use, with 2,858 seats to fill (although in practice only part of the auditorium was opened), it took a real blockbuster to drum up satisfactory audiences: *Star Wars*, for the week ending 18 February 1978, created a record in later years of 20,560 admissions. Although live events were profitable, there were not enough of them to make the theatre financially viable. In 1977, Rank announced plans to turn Lewisham over to bingo. Some hesitation followed, apparently because of the damage that might be done to existing Rank bingo halls nearby, but in 1979 the company sought planning permission and was refused. Live shows continued until nearly the day the cinema closed — The Who performed to a capacity audience, preceded by Hawkwind and Adam and the Ants. In the basement of the closed cinema lay a heap of umbrellas with fine wooden handles and the word Gaumont printed on the fabric, left over from the time when a doorman escorted patrons from their cars on rainy days...

Even though the auditorium had suffered from a fire in the early Sixties, it remained an awe-inspiring space and the building deserved a better fate than to sit derelict for twelve years before being demolished. It should have become the South London equivalent to Hammersmith with live shows, or at least tried again for a bingo licence, or even been belatedly converted to a triple cinema after Lewisham's other cinema closed in 1986.

1981 went on to become, to borrow a phrase from the Queen, an *annus horribilis*. On 19 June, Rank announced the closure of twenty-nine of its 123 cinemas in a few months' time.

Even before that took effect, the Gaumont Taunton, long known as the Odeon, was turned over to Rank's bingo side, bringing to an end substantial live show usage as well as films (Showaddywaddy gave the last concert the day before *Herbie Goes Bananas* became the last picture show). There had been talk of this building becoming a performing arts centre in the late Seventies but it underwent a substantial refurbishment for bingo, so it can still be counted among the survivors.

As for the twenty-nine, Rank were at least prepared to let others run some of the properties and even reprieved one or two itself. Single-screen properties from the former Gaumont circuit were the Odeon Ashton-under-Lyne (which was taken over by an independent and has remained in operation, re-

named the Metro); the Odeon Dundee (a plain modern cinema in the shell of an old theatre which went over to bingo and continues in this use); the Odeon Eglinton Toll, Glasgow (which still seated 2,003 although only the circle was usually opened — this closed and was eventually demolished); the Odeon Chelsea (the circle of the former Gaumont, this remained closed for nearly two years before being taken over for art house use); and the small screen at the Kilburn State in the former restaurant (which closed but was re-opened by Rank between 1985 and 1990). Also on the list was the Odeon Rayners Lane (an Odeon property which had taken the Gaumont name and release for many years). This had been in dire straits for some months, closed on Mondays and Tuesdays outside of school holidays as an economy measure. It passed to the independent Ace chain for a few years' further life as a cinema. Then, most surprisingly, the list also included the former Majestic at Rochester, Kent, which as the Odeon had been tripled only seven years earlier and was in excellent condition. This shut down and stood derelict for many years.

At the same time, Rank invested in some of its surviving cinemas. These included the Edinburgh Odeon, ex New Victoria, which was converted to three screens, using the rear stalls for two new cinemas. 1982 was a year of respite, then the slimming began again.

In 1983, the three-screen Odeon, ex Gaumont Palace, at Derby was sold to rivals EMI who were anxious to replace a popular bingo hall lost in a fire. The new owners retained a cinema upstairs, extending the old circle forwards, but removed the two mini-cinemas beneath the circle to use the entire stalls for bingo. Derby was left with just one mainstream screen.

And then Rank closed the very first Gaumont, in Birmingham, which still carried its name in the same scroll lettering it had on opening in 1931 (this having been centred after the suffix Palace was taken down). In the late Seventies, when 70mm spectaculars were no longer pouring out, the Gaumont had lost the biggest screen in Europe and the maximum picture size became 52 ft. by 22 ft. In 1981, plans had been announced to convert it to three screens but the national decline in attendances made the scheme seem uneconomic. By 1983, its entrance no longer faced onto a busy street — it was largely approached by pedestrian subways and had become stranded in an area of redevelopment. Even so, it attracted huge queues in its final summer of operation with the *Star Wars* picture, *Return of the*

The last Gaumonts. Above: Bournemouth (from 1967 slide by John Squires). Below: left, Ipswich (in 1975) and, right, Doncaster with its modernised frontage (taken circa 1980) (both photographs by Allen Eyles).

*Above, Doncaster's last
programmes as a Gaumont in
January 1987 (poor quality image
from microfilm). Right, the end of
an era. Note the number of live
shows despite a drop-wall
conversion to three screens. (Also
from microfilm.)*

Jedi, to be balanced by the absence of any customers at all for one showing of *The Legend of the Lone Ranger*. Instead of converting the building to three cinemas, Rank took the cheaper option of acquiring two closed cinemas adjacent to its Odeon Queensway to create a triple there, retaining the town's huge Odeon for major film attractions between live shows.

When, in the same month, Rank closed the former Gaumont in the centre of Watford, the company's commitment to any kind of national circuit seemed questionable. As the three screen Odeon, it was the leading cinema in the town, in an excellent state of repair, and should have been profitable. It seems that an offer for the site was irresistible. This left only the small two-screen Empire (an EMI property) at an out-of-the-way location.

More understandable was the closure of the former Gaumont at Wood Green, North London, in early 1984. As an Odeon triple screen operation, the main auditorium had become very tatty with its huge circle foyer a wasted and inhospitable space. Attendances had plunged to around 2,000 per week in the kind of unsophisticated district where video reigned and cinema seemed practically dead and buried. Bingo was the solution that has put the building among the survivors.

The huge, undivided Gaumont Southampton was proving a liability (the town's Odeon had been twinned) and Rank sought permission to turn it over to bingo. This was refused and in 1986 after protracted negotiations the company agreed to sell the freehold of the building, which had started life as the Empire live theatre, to the City Council for £650,000. It has since been thoroughly refurbished and re-opened as the Mayflower Theatre.

A turnaround came when Odeon chiefs resisted attempts by Rank's bingo executives to turn the three-screen Holloway Odeon, ex Gaumont, in north London over to the eyes-down crowd. Instead, the circle was divided up into two cinemas and the front stalls converted into another new screen, while more recently another screen has been added over the front entrance, making six cinemas in all. A further two cinemas were being contemplated in 1995, thought to be in disused basement space.

The very last Gaumont

By 1986, the Gaumont name hung on only at Bournemouth, Doncaster and Ipswich, and Rank decided to retire it for good. At Bournemouth and Doncaster, the main name signs were modern ones in red, but at Ipswich a blue sign still survived.

At Bournemouth, the Gaumont twins became the Odeon 1 and 2 in October 1986. The Odeon name returned to the town after a gap of nearly thirteen years. Since the old Odeon still stood as a bingo hall, there was some initial confusion among cinemagoers as to whether that might have re-opened as a cinema.

Then Rank stayed its hand for a couple of months, as though reluctant to finally banish a name that had been so much a part of its heritage. But in January 1987, it was consigned to history.

First the Odeon name returned to Ipswich where, in similar circumstances to Bournemouth, the former Odeon, closed four and a half years earlier, was still operating as a bingo club.

And that left Doncaster. With the town's Odeon having closed back in 1973 and long been demolished, there had existed an opportunity for many years to transfer the name to the Gaumont. But the Gaumont sign had remained, lit up in red from its prominent position on the bland modernised frontage. Then, on 22 January 1987, the men from Pearce Signs drew up and this too became an Odeon. An era was over.

15: REMAINS TO BE SEEN

Cinemas still

The arrival of the multiplex and the resurgence in attendances from the mid-Eighties prompted Rank to expand its number of cinemas. This has been achieved both by building new multiplexes and by adding new screens within existing buildings to create as many as six auditoria — the equivalent of the smaller multiplex. (Despite all the slimming down, the Rank Odeon chain remains a potent force in British exhibition. With Disney, the parent Rank Organisation is a very rare example of a film industry company that has never undergone a change of ownership.)

Several Gaumont cinemas remain in operation as Odeons in the autumn of 1995, although little or nothing of the original interiors survives at Bournemouth, Bradford, Cheltenham, Coventry, Doncaster, or Wimbledon (or, to be inclusive, the postwar cinema at Barnsley). However, the exteriors have been little altered, except in the case of Doncaster. At Cheltenham, the bas-relief figures supporting the original name sign have been picked out in colour but with an awkward gap between them where the name sign has been removed: the Odeon sign in the current red and dark blue style is now to one side rather than centred on the facade. At Holloway, the outside is as striking as ever while the entrance hall still displays some of its original splendour — but here a sixth screen has been opened in the balcony area over the main foyer and entrance doors, while the postwar auditorium has been superseded by subdivision.

The former Gaumont cinemas, now Odeons, in Edinburgh and Salisbury, were listed buildings and an effort has been made to retain the original auditorium atmosphere in the process of obtaining consent for major subdivision.

The Edinburgh cinema underwent some modernisation around 1960. The entrance hall was completely updated. The decorative plasterwork in the centre of the stalls lounge ceiling was covered up and new spray light fittings installed. In the auditorium, a much bigger screen was placed in front of the

inner proscenium arch, hiding the freize just above it, while the columns above the side exits supporting the pediment were covered over by drapes and the coffered underside of the pediment became a plain surface. Stereophonic speakers which replaced the lights on the side walls of the auditorium had already been installed along with CinemaScope.

There was one substantial bonus to this set of alterations. 506 lights were inserted into the huge expanse of plain ceiling to enhance the sky-at-night effect. The result was twenty-six large white stars, 360 smaller white stars, and 120 small blue ones. These lights did not twinkle: they were either on or off.

In more recent years, the cinema has been subdivided so that it now contains five cinemas. The first stage was a late tripling when two cinemas were created side by side in the rear stalls area. One has retained two of the twelve private boxes that were set across the back of the stalls: they now have two seats each (many of the other boxes are used for storage). Since then further cinemas have been built in the former front stalls area and on the stage.

The largest cinema at the Edinburgh Odeon occupies the old balcony and retains the historic character of the building. The original proscenium arch has been replicated to surround the new screen installed in front of the circle. New walls reach inwards to join the arch, extending the side wall decoration. The rear three statues remain on display in their niches along each side wall, lit by white light rather than red as before. Redecoration was carried out in white and Wedgewood blue, replacing yellow ochre, and creates a cool, relaxing atmosphere. Half of the star-studded ceiling remains, the lights still working.

The size and shape of the original auditorium were very much part of the impression it made. The upstairs cinema is now awkwardly wide, providing a dismal view of the screen from the seats at the far sides. The latest alterations are fully reversible: two further statues in niches on each side may now be

The Odeon Cheltenham with some Christmas lights in 1988. The new vertical sign leaves Newbury Trent's ladies twirling their strips of film out of any context (compare with 1933 photograph as the Gaumont Palace on page 60).

The Edinburgh Odeon (ex New Victoria) is seen here after the 1960 modernisation with its new starry ceiling. In recent years, a new screen within a reproduction of the far proscenium arch has been erected in front of the circle. The old auditorium remains partly on view, from the rear three statues on the side walls backwards, including the rear part of the sky ceiling.

hidden from view but they remain in place, dusty but undamaged. As the building was designed for stage use, the happiest scenario would be that at some future date Odeon could move to a purpose-built multiplex and the building be fully restored for use as a theatre or performing arts centre with occasional special film presentations.

At Salisbury, the "listed" former Gaumont Palace almost fell victim to a redevelopment scheme in 1986 which would have demolished the auditorium for commercial redevelopment while preserving the old Halle of John Halle. By this time, the auditorium had been subdivided into a main cinema seating 471 in the former circle, using the old screen, plus two small cinemas each seating 120 underneath the balcony.

Public uproar made the developers include two very small cinemas in their plans. Conservation groups, wanting to keep the listed building as it was, forced a public inquiry, by which time the proposed new cinemas had been enlarged to provide a still modest total of 500 seats. In his Proof of Evidence, Tony O'Ferrall, then managing director of the Odeon chain, declared: "...the general pattern of declining audiences has led Rank Theatres to believe that there is no future for the Odeon Salisbury in its present form. Financial results from the Odeon have never been satisfactory and in the past ten years profitability has been minimal... Estimates provided by Rank Theatres Technical Services Department indicate that the cost of refurbishment of the interior of the cinema auditorium alone currently stands at £300,000 ... a further £210,000 would be required to put the fabric of the building into good and substantial repair. These are not costs that I could recommend to the Board of Rank Theatres in the light of the past and projected trading performance of the cinema. The building cannot be left in its present state for much longer without major work being undertaken. Refurbishment alone cannot be justified in financial terms and even if the building were refurbished I doubt its viability in view of its high operating costs, brought about by the very nature of the building. If the proposed redevelopment does not proceed, therefore, we shall eventually in all likelihood have to close the cinema."

Accompanying figures showed that annual attendances (November to October) had remained fairly steady between 1964/65 and 1970/71 averaging around 250,000, then declined badly to 152,793 in 1980/81, dropped even further to 106,900 in 1981/82, recovered to 130,907 in 1982/83, and dropped again to only 84,806 in 1983/84 before recovering (apparently almost entirely thanks to *Ghostbusters*) to 122,763 in 1984/85.

The Inspector refused consent for the listed building to be demolished. The Odeon stayed open. Repairs were carried out to the roof. Rank have since converted the disused but still intact area of the former café into a fourth cinema and the empty front stalls area into a fifth screen, gaining listed building consent in exchange for refurbishing many of the surviving features. A new screen has been mounted above a false floor extending over the stalls area

There a couple of former Gaumonts that are now listed buildings in the hands of independent operators. The Gaumont Barnstaple was split for films and bingo, but evidently still retains enough of interest to be considered worthy of protection. The Gaumont Notting Hill Gate survived a threat to turn it into a McDonalds fast food outlet thanks to spot listing and continues as the Coronet, using its original name from when it opened as a legitimate theatre.

Live theatres

Other Gaumonts that were designed essentially as theatres have been restored to live use. These include the Dominion Tottenham Court Road and the Empire/Gaumont Southampton. Live use has also saved some of the cinemas.

As an Odeon, the Hammersmith cinema had slowly moved over to operating solely as a concert venue, retaining the Odeon name and becoming a listed building. It was then acquired by Apollo Leisure and renamed the Apollo. Since then it has become Labatt's Apollo, reflecting a sponsorship tie-in, and been well looked after, especially where its art deco features are concerned. Substantial redecoration of the auditorium took place in August 1995.

The London New Victoria is now also part of the Apollo group, and has gained a new lease of life as the home of the stage musical *Starlight Express*. While still a cinema, some alterations had taken place. On the frontage, the pierced stone grilles had been removed along with the lower stretches of canopy. A short, wide lightbox carrying the title of the current film attraction was mounted on the canopy, replacing the much larger display of lettering that had been placed higher up in the specially provided frame. The auditorium had been repainted in inappropriate red and beige hues and the faded design on the safety curtain painted out.

The Odeon (ex Gaumont Palace Salisbury), showing work in progress in Spring 1995 installing a new screen in front of the circle, and the opening of the cinema established in the previously disused front stalls underneath. (Courtesy of Graham Dilks/Odeon Salisbury.)

When, in 1984 as a listed building, permission was granted to conceal much of the original auditorium behind the ramps, supporting steelwork and other paraphernalia associated with *Starlight Express*, no one thought it would have such a long run. While the musical has given the building a new lease of life and hopefully established it as a theatre for many future shows, it is deeply regrettable that the auditorium cannot be properly appreciated while this particular show is in residence, not only because so much is hidden from view but because other fittings — like the two glass fountains on the side walls — have been removed for safe keeping. Apollo have done some work to improve the Wilton Road frontage of the building, reinstating the underside of the surviving canopy and the two black columns above it, while an Apollo Victoria sign has acceptably replaced the New Victoria one in the same style of blue neon outline lettering. However, even here more needs to be done: the blank space between the columns needs to be used for its original advertising purpose, and the Vauxhall Bridge Road frontage remains very drab and neglected.

A full refurbishment of the auditorium has been promised once *Starlight Express* finally comes to a halt. Considering the long period that this magnificent interior — in what is certainly the most innovative and very arguably the single most important piece of cinema design in this country — has been relegated from view, nothing less than complete reinstatement in the original colours will be acceptable, while it would be a nice gesture if the long missing set of stalactite light fittings around the edge of the ceiling could be replicated.

In Ipswich, Rank had tripled its Odeon in 1975 and still retained the Gaumont with a large, single auditorium that was frequently used for live shows as the largest such venue (or stage) in East Anglia. Unfortunately, various changes had occurred over the years to the former Regent. By 1965, the large paintings by Frank Baines on the side walls of the auditorium had all been removed or covered over, leaving blank spaces illuminated from the back edge. Subsequently, the grillework on the splay walls was hidden or taken out and the suspended art deco light fittings replaced by cheap-looking round fixtures directly attached to the ceiling. In the lounge, the original pattern of Gaumont/PCT carpet, which was there in 1965, has long gone; the row of modern cylindrical light fittings has given way to a smaller number of old-fashioned chandelier-type ones; and the moulded ceiling has been replaced or covered over by plain

surfaces. The entrance hall was totally modernised with a new false ceiling.

In 1980, Rank wanted to go over to bingo but it became clear from the reaction of the local authorities and the public to the loss of live shows that this wouldn't be allowed. Instead, Rank gained permission for bingo at the Odeon which was detripled, and decided to build up live shows at the Gaumont, mixed with major film attractions. The seating was even increased to 1,813 to make live shows more profitable, while the former ballroom was converted into a small cinema. In 1987, after Rank renamed the building the Odeon, the company declared its intention to scrap live shows and convert the main auditorium into five smaller cinemas. The town was again in an uproar over the threatened loss of the live venue and the local authority, prompted by a 22,000 signature petition, made a deal with Rank by which it took over the existing building in exchange for paying £3.7 million for the construction of the outside shell of a new five-screen cinema on an adjacent site which had been in use as a car park. Rank met the cost of fitting out the new cinema complex (nicely designed in a modern version of streamlined art deco) and retained the old cinema until its successor was completed.

The new cinema opened as the Odeon in 1991 and the old building re-opened after a few months of refurbishment for live shows, reverting to its original name of the Regent. Details of any reinstatement of old features are not to hand. It is pleasant to find the PCT name surviving in such circumstances, and one hopes that the former Regent Hanley will also regain its original name when it reopens as a live theatre (see below).

Besides concert and theatre use, some old cinemas have been converted to nightclubs and discos, usually burying the original decor. No information is available on the current state of the former Gaumont Chippenham as a nightclub. Considerable disquiet exists over the state of the former Grosvenor/Odeon/Gaumont at Rayners Lane, West London, where listing has failed to keep its unique auditorium ceiling with elaborate cove lighting in use while it functions as a club.

In limbo

In Hanley, the former Regent/Gaumont, by then Odeon, was replaced during 1989 by a new eight-screen Odeon multiplex in a leisure park at Stoke-on-Trent. The old cinema closed a few days before the new one opened. It was little altered from the time it opened in 1929 apart from a drop wall conversion to create two mini-cinemas beneath the balcony. This did not affect the main auditorium as viewed from the balcony, with its 1929 decorative scheme intact and concealed lighting still in use in the central ceiling dome and around the proscenium arch. It had been extensively and sensitively redecorated only two years earlier with new seating, carpeting, curtains and drapes. The front stalls had retained seating for use by overflow audiences or the elderly unwilling to climb the stairs. Some of the doors were original with elaborate etched glass designs. Outside, the building still retained its cartouches on the stage end wall, carrying the letters PCT as a reminder of its origins, as well as its original name of The Regent for all to see. After the building was put up for sale, an application for listing resulted in its being given Grade II status a few weeks later, the Schedule stating that it was "included as a late 1920s cinema of unusual richness and completeness and as one of only two surviving cinemas belonging to the historically important Provincial Cinematograph Theatres circuit, who pioneered the 'super cinema' along American lines in Britain". Listing has raised hopes that the building could become an arts, conference and exhibition centre for North Staffordshire. The Regent Theatre Trust was established, hoping to acquire the building, but it has remained out of use for several years, although its listing was upgraded to II* in late 1992/early 1993.

Bingo clubs

It is customary to applaud the bingo industry for the way it has given new life to expired cinemas. And certainly it is hard to see how many important cinemas could have survived to the present day without the arrival of bingo clubs. Yet many buildings have now operated longer as bingo halls than as cinemas and have inevitably been altered over the years to make them more suitable for their new use. The introduction of more powerful, direct lighting has ruined the subtle schemes of many cinema designers. The levelling off of the stalls floor and the replacement of seats with tables inevitably damages the original look of the building, as do new staircases from the front of circle to the ground floor, the opening up of stages and the introduction of false ceilings. Although, for example, the Gaumont Palace Peckham still stands as a Top Rank Club, from the entrance doors inwards it is no longer recognisable as the cinema it once was. In the case of Peckham, this is not a matter of great regret — nor is it surprising, for the leisure industry has never been sentimental about its past. After all, Gaumont did not think twice about demolishing the former theatre on the Peckham site for its new cinema. But at other former Gaumonts — such as Chadwell Heath, Dudley, Exeter, Rose Hill, Smethwick — enough has been retained (or had, when seen by the author over the past decade) — to give an impression of their atmosphere when they were cinemas.

In fact, the main drawback to bingo as an alternative use for cinemas or theatres is that it prevents even their occasional use for their original purpose. The more impressive cinemas are as bingo halls, the more one would like an opportunity to see them returned to film use for an occasional special event.

In many instances, money has been available to refurbish cinemas for new lives as bingo halls that was not there to spend on them as cinemas. Top Rank Clubs in particular has done an impressive job in launching some of its bingo halls. The reinstatement of the Troxy Stepney (complete with the Troxy name on the facade) after more than thirty years of non-public use and drastic alterations was little short of miraculous. As a Top Rank Club, the incisive interior decorative scheme at the Gaumont Palace Taunton is well preserved. At Kilburn, the giant State was ably refurbished to become a Top Rank Club (more recently renamed Mecca).

Best of all, one can still soak up the splendour of a major Gaumont Palace at the Wood Green Top Rank Club in North London. In its latter days as a triple cinema, it was a discouraging place to visit: the balcony needed redecoration, the seating was old, the huge circle lounge was hardly used, there were acres of empty passageways and empty seats. As a bingo club, it has been lavishly restored and brought back to life. Old signs to "Circle" and "Stalls" have been reinstated and backlit in the foyer; the spherical lights on the side walls of the auditorium have been restored; and, under the bright lights of bingo, there is much to delight the eye in the lines and decorative detail. Indeed, one does not have to wait until the lights come up at an interval to see its splendour. And, with the mini-cinemas in the rear stalls removed, one can appreciate the huge dimensions of the auditorium and sense the confidence that accompanied its construction in the Thirties. And, outside, in place of the Odeon sign, the name Gaumont Palace has been restored at the top of the frontage. So it is that the Gaumont name survives on public display after all, in this one place only within the United Kingdom, sole testament to a once vast enterprise.

The Gaumont State Kilburn still blazes the last half of its name in red neon from its tower in 1995 after being renamed a Mecca bingo club at canopy level. Below, an interior view shows levelled stalls floor and new staircase down from balcony. (Courtesy of Top Rank.)

Top Rank have reinstated the Gaumont Palace name at the top of the front elevation at Wood Green. (Photograph by Barry Chandler). Below, the auditorium retains much of its original splendour as a bingo hall (Courtesy of Top Rank.)

THE CIRCUIT RELEASES: 1932–1959

This is a listing of the Gaumont circuit releases in order of appearance. Main features would have played in the West End (and sometimes in key cities, seaside locations, etc.) prior to the general release listed here. Double bills are shown and, from 1937 onwards, B features became fixed enough to be named in brackets, although these were still flexible and would often have varied, especially outside London. My original intention was to start this record at 1937 in parallel with the titles in *ABC The First Name in Entertainment* and from a date when an Odeon circuit release became clear-cut. But an opportunity arose to include several preceding years for which the following credit is due:

1932-36 circuit releases researched by John Billington

1932
The Ghost Train
Bad Girl
Dirigible *or* The Secret Six
Carnival
Bought *or* Dishonoured
The Calendar
Splinters in the Navy
Merely Mary Ann
Hindle Wakes *or* City Streets
Blonde Reporter
Michael and Mary
Mischief
Bad Company
The Yellow Passport + The Cisco Kid
Congress Dances
Sunshine Susie
The Blue Danube *or* A House Divided
Murder at Covent Garden
Surrender *or* Top of the Bill
Around the World in 80 Minutes

Frankenstein
Condemned to Death
Charlie Chan's Chance
Forbidden
Business and Pleasure
The Silent Witness
Hotel Confidential *or* The Lost Lady
In a Monastery Garden
Determination
Panama Flo
Delicious
She Wanted a Millionaire
The Frightened Lady
The Lost Squadron
A Night Like This
Hell Divers
Goodnight Vienna
The Faithful Heart
Arrowsmith
Melody of Life
The Mayor's Nest
Jack's the Boy
Congorilla
Thark
What Price Hollywood?
Bring 'Em Back Alive +/*or* As You Desire Me
Love on Wheels
Leap Year
The Love Contract
The Lodger *or* Impossible Lover
Tom Brown of Culver
The First Year

1933
The Flag Lieutenant
One Hour With You *or* Tell Me Tonight
There Goes the Bride
Bird of Paradise
The Old Dark House
Rome Express
Happy Ever After

The Midshipmaid
Baroud
Way of Life *or* Payment Deferred *or* Movie Crazy
Tess of the Storm Country
The Sporting Widow +/*or* After the Ball
Sherlock Holmes +/*or* Blonde Venus
Yes, Mr. Brown
Air Mail + Call Her Savage
It's a King
Handle With Care *or* Soldiers of the King *or* Love Me Tonight
Trouble in Paradise +/*or* Beneath the Sea
The Mummy
What — No Beer? + The Match King *or* Night After Night
Hot Pepper
The Conquerors
Dangerously Yours
Her Reputation + He Learned About Women
The Man from Toronto
Undercover Man
Humanity *or* Madame Butterfly
The Penguin Pool Mystery
Employee's Entrance *or* Ironmaster *or* Billion Dollar Scandal
Grand Slam *or* Tonight Is Ours *or* Air Hostess
Pleasure Cruise
State Fair
King of the Ritz
When Strangers Marry *or* Crime of the Century
Pilgrimage
Waltz Time
Zoo in Budapest
Falling for You
The Good Companions
F.P.1
Cavalcade

The Ghoul
Adorable
Sleeping Car
Just Smith
Britannia of Billingsgate *or* The Working
    Man
I Was a Spy
Prince of Arcadia
The Only Girl *or* Jennie Gerhardt
Channel Crossing
My Lips Betray
A Cuckoo in the Nest

1934
Paddy The Next Best Thing
Orders Is Orders
It's a Boy
Another Language
I Lived With You
Friday the 13th
Dinner at Eight
Power and Glory
The Wandering Jew
Aunt Sally
The Bowery
My Weakness
The Constant Nymph
Jack Ahoy
Turkey Time
I'm No Angel
Broadway Thru' a Keyhole
Waltzes from Vienna
The Invisible Man
Little Women
Only Yesterday
Gallant Lady +/*or* Going Hollywood
Sealed Lips
The Women in His Life
Right to Romance
Bottoms Up
Wild Boy
Blood Money
I Believed in You
All Men Are Enemies
Man of Aran
This Side of Heaven +/*or* Search for Beauty
    +/*or* Two Hearts in Waltz Time
George White's Scandals
Princess Charming
The Battle
Queen Christina
Evergreen
Lady of the Boulevards

Meet JACK HULBERT

of the cheery grin and the breezy demeanour in his latest laughter vehicle

BULLDOG JACK

with

FAY WRAY
CLAUDE HULBERT
(By courtesy of Warner Bros. First National Productions, Ltd.)

RALPH RICHARDSON

A
GAUMONT-BRITISH
PICTURE

Directed by
WALTER FORDE
Cert. "U"

At these Cinemas September 16th week

ACTON	Globe	HARROW ROAD	Prince of Wales	REGENT STREET	Polytechnic
BURNT OAK	Regent	HIGHBURY	Imperial	RICHMOND	Royalty
CAMDEN TOWN	Hippodrome	HOLLOWAY	Marlborough	ROMFORD	Plaza (from Sept. 19th)
CANNING TOWN	Grand	HORNCHURCH	Tower	SHEPHERD'S BUSH	Pavilion
CHADWELL HEATH	Embassy	HOUNSLOW	Dominion	SOUTHALL	Palace
CHELSEA	Gaumont Palace	HOXTON	Britannia	ST. ALBANS	Capitol
CLAPTON	Rink	HOXTON	Variety (from Sept. 19th)	STAMFORD HILL	Regent
CRICKLEWOOD	Queen's	ILFORD	Super	STRATFORD	Broadway
CROUCH END	Hippodrome	ISLINGTON	Angel	SURBITON	Coronation
DALSTON	Picture House	KENSAL RISE	Pavilion	TOTTENHAM	Palace
EALING	Broadway Palladium	KENTISH TOWN	Palace	TWICKENHAM	Luxor
EAST HAM	Premier Super	KILBURN	Grange	UXBRIDGE	Savoy
EDGWARE ROAD	Grand	KING'S CROSS	Cinema	WALHAM GREEN	Red Hall
EDMONTON	Empire	KINGSTON	Regal	WALTHAMSTOW	Granada
ENFIELD	Rialto	KINGSWAY	Stoll	WATFORD	Plaza
FINCHLEY	Grand	LEYTON	Savoy	WEST KENSINGTON	Super
FINSBURY PARK	Rink	LEYTONSTONE	Rialto	WHITECHAPEL	Rivoli
FOREST GATE	Queen's	LOUGHTON	Cinema	WILLESDEN	Empire
GLOUCESTER	Hippodrome	MAIDENHEAD	Rialto	WINDSOR	Playhouse
HACKNEY	Pavilion	NOTTING HILL	Coronet	WOOD GREEN	Gaumont Palace
HAMMERSMITH	Gaumont Palace	PALMER'S GREEN	Palmadium		

Gaumont chief Isidore Ostrer also controlled the national newspaper The Sunday Referee, *so it is not surprising to find half-page advertisements for Gaumont British films, as here in successive weeks in September 1935. Areas listed are primarily North London then South London, and include non-Gaumont cinemas showing the film.*

At these Cinemas September 23rd week

BALHAM	Palladium	ISLINGTON	Annexe	RHYL	Plaza
BENWELL	Adelaide (from Sept. 26)	KENNINGTON	Princes	ROTHERHITHE	Lion
BENWELL	Majestic	KENTON	Odeon	RUSHEY GREEN	Queen's
BEXHILL	Playhouse	LAVENDER HILL	Pavilion	SOUTH HARROW	Odeon
BISHOP AUCKLAND	Hippodrome	LEEDS	Tower	STOCKTON	Regal
BISHOP'S STORTFORD	Regent	LEWISHAM	Gaumont Palace	STREATHAM	Gaumont Palace
BRENTWOOD	Palace	MANCHESTER	Piccadilly	SUTTON	Surrey County
BRIXTON	Astoria	MATLOCK	Cinema (from Sept. 26th)	SYDENHAM	Rink
BROMLEY	Grand	NEWCASTLE	Brighton Electric	TOOTING	Granada
CATERHAM	Capitol	NEW CROSS	Kinema	UPPER NORWOOD	Rialto
CLAPHAM	Majestic	OLD KENT ROAD	Picture House	WANDSWORTH	Palace
CROYDON	Davis	PECKHAM	Gaumont Palace	WEALDSTONE	Odeon
DARTFORD	Scala	PECKHAM	Annexe	WELLINGBOROUGH	Palace
DUBLIN	Carlton	PENGE	King's Hall	WESTMINSTER BRIDGE ROAD	Canterbury (from Sept. 26)
EASINGTON	Rialto (from Sept. 26)	PLUMSTEAD	Kinema	WEST WICKHAM	Plaza
EAST GRINSTEAD	White Hall (from Sept. 26)	PLYMOUTH	Gaumont Palace	WIMBLEDON	Elite
FULWELL	Marina	PUTNEY	Palace	WOOLWICH	Hippodrome

Cup of Kindness *or* Viva Villa
It Happened One Night
Chu Chin Chow
When New York Sleeps + Mala the
    Magnificent
House of Rothschild
My Song for You + Sadie McKee
Little Friend + Such Women Are Dangerous
My Old Dutch + The Thin Man
The Unfinished Symphony
Evensong
Stamboul Quest *or* Baby Take a Bow
Forbidden Territory *or* Paris Interlude
She Learned About Sailors
Treasure Island
The Camels Are Coming

1935
Jew Suss
One Night of Love
Belle of the Nineties + Bella Donna
The Cat's-Paw + Man with the Electric Voice
The Man Who Knew Too Much + Mrs.
    Wiggs of the Cabbage Patch
The World Moves On + Her Sacrifice
Dirty Work + Ladies Should Listen
The Count of Monte Cristo
A Lady in Danger + College Rhythm
We Live Again + Peck's Bad Boy
The Iron Duke
Caravan
My Heart Is Calling
The Gay Divorce
The White Parade
Things Are Looking Up
Strictly Confidential
Oh, Daddy + Marie Galante
Great Expectations
The King of Paris
Wednesday's Child *or* Vanessa
The Captain Hates the Sea
Imitation of Life
Dangerous Corner
Wings in the Dark *or various*
Anne of Green Gables + Fugitive Lady
Mystery Woman
Romance in Manhattan
Ruggles of Red Gap
Grand Old Girl + Murder on a Honeymoon
The Phantom Light + Uniform Lovers
The Little Minister
Mississippi *or* Carnival Nights
The Silver Streak

Music in the Air
Love Affair of the Dictator
Clive of India
Bulldog Jack
Roberta + *(selected)* The Scarlet Pimpernel
Bride of Frankenstein
Les Miserables
Me and Marlborough
Kid Millions + The Case of Gabriel Perry
Becky Sharp
Cardinal Richelieu
For Ever England (*shown in West End as*
    Brown on Resolution)
The 39 Steps + Call of the Wild
The Clairvoyant
Dante's Inferno + False Faces
Boys Will Be Boys
Car of Dreams + R.A.F.
Ginger
Our Little Girl + Charlie Chan in Egypt

1936
Stormy Weather + Murder by Television
On Wings of Song
Where's George? + She
The Passing of the Third Floor Back
First a Girl + Peg of Old Drury
Barbary Coast
Foreign Affaires + While Parents Sleep
Curly Top
The Guvnor + Dark Angel
The Ghost Goes West
The Tunnel
No Limit
King of the Damned
Thanks a Million + Storm Over the Andes
Jack of All Trades
Charlie Chan in Shanghai + Metropolitan
The Man Who Broke the Bank at Monte
    Carlo
Captain Blood
Pot Luck
Remember Last Night? *or* Anything Goes
Public Nuisance No. 1
Woman Trap + Improper Duchess *or*
    Improper Duchess + Java Seas
The Melody Lingers On
Klondike Annie *or* Forced Landing
Miss Pacific Fleet + Paddy O'Day
Next Time We Live
The Music Goes Round
It Had to Happen
Wolf's Clothing + Dangerous Waters

Soft Lights and Sweet Music
The Littlest Rebel
Where There's a Will
Love Before Breakfast
Tudor Rose
The Prisoner of Shark Island
Rhodes of Africa + Limelight
When Knights Were Bold + The Petrified
    Forest
Mutiny on the Bounty
Secret Agent
The Country Doctor
It's Love Again + The Story of Louis
    Pasteur
Modern Times (+ Boulder Dam)
Ceiling Zero + East Meets West
Under Two Flags
The Man Who Changed His Mind + I
    Married a Doctor
Secret Interlude + Sutter's Gold
Everything Is Thunder (+ Murder by an
    Aristocrat)
Seven Sinners + Little Miss Nobody
Everybody Dance + Murder in the Big House
Sins of Man + The Marriage of Corbal
All In + Hot Money
Poor Little Rich Girl

1937
Windbag the Sailor (+ Case of the Velvet
    Claws)
Anthony Adverse (+ Ticket to Paradise)
White Angel (+ Strangers on Honeymoon)
Show Boat (+ Crime of Dr. Forbes)
Three Maxims + The Golden Arrow
Sabotage (+ Modern Madness)
Dodsworth (+ Thank You Jeeves)
His Lordship + Sing, Baby, Sing
Ramona (+ G-Man's Wife)
O.H.M.S. (+ Bengal Tiger *or various*)
Keep Your Seats Please + Harmony Parade
Sweet Aloes (+ Wives Never Know)
Head Over Heels + The Man in the Mirror
Good Morning, Boys (+ Lady Be Careful)
Libelled Lady + China Clipper
The General Died at Dawn (+ 15, Maiden
    Lane)
The Great Barrier + Stage Struck
Come and Get It (+ King of the Ice Rink)
Champagne Waltz (+ The King's People)
Cain and Mabel (+ One for All)
Three Smart Girls + The Big Broadcast of
    1937

Go West, Young Man (+ Fugitive in the Sky)
Love from a Stranger (+ Hideaway Girl)
Three Men on a Horse (+ Lady Reporter)
Pluck of the Irish (+ Cafe Colette)
The Plainsman (+ Melody for Two)
Crack Up (+ The Luckiest Girl in the World)
Splinters in the Air (+ Mind Your Own Business)
Feather Your Nest (+ Black Legion)
Jungle Princess (+ Once a Doctor)
Stowaway (+ Off to the Races)
Calling All Stars + John Meade's Woman
Wings of the Morning (+ Smart Blonde)
O-Kay for Sound (+ A Doctor's Diary)
Stolen Holiday + For Valour
Take My Tip (+ Midnight Court)
Lloyds of London (+ Woman in Distress)
King Solomon's Mines (+ Midnight Taxi)
The Prince and the Pauper (+ The Gap)
For You Alone (+ Her Husband's Secretary)
Seventh Heaven (+ Step Lively, Jeeves)
Lost Horizon (+ Speed to Spare)
The Frog + The Show Goes On
His Affair (+ The Perfect Crime)
Farewell Again (also Odeon circuit main feature release) (+ Night Key)
Wake Up and Live + Call It a Day
The Road Back (+ The Devil Is Driving)
As Good As Married (+ Think Fast, Mr. Moto)
Love Is News (+ That I May Live)
Hotel Haywire (+ Criminals of the Air)
Said O'Reilly to McNab + Slim
Wee Willie Winkie (+ Big Business)

1938
Oh, Mr Porter! (+ Let's Get Married)
Knight Without Armour (also Odeon circuit main feature release) (+ The Go Getter)
A Star Is Born (+ California Straight Ahead)
High, Wide and Handsome (+ Born Reckless)
Gangway (+ Love Under Fire)
Lovely to Look At (+ Blonde Trouble)
Doctor Syn (+ The Squeaker)
The Firefly (+ A Man Betrayed)
It's Love I'm After (+ Sing and Be Happy or Keep Fit)
Ali Baba Goes to Town + The Singing Marine
One Hundred Men and a Girl (+ The Man Who Cried Wolf)

Non-Stop New York + Charlie Chan on Broadway
Confession (+ School for Husbands)
Dead End (+ Dinner at the Ritz)
Smash and Grab + Stand-In (Odeon circuit main feature release) or (+ Don't Pull Your Punches)
The Return of the Scarlet Pimpernel (also Odeon circuit main feature release) (+ On Such a Night)
Paradise for Two (also Odeon circuit main feature release) + Second Honeymoon; or Second Honeymoon (+ The Invisible Menace)
Young and Innocent (+ Submarine D.1)
45 Fathers + A Girl with Ideas
Charlie Chan at Monte Carlo + Partners in Crime
Alcatraz Island + Prescription for Romance
Wells Fargo (+ Easy Money)
Bank Holiday (+ Thank You, Mr. Moto)
Wise Girl (+ Who Killed John Savage?)
Tarzan's Revenge (+ City Girl)
You're a Sweetheart (+ The Informer)
Sweet Devil (+ Change of Heart)
I See Ice (+ He Couldn't Say No)
Second Best Bet + The Black Doll
She's Got Everything (+ Crashing Hollywood)
Rebecca of Sunnybrook Farm (+ Love on a Budget)
Owd Bob + Radio City Revels
Bringing Up Baby (+ Everybody's Doing It)
International Settlement + South Riding (Odeon circuit main feature release) or (+ Under Suspicion or Swing It, Sailor or other)
Sailing Along (+ The Daredevil Drivers)
The Hurricane (Odeon circuit main feature release) + Sally, Irene and Mary; or Sally, Irene and Mary (+ Here's Flash Casey)
Tovarich (+ Double Danger)
Snow White and the Seven Dwarfs (+ Rhythm on the Ranch)
Convict 99 (+ Start Cheering)
In Old Chicago (+ Maid's Night Out)
Nothing Sacred (also Odeon circuit main feature release) + Who Goes Next
Alf's Button Afloat (+ Island in the Sky)
The Drum (Odeon circuit main feature release); or Yellowjack (+ Follow Your Star)
We're Going to Be Rich (+ One Wild Night)
Goldwyn Follies (Odeon circuit main feature release) (+ Tip-Off Girls)

Dr. Rhythm + Strange Boarders
The Adventures of Marco Polo (also Odeon circuit main feature release) (+ Hunted Men)
Kidnapped + Blockade (Odeon circuit main feature release) or (+ Mr. Moto's Gamble)
Crime School (+ Red Lights Ahead)
Josette (+ No Parking)
Three Men and a Girl (+ Hollywood Stadium Mystery)
Hey Hey USA + Fools for Scandal

1939
The Lady Vanishes (+ The Affairs of Anabel)
The Adventures of Tom Sawyer (Odeon circuit main feature release) (+ My Bill or Gangs of New York); or My Bill + Gangs of New York
The Amazing Dr. Clitterhouse (+ The Cheat)
The Rage of Paris + Algiers (Odeon circuit main feature release)
That Certain Age (+ The Devil's Party)
Marie Antoinette (also Odeon circuit main feature release)
Carefree (+ Wives Under Suspicion)
My Lucky Star (+ Penny Paradise)
It's in the Air (+ Breaking the Ice)
Suez (+ Road Demon)
You Can't Take It With You (+ Little Adventuress)
Old Bones of the River (+ While New York Sleeps)
The Young in Heart (also Odeon circuit main feature release) (+ The Return of Carol Deane or various)
The Gladiator + Crackerjack (latter soon replaced by Valley of the Giants or by Stolen Life [Odeon circuit main feature release])
Just Around the Corner (+ Down on the Farm)
Kentucky (+ The Gaunt Stranger)
The Cowboy and the Lady (also Odeon circuit main feature release)(+ Pardon Our Nerve)
So This Is London + Hold That Girl
Climbing High (+ Stranded in Paris) or + The Ware Care (Odeon circuit main feature release)
Son of Frankenstein (+ Exposed)
Trade Winds (+ Lightning Conductor)
Cafe Society + The Duke of West Point (Odeon circuit main feature release)

Topper Takes a Trip (*also Odeon circuit main feature release*) + Storm Over Bengal

Thanks for Everything (+ Mr. Moto's Last Warning *or various*)

The Sisters (+ Nancy Drew — Detective *or* Convict's Code)

The Great Man Votes (+ Homicide Bureau)

Ambush + Let's Be Famous

The 39 Steps *revival* (+ Blackwell's Island)

Tail Spin (+ Tarnished Angel)

Trouble Brewing (*also Odeon circuit main feature release*) (+ Gambling Ship)

Off the Record + I Was a Spy (*revival*)

The Little Princess (+ Everybody's Baby)

Inspector Hornleigh + Miss Fix-It

Jesse James (+ The Rudd Family Goes to Town)

Ask a Policeman (+ Exile Express + Ferdinand the Bull + The March of Time 4: March of the Movies)

The Four Feathers (*also Odeon circuit main feature release*)(+ The Family Next Door)

The Hound of the Baskervilles + Man's Heritage

Gunga Din (+ Winner Take All)

A Girl Must Live + Mr. Moto on Danger Island

The Story of Vernon and Irene Castle (+ Swift Vengeance)

The Modern Miracle (+ The Jones Family in Hollywood + Donald's Cousin Gus)

Shipyard Sally (+ Double Daring)

Good-Bye Mr. Chips! (*also main feature at many Odeons*)

Wuthering Heights (*also main feature at many Odeons*) (+ Flying Fifty Five)

Rose of Washington Square + The Four Just Men

Union Pacific (+ The Lion Has Wings [*also Odeon circuit second feature release*])

Five Came Back + That Girl from College

The Sun Never Sets (+ Man About Town *or* Code of the Streets *or* What Would You Do, Chums?)

The Saint in London + Maisie; *or* The Saint in London + Career; *or* Maisie + Career

Stanley and Livingstone (+ Mr. Moto Takes a Vacation)

1940

The Frozen Limits (+ The Silent Battle)

Where's That Fire? (+ The Spellbinder)

When Tomorrow Comes (+ The Missing People)

Bachelor Mother (+ The Man Who Knew Too Much *revival*)

Susannah of the Mounties (+ News Is Made at Night)

In Name Only (+ All at Sea)

The Rains Came (+ Stop, Look and Love)

The Arsenal Stadium Mystery + Wife, Husband and Friend

Babes in Arms (+ The Day the Bookies Wept)

First Love (+ Tropic Fury)

Hotel for Women + Charlie Chan at Treasure Island

Fifth Avenue Girl (+ The Escape)

Band Waggon (+ Mr. Wong in Chinatown)

Escape to Happiness (+ Full Confession)

The Proud Valley (+ Everything's On Ice)

Daytime Wife + The Spider

The Hunchback of Notre Dame

I Stole a Million + Sons of the Sea

For Freedom (+ Hawaiian Nights)

Drums Along the Mohawk (+ The Honeymoon's Over)

Spirit of the People + 20,000 Men a Year

On the Night of the Fire (+ Mutiny on the Blackhawk)

A Chump at Oxford + That's Right, You're Wrong

They Came by Night + Charlie Chan in the City of Darkness

A Window in London (+ The Forgotten Woman)

Swiss Family Robinson + We're in the Army Now

Barricade + Married and In Love

Vigil in the Night + Law and Disorder

Remember the Night (+ Mexican Spitfire)

Untamed (+ The Marines Fly High)

Top Hat *revival or* The First Rebel (+ Two Thoroughbreds) (*Odeon main feature release* Typhoon *substituted at many cinemas*)

Swanee River (+ City of Chance)

The Primrose Path (+ Glamour Boy)

Let George Do It (+ Fighting Mad)

Bill of Divorcement + Tilly of Bloomsbury

Charley's Aunt (+ The Saint's Double Trouble)

Irene (+ In the Nick of Time *or* Three Silent Men)

Rebecca (+ The Courageous Dr. Christian)

Pinocchio (+ Little Orvie)

Gangs of Chicago (+ Curtain Call)

My Favourite Wife (+ The Marshal of Mesa City)

Turnabout + Gentleman of Venture

South of Pago Pago (+ You Can't Fool Your Wife)

Tom Brown's Schooldays (+ Crashin' Thru)

Saloon Bar + Saps at Sea

Convoy + Anne of Windy Willows

Foreign Correspondent (+ The Saint Takes Over)

Dance, Girl, Dance (+ Wildcat Bus)

The Boys from Syracuse (+ You're Not So Tough)

Our Town (+ Millionaires in Prison)

Sailors Three (+ The Villain Still Pursued Her)

When the Daltons Rode (+ Little Accident)

Lucky Partners (+ Pop Always Pays)

1941

Neutral Port (+ Cross Country Romance)

Kit Carson (+ Dr. Christian Meets the Women)

The Return of Frank James (+ Come Up Smiling)

Brigham Young

Gasbags (+ Dreaming Out Loud)

The Girl in the News (+ One Crowded Night)

Public Debutante No. 1 (+ Pier 13)

The Great Dictator (*also Odeon circuit main feature release*)

Old Bill and Son (+ Meet the Wildcat)

The Thief of Bagdad (*also Odeon circuit main feature release*) (+ Danger Ahead)

The Long Voyage Home (+ Dad Rudd, M.P.)

Spring Parade (+ Honeymoon Deferred)

No, No, Nanette (+ Before I Hang)

The Son of Monte Cristo (+ Girl from Havana)

Spare a Copper (+ Yukon Flight)

Diamond Frontier (+ Sandy Is a Lady)

Mr. and Mrs. Smith (+ Charter Pilot)

The Ghost Train (+ Let's Make Music)

So Ends Our Night (+ Remedy for Riches)

Inspector Hornleigh Goes To It (+ The Gay Caballero)

The Saint's Vacation (+ You'll Find Out)

The Philadelphia Story

Kitty Foyle (+ Old Mother Riley's Ghosts)

Captain Caution (+ Playgirls)(*Odeon circuit main feature release* Chad Hanna *at some cinemas*)
Virginia (*also Odeon circuit main feature release*)(+ Meet the Missus) *or* Rebecca *revival* (+ Meet the Missus) *or* Virginia + Rebecca
Kipps
The Navy Steps Out + The Ramparts We Watch
That Uncertain Feeling (+ Sleepers West)
Western Union (+ You're the One)
Topper Returns (+ Magic in Music)
Turned Out Nice Again (+ Doomed Caravan)
I Wanted Wings
The Devil and Miss Jones (+ Target for Tonight)
Andy Hardy's Private Secretary (+ Footlight Fever)
Cottage to Let + Road Show
The Great American Broadcast (+ The Cowboy and the Blonde)
The Golden Hour (+ Dead Men Tell)
Sunny (+ Melody for Three)
The Flame of New Orleans (+ Meet the Chump)
The Reluctant Dragon + A Very Young Lady
Tall, Dark and Handsome (+ Repent at Leisure)
I Thank You (+ Behind the News *or* Murder on the Yukon)
Forty Thousand Horsemen + Model Wife
Parachute Battalion + Father Takes a Wife
The Black Cat (+ Give Us Wings)
International Lady (+ Hurry, Charlie, Hurry)
My Life with Caroline (+ The Night of January 16th)
The Great Awakening (+ Tanks a Million)
The Saint Meets the Tiger (+ They Meet Again)
The Common Touch (+ Lady Scarface)
Tom, Dick and Harry (+ Dressed to Kill)
Hi! Gang (+ Burma Convoy)

1942

It Started with Eve (+ Bombay Clipper)
Ships with Wings (+ Moonlight in Hawaii)
Suspicion (*also Odeon circuit main feature release*)(+ Wild Geese Calling *or* We Go Fast)

Sun Valley Serenade (+ Riders of the Purple Sage)
Citizen Kane (+ Marry the Boss's Daughter)
Sundown (+ Old Mother Riley's Circus)
A Yank in the R.A.F. (+ Broadway Limited)
Appointment for Love (+ Ferry Pilot + Niagara Falls)
The Little Foxes (+ Charlie Chan in Rio)
Ride 'Em Cowboy (+ Flying Cadets)
Hellzapoppin' (+ In the Rear of the Enemy)
The Big Blockade (+ Badlands of Dakota)
Dumbo (+ Obliging Young Lady)
The Corsican Brothers (+ Miss Polly)
The Man Who Came Back (+ A Date with the Falcon)
Hot Spot (+ Small Town Deb)
Back Room Boy (+ Mob Town)
H. M. Pulham Esq. (+ Melody Lane)
The Men in Her Life (+ Sing Another Chorus)
Ball of Fire (+ Hard Steel)
Weekend in Havana (+ The Night Has Eyes)
Next of Kin (+ The Perfect Snob)
The Shanghai Gesture (+ All American Co-Ed)
How Green Was My Valley (+ Hay Foot)
Wake Up and Scream (+ Call Out the Marines)
To Be Or Not To Be (+ Frontline Kids)
Joan of Paris (+ Caravan)
Gentleman After Dark + The Defeat of the Germans Near Moscow
Broadway + This Woman Is Mine
Charley's American Aunt (+ On the Sunny Side)
Jungle Book (+ 'Frisco Lil)
Roxie Hart (+ Right to the Heart)
Uncensored (+ The Man Who Wouldn't Die)
Son of Fury (+ The Night Before the Divorce)
Twin Beds (+ Women in War)
Pardon My Sarong (+ Red Flyer)
To the Shores of Tripoli (+ Suspected Person)
The Young Mr. Pitt (+ Brooklyn Orchid)
Eagle Squadron (+ Strictly in the Groove)
Secret Agent of Japan (+ Sleepytime Gal)
Invisible Agent (+ Born to Sing)
Ten Gentlemen from West Point (+ A Dangerous Game)
This Above All (+ Wild Cat)
Between Us Girls + Adventures of Martin Eden

Moontide (+ Give Out Sisters)
Coastal Command + Jackass Mail
Priorities on Parade + Dangerous Moonlight *revival*
She's My Lovely (+ Eyes of the Underworld)
Went the Day Well? (+ The Postman Didn't Ring)
Queen Victoria (+ Old Bones of the River *revival*)
The War Against Mrs. Hadley (+ The McGuerins from Brooklyn)
King Arthur Was a Gentleman (+ One Thrilling Night)

1943

indicates main film in box-office Top Six of the year

The Big Street (+ The Devil with Hitler)
Sin Town (+ A Date with an Angel)
Women Aren't Angels (+ Highways by Night)
Seven Days' Leave (+ Mexican Spitfire's Elephant)
My Sister Eileen (+ Stand-By All Networks)
Rookies (+ Sherlock Holmes in Washington)
Pride of the Yankees
Nine Men (+ Rubber Racketeers)
You Were Never Lovelier (+ Berlin Correspondent)
Pittsburgh (+ Lucky Legs)
Silver Queen + Desert Victory
I.T.M.A. (+ A Man's World)
Arabian Nights (+ Hi, Buddy)
Eyes in the Night (+ The Daring Young Man)
Katina + Fires Were Started
Andy Hardy's Double Life (+ Flying with Music)
Springtime in the Rockies (+ Operational Height)
Get Cracking (+ Quiet, Please, Murder)
Money for Jam (+ City of Silent Men)
Commandos Strike at Dawn (+ Blackie Goes Hollywood)
A Night to Remember + The Magnificent Ambersons
China Girl + When Johnny Comes Marching Home
The Light of Heart (+ The Lido Mystery)
Miss London Ltd. (+ Time to Kill)
Something to Shout About (+ Troubles Through Billets)

Thunderbirds (+ How About It?)
Desperadoes (+ Laugh Your Blues Away)
Hangmen Also Die (+ No Place for a Lady)
Girl Trouble + The Meanest Man in the World
Hello, Beautiful + Strange Incident
*Hello, 'Frisco, Hello (+ Power of the Press)
The More the Merrier (+ After Midnight)
The Moon Is Down + I'll Walk Beside You
*The Man in Grey (+ Reveille with Beverly)
Crash Dive (+ Redhead from Manhattan)
Clive of India *revival* + They Came To Blow Up America
Bataan (+ One Dangerous Night)
Dear Octopus (+ Murder in Times Square)
Fired Wife + In the Navy *revival*
Hers to Hold (+ Youth Takes a Hand)
Rhythm Serenade (+ Battle of Britain)
Stormy Weather (+ Jitterbugs)
Mister Big + Somewhere in Civvies
Heaven Can Wait (+ Mantrap)
Victory Through Air Power (+ Someone to Remember)
Millions Like Us (+ All By Myself)
Holy Matrimony (+ Henry Gets Glamour)
The Lamp Still Burns (+ Crime Doctor)
Chetniks + Alexander's Ragtime Band *revival*
First Comes Courage (+ Two Senoritas)
Hi, Diddle, Diddle + Alf Button's Afloat *revival*
Wintertime (+ A Gentle Gangster)

1944
indicates main film in box-office Top Twelve of the year

Flesh and Fantasy (+ What's Buzzin' Cousin?)
Bell Bottom George (+ Appointment in Berlin)
Destroyer (+ It's a Great Life)
*Sweet Rosie O'Grady (+ Honeymoon Lodge)
Journey into Fear + The Garden of Allah *revival*
Guadalcanal Diary + The Man Who Broke the Bank at Monte Carlo *revival*
Happy Land (+ Dangerous Blondes)
Texas to Tokyo (+ Never a Dull Moment)
Sahara (+ Is Everybody Happy?)
Crazy House (+ You're a Lucky Fellow, Mr. Smith)

The Lodger (+ Yanks Ahoy)
Bees in Paradise (+ So's Your Uncle)
Tarzan's Desert Mystery (+ Doughboys in Ireland)
Snow White and the Seven Dwarfs *revival* (+ Here Comes Kelly)
Heaven Is Round the Corner (+ Sherlock Holmes Faces Death)
The Mark of Zorro *revival* (+ Dancing Masters)
Jack London (+ Old Mother Riley Overseas)
Ali Baba and the Forty Thieves (+ She's For Me)
The Beautiful Cheat (+ O, My Darling Clementine)
Gung Ho + Swing Fever
Four Jills in a Jeep + The Hound of the Baskervilles *revival*
Buffalo Bill (+ Nobody's Darling)
The Purple Heart (+ Henry's Little Secret)
Fanny by Gaslight (+ Mardi Gras)
Tampico + Demobbed
Pygmalion *revival* + Weird Woman
None Shall Escape + Tropicana
Lady Hamilton *revival* (+ Week-End Pass)
Phantom Lady (+ Moonlight and Cactus)
Various revivals including The Rains Came, The Prisoner of Zenda, Holiday Inn, The Adventures of Tom Sawyer, New Moon *and* The Hard Way
Knickerbocker Holiday + Johnny Apollo *revival*
*This Happy Breed
Up in Mabel's Room + The Man in the Iron Mask *revival*
A Canterbury Tale (+ Caribbean Romance)
Pin-Up Girl (+ Here Comes Elmer)
*Cover Girl
*The Song of Bernadette
Give Us the Moon (+ Hey Rookie)
Once Upon a Time + That Night in Rio *revival*
Mr. Emmanuel (+ Lady in the Death House)
Christmas Holiday (+ Hi! Good Looking)
Sweet and Low-Down (+ Bermuda Mystery)
Song of the Open Road + Eternally Yours *revival*
The Hairy Ape (+ Beautiful But Broke)
2,000 Women + Stella Dallas *revival* (or + The Silver Key)
Address Unknown + The Kid from Spain *revival*
Love Story (+ She Has What It Takes)

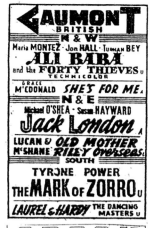

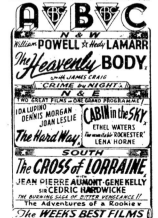

Competing attractions of the three major circuits in London during 1944.

Arms and the Woman (+ Jam Session + Left of the Line)
Abroad with Two Yanks (+ Gambler's Choice)
*Fanny By Gaslight (+ Her Primitive Man)
In Society (+ Kansas City Kitty)
Irish Eyes Are Smiling (+ Sons of the Air)

1945
*indicates main film in box-office Top Twenty-Three of the year

Gipsy Wildcat (+ Allergic to Love)
He Stoops to Conquer (+ Two Man Submarine)
Secret Command (+ Take It or Leave It)
Madonna of the Seven Moons (+ Music in Manhattan)
The Impatient Years (+ Louisiana Hayride)
Summer Storm (+ Pass to Romance)
The Merry Monahans (+ Pearl of Death)
Down Argentine Way revival (+ The Big Noise or Bulldog Drummond Strikes Back revival)
Winged Victory (+ Halfway to Heaven)
Together Again (+ Cry of the Werewolf)
Three's a Family + Dodsworth revival
Kid Millions revival + If I Had My Way revival; or This Happy Breed revival
Bowery to Broadway (+ Secrets of Scotland Yard)
*A Song to Remember
Hangover Square (+ Ever Since Venus)
*Since You Went Away
The Keys of the Kingdom
Belle of the Yukon (+ Marked Man)
See My Lawyer + Tall in the Saddle
Bride by Mistake + Give Me the Stars
*Tonight and Every Night (+ Behind Closed Doors)
For You Alone (+ The Missing Juror)
Moon Over Miami revival + The Fighting Lady
A Tree Grows in Brooklyn (+ Road to Russia + Showboat Serenade)
Sudan + Carolina Blues
Tarzan and the Amazons (+ Leave It to Blondie)
*They Were Sisters (+ Knight and a Blonde)
The Fifth Chair (+ Betrayal from the East)
Thunderhead, Son of Flicka + Dreaming
I Didn't Do It + Flame of the Barbary Coast
I'll Be Your Sweetheart (+ Passport to Suez)

Salome, Where She Danced + The Last Gangster
A Man Called Sullivan + Bluebeard
Frisco Sal + The Woman in Green
Blood on the Sun (+ Blonde Ransom)
Junior Miss (+ Steel + Bombalero)
The Naughty Nineties + Strange Illusion
Waterloo Road revival + Cover Girl revival
The Three Caballeros (+ Boys of the Old Brigade + Guess What No. 5 + Ugly Duckling)
*Nob Hill (+ The Doctor's Courage)
One Against Seven + Strange Affair
Dead of Night (+ The Bullfighters)
Lady on a Train (+ On Stage Everybody)
Ten Little Niggers + Home Sweet Home
Over 21 (+ Crime Inc.)
Don Juan Quilligan + Divorce
Blood and Sand revival (+ Caribbean Mystery)
Guest Wife (+ Enter Arsene Lupin)
Kiss and Tell (+ The Power of the Whistler)
Johnny Angel + Bedside Manner
Love, Honour and Goodbye + Wings of the Morning revival (order reversed after first two weeks)
State Fair (+ Land of the Outlaws)
A Thousand and One Nights (+ Racket Man)

1946
Pink String and Sealing Wax (+ Girl on the Spot)
Fallen Angel (+ Booked on Suspicion)
The Wicked Lady (+ Isle of Tabu + Who's Who in Animal Land)
Those Endearing Young Charms + Here Comes the Sun
Pardon My Past + Going My Way revival
Brief Encounter (+ Pillow Talk)
Come Back to Me (+ Having Wonderful Crime)
Tarzan and the Leopard Man + Swingin' on a Rainbow
They Knew Mr. Knight + Shady Lady
The Dolly Sisters (+ The Peke's Sold a Pup)
She Wouldn't Say Yes + My Name Is Julia Ross
Scarlet Street (+ What a Woman)
Shock + My Gal Sal revival
Pinocchio (+ Dakota or The Man from Oklahoma)
The Spanish Main (+ Bothered by a Beard)

The Bandit of Sherwood Forest (+ Life with Blondie)
Song of Old Wyoming (+ Scotland Yard Investigator) (but ABC release The Harvey Girls at many cinemas)
Whistle Stop + Under New Management
Tangier + The Daltons Ride Again
The Son of Monte Cristo + Brewster's Millions
Gilda (+ Voice of the Whistler)
Caravan
Renegades (+ Blondie's Lucky Day)
Wanted for Murder (+ The Crimson Canary)
A Scandal in Paris (+ The Doctor's Warning or The Real Glory revival or The Westerner revival)
The Dark Corner + Stars and Spars
The Years Between (+ Terror by Night)
From This Day Forward + Madame Pimpernel
Somewhere in the Night (+ Hit the Hay)
Johnny Eager revival + Jane Eyre revival
Spellbound
The Way to the Stars revival + The Seventh Veil revival
Do You Love Me (+ Blackie's Rendezvous)
A Genius in the Family (+ Sherlock Holmes and the Secret Code)
Caesar and Cleopatra (Odeon circuit main feature release); or Abilene Town + Love Story revival
Men of Two Worlds
The Bells of St. Mary's
Concerto (+ Behind Green Lights)
Anna and the King of Siam
Centennial Summer
Theirs Is the Glory
The Stranger + Man of the Hour
A Night in Casablanca (+ The Phantom Thief)
Kentucky + Home Sweet Homicide
The Time of Their Lives + Week End in Havana revival
Canyon Passage + The Runaround
The Citadel revival + Black Beauty
Carnival (+ Man Who Lost Himself)
A Song to Remember revival + Adam Had Four Sons revival
Badman's Territory + Princess and the Pirate revival
Three Little Girls in Blue (+ Send for Paul Temple)

London-area advertising for the Gaumont circuit during 1947.

A Matter of Life and Death

1947
indicates main film in box-office Top Nine of the year

*The Jolson Story (+ Fear)
The Killers (+ Slightly Scandalous)
13 Rue Madeleine (+ Melody Maker)
*Great Expectations
The Kid from Brooklyn (+ Candy's Calendar)
Hungry Hill (+ Genius at Work + This Modern Age No. 5 Thoroughbreds for the World)
The Strange Woman (+ Loyal Heart)
The Outlaw
Boomerang (+ Blondie's Big Moment)
Green for Danger (+ Detour)
Nocturne + Lady Luck
Margie (+ Game of Death + This Modern Age No. 7 Coal Crisis)
White Tie and Tails + A Cage of Nightingales
Song of the South (+ In Old Sacramento)
The Root of All Evil (+ Split Face *or* King Kong *revival or* Beau Geste *revival*)
Dead Reckoning (+ Blondie's Holiday)
The Scarlet Pimpernel *revival* + The High Window
Magnificent Doll + Son of Dracula
Johnny O'Clock + Caught in the Draft *revival*
The Man Within
It's a Wonderful Life
Young Widow + School for Danger
Hue and Cry (+ That Brennan Girl)
I'll Be Yours + The Michigan Kid
The Locket + Rendezvous 24
The Ghost and Mrs. Muir (+ Headline)
The Brothers (+ Down Cuba Way + This Modern Age No. 9 Development Areas)
The Loves of Joanna Godden (+ Cigarette Girl)
Carnival in Costa Rica (+ Blackie and the Law)
Tarzan and the Huntress (+ Born to Speed)
The Upturned Glass (+ The Falcon's Alibi)
Lost Honeymoon + Swell Guy
The Egg and I (+ The Cat Creeps)
Bob, Son of Battle (+ It Happened Tomorrow *revival*)
Down to Earth (+ The Thirteenth Hour)

Two Men and a Girl + The Guilt of Janet Ames
*Holiday Camp (+ The Lone Wolf in Mexico)
The Web (+ The Vigilantes Return)
The Birth of a Baby (*shown under local certificates*)
The October Man (+ Keeper of the Bees)
Copacabana + Secret Mission *revival*
The Long Night + They Got Me Covered *revival*
Captain Boycott
Piccadilly Incident *revival* + Wake Up and Dream
Uncle Silas (+ The Little Ballerina)
The White Unicorn
The Big Heart + High Conquest
The End of the River (+ San Quentin + This Modern Age No. 13 Will Britain Starve?)
Dishonoured Lady + Her First Romance *revival*
Trail Street + Frieda *revival*
Slave Girl + Hellzapoppin *revival*
The Macomber Affair (+ Little Iodine)

1948
indicates main film in box-office Top Ten of the year

Christmas Eve (+ Mystery of the Wentworth Castle *revival*)
Blithe Spirit *revival* + Song of the Islands *revival*
*It Always Rains on Sunday (+ A-Haunting We Will Go *revival*)
Monsieur Verdoux
When the Bough Breaks (+ Circus Boy)
Crossfire (+ Stork Bites Man + This Modern Age No. 4 Fabrics of the Future)
Heaven Only Knows (+ Atlantic Episode *revival, formerly* Catch As Catch Can)
Easy Money (+ Flight to Nowhere + This Modern Age No. 15 Land Short of People)
Millions Like Us *revival or* Vice Versa (*main feature Odeon circuit release*) + One Night in the Tropics
Personal Column (+ Perilous Holiday *revival or* Devil on Wheels)
Mark of Cain + Topper *revival*
Indian Summer + The Spiral Staircase *revival*
Against the Wind (+ Death in the Hand)

Pygmalion *revival* + The Captive Heart *revival*; or *The Best Years of Our Lives (*Odeon circuit main feature release*)

Up in Arms *revival* + Bambi *revival*

The Lady from Shanghai + A Girl Must Live *revival*

The Return of Frank James *revival* + Where There's Life *revival*

Blue Skies *revival* (+ Black Memory)

Bandit of Sherwood Forest *revival* (+ Dick Barton Special Agent)

Escape + The Glass Key *revival*

Odd Man Out *revival* + Bedelia *revival*

Broken Journey + Keep 'Em Flying *revival*

Nothing Sacred *revival* + Deadline at Dawn *revival* (+ This Modern Age No. 13 Ceylon)

The Seventh Veil *revival* + The Life and Death of Colonel Blimp *revival*

The Assassin + The Corpse Came C.O.D.

The Gentle Sex *revival* + The Miracle of Morgan's Creek *revival* (*Odeon release A Double Life at many Gaumonts*)

The Calendar + The Four Feathers *revival*

Three Weird Sisters + Springtime in the Rockies *revival*

The Jolson Story *revival* (+ Olympic Preview)

Gentleman's Agreement (+ Too Busy to Work)

My Sister and I + Are You With It?

I Love Trouble + The Moon and Sixpence *revival*

Ride the Pink Horse + The Edge of the World *revival*

You Were Meant for Me + Black Narcissus *revival*

The Bishop's Wife (+ Caged Fury + This Modern Age No. 8 Sudan Dispute)

*The Red Shoes (+ This Modern Age No.19 Challenge in Nigeria)

Nightmare Alley + Hold That Ghost

XIVth Olympiad (*also at many Odeons*)

Forever Amber

Saraband for Dead Lovers (+ This Modern Age No. 21 Shadow of the Ruhr + The Little Witch)

All My Sons (+ Fortune Lane)

The Blind Goddess (+ Heading for Heaven)

Girl from Manhattan + London Town *revival*; or *Oliver Twist (*Odeon circuit main feature release*)

Esther Waters + Merrily We Live *revival*

Sleeping Car to Trieste (+ The Cobra Strikes + The Thames)

The Wistful Widow (+ The Little Foxes *revival*)

Ruthless + The Adventures of Casanova

A Foreign Affair (+ A Piece of Cake + This Modern Age No. 10 The Rape of the Earth)

Here Come the Huggetts (+ 13 Lead Soldiers + This Modern Age No. 23 Lancashire's Time for Adventure)

River Lady + Secret Beyond the Door

Call Northside 777 (+ Secret Tunnel)

It's Hard to Be Good (+ Man-Eater of Kumaon)

1949

Mother Wore Tights (+ The Checkered Coat)

Caesar and Cleopatra *revival* (+ House Cat + This Modern Age No 12 Antarctic Whale Hunt)

Look Before You Love (+ Secret Service Investigator + This Modern Age No.14 Jamaica Problem)

Once a Jolly Swagman (+ The Connors Case)

Tap Roots (+ The Fool and the Princess)

The Luck of the Irish (+ The Counterfeiters + The Cuckoo)

Whispering City + San Demetrio, London *revival*

The Saxon Charm (+ Feudin' Fussin' and A-Fightin')

Eureka Stockade (+ Badger's Green)

The Paradine Case (+ This Modern Age No. 16 The British — Are They Artistic?)

Blood on My Hands + Pirates of Monterey

Britannia Mews (+ So This Is London *revival* + This Modern Age No. 25 Struggle for Oil)

The History of Mr. Polly (+ Kings of the Turf)

Whispering Smith (+ Speed to Spare)

*The Blue Lagoon (+ Rolling Home)

A Yankee in King Arthur's Court (+ Dynamite)

Unfaithfully Yours (+ The Tender Years)

Floodtide + Canon City

Mr. Blandings Builds His Dream House (+ The Window)

It's Not Cricket + The Lost Moment

Enchantment (+ Chisoko the African + The Ostrich)

The Perfect Woman + Jigsaw (+ This Modern Age No. 27 Education for Living)

Wake of the Red Witch (+ Special Agent)

Marry Me! + Dear Octopus *revival*

A Boy, A Girl and a Bike + The Years Between *revival*

Mexican Hayride + Criss Cross (+ This Modern Age No. 18 The Future of Scotland)

A Letter to Three Wives (+ Jungle Patrol)

Good Sam (+ Strange Bargain)

Whisky Galore! (+ My Dog Shep + This Modern Age No. 20 Fate of an Empire)

Sorrowful Jones (+ Two Blondes and a Redhead + Yorkshire Ditty)

Kind Hearts and Coronets (+ Fiddlers Three *revival*)

That Lady in Ermine + Chicken Every Sunday

The Huggetts Abroad + Illegal Entry

Don't Ever Leave Me + Family Honeymoon

Champion (+ The Fabulous Joe + This Modern Age No. 22 Women in Our Time)

Mr. Belvedere Goes to College (+ I Cheated the Law)

Trottie True (+ Johnny Stool Pigeon)

Magic Town + Race Street

The Lost People + Escape to Happiness *revival*

Chicago Deadline (+ Follow Me Quietly)

Dear Mr. Prohack + Take One False Step

A Song Is Born (+ Forty Minutes at the Zoo)

Diamond City + Abandoned

House of Strangers (+ The Winner's Circle + Sketches of Scotland)

Abbott and Costello Meet the Ghosts + City Across the River

Red, Hot and Blue (+ Prison Warden + This Modern Age No. 31 India and Pakistan)

Slattery's Hurricane (+ Rusty's Birthday *or* Up in the Air)

Tokyo Joe (+ Hitting the Jackpot *or* The Big Deal)

Lust for Gold (+ Mary Lou)

Old Mother Riley's New Venture + The Countess of Monte Cristo (*order reversed in second week; The Countess of Monte Cristo replaced by* Rogue's Regiment *from third week*)

So Dear to My Heart + Kidnapped
A Run for Your Money (+ The Big Cat +
    Ginger Mutt's Christmas Circus)

1950
*indicates main film in box-office Top Ten of the
year*

The Romantic Age + The Story of Molly X
Mighty Joe Young (+ Duke of Chicago)
Abbott and Costello Meet the Killer Boris
    Karloff + The Gal Who Took the West
    (+ Canterbury Road)
Boys in Brown + Miss Pilgrim's Progress
Prince of Foxes (+ Search for Danger + This
    Modern Age No. 33 When You Went
    Away)
Holiday Affair + A Dangerous Profession
Paid in Full + Dear Wife
Come to the Stable + Sand
Woman in Hiding + Francis
Golden Salamander (+ Project X)
The Rugged O'Riordans + Buccaneer's Girl
The Reckless Moment + Innocence Is Bliss
Three Came Home + It Happens Every
    Spring
Bagdad + Borderline
Morning Departure (+ Meet Simon Cherry)
Africa Screams + Outpost in Morocco
The Beautiful Blonde from Bashful Bend +
    The Prisoner of Zenda *revival*
Appointment with Danger (+ Beware of
    Blondie + A Fantasy of London Life
    [Musical Paintbox])
Lost Boundaries + The Body Said No!
Oh, You Beautiful Doll + Mother Didn't Tell
    Me
All the King's Men (+ Beauty on Parade)
Champagne for Caesar + D.O.A.
Under My Skin + Canadian Pacific
The Big Lift (+ The Dream of Olwen *revival,*
    formerly While I Live)
Double Crossbones + Deported
The Capture + Ichabod and Mr. Toad (+
    Ginger Nutt's Forest Dragon)
The Dividing Line + The Eagle and the
    Hawk
Night and the City (+ Trophy Island)
Louisa + Comanche Territory (+ This
    Modern Age No. 36 Where Britain
    Stands)
Dance Hall (+ The Overlanders)

A Ticket to Tomahawk + Old Mother Riley
    Headmistress
So Long at the Fair (+ The Great Plane
    Robbery)
Abbott and Costello in the Foreign Legion
    (+ Shakedown)
Tony Draws a Horse (+ Never Fear)
Waterfront + The Man in Grey *revival*
*Fancy Pants (+ Highway 13)
Rogues of Sherwood Forest + Cargo to
    Capetown
Nancy Goes to Rio (+ Right Cross)
Destination Moon + High Lonesome
Broken Arrow (+ Dick Barton at Bay)
Shadow of the Eagle + Port of New York
Mister 880 + Kill the Umpire
Cage of Gold + The Great Rupert
Seven Days to Noon (+ Tough Assignment)
My Blue Heaven + State Penitentiary
A Life of Her Own + When You're Smiling
Woman on the Run + Wyoming Mail (+
    This Modern Age No. 39 The Future of
    One Million Africans)
Her Favourite Husband (+ The Glass
    Mountain [revival])
Two Flags West (+ Federal Man)
Frightened City + Girl of the Year
Mr. Music (+ Operation Hay Lift)
The Mudlark (+ Shooting Stars)

1951
*indicates main film in box-office Top Ten of the
year*

Harriet Craig + Between Midnight and
    Dawn
Union Station + Tripoli
Lilli Marlene + The Underworld Story
Mystery Submarine + The Desert Hawk (+
    This Modern Age No. 41 Turkey: Key to
    the Middle East)
I Shall Return (+ The Rossiter Case)
Where Danger Lives + Born to Be Bad
To Please a Lady (+ Counterspy Meets
    Scotland Yard)
I'll Get By (+ The Man Who Cheated
    Himself)
The Dark Man + Kansas Raiders
Battle of Powder River + The Fat Man
I'll Get You For This (+ Hi-Jacked + This
    Modern Age No. 30 Fight For a Fuller Life)
Pool of London (+ The Count *revival*)
The 13th Letter (+ The Tattooed Stranger)

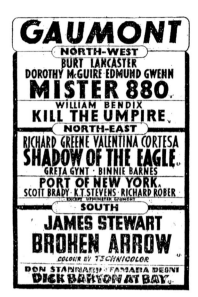

*London-area advertising for the Gaumont
circuit in 1950 and early 1952.*

The Mating Season + The Great Missouri Raid
The Adventurers + The Admiral Was a Lady
Fourteen Hours (+ The Tougher They Come + This Modern Age No. 29 Gambling)
This Is My Affair (+ The Dark Light)
Pagan Love Song + Cause for Alarm
Traveller's Joy + Smuggler's Island
*Cinderella (+ Mysterious Desperado or Riders of the Range)
Circle of Danger + The Company She Keeps
You're in the Navy Now (+ Fugitive Lady)
Abbott and Costello Meet the Invisible Man + Hollywood Story (+ This Modern Age No. 26 Europe's Fisheries in Danger)
A Tale of 5 Cities + The Scarf
Payment on Demand (+ Hunt the Man Down)
Bonaventure + The Groom Wore Spurs
Call Me Mister + House on Telegraph Hill
There Is Another Sun + Apache Drums
Ace in the Hole (+ Dear Brat)
Hell Is Sold Out + When I Grow Up
Up Front + Cattle Drive
Bird of Paradise + No Room at the Inn
Lorna Doone + The Big Gusher
Calling Bulldog Drummond + Kind Lady
Comin' Round the Mountain + The Prince Who Was a Thief
Red Mountain (+ Bunco Squad)
The Man in the White Suit (+ Double Deal)
His Kind of Woman (+ Rhythm Inn)
Half Angel + As Young As You Feel
Decision Before Dawn (+ Father's Wild Game)
Chicago Masquerade + Iron Man
Mr. Belvedere Rings the Bell (+ Night Beat)
He Ran All the Way + Madame Louise
Submarine Command + Rhubarb
Let's Make It Legal + Peking Express
High Treason (+ The Showdown)
Oliver Twist revival + Cave of Outlaws
The Secret of Convict Lake + The Guy Who Came Back
Meet Danny Wilson (+ The Lady from Texas)
The Stooge (+ High Vermilion)
My Favourite Spy (+ Mine Own Executioner revival)
Scrooge (+ Carlotta)
I Want You (+ Cry Danger)

1952
indicates main film in box-office Top Ten of the year

*Where No Vultures Fly (+ Father Takes the Air)
Week End with Father (+ The Raging Tide)
The Day the Earth Stood Still (+ Love Nest) in London area; The Magic Box (+ The Blue Blood) outside London
The House in the Square (+ Yellow Fin)
Two Tickets to Broadway + The Racket
Something to Live for (+ Hong Kong)
Anne of the Indies + The Small Back Room revival
Painting the Clouds with Sunshine + Tomorrow Is Another Day
Phone Call from a Stranger (+ Fingerprints Don't Lie)
Sailor Beware (+ Warpath)
Hunted (+ On the Loose)
Steel Town + Flesh and Fury
I Believe In You (+ Finders Keepers)
Red Skies of Montana (+ Japanese War Bride)
Robin Hood and His Merrie Men (+ Hammer the Toff)
Force of Arms + Close to My Heart
Song of Paris + The Dark Page
5 Fingers (+ FBI Girl)
The River + The Fighter
With a Song in My Heart (+ The Girl on the Bridge)
Wings of Danger + The Atomic City
That's My Boy (+ Denver and Rio Grande)
The Silent Voice + The Family Secret
Down Among the Sheltering Palms + Return of the Texan
Stolen Face + Has Anybody Seen My Gal?
This Woman Is Dangerous + The Fallen Idol revival
Treasure Hunt (+ The Captive City)
Wait 'Til the Sun Shines, Nellie + The Outcasts of Poker Flat
Scarlet Angel + Brandy for the Parson
Little Big Shot (+ The Chiltern Hundreds revival)
Kangaroo (+ The Guinea Pig revival)
You're Only Young Twice! + Sound Off
Untamed Frontier (+ Mother Riley Meets the Vampire)
*Mandy (+ Passport to Pimlico revival)
Clash by Night (+ Slaughter Trail)

The Brave Don't Cry + The Duel at Silver Creek
Dreamboat (+ Let's Go to Paris)
Affair in Trinidad (+ Montana Territory)
Just for You (+ Distant Trumpet)
Abbott and Costello Lost in Alaska + The Red Ball Express
Lure of the Wilderness (+ Lady in the Fog)
*The Planter's Wife (+ Woman in the Dark)
It Grows on Trees + Son of Ali Baba
Venetian Bird (+ Ma and Pa Kettle Go to Paris)
The Happy Time (+ Brave Warrior)
The Gentle Gunman (+ Young Paul Baroni)
Monkey Business (+ Paul Temple Returns)
The Turning Point + The Savage
Don't Bother to Knock + A Millionaire for Christy!
Yankee Buccaneer + The Thief
Made in Heaven (+ The Big Top)
*Road to Bali (+ Potter of the Yard)

1953
indicates main film in box-office Top Ten of the year

My Pal Gus + What Price Glory
The Ringer + The Blazing Forest
Montana Belle + Angel Face
The Man Who Watched Trains Go By (+ Confidence Girl)
Somebody Loves Me + Caribbean Gold
Escape Route + The Redhead from Wyoming
Against All Flags (+ Francis Goes to West Point)
Marching Along (+ Hot Ice)
The Net (+ Royal Journey)
Blackbeard the Pirate + Time Gentlemen Please!
Appointment in London (+ Frank James Rides Again)
Ruby Gentry + Taxi
Rough Shoot (+ The Magnetic Monster)
Military Policemen (+ Now Barabbas Was a Robber... revival)
Street Corner (+ Varieties on Parade)
Desert Legion (+ Black Orchid)
*The Cruel Sea
The "I Don't Care" Girl + The Silver Whip
Niagara (+ Fargo)

Grand National Night + Seminole
City Beneath the Sea (+ Willie and Joe in Tokyo)
Turn the Key Softly (+ The Cimarron Kid)
*A Queen Is Crowned (+ No Escape) (*both films also Odeon circuit release same week*)
Stalag 17 (+ Tropic Zone)
Fair Wind to Java (+ City That Never Sleeps)
Man on a Tightrope + The Farmer Takes a Wife
Twice Upon a Time + The Man Behind the Gun
Abbott and Costello Go to Mars + Gunsmoke
Peter Pan (+ Nature's Half Acre + The Avenging Rider)
Single-Handed (+ Your Witness *revival*)
Thunder Bay (+ Wheel of Fate)
Pickup on South Street + MacDonald of the Canadian Mounties

Scared Stiff (+ The Vanquished)
*Genevieve (+ Murder at 3 a.m.)
The Desert Song + The System
Dangerous Crossing + Powder River
Always a Bride (+ Law and Order)
Affair with a Stranger + Forbidden
Little Boy Lost + Anything Can Happen
Take Me to Town + East of Sumatra
White Witch Doctor (+ The Saint's Return)
Laughing Anne (+ Army Capers)
*Shane
Mr. Scoutmaster (+ City of Bad Men)
Background + The Lone Hand
The Girl in Room 17 (+ There Was a Young Lady)
Albert R.N. (+ Love in Pawn)
Back to God's Country + The Veils of Bagdad
Vicki + The Girl Next Door
Flight to Tangier + Those Redheads from Seattle

A Day to Remember + Column South
*Trouble in Store (+ The Glass Web)

1954

indicates main film in box-office Top Ten of the year

Wings of the Hawk (+ Francis Covers the Big Town)
Houdini (+ Arrowhead)
Meet Mr. Lucifer (+ The Golden Blade)
*From Here to Eternity
Our Girl Friday (+ Tom Brown's School Days *revival*)
Money from Home (+ Park Plaza 605)
Hell Below Zero (+ Desert Patrol)
Border River + The Runaway Bus
The Love Lottery (+ Royal New Zealand Journey)
Lost Treasure of the Amazon + Cease Fire!
War Arrow + Fast and Loose
Jubilee Trail (+ Hell's Half Acre)
Star of India (+ River Beat)
3 Sailors and a Girl (+ It Happened in Paris)
An Inspector Calls + Bang! You're Dead
The Shanghai Story + Make Haste to Live
*Doctor in the House (+ Life in the Arctic + Two Gun Goofy)
Casanova's Big Night (+ Blood Orange)
Conflict of Wings (+ Geraldine)
Act of Love (+ Shark River)
The French Line (+ Tembo)
Beachhead + Riders to the Stars
The Rainbow Jacket (+ That Kind of Girl)
Drums of Tahiti + The Miami Story
Miss Sadie Thompson (+ Dangerous Cargo)
Crossed Swords + The Lone Gun
The Stranger's Hand (+ Who Goes There? *revival*)
The Long Wait + Camels West
Battle of Rogue River + The Saracen Blade
Trouble in the Glen (+ Untamed Heiress)
Up to His Neck (+ Ricochet Romance)
Secret of the Incas (+ The Stranger Came Home)
Indiscretion + Adventures of Robinson Crusoe
Elephant Walk (+ Man of Conflict)
Beautiful Stranger (+ Stormswept)
Black Horse Canyon + Naked Alibi
The Beachcomber (+ Profile)
Apache (+ Captain Kidd and the Slave Girl)
The Young Lovers (+ Stolen Identity)

HIGH AND LOWS OF GAUMONT ATTENDANCES AT GAUMONT SHEFFIELD

It is important to note that these totals include a separate Sunday revival double-bill programme that attracted significant attendances. Years are those each circuit release started out, and some year-end films may have reached Sheffield in the following year. It should also be remembered that the Gaumont Sheffield did not play every Gaumont circuit release and avoided some films that probably would have done worse business than those listed below. The cinema was closed on Xmas Day so takings for that week could be adversely affected. Generally, the weather, time of year and the films playing at opposition halls will have affected figures.

1947
47,741 The Birth of a Baby (first week)
47,488 Great Expectations (first week)
17,761 Song of the South
1948
39,506 Forever Amber (first week)
11,761 Esther Waters + Merrily We Live (Xmas week)
1949
34,666 The Snake Pit (Odeon release)
28,488 Chicago Deadline
11,252 Floodtide + Canon City
1950
46,250 Jolson Sings Again (Odeon release)
35,822 The Mudlark

13,973 Shadow of the Eagle + Port of New York (Xmas week)
1951
43,163 Cinderella
14,836 A Tale of 5 Cities + The Scarf
1952
35,667 Where No Vultures Fly
13,565 Treasure Hunt
1953
43,051 The Cruel Sea
12,879 Twice Upon a Time + The Man Behind the Gun
1954
37,944 Doctor in the House
10,649 Men of Sherwood Forest + Private Hell 36
1955
28,475 The Man from Laramie
 9,741 The Girl Rush + The Blue Peter (Xmas week)
1956
35,571 The Lady and the Tramp
 9,531 Pacific Destiny
1957
31,816 Doctor at Large
 7,237 After the Ball + Time Lock
1958 (Jan/June only)
20,114 Dracula
 5,754 6.5 Special

The choice between the three major circuits in late 1952 and a good indication of the cinemas taking the Gaumont release in the so-called Northeast London area in early 1955.

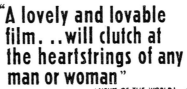

Pushover + The Iron Glove
Sabrina Fair (+ *various supporting features*)
The Purple Plain (+ Johnny on the Run *or various*)
Dawn at Socorro + Francis Joins the WACs
A Bullet Is Waiting (+ Massacre Canyon)
The Black Shield of Falworth (+ The Yellow Mountain)
Rear Window (+ The Link)
Down Three Dark Streets + The Yellow Tomahawk
The Teckman Mystery (+ Into the Blue *revival*)
Men of Sherwood Forest + Private Hell 36
The Living Desert (+ *various supporting features*)
Magnificent Obsession (+ Double Profile)
The Divided Heart (+ Mask of Dust)

1955

*indicates main film in box-office Top Ten of the year

Phffft! (+ Three Hours to Kill)
The Sea Shall Not Have Them (+ 3 Steps to the Gallows)
Svengali (+ Navajo)
3 Ring Circus (+ The Delavine Affair)
Khyber Patrol + The Golden Mistress
To Paris with Love (+ Shield for Murder)
Rough Company (+ The Bamboo Prison *or* Jungle Moon Men)
Six Bridges to Cross + Before I Wake
Sitting Bull (+ Little Fugitive)
Timberjack (+ The Atomic Kid)
Tight Spot (+ Ten Wanted Men)
A Prize of Gold (+ The Other Woman)
Vera Cruz (+ Black Forest)
Man Without a Star (+ Third Party Risk)
As Long As They're Happy (+ Armand and Michaela Denis on the Barrier Reef)
The Eternal Sea + Where There's a Will
A Bullet for Joey (+ The White Orchid)
Conquest of Space + Hell's Island
*Above Us the Waves (+ Police Dog)
Top of the World + Canyon Crossroads
The Ship That Died of Shame (+ I Cover the Underworld)
Valley of Fury + Lady Godiva of Coventry
Mambo (+ Reluctant Heroes *revival*)
5 Against the House + Chicago Syndicate
Escape to Burma + The Secret
Female on the Beach + This Island Earth

The Far Horizons (+ The Big Chase)
There's Always Tomorrow (+ Francis in the Navy)
You Lucky People! + The Naked Street
Pearl of the South Pacific (+ Barbados Quest)
Bring Your Smile Along (+ Wyoming Renegades)
The Private War of Major Benson (+ The Outlaw's Daughter)
The Last Command (+ City of Shadows)
Escapade (+ Windfall)
The Seven Little Foys (+ Crooked Ring)
The Shrike (+ The Hornet's Nest)
Footsteps in the Fog (+ The Gun That Won the West)
The Man from Laramie (+ A Life at Stake)
The Woman for Joe (+ Santa Fe Passage)
The Spoilers (+ The Kettles in the Ozarks)
Man of the Moment (+ One Way Out)
Gentlemen Marry Brunettes (+ Robbers' Roost)
Lucy Gallant (+ The Silver Star)
Touch and Go (+ Armand and Michaela Denis Among the Headhunters)
Summer Madness (+ Murder Is My Beat)
The Second Greatest Sex (+ The Vanishing American)
Desert Sands + Storm Fear
Texas Lady + Bengazi
The Girl Rush + The Blue Peter
Count 3 and Pray (+ I Had 7 Daughters)
Portrait of Alison + Tennessee's Partner
Simon and Laura (+ Running Wild)

1956

(no films were in the box-office Top Ten of the year)

Lady and the Tramp (+ Laughing in the Sunshine)
The Big Knife (+ Top Gun)
Josephine and Men (+ The Big Bluff)
Artists and Models (+ Gateway to the Antarctic)
The Last Frontier + The Gamma People
To Hell...and Back (+ The Square Jungle)
Jumping for Joy (+ A Lawless Street)
The Benny Goodman Story (+ Cloak Without Dagger)
The Indian Fighter (+ Timetable)
Lost (+ Star in the Dust)
Come Next Spring + Ali-Baba
The Rose Tattoo (+ Flight from Vienna)

Who Done It? (+ A Day of Fury)
Davy Crockett, King of the Wild Frontier (+ Tons of Trouble)
The Black Tent (+ Crime Against Joe)
Jubal (+ Nigeria Greets the Queen)
While the City Sleeps + Great Day in the Morning
Safari (+ Inside Detroit)
The Vagabond King (+ Toughest Man Alive)
Alexander the Great
Keep It Clean + Dakota Incident
The Trouble With Harry (+ The Scarlet Hour)
Toy Tiger + The Intimate Stranger
Guilty? (+ Battle Stations!)
Port Afrique (+ The Houston Story)
The Bold and the Brave (+ Race for Life)
Congo Crossing + Raw Edge
The Birds and the Bees (+ The Leather Saint)
Pacific Destiny (+ Night Freight)
Foreign Intrigue (+ The Killing)
Various revivals including Doctor in the House + The Glenn Miller Story
Away All Boats! (+ Behind the Headlines)
Eyewitness (+ Jedda)
Anything Goes (+ Innocents in Paris *revival*)
Rock Around the Clock + One Good Turn *revival or* Doctor at Sea *revival or other revival*
The Ambassador's Daughter (+ The Broken Star)
The Long Arm (+ Edge of Hell)
He Laughed Last + The Last Man to Hang
Child in the House (+ Passport to Treason)
Back from Eternity (+ The High Terrace)
The Proud and Profane (+ Zanzabuku)
Run for the Sun (+ Rebel in Town)
A Hill in Korea (+ Raising a Riot *revival*)
Beyond Mombasa (+ Miami Expose)
You Can't Run Away from It (+ Blackjack Ketchum, Desperado)
Beyond a Reasonable Doubt + A Touch of the Sun
Nightfall + Bermuda Affair
The Great Locomotive Chase (+ Mam'zelle Pigalle)
Death of a Scoundrel + Tension at Table Rock
Up in the World (+ The Hide-Out)
Dance With Me, Henry + Frontier Scout
Dry Rot + Affair in Reno

These advertisements from 1956 (left) and 1957 (above) show the cinemas taking the Gaumont release in the first week (Northwest London) and the third (South). The print of Safari *moved midweek from the West Wickham Gaumont (place name misspelt) to the Elmers End Odeon. The pre-release of* Doctor at Large *at two large Northeast London (second week) cinemas was an experiment.*

Reach for the Sky *revival* + World in My Corner *or* A Town Like Alice *revival* + Johnny Dark *or various revivals*

1957

indicates main film in box-office Top Fifteen of the year

Kelly and Me + Gun for a Coward
Checkpoint (+ Christine)
Three Violent People + Escape in the Sun
The Spanish Gardener (+ Behind the High Wall)
Don't Knock the Rock + The Counterfeit Plan
The King and Four Queens (+ Hit and Run)
Town on Trial (+ Reprisal)
The Great Man + The Killers *revival*
*Ill Met by Moonlight (+ Once Upon a Time)
The Silent World + The Man from Del Rio
The Rainmaker (+ Crowded Paradise)
The Secret Place (+ The Halliday Brand)
The Hunchback of Notre Dame (+ There's Always a Thursday)
Seven Waves Away (+ Sierra Stranger)
Tammy + Appointment with a Shadow
The Monte Carlo Story (+ Bale Out at 43,000)
*Doctor at Large (+ Lovers and Lollipops)
The Day They Gave Babies Away + The Silken Affair
Time Without Pity (+ The Guns of Fort Petticoat)
Cockleshell Heroes *revival* + From Here to Eternity *revival*
Drango (+ The Girl in Black Stockings)
The Oklahoman + That Woman Opposite
Valerie + The Shadow on the Window
Fear Strikes Out (+ The Buster Keaton Story)
The Incredible Shrinking Man (+ O'Rourke of the Royal Mounted *revival*)
The Garment Jungle (+ The Burglar)
The Vintage + Diane
How to Murder a Rich Uncle (+ The Tall T)
The Bachelor Party + Monkey on My Back
Fire Down Below (+ Ride the High Iron)
Sweet Smell of Success (+ Jungle Heat)
Beau James + Second Fiddle
After the Ball + Time Lock
The Seventh Sin + Lust for Life
Across the Bridge (+ Account Rendered)
Operation Mad Ball (+ Domino Kid)

Manuela (+ Hell's Crossroads)
The Vicious Circle (+ The Wayward Girl)
The Long Haul (+ Calypso Heat Wave)
Loving You (+ Short Cut to Hell)
Man of a Thousand Faces (+ *various revivals*)
Seven Thunders (+ Short Head)
Lucky Jim (+ Last Stagecoach West)
Jet Pilot (+ Naked Sea)
The One That Got Away (+ The Captain's Paradise *revival*)
End As a Man + Full of Life
The Delicate Delinquent (+ Mister Rock and Roll)
Private's Progress *revival* + The Baby and the Battleship *revival*
The Lady Takes a Flyer (+ The Monolith Monsters)
Johnny Tremain + Bambi *revival*
The Tin Star (+ Spanish Affair)
The Tarnished Angels (+ Damn Citizen!)

1958

(no films were included in the box-office Top Fourteen of the year)

Time Limit (+ The Depraved)
The Devil's Hairpin + Zero Hour!
Windom's Way (+ Distant Neighbours)
Paths of Glory (+ Baby Face Nelson)
Man on Fire (+ Bhowani Junction *revival*)
Cowboy (+ The Tijuana Story)
Escapade in Japan (+ Day of the Badman)
The Gypsy and the Gentleman (+ An Eye for an Eye)
Legend of the Lost (+ Son of a Stranger)
The Brave One + Rommel's Treasure
The Female Animal + The Big Beat
Wild Is the Wind (+ Red Garters *revival*)
Innocent Sinners (+ The Clouded Yellow *revival*)
Violent Playground (+ Crash Landing)
6.5 Special (+ The Strange Awakening)
Rooney (+ Running Target)
The Quiet American (+ The Toughest Gun in Tombstone)
Bonjour Tristesse (+ Escape from San Quentin)
No Time to Die (+ The World Was His Jury)
The Gift of Love + Showdown at Boot Hill
The Sea Wall (+ Blazing a Trail to the Stars)
Another Time, Another Place (+ The Naked Jungle *revival*)
China Doll (+ Fort Massacre)

Dracula (+ There's Always a Price Tag)
The Caine Mutiny *revival* + Father Brown *revival*
St. Louis Blues (+ High Hell)
Fraulein (+ Undersea Girl)
Law and Disorder (+ The Spaniard's Curse)
Run Silent, Run Deep (+ On the Run)
Sierra Baron + How to Rob a Bank
The Whole Truth (+ Return to Warbow)
The Wind Cannot Read (+ Last of the Desperadoes)
Blackboard Jungle *revival* + Rogue Cop *revival*
The Missouri Traveller (+ The Fearmakers)
Tread Softly Stranger (+ The Bride Is Too Beautiful)
A Time to Love and a Time to Die (+ Quantez)
The Gun Runners (+ Terror in a Texas Town)
Sea Fury (+ A Dangerous Age)
The Fiend Who Walked the West (+ The Case Against Brooklyn)
God's Little Acre (+ Island Women)
The Man Upstairs + Chain of Events
Rockets Galore (+ Ghost of the China Sea)
Rock-A-Bye Baby (+ Links of Justice)
Escort West (+ Guns, Girls and Gangsters)
Virgin Island (+ The Intruder *revival*)
Sea of Sand (+ Hong Kong Affair)
In Love and War (+ Lone Texan)
The Fantastic Disappearing Man + The Moon Is Blue *revival*
The Light in the Forest (+ The Sign of Zorro)
Timbuktu (+ The Lost Missile)
Strictly for Pleasure (+ Wild Heritage)
Bell Book and Candle (+ Keep It Cool)

1959

indicates main film in box-office Top Ten of the year

*The Square Peg (+ Fury Unleashed)
Man of the West (+ Hong Kong Confidential)
The Seventh Voyage of Sinbad (+ The Hard Man)

The Gaumont release then ended, cinemas playing the new Rank or National release programme

ALL THE GAUMONTS: FROM A TO Z

In this list of the Gaumont-British Picture Corporation's cinemas, information in brackets refers to details outside the period of cinema operation by the company. Cinemas operated in Dublin and Paris are also included, along with cinemas belonging to the Odeon circuit that were attached to the Gaumont chain and often, but not always, renamed Gaumont.

Cinemas are listed by the district in which they were located and with which they were usually associated in advertising, and by the name they had when taken over or opened by Gaumont.

In places where Gaumont had more than one cinema, they are listed as far as possible in the order in which they became part of the circuit.

Seating figures have been particularly difficult to ascertain in the case of the Gaumont circuit, even for the cinemas the company built and opened. In some instances, figures are quoted from plans but the actual number of seats installed may have varied. No detailed company records have been found and it has not been practicable to consult licensing records. In any case, the number of seats varied over the years, often increased to the maximum in the boom years, usually reduced when wide screens were installed.

Opening dates given for former live theatres and music halls always refer to when they became full-time cinemas, *not* to when they first opened.

This listing has drawn heavily on the information contained in the *CTA Bulletin*, *Kinematograph Year Books* and numerous other sources, including those listed in the Bibliography. Some details, especially of current site use, were provided by CTA members following a request for specific information published in the March/April 1995 *Bulletin* (those who kindly responded are listed in the Acknowledgements).

Other information concerning some recent changes came from Odeon Cinemas (as also noted in the Acknowledgements).

I have gone to some lengths to check the information concerning the following cinemas during the period when they were operated by Gaumont and (later) Rank, but (local historians, please note) it has not been possible to double check every fact, especially of post-cinema usage.

Abbreviations

APPH: Associated Provincial Picture Houses
GTC: General Theatre Corporation
PCT: Provincial Cinematograph Theatres.

ABBEYMOUNT Edinburgh

REGENT 12 Abbeymount. (Opened 1.8.27, architect: T. Bowhill Gibson, 1700 seats. Taken over by GTC 3.28.) Taken over 5.28 as part of GTC circuit. Closed 2.5.70.

ABERDEEN Grampian

PICTURE HOUSE 181 Union Street. (Opened 14.4.14 by APPH, architect: Robert Atkinson, 877 seats.) Taken over 2.29, part of PCT/APPH circuit. Renamed GAUMONT 15.5.50. Closed 6.10.73. (Facade retained, entrance converted to shops. Auditorium demolished for office block.)

ACTON West London

GLOBE 128 High Street. (Opened 26.3.21 by PCT, architect: G. Percy Pratt, 2136 seats.) Taken over 2.29 as part of PCT. Renamed GAUMONT 1949. Closed 4.4.59. (Demolished. Part of shopping precinct.)

AIGBURTH Liverpool

RIVOLI 192 Aigburth Road between Tramway Road and Burdett Street. (Opened 1906 as Aigburth Assembly Picturedrome, former Assembly Rooms. Renamed Rivoli 1921.) Taken over c5.28 by Denman/Gaumont. 602 seats. Closed 5.1.57. (Church hall and school annexe. Fitted kitchen centre.)

ALLERTON Liverpool

PLAZA Allerton Road. (Opened 31.3.28 by GTC, architect: A. Ernest Shennan, 1432 seats.) Taken over 5.28 as part of GTC circuit. Renamed GAUMONT 11.9.50. Renamed ODEON 25.11.62. (Taken over by Classic 9.12.67, renamed Classic. Closed 19.4.71. Demolished. New Classic opened 28.7.73 above supermarket in redevelopment. Open in 1995 as Cannon. 493 seats.)

ALLOA Central Scotland

LA SCALA Mill Street. (Part of Thomas Ormiston circuit.) Taken over 3.28 by Denman/Gaumont. Almost immediately transferred to Gaumont/PCT control. 717 seats. Closed 2.7.38. (Demolished for new Gaumont.)

GAUMONT Mill Street (site of La Scala). Opened 29.4.39 by Gaumont/PCT, architect: W. E. Trent, 1000 seats. Renamed ODEON 18.10.64. (Taken over by Classic 16.12.67, renamed Classic. Taken over by independent, renamed De Luxe, with partweek bingo. Closed 30.7.71, except for children's shows to 13.6.75. Bingo only, open in 1994.)

ANFIELD Liverpool

KING'S HALL Oakfield Road. (Opened c1912. 1000 seats plus billiard hall. Taken over by GTC.) Taken over 5.28 as part of GTC circuit. Closed 10.30. (Demolished for new Gaumont Palace.)

GAUMONT PALACE Oakfield Road and St.

Domingo Vale (site of King's Hall). Opened 21.12.31 by Gaumont/GTC, architects: Gray and Evans, 1600 seats: 1100 stalls & 500 balcony. Renamed GAUMONT. Closed 26.11.60. (Warehouse.)

ANNIESLAND Glasgow

ASCOT 1544 Great Western Road and Ascot Avenue. (Opened 6.12.39, associated with Alexander B. King, architects: Charles J. McNair and Elder, 1963 seats.) Taken over 31.5.43 by Gaumont/PCT. Renamed GAUMONT c1949. Renamed ODEON 23.3.64. Closed 25.10.75. (Bingo, open in 1994.)

ASHTON-UNDER-LYNE Greater Manchester

MAJESTIC Old Street and Delamere Street. (Opened 22.4.20 by PCT, architect: Arnold England, 1233 seats.) Taken over 2.29 as part of PCT circuit. Renamed GAUMONT c1946. Renamed ODEON 11.11.62. (Taken over 1.11.81 by independent, renamed Metro. 945 seats. Open in 1995.)

AYR Strathclyde

PICTURE HOUSE 131 High Street. (Opened 13.10.21, architects: Lennox and MacMath.) Taken over 5.28 by Denman/Gaumont. Enlarged 12.28, 1800 seats. Renamed GAUMONT 1.5.50. Closed 8.6.68. (Demolished. Littlewood's store.)

BALHAM South London

PAVILION 75 High Road. (Opened c7.07 as Empire, former Balham Music Hall, conversion of swimming pool. 900 seats. Renamed Theatre De Luxe in 1909. Closed for alterations, re-opened 8.15 as Olympia. Renamed Pavilion c1922. Part of National Electric circuit.) Taken over 3.28 by Denman/Gaumont. 1037 seats. Renamed GAUMONT 28.11.49. Closed 5.11.60. (Bingo. Demolished. Open-air car sales.)

PALLADIUM 177 High Road. (Opened pre-1914, 1180 seats. Taken over by GTC 3.28.) Taken over 5.28, part of GTC circuit. Enlarged 1928 with full stage, architect: Cecil Masey. Closed 9.40 by World War Two bomb damage. (Site cleared in 1950s. Station Motors. Office block: Station House.)

BARNET Hertfordshire

CINEMA 122 High Street, High Barnet. (Opened 26.12.12 as Cinema Palace, one floor. Renamed Cinema 9.10.26. Balcony added and opened 10.26. Redecorated 7.33. Taken over by Odeon 12.36. 1038 seats.) Renamed GAUMONT 10.1.55. Closed 8.8.59. (Demolished 1961. Supermarket.)

BARNSLEY South Yorkshire

PRINCESS Racecommon Road, Townend. (Opened 19.12.10, architect: W. T. Turner. 850 seats. Part of New Century Pictures circuit.) Taken over 3.28 by Denman/Gaumont. 817 seats. Closed 29.9.56. (Warehouse. Demolished 1986.)

EMPIRE Eldon Street. (Opened 1917 as Empire Super, former live theatre with some film use. Part of New Century Pictures circuit.) Taken over 3.28 by Denman/Gaumont. 1148 seats. Renamed GAUMONT 15.5.50. Closed 2.1.54 by fire. (Demolished for new Gaumont.)

GAUMONT Eldon Street (site of Empire). Opened 27.2.56, architect: T. P. Bennett & Son, 1238 seats: 706 stalls & 532 balcony. Renamed ODEON 9.9.62. Closed 1.80 for twinning. Re-opened 26.4.80, 419 & 636 seats. Open in 1995.

BARNSTAPLE Devon

THEATRE ROYAL Boutport Street. (Part of Albany Ward/PCT circuit.) Taken over 2.29, part of PCT circuit. Closed. (Demolished for Gaumont Palace.)

GAUMONT PALACE Boutport Street (site of Theatre Royal). Opened 3.8.31 by Gaumont/Albany Ward-PCT, architect: W. H. Watkins (Percy Bartlett), 1124 seats: 702 stalls & 422 balcony. Renamed GAUMONT c1937. Renamed ODEON 21.10.62. (Taken over by Classic 9.12.67, renamed Classic. Partweek bingo. Twinned for films and bingo. Taken over c1982 by independent, renamed Astor. Grade II listed building. Open in 1995. 360 seats.)

BELFAST Antrim

CLASSIC 13/25 Castle Lane. (Opened 24.12.23. Taken over by PCT c8.26, 1810 seats.) Taken over 2.29, part of PCT circuit. Renamed GAUMONT 3.7.50. Closed 30.9.61.)

BELLSHILL Strathclyde

PICTURE THEATRE Main Street. (Opened 9.11. Part of Thomas Ormiston circuit.) Taken over 3.28 by Denman/Gaumont. 629 seats.

Closed 20.12.58. (Frontage demolished. Auditorium extensively altered for indoor market, open in 1995.)

BERMONDSEY South London

TROC-ETTE Tower Bridge Road and Bermondsey Street. (Opened 1929 as Super by George Smart. Taken over by Hyams & Gale. Closed 1.2.32 for alterations, architect: George Coles. Re-opened 8.2.32 as Troc-ette, 2278 seats.) Taken over 10.35 by Gaumont Super Cinemas. Closed by 1.41 by war conditions. Re-opened 18.2.41. Fully taken over 28.2.44. Renamed TROCETTE. Closed 7.1.56. (Disused. Demolished 10/12.75. Public space. Redeveloped in 1989.)

BETHNAL GREEN Northeast London

FORESTERS 93 Cambridge Heath Road. (Opened c9.26, former music hall reconstructed, architect: George Coles. Taken over by Odeon 10.6.37, 1057 seats. Closed 4.47 for restoration after war damage. Re-opened 10.10.49. Advertised as part of Gaumont circuit as it played Gaumont release, but never owned by Gaumont. Closed 20.8.60. Demolished.)

BIRKENHEAD Merseyside

SUPER Conway Street. (Opened 26.6.16 as the Picture House, architect: T. T. Rees, 730 seats. Renamed Super. Taken over by GTC 3.28.) Taken over 5.28, part of GTC circuit. 751 seats. Closed 29.9.56. (Ballroom. Furniture store.)

PARK 1a Park Road East. (Opened 2.11 as the Electric Palace, conversion of skating rink. 1100 capacity. Renamed Park. Taken over by GTC 1.5.28.) Taken over 5.28, part of GTC circuit. 928 seats. Closed 5.6.37. (Demolished for Gaumont.)

QUEEN'S 19-21 Claughton Road, corner of Kendall Street. (Opened 10.11.13, former Queen's Hall music hall heavily altered. 1300 seats. Taken over by GTC.) Taken over 5.28, part of GTC circuit. 918 seats. Closed 5.49. (Ballroom from 31.5.52. Demolished. Car park.)

GAUMONT Park Road East (site of Park cinema). Opened 30.5.38 by Gaumont/GTC, architects: W. E. Trent and Daniel Mackay, 1694 seats. Closed 4.1.64. (Re-opened 16.4.64 as Top Rank Club for bingo. Closed 1.11.86. Snooker hall. Closed 1990. Major fire damage. Roller rink from 12.93.)

BIRMINGHAM West Midlands
see also Harborne and Smethwick

HIPPODROME Hurst Street. (Operated as live theatre by GTC. Taken over 5.28 as part of GTC circuit. No apparent film use. Open in 1995.)
WEST END Suffolk Street. (Originally Curzon Hall with some film use from 1899 or earlier. Re-opened 9.3.25 as West End following conversion work, architect: Frederick J. Pepper, 1385 seats. Taken over by PCT 1.5.26.) Taken over 2.29, part of PCT circuit. Closed 27.3.65. Re-opened 1965. Closed 18.3.67. (Demolished. ATV Centre.)
GAUMONT PALACE Steelhouse Lane/Colmore Circus, corner of Weaman Street. Opened 9.2.31 by Gaumont, architect: William T. Benslyn, 2034 seats. Renamed GAUMONT c1937. Closed 7.42 by bomb damage. Re-opened 23.8.42. Modernised summer 1961. Completely reconstructed internally and Cinerama installed, re-opened 14.10.63. Closed 6.8.73 for ceiling repairs and redecoration. Re-opened 26.8.73, 1212 seats. Closed 29.10.83. (Demolished. Office building: Wesleyan & General Insurance Co.)

BOOTLE Merseyside
STRAND Irlam Road. (Opened 19.8.12 as New Princes Theatre with cine-variety, former Royal Muncaster Theatre. Renamed Strand 19.9.21. Taken over by Bedford Cinemas. Taken over by GTC.) Taken over 5.28, part of GTC circuit. 975 seats. (Leased to independent c8.36. 750 seats. Closed 11.40. Re-opened c1941 by independent. Closed c1948. Warehouse. Destroyed by fire 7.64.)
BROADWAY Stanley Road. (Opened 25.7.12 as Picture House, 1200 seats. Renamed Broadway 26.12.21. Taken over by GTC 1.5.28. Billiard hall attached.) Taken over 5.28, part of GTC circuit. Closed 8.5.41 by wartime bomb damage. (Site cleared for Gaumont.)
GAUMONT Stanley Road (site of Broadway). Opened 23.1.56 by Rank, architects: T. P. Bennett & Son, 1312 seats, one floor. Renamed ODEON 28.4.64. Open partweek only from 7.74 except during school holidays. Closed 1.11.75. (Skateboard centre. Snooker centre.)

BOSCOMBE Bournemouth
HIPPODROME Christchurch Road. (Operated as live theatre by GTC. Taken over 5.28 as part of GTC circuit. No apparent film use. Dance hall. Academy nightclub in 1992.)

BOURNEMOUTH Dorset
see also Boscombe

REGENT Westover Road. Opened 13.5.29 by Gaumont/PCT, architects: W. E. Trent and Seal & Hardy, 2267 seats. Renamed GAUMONT 22.8.49. Closed 16.11.68 for twinning, architects: Dry, Halasz & Associates. Re-opened 15.7.69 as GAUMONT 1 & 2, 754 seats upstairs & 1158 downstairs. Renamed ODEON 1 & 2 30.10.86. ODEON 2 downstairs closed 6.3.89 for subdivision. Re-opened 6.89 as ODEON 2, 3, 4 & 5, 359 & 267 & 119 & 121 seats. ODEON 6 opened 24.2.95 in former circle bar, 140 seats. All open in 1995.

BRADFORD West Yorkshire
see also Saltaire

ST. GEORGE'S HALL Bridge Street. (Films shown from c1902 on occasion. Full-time cinema from c1913. Taken over 1.26 by New Century Pictures circuit.) Taken over 3.28 by Denman/Gaumont. Closed 3.49. (Civic hall.)
MORLEY STREET PICTURE HOUSE. (Opened 2.4.14 by PCT as Bradford Picture House, conversion of hall opened in 1913. Taken over by independent c1922. Renamed Picture House in 1924. Taken over 13.4.27 by New Century Pictures circuit.) Taken over 3.28 by Denman/Gaumont. Closed 27.10.56. (Re-opened as Majestic Ballroom 25.10.57. Top Rank Club for bingo from 7.3.65. Closed 1970. Sold 29.9.71. Re-opened as Majestic cinema with Indian films. Closed. Rehearsal studio, extra dressing rooms, wardrobe and offices plus enlarged back stage for adjacent Alhambra Theatre.)
EMPIRE Great Horton Road. (Opened 11.2.18, former Empire Theatre. Renamed Empire Super Cinema in 1926. Part of Biocolour circuit.) Part of original Gaumont circuit in 3.27. 1381 seats. (Taken over by independent c3.37, renamed New Empire. Closed 25.1.52 by fire. Auditorium demolished. Front converted to part of Bradford College.)
NEW VICTORIA Brewery Street (now Prince's

Way), Thornton Road and Quebec Street. Opened 22.9.30 by Gaumont/PCT, architect: William Illingworth, 3318 seats. Renamed GAUMONT 22 or 25.9.50. Redecorated early 1954. Closed 30.11.68 for twinning plus bingo in stalls, architects: Gavin Peterson & Sons, interior designers: Trevor & Mavis Stone. Re-opened 21.8.69 as ODEON 1 & 2, 467 + 1207 seats. ODEON 3 opened 6.87 in former ballroom, 244 seats. All open in 1995.

BRIDGWATER Somerset
BIJOU Behind 27 St. Mary Street. (Taken over by Albany Ward/PCT.) Taken over 2.29, part of PCT circuit. Closed c1934.
PALACE Penel Orlieu. (Opened 1916 as theatre or cinema. Taken over by Albany Ward/PCT.) Taken over 2.29, part of PCT circuit. 684 seats. Closed 9.4.38, refused licence for inadequate exits. (Used 1939-44 by ENSA for entertaining troops. Taken over by independent and re-opened 24.4.50. 551 seats. Some theatre use. Closed c10.86. Disused in 1995.)

BRIGHTON East Sussex
ACADEMY West Street. (Opened 3.6.11, former Turkish baths. Enlarged and re-opened 27.9.13. Taken over by Biocolour circuit.) Part of original Gaumont circuit in 3.27. 1012 seats. Renamed TATLER 7.9.31. Renamed ACADEMY 18.1.32. Closed 24.1.73. (Demolished. Academy House office block.)
HIPPODROME Middle Street. (Operated as live theatre by GTC. Taken over 5.28 as part of GTC circuit.) Films shown on Sundays from 3.2.29 to 23.6.29 during closure of Regent. (Closed as theatre 1964. Bingo, open in 1995 as Mecca Club.)
COURT THEATRE New Road. (Opened 1909, former Coliseum theatre/music hall.) Taken over 5.28, part of GTC circuit. (Taken over 1.30 by independent. 800 seats. Re-opened 1947 as Dolphin live theatre. Renamed Her Majesty's in 1952. Closed 20.1.55. Re-opened 6.4.55 as Paris Continental cinema. Closed 2.1.62. Demolished 1967. Office block.)
REGENT Queens Road and North Street. (Opened 27.7.21 by PCT, architect: Robert Atkinson, interior decorations with Walter Bayes. 2200 seats. Closed by fire 25.1.29. Re-opened 1.7.29 with proscenium arch area re-

designed.) Taken over 2.29, part of PCT circuit. Closed 13.4.55 for alterations to circle for CinemaScope. Re-opened 19.5.55. Closed 25.4.62 for 70mm installation with new screen and proscenium arch. Re-opened 7.6.62. Closed 14.4.73. (Demolished 1973. Boots the Chemist opened 1977.)

BRISTOL Avon

PALACE Baldwin Street. (Opened 2.12 as full-time cinema, the People's Palace, formerly music hall. Taken over 1920 by Biocolour circuit.) Part of original Gaumont circuit in 3.27. Closed 30.6.27 for reconstruction behind front wall, architect: Frank T. Verity. Re-opened 14.2.28 as NEW PALACE, 1574 seats. Renamed PALACE. Renamed GAUMONT c1952. Modernised c1960, 1245 seats. Closed 15.3.80. (Listed facade. Nightclub.)

REGENT Castle Street. (Opened 30.7.28 by PCT, architect: W. H. Watkins [Percy Bartlett], 2036 seats.) Taken over 2.29, part of PCT circuit. Destroyed by bomb 24.11.40. (Site cleared in 1963.)

BROMLEY Southeast London

GRAND THEATRE 111 High Street. (Opened 22.3.09 as the Grand Hall cinema. former hall and theatre built over swimming pool. Closed 31.5.24 for reconstruction. Re-opened 4.10.26 as the Grand Theatre, cinema with occasional live shows.) Taken over by Denman/Gaumont 1934. 900 seats. Closed 29.5.37. (Re-opened 6.9.37 as live theatre. Used during World War Two as air-raid shelter, store, civil defence centre, etc. Re-opened 27.12.47 as New Theatre. Destroyed by fire early on 6.5.71.)

PALAIS DE LUXE CINEMA High Street. (Opened 1911.) Taken over by Denman/Gaumont 1934. 881 seats. Closed 1940. (Food store.) Used for experimental large-screen TV until 12.48. (Taken over by independent and re-opened 1949 as Palais, 760 seats. Renamed Pullman 7.11.54. Modernised and re-opened 18.8.63 as Astor. Closed 24.9.77. Bingo. Closed 4.85. Auditorium demolished in 1985. Facade demolished 1988. Metropolitan Building Society on front, car park/Sainsbury's supermarket at rear.)

GAUMONT High Street, corner of Ravensbourne Road. Opened 23.11.36 by Gaumont/PCT, architect: W. E. Trent, 2583

seats. Closed 18.2.61. (Largely demolished for Debenham's store, parts of facade retained. Habitat and other shops in 1995.)

BURNT OAK North London

REGENT The Broadway, High Road. (Opened 25.2.29, architect: George Coles, 900 seats. Enlarged 1932 with addition of balcony, architect: George Coles. Taken over by Odeon 16.7.36. Renamed Odeon 30.7.37.) Renamed GAUMONT 1949. Renamed ODEON 16.12.62. Closed 12.2.72. (Demolished. Shops and flats.)

BURSLEM Stoke-on-Trent

COLISEUM Cleveland Street/Bournes Bank. (Full-time cinema from 1921, former live theatre. Part of Biocolour circuit.) Part of original circuit in 3.27. 1782 seats. Renamed GAUMONT 2.5.55. Closed 12.11.60. (Club. Demolished.)

BURTON-ON-TRENT Staffordshire

ELECTRIC 165 High Street. (Opened 25.10.10, architect: Thomas Jenkins. Part of National Electric circuit.) Taken over 3.28 by Denman/Gaumont. Interior reconstructed, re-opened 10.9.28, 1025 seats. Renamed GAUMONT 28.11.49. Closed 29.9.56. (Entrance converted to shops, auditorium to warehouse.)

RITZ Guild Street and George Street (site of Opera House, retaining facade as rear wall). (Opened 11.3.35, architects: Thomas Jenkins and John Fairweather, 1600 seats.) Taken over by Rank 5.9.55. 1355 seats. Renamed GAUMONT 24.2.57. Renamed ODEON 14.11.66. Triple from 14.4.74. 502 & 110 & 110 seats. Open in 1995.

BYKER Newcastle

GRAND THEATRE Wilfred Street. (Former theatre with films from 1899. Part of Thompson and Collins' Enterprises circuit, on cinevariety.) Taken over 3.28 by Denman/Gaumont. 650 seats. (Leased to independent 1935. Live theatre from 9.3.36. Cinema again from 9.10.39. Closed 17.3.41. Variety theatre. Closed 27.8.54. Builders' store. Demolished 1964.)

CALNE Wiltshire

PALACE THEATRE Mill Street. (Opened 1918

as Taylor's Electric Theatre. Taken over c1924 by Award circuit. Taken over 9.27 by PCT.) Taken over 2.29, part of PCT/Albany Ward circuit. 500 seats. (Taken over by independent 1931. Renamed Regent 13.3.58. Closed 10.5.69. Demolished.)

CAMDEN TOWN North London

HIPPODROME High Street, corner of Crowndale Road. (Former live theatre. Cinema by 1924. Part of United Pictures Theatres circuit from 1.28.) Under Gaumont management from 7.30 as part of UPT circuit. Closed 1940. (Leased out for BBC studio. Sold 17.10.60. Grade II listed building. Nightclub in 1995.)

GAUMONT PALACE 14 Parkway. Opened 25.1.37 by Gaumont/PCT, architects: W. E. Trent, W. Sydney Trent & Daniel Mackay, 2742 seats. Renamed GAUMONT c1937. Renamed ODEON 30.5.64. Closed 4.11.67 for stalls bingo and new Odeon in circle, opened 26.2.68, 1198 seats. Closed 29.9.79. (Re-opened 9.10.80 as Gate 3, 424 seats. Closed 19.7.82. Re-opened 15.12.83 as Camden Parkway, 1000 seats. Former projectionists' training school area converted to Regency cinema, 90 seats, main auditorium known as King's. Both closed 2.3.87. King's re-opened 15.12.89. Regency re-opened 9.2.90. Both closed 30.8.93. Bingo open as Top Rank Club in 1995.)

CANNING TOWN Northeast London

CINEMA 317 Barking Road. (Opened 7.11. Part of Gale and Repard circuit.) Taken over 3.28 by Denman/Gaumont. 840 seats. Closed 13.4.57. (Sold 1.11.60. Shops.)

GRAND THEATRE 90 Barking Road. (Opened 1913. Part of Gale and Repard circuit.) Taken over 3.28 by Denman/Gaumont. 1346 seats. Closed 1940 by bomb damage. (Demolished.)

CAPE HILL Smethwick — see Smethwick

CARDIFF South Glamorgan

HIPPODROME Westgate Street. (Part of Biocolour circuit.) Part of original circuit in 3.27. 1300 seats. (Leased to independent by 1933, renamed New Hippodrome. Demolished March 1939 for new garage.)

EMPIRE THEATRE Queen Street. Opened 7.9.31 by Gaumont, former live theatre, 2820 seats. Reverted to live shows from 19.9.32 to 10.10.32. Closed 3.6.33 for extensive alterations. Re-opened 8.33, 2599 seats. Renamed GAUMONT c1958. Closed 30.12.61. (Sold 17.1.62. Demolished. C&A store.)

CARLISLE Cumbria
PICTURE HOUSE 37 Botchergate. (Opened 8.15, architect: George Gunn. 1006 seats.) Taken over by Rank 5.9.55, renamed GAUMONT. Renamed ODEON 13.1.64. Closed 17.5.69. (Auditorium demolished. Supermarket.)

CARSHALTON South London — see Rose Hill

CATFORD Southeast London — see Rushey Green

CHADWELL HEATH Northeast London
EMBASSY High Road. (Opened 17.5.34, architect: Harry Weston, 1812 seats: 1232 stalls & 580 balcony.) Taken over Gaumont/PCT 19.10.34, renamed GAUMONT PALACE. Renamed GAUMONT c1937. Renamed ODEON 24.2.64. Closed 28.7.66. (Bingo, open as Top Rank Club in 1995.)

CHARING CROSS ROAD London — see London West End

CHATHAM Kent
NATIONAL ELECTRIC 205 High Road. (Opened 15.4.11. Part of National Electric circuit.) Taken over by 3.28 by Denman/Gaumont. 836 seats. Renamed ELECTRIC. Closed 25.2.51. (Sold 1.3.51. Wilson's Fashion Store until 1983.)
PALACE Watling Street & Beechwood Avenue. Opened 30.11.36 by Kent Proprietary Holdings, controlled by Gaumont, architect: Arthur W. Kenyon, 1864 seats. Renamed GAUMONT 18.12.50. Closed 4.2.61. (Bowling alley from 21.8.61. Closed c1970. B&Q DIY centre from 1978. Church.)

CHELSEA West London
GAUMONT PALACE 206/222 King's Road, corner of Upper Manor Street (site of William Friese-Greene's studio & laboratory). Opened 8.12.34 by Gaumont/PCT, architects: W. E. Trent & Ernest F. Tulley, 2502 seats. Renamed

GAUMONT c1937. Modernised c1960. Renamed ODEON 7.1.63. Closed 11.3.72. (Converted to Habitat store, offices, flats in old flytower, plus smaller cinema.) New Odeon in former circle with new entrance (former exit) opened 9.9.73, 739 seats. (Closed 21.11.81. Re-opened 15.9.83 as Chelsea Cinema by Artificial Eye. Open in 1995.)

CHELTENHAM Gloucestershire
GAUMONT PALACE Winchcombe Street. Opened 6.3.33 by Gaumont/Albany Ward-PCT, architect: W. E. Trent, 1774 seats. Renamed GAUMONT c1937. Renamed ODEON 16.12.62. Triple from 1.1.73, 756 seats (old circle) & 110 & 110 seats (both in former rear stalls). ODEON 2 (downstairs) enlarged to 129, ODEON 3 (downstairs) reduced to 104. ODEON 4 opened late 1987 in former café/ballroom, 90 seats. ODEON 5 opened 6.10.89 in former front stalls & stage area, 204 seats. All open in 1995.

CHEPSTOW Gwent
PALACE THEATRE Bridge Street. (Part of Albany Ward/PCT circuit.) Taken over 2.29, part of PCT circuit. 424 seats. Closed 5.38.
GAUMONT Beaufort Square (west side, part of Beaufort Hotel). Opened 16.5.38 by Gaumont/Albany Ward-PCT, architect: Enoch Williams, modifications: W. E. Trent, 825 seats. Taken over 5.1.58 by independent, renamed Regal. Closed 3.4.71. Café & shop in foyer, builders' warehouse in auditorium. Disused. Demolished c1989. TSB bank and shops in 1995.)

CHESTER Cheshire
MUSIC HALL St. Werburgh's Street (rear exit onto Northgate Street). (Opened 1910, former church & theatre. Reconstructed, architects: E. J. Muspratt & G. E. Tonge, and re-opened 12.21. Taken over by GTC 3.28.) Taken over 5.28, part of GTC circuit. 870 seats. Closed 29.4.61. (Retail use - Reject shop in 4.95.)
GLYNN 110 Foregate Street. (Opened 19.6.11, architects: Marshall & Muspratt, 750 seats. Taken over 3.28 by GTC.) Taken over 5.28, part of GTC circuit. Closed 5.9.31. (Retail use. Disused in 4.95.)
MAJESTIC Brook Street. (Opened 2.21. Taken over by GTC 3.28.) Taken over 5.28, part of

GTC circuit. 1084 seats. Closed 29.9.56. (Ballroom from 15.3.57. Bingo from 22.8.65. Sold to town 22.1.73. Retail use.)
GAUMONT PALACE Brook Street. Opened 2.3.31 by Gaumont/PCT, architect: William T. Benslyn, 1997 seats. Renamed GAUMONT. Closed 9.12.61. (Bowling alley from 9.7.62. Bingo from c1967, open in 1995 as Top Rank Club.)

CHESTERFIELD Derbyshire
VICTORIA PICTURE HOUSE Knifesmithgate. (Opened 1.12.24, architect: W. Cecil Jackson, replacing old Victoria adjacent. 1298 seats.) Taken over by Rank 28.5.56, renamed GAUMONT. 1148 seats. Closed 30.1.65. (Bingo. Closed 29.12.68. Supermarket.)

CHICHESTER West Sussex
GAUMONT East Street and St. Pancras, Eastgate Square. Opened 20.9.37 by Gaumont, architect: Harry Weston, 1278 seats: 874 stalls, 404 raised rear section. Closed 15.10.60. (Sold 29.12.61. Auditorium reconstructed as swimming baths, frontage and entrance retained. Closed. Old café open as Indian restaurant in 1995.)

CHIPPENHAM Wiltshire
PALACE THEATRE Station Hill. (Opened 1910 as Chippenham Public Hall for skating and films. Taken over 1913 by Albany Ward, converted to fulltime cinema, architect: Percival Rigg, renamed Palace. Enlarged 1921 after gale damage. Part of Albany Ward/PCT circuit.) Taken over 2.29, part of PCT circuit. Closed 7.11.36. (Warehouse in 1980.)
GAUMONT PALACE Timber Street. Opened 14.11.36 by Gaumont/Albany Ward-PCT, architects: W. E. Trent & W. Sydney Trent, 1084 seats. Renamed GAUMONT c1937. Renamed ODEON 21.10.62. (Taken over by Classic 8.12.67, renamed Classic. Closed 27.4.74. Store. Nightclub.)

CHORLTON-CUM-HARDY Greater Manchester
SAVOY Manchester Road, corner of Nicholas Road. (Opened 8.11.20 as Picture House by PCT. Leased by Savoy Cinemas and renamed Savoy. Part of ABC circuit from formation in

1928. 1500 seats.) Taken back 25.3.46 by Gaumont/PCT, re-opened 1.4.46 as GAUMONT. 1250 seats. Closed 6.1.62. (Co-Op Funeral centre with new frontage.)

CINDERFORD Gloucestershire
PALACE Belle Vue Road. (Opened 1.24 by Albany Ward on site of former Palace. Part of Award circuit. Taken over 9.27 by PCT.) Taken over 2.29, part of PCT/Albany Ward circuit. 443 seats. Closed 1957 by fire. (Taken over by independent 5.1.58. Closed 1966. British Legion hall.)

CIRENCESTER Gloucestershire
PICTURE HOUSE Victoria Road. (Opened 13.9.26 by Albany Ward, 700 seats. Taken over 9.27 by PCT as part of Award circuit.) Taken over 2.29, part of PCT/Albany Ward circuit. Renamed GAUMONT c1952. Closed 1.12.56. (Demolished. Flats.)

CLAPHAM South London
MAJESTIC 146 High Street. (Opened 1914, architect: J. Stanley Beard. Taken over c10.28 by PCT.) Taken over 2.29, part of PCT circuit. 1556 seats. Closed late 10.40. Re-opened 9.2.41. Renamed GAUMONT 19.6.50. Closed 5.11.60. (Bingo from 1969. Nightclub in 1995.)

CLAPHAM JUNCTION South London
SHAKESPEARE Lavender Hill, corner of Theatre Street. (Opened 4.15, former live theatre. Part of United Pictures Theatres circuit from 1.28.) Under Gaumont management from 7.30 as part of UPT circuit. 1175 seats. Closed 27.9.40 by World War Two bomb damage. (Taken over 1955 by Compulsory Purchase Order. Surviving frontage demolished c1.57 for proposed Battersea Town Hall extension. Foxton's office block in 1995 with flats behind.)
PAVILION 222 Lavender Hill. (Opened 1.16 as Electric Pavilion by Israel Davis. Part of Davis circuit.) Part of original Gaumont circuit in 3.27. 1250 seats. Closed late 9.40. Re-opened 29.12.40. Closed 17.8.44 by World War Two flying bomb. (Part of Asda supermarket car park & open space in 1995.)

CLAPTON North London
RINK 137 Lower Clapton Road. (Opened 8.11, former skating rink. Taken over by GTC 3.28).

Taken over 5.28, part of GTC circuit. 2000 seats. Closed 1942 by bomb damage. (Demolished in 1950s. Fina petrol station in 1995.)

COATBRIDGE Strathclyde
B.B. PICTURE HOUSE Water Street. (Opened pre-1917, 800 seats. Part of BB group.) Taken over 12.28. Closed 28.11.56. (Demolished. Supermarket.)

COLCHESTER Essex
EMPIRE Mersea Road. (Opened as Vaudeville Electric music hall before World War One. Taken over by Biocolour circuit.) Part of original Gaumont circuit in 3.27. 673 seats (Taken over c1942 by independent. 662 seats. Closed c1959. Warehouse. Demolished for roadway.)
HIPPODROME High Street. (Opened 12.7.20, former live theatre with some film use. Part of Biocolour circuit.) Part of original Gaumont circuit in 3.27. 1000 seats. Closed 23.12.61. (Top Rank Club, bingo from 29.12.61. Closed 1985. Disco from 1988.)

COMMERCIAL ROAD Northeast London –
see Stepney

COVENTRY West Midlands
GAUMONT PALACE Jordan Well. Opened 5.10.31 by Gaumont, architect: W. H. Watkins (Percy Bartlett), 2517 seats. Renamed GAUMONT 10.1.37. Closed 14.11.40 by bomb damage. Re-opened 23.12.40. Restored and redecorated 1949 without closing, architect: Harry Weedon. Modernised 1960. Modernised again and re-opened 31.7.67 as ODEON. Triple from 16.11.75, 716 seats (old circle) & 170 & 172 seats (both in former rear stalls). ODEON 4 and 5 opened 8.2.90, 390 seats (former front stalls area) & 121 seats (former café). All open in 1995: 714 & 178 & 213 & 390 & 121 seats.

CREWE Cheshire
PLAZA High Street. (Opened 11.11.33, 1400 seats.) Taken over by Rank 12.12.55, renamed GAUMONT. Closed 12.8.61. (Majestic Ballroom. Top Rank Club for bingo from 8.8.65. Sold 2.9.71. Apollo cinemas opened 24.5.90 in circle and circle foyer: 110 & 110 & 93 seats. Bingo continued on ground floor. Open in 1995.)

CRICKLEWOOD North London
QUEEN'S HALL Cricklewood Lane. (Opened 12.20. Operated by Catwood Cinemas.) Taken over 3.28 by Denman/Gaumont, 1904 seats. Renamed GAUMONT 1949. Closed 16.1.60. (Demolished. Supermarket - Kwiksave in 1995.)

CROSBY Merseyside
CORONA College Road. (Opened 21.5.20.) Taken over 3.28 by Denman/Gaumont, 1150 seats. Closed 1.12.56. (Demolished. Shops.)

CROUCH END North London
HIPPODROME 31 Topsfield Parade, Tottenham Lane. (Opened c1915, former public hall and opera house. Alterated in 1920, architect: E. A. Stone. Altered in 1926, architect: W. C. Thomerson. Taken over by GTC.) Taken over 5.28, part of GTC circuit. Altered in 1929, architect: W. E. Trent. Further alterations 1933. 1000 seats. Closed 1941/42 by severe bomb damage to auditorium in World War Two. (Sold 1950. Frontage intact but re-built, entrance becoming shop.)

DAGENHAM Northeast London
HEATHWAY Heathway. (Opened 29.7.36 by Kay Bros., architect: George Coles, 2198 seats. Taken over by GCF 1936. Taken over by Odeon c1943.) Renamed GAUMONT 14.11.49. Renamed ODEON 30.5.64. Closed 20.2.71. (DIY store. Shopping centre. Destroyed by fire night of 21/22.7.83.)

DALSTON North London
PICTURE HOUSE 12 Dalston Lane. (Opened 6.12.20, conversion of Dalston Theatre, architect: F. Edward Jones [Robert Cromie], 2157 seats. Part of Biocolour circuit.) Part of original circuit in 3.27. Renamed GAUMONT 9.4.51. Closed 19.11.60. (Warehouse. Foyer into club, stalls area into car auction room entered from rear, later converted into another club. Both open in 1995 as Four Aces in foyer and Roseberry's in auditorium.)

DARLINGTON County Durham
ARCADE Skinnergate. (Opened 1908. Taken over by PCT c1919. 1300 seats.) Taken over 2.29, part of PCT circuit. Closed 11.8.56. (Majestic Ballroom. Bingo, open in 1995.)

COURT Skinnergate. (Opened 2.13. Taken over by PCT c1921. 1200 seats.) Taken over 2.29, part of PCT circuit. Modernised and re-opened 26.12.32, 1007 seats. Closed 8.47, destroyed by fire. (Frontage remains, auditorium into shops.)

ALHAMBRA Northgate. (Opened 9.13, 1000 seats. Taken over by PCT 5.1.25. 1000 seats.) Taken over 2.29, part of PCT circuit. Renamed GAUMONT 11.12.50. Closed 15.2.64. (Demolished in 1973. Office block.)

DENNISTOUN Glasgow

PARADE 184/200 Meadowpark Parade. (Opened 25.2.21, architect: P. Mackay Stoddart of Paterson & Stoddart. Enlarged 8.26, 1400 seats.) Taken over by Denman/Gaumont c10.28. 1400 seats. Closed 5.8.61. (Bingo. Re-opened as New Parade cinema 30.6.69. Closed 7.4.86. Auditorium largely demolished. Parade Lounge and Bar in front in 1994.)

DEPTFORD Southeast London

BROADWAY Broadway (496 New Cross Road). (Opened 4.3.16, former live theatre, 1300 seats. Part of United Pictures Theatres circuit from 1.28.) Under Gaumont management from 7.30 as part of UPT circuit. (Taken over 1934 by independent. Taken over c6.48 by Granada. Re-opened 12.49. Renamed Century 15.8.55. Closed 30.4.60. Demolished 3.63.)

DERBY Derbyshire

GAUMONT PALACE London Road. Opened 17.9.34 by Gaumont/PCT, architects: W. E. Trent & W. Sydney Trent, 2175 seats. Renamed GAUMONT c1937. Modernised 1962. Renamed ODEON 8.10.65. Triple from 29.12.74, 800 seats (old circle) & 138 seats & 138 seats (both in former rear stalls). Closed 4.5.83. (Taken over by EMI, re-opened 26.8.83 as New Trocadero Entertainments Centre with stalls converted to bingo, new cinema with 559 seats in old circle area. Cinema closed 19.12.88 after part of ceiling collapsed.)

DINGLE Liverpool

PICTUREDROME Park Road. (Opened c12.12. 770 seats.) Taken over 3.28 by Denman/Gaumont. Closed by 11.29. (Demolished 1935. New Gaumont on enlarged site.)

BERESFORD Park Road. (Opened c1.22, 1047 seats.) Taken over 3.28 by Denman/Gaumont. Closed 29.9.56. (Demolished in road widening.)

GAUMONT Park Road and Dingle Road (Prince's Park). Opened 29.3.37 by Gaumont/Denman on site of old Picturedrome, architect: W. E. Trent (assistant: Daniel Mackay), 1503 seats. Closed 17.9.66. (Top Rank Club for bingo, open in 1995.)

DONCASTER South Yorkshire

MAJESTIC Hallgate, corner of Thorne Road. (Opened 9.12.20 as South Parade Cinema. Renamed Majestic 9.22. Taken over 2.28 by PCT and improved.) Taken over 2.29, part of PCT circuit. 1200 seats. Closed 17.6.33. (Demolished for new Gaumont Palace.)

GAUMONT PALACE Hallgate, corner of Thorne Road (enlarged site of old Majestic). Opened 3.9.34 by Gaumont/PCT, architects: W.E. Trent & W. Sydney Trent, 2020 seats. Renamed GAUMONT. Modernised 1968. Triple from 8.4.73, 1003 seats (old circle and front stalls), 144 & 144 seats (both in former rear stalls). Renamed ODEON 22.1.87. All open in 1995.

DORCHESTER Dorset

PALACE THEATRE Durngate Street. (Opened 1920, former live theatre. Taken over by Albany Ward c1921. Taken over by PCT 9.27.) Taken over 2.29, part of PCT circuit. 379 seats. Closed 4.5.57. (Motor accessories store. Demolished mid-1970s. Old people's flats: Palace Court.)

DORKING Surrey

GAUMONT Reigate Road. Opened 28.2.38 by Gaumont/PCT and local company, architect: Harry Weston, 1290 seats. (Taken over 4.9.38 by Shipman and King with local company, renamed Embassy. Closed 14.4.73. Jehovah's Witness Meeting Hall. Closed 1983. Demolished 8.83. Council offices.)

DOVER Kent

KING'S HALL 49 Biggin Street. (Opened 21.10.11, architect: A. H. Steele, 800 seats. Variety theatre from c1913 to 6.4.31. Closed 29.12.37 by fire. Rebuilding started 8.39, architects: Verity and Beverley. Naval training

establishment during World War Two. Taken over by Odeon 19.7.43. Re-opened 14.7.47, 1050 seats.) Renamed GAUMONT 15.1.50. Closed 26.11.60. (Bingo from 19.3.61.)

DUBLIN Co. Dublin, Ireland

GRAFTON 72 Grafton Street. (Opened 17.4.11 by PCT, 450 seats. Closed 6.13 for enlargement. Re-opened c2.14, 800 seats.) Taken over 2.29, part of PCT circuit. (Seems to have been taken over by a local independent by the late 30s, perhaps when original lease expired in 1939. Closed. Re-opened 19.9.59 as Grafton News and Cartoon Cinema by Classic. Closed c1970. Shopping arcade.)

DUDLEY West Midlands

EMPIRE Hall Street. (Opened 8.1.12, former music hall. Taken over 1920 by Shapeero circuit.) Taken over 3.28 by Denman/Gaumont. 1300 seats. Closed 2.11.40. (Factory and warehouse. Engineering company. Demolished early 1970s. Supermarket.)

CRITERION 42 High Street. (Opened 17.11.23, architect: Joseph Lawden, incorporating old Criterion as entrance hall and cafe, 1200 seats. Taken over 12.27 by APPH.) Taken over 2.29, part of PCT/APPH circuit. Closed 29.9.56. (Front into shop, rear on King Street into warehouse. Demolished c1980.)

REGENT 171 High Street. (Opened 3.9.28 by APPH, architect: W. E. Trent, 1235 seats, stadium plan.) Taken over 2.29, part of PCT/APPH circuit. Renamed GAUMONT 6.3.50. Closed 15.7.61. (Top Rank Club for bingo from c24.7.61, open in 1995.)

DUNDEE Tayside

KING'S 27 Cowgate, corner of St. Andrews Street. (Opened 24.9.28 by PCT, former King's Theatre, 1458 seats.) Taken over 2.29, part of PCT circuit. Renamed GAUMONT 8.5.50. Interior completely rebuilt 1961, 1265 seats. Renamed ODEON 2.9.73. Closed 24.10.81. (Bingo from 5.83, open in 1994.)

EALING Northwest London

PALLADIUM 22 Broadway. (Opened 3.11.08 as Broadway, former variety theatre. Renamed Palladium c1923. Taken over by Scala circuit. Taken over by PCT. Transferred 5.27 to APPH.) Taken over 2.29, part of PCT/APPH circuit, 1260 seats. Closed 1.2.58. (Demolished. W. H. Smith store.)

EAST HAM Northeast London

EMPIRE Barking Road. (Opened 1914.) Taken over 3.28 by Denman/Gaumont, operated by Bernstein/Granada. Closed 23.5.36. (Demolished for Granada.)

PREMIER SUPER 79/81 High Street North. (Opened 12.3.21, interior decorator: Val Prince, incorporating former Premier Electric cinema as entrance hall, café and lounge area, 2468 seats. Taken over by PCT.) Taken over 2.29, part of PCT circuit. Renamed SUPER. 2118 seats. Renamed GAUMONT 21.4.52. Closed 6.4.63. (Top Rank Club for bingo, open in 1995.)

GRANADA Barking Road (enlarged site of Empire). Opened 30.11.36 by Denman/Gaumont, operated by Granada, architect: W. E. Trent, interior decorator: Theodore Komisarjevsky, 2468 seats. (Fully acquired by Granada 3.65. Closed 1.11.74. Bingo.)

EASTON, Isle of Portland, Dorset
see also Portland, Isle of

PALACE Victoria Square. (Part of Albany Ward circuit. Taken over by PCT.) Taken over 2.29, part of PCT circuit. Closed c1931. (Re-opened c1947 by independent. Closed c1960. Youth club. Demolished. Housing.)

EDGWARE North London — see Burnt Oak

EDGWARE ROAD North London

GRAND 280/284 Edgware Road. (Opened 18.10.26, second enlargement of existing Grand cinema, architect: E. A. Stone.) Taken over c5.28 by Denman/Gaumont. 1942 seats. Renamed GAUMONT 23.7.51. Closed 1.4.61 by Compulsory Purchase Order. (Demolished for road widening.)

EDINBURGH Lothian
see also Abbeymount and Leith

CINEMA HOUSE 18 Nicolson Street. (Opened 9.6.11 as North British Electric Theatre. Taken over by Thomas Ormiston circuit.) Taken over 3.28 by Denman/Gaumont. Closed 24.5.30. (Salvation Army citadel from c1940.)
NEW PICTURE HOUSE 56/57 Princes Street.

(Opened 21.10.13 by PCT, architects: Anderson and Alexander, constructed within banqueting hall of Royal Hotel, 850 seats.) Taken over 2.29, part of PCT circuit. 958 seats. Closed 26.5.51. (Demolished with Royal Hotel. Marks and Spencer store from 6.57 plus new Mount Royal Hotel.)

ST. ANDREW'S SQUARE PICTURE HOUSE Clyde Street and North Clyde Street. (Opened 1.1.23, converted from Royal Veterinary College. Taken over by GTC.) Taken over 5.28, part of GTC circuit. 1421 seats. Closed 12.11.52 by fire in the afternoon. (Demolished. Bus station.)

RUTLAND Canning Street, corner of Torpichen Street. Opened 28.4.30 by Gaumont/GTC, architect: T. Bowhill Gibson, 2187 seats. Renamed GAUMONT 6.3.50. Closed 30.5.62 by fire. (Demolished. Part of Lothian Regional Education offices.)

NEW VICTORIA 7 Clerk Street. Opened 25.8.30 by Gaumont/PCT, architects: W. E. Trent and J. W. Jordan, 2058 seats: 1226 stalls + 772 balcony + 60 in boxes. Modernised 1960 with proscenium arch modified. Renamed ODEON 6.4.64. 1784 seats. Listed building. Triple from 3.4.82, 695 seats (old balcony) + 293 + 201 seats (both in former stalls). ODEON 4, 259 seats in former front stalls, and ODEON 5, 182 seats on former stage, both opened 12.89. All open in 1995.)

EDMONTON North London

EMPIRE 10 New Road. (Opened 18.4.27 by Bernstein Theatres, former music hall with some film use.) Taken over by Denman/Gaumont, operated by Bernstein/Granada. Reconstructed, architect: Cecil Masey, interior decorator: Theodore Komisarjevksy, and re-opened 28.8.33, 2500 seats. Renamed GRANADA 1.1.51. (Fully acquired by Granada 3.65. Closed 13.7.68. Bingo. Closed and demolished.)

REGAL Silver Street and Fore Street. (Opened 8.3.34 by A. E. Abrahams' circuit, architect: Clifford Aish, 2940 seats. Leased by Hyams & Gale 12.3.34.) Taken over 10.35 by Gaumont Super Cinemas. Taken over fully 28.2.44. Closed 15.7.72. (Sundown discotheque. Films returned. Closed 3.8.74. Top Rank Club for

bingo. Closed c1985. Demolished 1985. Supermarket.)

EGLINTON TOLL Glasgow

B. B. CINERAMA 201 Victoria Road, corner of Butterbiggins Road. (Opened 7.8.22 by J. J. Bennell circuit, architect: McInnes Gardner.) Taken over 12.28 by Gaumont. Auditorium extended at screen end, architect: James L. Ross, and re-opened 1931, 2662 seats. Renamed NEW CINERAMA c1940. Renamed ODEON 24.2.64. 2003 seats. Then circle only for film shows. Closed 17 or 24.10.81. (Demolished late 1986. Petrol station in 1994.)

EGREMONT Wallasey

LYCEUM King Street. (Opened 1.10, former church. Operated by Bedford Cinemas circuit. Taken over 3.28 by GTC.) Taken over 5.28, part of GTC circuit. 700 seats. Destroyed by fire morning of 30.12.31. (Demolished 3.33 for new Gaumont Palace.)

GAUMONT PALACE King Street. Opened 13.11.33 by Gaumont/GTC, architect: W. E. Trent, 1209 seats, stadium plan. Renamed GAUMONT. (Taken over by Classic 2.12.67, renamed Classic. Bingo briefly in 1969. Taken over by Unit 4 cinemas 29.9.74. Divided into four cinemas — three in former stalls area, one in raised rear section — from 30.3.75 and re-named Unit 4. Unit 5 & 6 added 20.5.79 by dividing rear section into three. Renamed Apollo 6. 181 & 127 & 177 & 105 & 91 & 92 seats. All open in 1995.)

ELEPHANT AND CASTLE South London
see also Kennington

TROCADERO 5 New Kent Road. (Opened 22.12.30 by Hyams and Gale, architect: George Coles, 3500 seats.) Taken over 10.35 by Gaumont Super Cinemas. Closed mid-10.40. Re-opened 2.11.40, initially weekends only. Closed 10.5.41 by bomb damage for several weeks. Taken over fully from 28.2.44. 3329 seats. Closed 19.10.63. (Demolished. New Odeon in redevelopment, opened 22.12.66. Taken over by Panton and renamed Coronet. Closed 28.7.88 and demolished. Car park.)

ELTHAM HILL Southeast London

ODEON Eltham Hill. (Opened 14.4.38 by Odeon, architect: Andrew Mather, 1711 seats, semi-stadium plan.) Renamed GAUMONT 28.11.49. Closed 16.9.67. (Top Rank Club for bingo from 26.10.67, open in 1995.)

ENFIELD North London
RIALTO Burleigh Way. (Opened 8.11.20, former live theatre. Part of Bernstein circuit.) Taken over 3.28 by Denman/Gaumont, operated by Bernstein/Granada. 1258 seats. (Fully acquired by Granada 3.65. Renamed Granada 7.67. Closed 10.7.71. Bingo, open in 1995.)

EXETER Devon
PALLADIUM 93/94 Paris Street. (Opened 7.9.12 as Queen's Hall, for variety/dancing, possibly with some films. Taken over by Albany Ward by 1.14, 1100 seats. Modernised and renamed Palladium 1921, full-time cinema, 800 seats. Taken over by PCT 9.27.) Taken over 2.29, part of PCT circuit. Closed 20.10.40. (Taken over by government for wartime use as store. Severely damaged by bombing 5.42. Site cleared for local council offices & road widening.)
GAUMONT PALACE 12 North Street. Opened 16.5.32 by Gaumont/Albany Ward-PCT, architect: W. H. Watkins (Percy Bartlett), 1449 seats, stadium plan. Renamed GAUMONT c1937. Closed 2.5.42 after World War Two bomb damage. Re-opened 24.5.43. Closed 4.5.63. (Top Rank Club for bingo from 16.5.63, open in 1995.)

FALKIRK Central Scotland
PAVILION Newmarket Street. (Opened 8.14, 950 seats. Taken over by Thomas Ormiston circuit.) Taken over 3.28 by Denman/Gaumont. Enlarged by 6.33, 1337 seats. Renamed GAUMONT 3.4.50. Renamed ODEON 16.12.62. Closed 22.9.73. (Demolished. Shops and offices.)

FINCHLEY North London
GRAND HALL Tally Ho Corner. (Part of National Electric circuit.) Taken over 3.28 by Denman/Gaumont. 1093 seats. Closed c1936.
NEW BOHEMIA Church End. (Opened 3.20, architect: C. Dudley Lewis, 1000 seats. Taken over c7.26 by National Electric circuit.) Taken over 3.28 by Denman/Gaumont. 1114 seats. Closed 4.4.59. (Demolished. Gateway House.)
GAUMONT Tally Ho Corner. Opened 19.7.37

by Gaumont/PCT, architects: W. E. Trent, W. Sydney Trent & R. Golding, 2165 seats: 1390 stalls & 725 balcony. Circle closed, stalls reduced to 831 in 70s. Closed 25.10.80. (Demolished c1986.)

FINSBURY PARK North London
CINEMA Stroud Green Road/Seven Sisters Road. (Opened 1.10.09 as the Rink, architects: Fair, Mayer & Marshall, designed as skating rink, adapted before opening for cinema use. Balcony added 1916, architect: E. A. Stone. Re-opened 17.5.20 by APPH with new entrance and foyer on Seven Sisters Road using former Pyke's Cinematograph Theatre, 2800 seats.) Taken over 2.29, part of PCT/APPH circuit. 2092 seats. Renamed GAUMONT 14.8.50. Closed 12.7.58. (Dance hall from 20.8.59. Bingo. Closed 1984. Snooker hall and bowling alley. Entrance on Seven Sisters Road demolished.)

FROME Somerset
PALACE THEATRE Church Slope. (Taken over by PCT.) Taken over 2.29, part of PCT circuit. Closed 4.2.39, replaced by new Gaumont.
GAUMONT Cork Street. Opened 6.2.39 by Gaumont/Albany Ward-PCT, architects: W. E. Trent, W. Sydney Trent & H. G. Payne, 1000 seats, stadium plan. (Taken over by Classic 9.12.67, renamed Classic. Closed 10.1.71. Demolished. New Westway cinema opened 21.3.74, 350 seats, in redevelopment. Open in 1995.)

FULHAM West London — see Walham Green

GAINSBOROUGH Lincolnshire
ELECTRIC Caskgate Street. (Opened 1.4.11, former chapel and theatre. Closed 1925. Re-opened 1925. Closed c9.27. Part of Gale and Repard circuit.) Taken over closed in 3.28 by Denman/Gaumont. Never re-opened.
GRAND 15 Market Place. (Opened 1.6.25. Part of Gale and Repard circuit.) Taken over 3.28 by Denman/Gaumont. 1260 seats. Renamed GAUMONT c1949. Modernised and re-opened 29.3.54. (Taken over by independent 1.5.60, renamed Grand. Closed 4.61. Part of Co-Op store with facade rebuilt.)
KING'S THEATRE Trinity Street. (Opened

1911, former Albert Hall and live theatre. Closed 22.1.25 by fire. Re-opened 5.9.27.) Taken over c10.28 by Denman/Gaumont. 750 seats. Closed 10.7.37. (Taken over 2.8.37 by J. F. Emery circuit. Repertory and variety theatre. Bingo in 1992.)

GATESHEAD Tyne and Wear
NEW PALACE THEATRE Sunderland Road. (Opened 1909, former live theatre. Part of Thompson and Collins circuit.) Taken over 3.28 by Denman/Gaumont, 700 seats. Renamed PALACE. Closed 24.9.60. (Sold 5.1.62. Warehouse, open in 1995 as Elders Glass.)
SCALA THEATRE High Street & Jackson Street. (Opened 11.2.19, former Metropole live theatre, 1250 seats. Part of Thompson and Collins circuit.) Taken over 3.28 by Denman/Gaumont. Closed 29.9.56. (Demolished 1960, except High Street entrance — shops in 1995.)

GILLINGHAM Kent — see Chatham

GLASGOW Strathclyde
see also Anniesland, Dennistoun, Eglinton Toll, Ibrox, King's Park, Partick and Townhead
NEW SAVOY PICTURE HOUSE Hope Street. (Opened 21.12.16, converted music hall, architect: George A. Boswell. Part of Biocolour circuit.) Part of original circuit in 3.27. Modernised and re-opened 9.7.34, 2000 seats. Renamed SAVOY 27.9.58. (Majestic Ballroom. Closed 15.1.72. Demolition started. Destroyed by fire 20.3.72. Part of Savoy Centre and Savoy Tower, shops and offices.)
PICTURE HOUSE 140 Sauchiehall Street. (Opened 19.12.10 by PCT, architects: Naylor & Sale. Reconstructed, architects: Naylor and Sale, and re-opened 12.12, 1084 seats. Reconstructed 1925, architect: Percy L. Browne.) Taken over 2.29, part of PCT circuit. 1600 seats. Renamed GAUMONT c1948. Modernised c1960. Closed 15.1.72. (Demolition started. Destroyed by fire 20.3.72, except for facade, retained in redevelopment. Part of Savoy Centre and Savoy Tower, shops and offices.)

GLOSSOP Derbyshire
PALACE THEATRE George Street. (Part of

PCT circuit.) Taken over 2.29, part of PCT circuit. Closed c1931. (Sold 12.36 to Glossop Corp. as site for new bus station and waiting rooms.)
EMPIRE THEATRE 60/64 High Street West. (Opened 4.21. Taken over by PCT in 1926.) Taken over 2.29, part of PCT circuit. 1022 seats. Closed 27.7.63. (Supermarket.)

GLOUCESTER Gloucestershire

HIPPODROME Eastgate Street. (Opened 20.6.11 as City. Renamed Hippodrome 1.3.15. Taken over 1922 by Poole's circuit. Reconstructed, architects: Chadwick, Watson, and re-opened 9.35, 1600 seats. Closed 23.10.55 by fire. Reconstructed and re-opened 18.6.56.) Taken over 1.10.56 by Rank. Renamed GAUMONT 1959. Closed 22.4.61. (Demolished 1964. British Home Stores.)

GORSE HILL Swindon — see Swindon

GORTON Greater Manchester

CORONA Birch Street. (Opened 4.15, 1000 seats. Part of New Century Pictures circuit.) Taken over 3.28 by Denman/Gaumont. 1100 seats. Closed 30.4.50. (Sold 31.5.50 to Snape circuit, continued as cinema. Closed c1957. Mayflower Cabaret Club. Derelict from c1980. Demolished 4 & 5.85.)

GOSFORTH Tyne and Wear

GLOBE THEATRE Salters Road. (Opened pre-1915. Taken over by GTC.) Taken over 5.28, part of GTC circuit. 883 seats. (Leased c1935 to E. J. Hinge circuit. Closed 25.11.61. Bingo until 1990. Reconstructed internally — shops and vacant space in 1995.)

GREENOCK Strathclyde

PICTURE PALACE 5/7 Brougham St. (Opened 30.12.29 as New Palace, adjacent to old Palace. 1700 seats.) Taken over 5.9.55 by Rank, renamed GAUMONT. 1395 seats. Closed 6.12.80 or 24.1.81.

GRIMSBY Humberside

SAVOY Victoria Street. (Opened 1920.) Part of original circuit in 3.27. 1430 seats. Renamed GAUMONT 10.4.50. Renamed ODEON 21.10.62. 1241 seats. (Taken over by Brent

Walker 5.10.75, renamed Focus. Closed 24.12.77. Shops from c1983.)

GUERNSEY Channel Islands —
see St. Peter Port

GUILDFORD Surrey

PLAYHOUSE High Street. (Opened c1922. Taken over by County 1929. Taken over by Odeon. 925 seats.) Played Gaumont release and listed as a Gaumont in 1950s. Closed 12.6.65.

HACKNEY North London

PAVILION 290 Mare Street. (Opened 5.14, 1500 seats. Taken over 4.28 by PCT.) Taken over 2.29, part of PCT circuit. 1117 seats. Closed 22.1.72. (Demolished. Barclays Bank in 1995.)

HALIFAX West Yorkshire

ELECTRIC 72 Commercial Street. (Opened 1911, former riding school, 800 seats. Part of National Electric circuit.) Taken over 3.28 by Denman/Gaumont. Improved and enlarged 1928, architects: Horsfall and Dawson, 1100 seats. Enlarged c1935, 1728 seats. Modernised with facade rebuilt, architect: W.E. Trent, re-opened 22.5.39, 1536 seats. Closed 29.9.56. (Foyer into car showroom. Snooker club from 1.9.83.)
PICTURE HOUSE Ward's End. (Opened 20.10.13 by PCT, 1300 seats. Taken over 1914 by APPH.) Taken over 2.28, part of PCT/APPH circuit. 1384 seats. Closed c4.47 by fire. Re-opened 1.48, renamed GAUMONT. Closed 26.11.60. (Bingo. Taken over by independent and re-opened 18.4.73 as Astra Entertainment Centre with bingo + Astra 1 & 2 cinemas in old circle, 200 + 200 seats. Cinemas closed 5.6.82. Nightclub & disco from c1987, open in 1994.)

HAMILTON Strathclyde

LA SCALA Keith Street. (Opened 3.21, architect: James McKissack. Part of Thomas Ormiston circuit.) Taken over 3.28 by Denman/Gaumont. 1297 seats. Renamed GAUMONT 10.4.50. Closed 5.11.60. (Bingo.)

HAMMERSMITH West London

GAUMONT PALACE Queen Caroline Street.

Opened 28.3.32 by Gaumont, architect: Robert Cromie, 3487 seats. Renamed GAUMONT c1937. Renamed ODEON 25.11.62. (Concert venue with very occasional films by early 1980s. Grade II listed building from 26.3.90. Taken over 6.92 by Apollo, renamed Apollo. Renamed Labatt's Apollo. Concert and show venue only, open in 1995.)

HANDSWORTH Birmingham

VILLA CROSS PICTURE HOUSE Heathfield Road. (Opened 5.13 or later. Part of Shapeero circuit.) Taken over 3.28 by Denman/Gaumont. 1200 seats. Closed 18.4.70. (Asian cinema. Bingo. Closed 1984. Badly damaged 9.9.85 in riots. Demolished c1989.)

HANLEY Stoke-on-Trent Staffordshire
see also Stoke-on-Trent

EMPIRE Piccadilly, Brunswick Street (also entrance on Trinity Street). (Opened 26.12.10. Part of Biocolour circuit.) Part of original Gaumont circuit in 3.27. 929 seats. Closed 29.9.56. (Demolished. Shops.)
REGENT Piccadilly. Opened 11.2.29 by Gaumont/PCT, architect: W. E. Trent, 2151 seats. Renamed GAUMONT 25.9.50. Triple from 12.5.74, 1137 seats (balcony + front stalls) + 159 + 159 seats (both in former rear stalls). Renamed ODEON 1, 2 & 3 from 6.6.76. Closed 12.10.89. (Grade II listed building from 30.11.89. Raised to Grade II*.)

HARBORNE Birmingham

PICTURE HOUSE Serpentine Road. (Opened 1914. Part of Shapeero circuit.) Taken over 3.28 by Denman/Gaumont, 714 seats. Closed 13 (or 27).4.57. (Harborne Village Social Club and Institute.)

HARLESDEN Northwest London

HIPPODROME High Street. (Opened 19.2.27 by Bernstein Theatres, former music hall, known as Willesden Hippodrome.) Taken over 3.28 by Denman/Gaumont, managed by Bernstein. (Taken over c1928 by Abrahams. Taken over c8.30 by ABC. 1900 seats. Closed 9.38. Re-opened as music hall, films on Sundays. Bombed 1940. Demolished 1957.)

HARROGATE South Yorkshire

SCALA Cambridge Street. (Opened 4.10.20,

part of New Century Pictures circuit. 1400 seats.) Taken over 3.28 by Denman/Gaumont. 1366 seats. Renamed GAUMONT 12.6.50. Closed 26.9.59. (Sold 29.9.59. Demolished 1962. Littlewood's store.)

HARROW North London — see Kingsbury and Rayners Lane

HAYMARKET London — see London West End

HEATON Newcastle
SCALA Chillingham Road and Tosson Terrace. (Opened 10.3.13, 1200 seats. Taken over 3.28 by GTC.) Taken over 5.28, part of GTC circuit. (Leased 4.36 by Essoldo. Closed 1.7.61. Demolished. Supermarket.)

HENDON North London
AMBASSADOR Hendon Central. (Opened 15.2.32 by London and Southern Super Cinemas, architects: Henry F. Webb and Ash [G. E. McLeavy], 1937 seats.) Taken over by Gaumont 12.33. Renamed GAUMONT 1949. (Taken over by Classic 16.12.67, renamed Classic. Triple from 15.2.73, 580 & 399 & 423. Renamed MGM in 1993. All open in 1995.)

HIGHBURY North London
IMPERIAL 2 Holloway Road. (Opened 26.12.12, architect: A. Constantine, 1750 seats. Taken over 3.28 by GTC.) Taken over 5.28, part of GTC circuit. Renamed PICTURE HOUSE c1945. Closed 11.4.59. (Demolished. Regent Lion petrol station. Majestic Wine warehouse.)

HINCKLEY Leicestershire
REGENT Rugby Road and Lancaster Road. (Opened 11.3.29, architect: Horace G. Bradley, 920 seats, as cinema and theatre, starting with live show. Taken over by Odeon 29.7.35.) Renamed GAUMONT 18.4.55. (Taken over by Classic 2.12.67, renamed Classic. Closed 30.6.68. Bingo.)

HOLBORN Central London
EMPIRE 242/5 High Holborn. (Music hall, with some films shown by 1914. Taken over 3.28 by GTC.) Taken over 5.28, part of GTC circuit. Music hall. (Bombed 1941. Projection-

ists' training centre. Taken over 1946 by Moss Empires. Demolished 1961 for extension of Pearl Assurance offices.)

HOLLOWAY North London
see also Highbury

EMPIRE 556/564 Holloway Road. (Opened 1916, former variety theatre with some films shown from 1902. 1210 seats. Part of Biocolour circuit.) Part of original Gaumont circuit in 3.27. 1140 seats. Closed 8.38. (Warehouse. Demolished. Office block.)

MARLBOROUGH THEATRE 383 Holloway Road. (Opened 28.5.18, former live theatre with some films shown earlier. Taken over 1925 by PCT, 2612 seats.) Taken over 2.29, part of PCT circuit. 1685 seats. Closed 9.40. (Taken over by Odeon, re-opened 9.3.42, 1500 seats. Closed 31.8.57. Demolished 1962. Marlborough House office block.)

GAUMONT 417/427 Holloway Road. Opened 5.9.38 by Gaumont/GTC, architect: C. Howard Crane, alterations: W. E. Trent, 3006 seats. Closed 11.8.44 by wartime bomb damage. Auditorium reconstructed, architects: T. P. Bennett & Son, and re-opened 21.7.58, 1987 seats. Renamed ODEON 25.11.62. Triple from 6.5.73, 614 (former balcony) & 216 & 216 seats (former rear stalls). ODEON 1 in former balcony closed 4.9.88 for subdivision into two cinemas plus new cinema in former front stalls area - all three opened 16.12.88. ODEON 6 opened 5.6.92 over main foyer, 78 seats. All open in 1995: 397 & 209 & 269 & 394 & 361 & 78 seats.

HOUNSLOW West London
DOMINION London Road, corner of North Drive. (Opened 28.12.31, architect: F. E. Bromige, 2022 seats. Taken over by Odeon c7.37.) Listed as a Gaumont theatre in 1950s. (Closed 30.12.61. (Top Rank Club for bingo from 3.62, open in 1995.)

HOXTON North London
BRITANNIA THEATRE Hoxton Street. (Opened 1923, former live theatre with some films shown earlier. Part of Biocolour circuit.) Part of original Gaumont circuit in 3.27. 2972 seats. Destroyed 1940 by wartime bomb.

YE OLDE VARIETIES 18-20 Pitfield Street.

(Opened 1910, former Hoxton Variety Theatre, also known as Raymond's Old Varieties, with some films shown. Taken over by Hyams circuit. Full-time cinema.) Taken over 3.28 by Denman/Gaumont. Renamed HOXTON CINEMA THEATRE. 572 seats. Closed 1941. (Sold 24.7.70 to Walmore Electronics. Demolished 1981. Houses.)

CINEMA 55 Pitfield Street. (Opened 20.1.14, architects: Lovegrove and Papworth. Taken over by Hyams circuit.) Taken over 3.28 by Denman/Gaumont. 866 seats. Closed during Blitz, re-opened 23.2.41. Closed 27.10.56. (Sold 3.6.60. Premises of delicatessen importers and wholesalers. Disused by 1990.)

HULL Humberside
HOLDERNESS HALL Holderness Road, Witham. (Opened 16.11.12.) Taken over 1931 by Gaumont. 1850 seats. Renamed GAUMONT 3.7.50. Closed 21.11.59. (Majestic dance hall. Closed 7.3.65. Bingo.)

HUNSLET Leeds
PAVILION 250 Dewsbury Road. (Opened c8.11, architect: G. Frederick Bowman, 820 seats. Part of North of England Cinemas circuit.) Taken over 3.28 by Denman/Gaumont. Closed 29.9.56. (Sold 10.11.58. Furniture warehouse.)

HYSON GREEN Nottingham
GRAND Radford Road. (Opened 19.10.25,, former live theatre with some film use. Part of Shapeero circuit.) Taken over 3.28 by Denman/Gaumont. 1026 seats. Closed 29.9.56. (Garden of Rest in 1995.)

IBROX Glasgow
CAPITOL 5 Lorne Street. (Opened 11.4.27, architect: John Fairweather, 2062 seats.) Taken over 6.28 by Denman/Gaumont. Renamed GAUMONT 1.56. Closed 5.8.61. (Bingo, open as Mecca Club in 1995.)

ILFORD East London
SUPER Ley Street and Balfour Road. (Opened 14.10.22, architect: W. E. Trent, interior decorator: Val Prince. Taken over c1924 by PCT.) Taken over 2.29, part of PCT circuit. 2336 seats. Closed 2.45.by wartime bomb damage. (Demolished 1956. Sold 4.6.58. C&A store.)

ILFRACOMBE Devon

ALEXANDRA HALL. Part of Albany Ward-PCT circuit in 3.29. Possibly same as Palace.

PALACE. Part of Albany Ward-PCT circuit in 3.29. Closed c1930. (Shown on 1952 property records as formerly Gaumont owned but let for non-cinema use, then recently sold.)

SCALA THEATRE Hill Street. (Opened 20.12.20. Part of Albany Ward circuit. Taken over 9.27 by PCT.) Taken over 2.29, part of PCT circuit. 1000 seats. Renamed GAUMONT 11.12.50. Closed late 1957. Re-opened for summer seasons. (Taken over c1961 by Clifton circuit, renamed Clifton. 666 seats. Basement cinema added 10.73, 120 seats. Both open summer season only by 1980. Both closed 1983. Demolished. Clifton Flats.)

IPSWICH Suffolk

REGENT Major's Corner/8 St. Helens Street. Opened 4.11.29 by Gaumont/PCT, architect: W. E. Trent, 1800 seats, stadium plan: 1070 stalls & 660 raised rear section & 70 from 14 boxes of 5 seats. Renamed GAUMONT 24.4.50. 1666 seats. Seating increased to 1813 in 1985, mostly live show use. GAUMONT 2 opened 22.8.83 in former restaurant/ballroom area, 186 seats. Both renamed ODEON 9.1.87. Both closed 20.3.91. (Main auditorium re-opened late 21.9.91 as live theatre, renamed Regent. Open in 1995.)

ISLINGTON North London

BLUE HALL 54 Upper Street (part of Royal Agricultural Hall). (Opened 1901 as Mohawk Hall, formerly St. Mary's Hall, some films shown earlier. Renamed Empire in 1902, films plus variety. Renamed Palace in 1908, full-time cinema. Renamed Blue Hall in 1918. Taken over 3.28 by GCT.) Taken over 5.28, part of GTC circuit, 1303 seats. Renamed GAUMONT 2.7.51. Closed 5.1.63. (Bingo. Grade II listed building. Closed 7.6.75. Demolished 1985. Open space.)

BLUE HALL ANNEXE 46 Essex Road, corner of Packington Street. (Opened 7.11 as Coronet, 740 seats, conversion of post office, architect: A. W. Hudson. Renamed Blue Hall Annexe in 1924. Taken over 3.28 by GTC.) Taken over 5.28, part of GTC circuit, 599 seats. Closed 1941. (William Bedford Antiques in 1995.)

ANGEL 7 High Street (stalls entrance in White Lion Street). (Opened 31.12.12 by Davis circuit, architect: H. Courtenay Constantine, 1463 seats. Taken over by APPH 8.26.) Taken over 2.29, part of PCT/APPH circuit, 1403 seats. Listed as an Odeon theatre in 1950s. Renamed ODEON 1.9.63. Closed 18.3.72. (Auditorium demolished 1974. Offices. Tower frontage Grade II listed building from 31.1.91.)

JERSEY Channel Islands — see St. Helier

KENNINGTON South London

KENNINGTON THEATRE Kennington Park Road, South Place and De Laune Street. (Opened 28.2.21, former live theatre. 1347 seats. Part of United Pictures Theatres circuit from 1.28.) Under Gaumont management from 7.30 as part of UPT circuit. Closed 1934. (Taken over by Odeon as site for new cinema, not re-opened. Bomb damaged in war. Demolition started 4.43. Site taken over by compulsory purchase order c1950. Block of flats.)

PRINCES 2/6 Kennington Park Road. (Opened 22.1.23 as Princes Picture Playhouse, architect: Cecil Masey. 1600 seats.) Taken over 1933 by Gaumont/PCT. Destroyed 10.5.41 by wartime bomb.

KENSINGTON Liverpool

CASINO 6 Prescot Road and Sheil Road, Fairfield. (Opened 4.8.23, 1659 seats. Taken over 3.28 by GTC.) Taken over 5.28, part of GTC circuit. Closed 30.12.61. (Top Rank Club for bingo in 1995.)

KENSINGTON London — see West Kensington

KENTISH TOWN North London

PALACE 197 Kentish Town Road. (Opened 8.12.13, architect: J. Stanley Beard, 1200 seats. Taken over 1920 by PCT.) Taken over 2.29, part of PCT circuit. 1058 seats. Renamed GAUMONT in 1948. Closed 4.4.59. (Offices.)

KETTERING Northamptonshire

ELECTRIC PAVILION High Street. (Opened 10.5.13, 650 seats, one floor. Taken over 1919 by Shapeero circuit.) Taken over 3.28 by Denman/Gaumont. 800 seats. Renamed

PAVILION 22.5.50. Closed 2.9.53 for modernisation. Re-opened 26.9.53 as GAUMONT. Closed 10.10.59. (Demolished. Boots store.)

KILBURN North London
see also Maida Vale

PICTURE PALACE 256 Belsize Road. (Opened 2.8.09, former Theatre Royal. 514 seats. Enlarged. Part of United Pictures Theatres circuit from 1.28.) Under Gaumont management from 7.30 as part of UPT circuit. 1775 seats. Closed late 1940. (Demolished. Offices on front of site.)

GRANGE High Road, Grangeway and Messina Road. (Opened 30.7.14, architect: Edward A. Stone. 2028 seats. Taken over by PCT/Scala. Transferred 5.27 to APPH.) Taken over 2.29, part of PCT/APPH circuit. Closed 14.6.75. (Re-opened 23.2.76 as Butty's cabaret and dance hall. National nightclub. Grade II listed building from 5.2.91.)

GAUMONT STATE 195/9 High Road and Willesden Lane. Opened 20.12.37 by Gaumont Super Cinemas, architect: George Coles, 4004 seats: 2648 stalls & 1356 balcony. Closed mid-10.40 by wartime conditions. Re-opened 2.11.40, initially weekends only. Fully taken over 28.2.44. Closed 16.1.60 for conversion of stalls area beneath balcony into ballroom, later bingo club. Re-opened, 1300 seats (+ 742 in front stalls if needed, later reduced by expansion of bingo club). Second cinema opened 23.11.75 in former restaurant/dance studio, 202 seats. Main cinema closed 18.9.80. Grade II listed building from 10.10.80. Second cinema closed 10.10.81. (Dividing wall removed and whole of main auditorium used for bingo. Second cinema re-opened 12.85 as Odeon. Closed 14.6.90. Bingo open as Mecca Club in 1995.)

KINGSBURY North London

ODEON Kingsbury Road. (Opened 30.5.34 by Odeon, architect: A. P. Starkey, 1003 seats.) Renamed GAUMONT 20.3.50. Renamed ODEON 30.5.64. Closed 9.9.72. (Demolished except for part of facade. Supermarket.)

KING'S CROSS North London

CINEMA 279 Pentonville Road, corner of King's Cross Road. (Opened 26.4.20, architect:

H. Courtenay Constantine, 1800 seats. Taken over by Davis circuit. Taken over 21.12.26 by APPH.) Taken over 2.29, part of PCT/APPH circuit. Closed 9.5.49 to repair wartime damage. Re-opened 17.3.52 as GAUMONT. Renamed ODEON 25.11.62. Closed 22.8.70. (Taken over by independent, re-opened 22.2.71 as King's Cross Cinema. Closed 29.3.75. Re-opened as the Primatarium. Stalls floor to snooker. Circle re-opened c6.81 with new screen as Scala, 350 seats. Closed 6.93. Church. Disused.)

KING'S PARK Glasgow

FLORIDA Ardmay Crescent and Millport Avenue. (Opened 28.12.31, architect: Hamilton Neil, 1640 seats.) Taken over 7.3.38 by Gaumont. Renamed GAUMONT 17.4.50. Closed 5.1.57. (Sold 13.11.61. Demolished.)

KIRKCALDY Fife

RIALTO 204 High Street. (Opened 2.24. Part of Thomas Ormiston circuit.) Taken over 3.28 by Denman/Gaumont. 1212 seats. Renamed GAUMONT 1.5.50. Renamed ODEON 16.12.62. Destroyed by fire morning of 26.12.74. (Demolished. Sold 28.8.75. House of Fraser store.)

KIRKINTILLOCH Strathclyde

PAVILION Oxford Street. (Part of Thomas Ormiston circuit.) Taken over 3.28 by Denman/Gaumont. 1000 seats. Closed c1943. (Re-opened c1945 by independent, 825 seats. Closed 29.7.61. Bingo.)

LANARK Strathclyde

PICTURE HOUSE Castlegate. (Part of Thomas Ormiston circuit.) Taken over 3.28 by Denman/Gaumont. 800 seats. (Taken over c1933 by independent. Renamed Rio c1945. Closed 6.60, gutted by fire. Demolished. Supermarket.)

LAVENDER HILL South London — see Clapham Junction

LEEDS West Yorkshire
see also Hunslet

COLISEUM Cookridge Street. (Opened 17.4.05, former concert and music hall used for film shows. Part of New Century Pictures circuit.) Taken over 3.28 by Denman/Gaumont. 2702 seats. Closed 30.4.38 for complete internal reconstruction, architects: W. E. Trent, W. Sydney Trent & Daniel Mackay. Re-opened 24.10.38 as GAUMONT, 1746 seats. Closed 23.12.61. (Top Rank bingo from 30.12.61. Closed 12.69. Rehearsal rooms and box-office for Playhouse company. Disused. Cinema interior removed. Listed 25.6.75 by City Council. Re-opened 12.80 as Norwood Studios at the Colosseum for film & TV production. Concert venue, the Colosseum, from 31.10.92.)

ASSEMBLY ROOMS New Briggate. (Opened 15.4.07, former concert hall with some films shown from 1903, 1100 seats. Part of New Century Pictures circuit.) Taken over 3.28 by Denman/Gaumont. 800 seats. Closed 5.4.58. (Taken over c8.58 by Star. Renamed Plaza 25.8.58. Closed 14.2.85. Studio space for rehearsals/exhibitions.)

SCALA Albion Place and Lands Lane. (Opened 24.7.22 by Sol Levy, 1692 seats.) Taken over 3.28 by Denman/Gaumont. Closed 31.8.57. (Sold 23.9.57. Waring and Gillow furniture store.)

HIPPODROME King Charles Croft. (Music hall. Taken over 3.28 by GTC.) Taken over 5.28, part of GTC circuit. No apparent film use. (Closed 1933. Demolished.)

SAVOY Boar Lane. (Opened 4.10.15 as City, architect: J. P. Crawford, 514 seats. Taken over by Savoy Cinemas. Closed 2.7.25 for redecoration. Re-opened 13.8.25 as Savoy. Taken over c9.28, renamed LEEDS REPERTORY CINEMA. (Taken back 30.9.29 by Savoy/ABC, renamed Savoy. Leased to Regent/ABC c5.33. Renamed Academy 19.9.33. Returned to main ABC circuit 1935. Sold. Reconstructed, architect: Peter Cummings, and re-opened 23.12.36 as Tatler, 350 seats, one floor. Closed 27.1.64. Demolished. Royal Exchange House.)

MAJESTIC City Square (Wellington Street and Quebec Street). (Opened 6.6.22, architects: Pascal J. Steinlet and J. C. Maxwell, 2392 seats. Taken over 12.25 by PCT.) Taken over 2.29, part of PCT circuit. Closed 10.7.69. (Top Rank Club for bingo. Grade II listed building from 14.6.93. Open in 1995.)

LEICESTER Leicestershire

PICTURE HOUSE 7 Granby Street (rear on Town Hall Square). (Opened 22.12.10 by PCT, architects: Naylor and Sale, 600 seats. Closed 5.5.24 for rebuilding. Re-opened 3.8.25, 1626 seats.) Taken over 2.29, part of PCT circuit. Closed 9.6.73. (Demolished from 1.81, except rear section, converted to offices. Lunn Poly travel shop and Pizzaland restaurant occupy new frontage in 1995. Rear elevation, 7-9 Town Hall Square, given Grade II listed building status.)

CITY Market Place. (Opened 3.11.24, architects: Burdwood & Mitchell, 2200 seats.) Taken over by Gaumont/PCT 4.11.29. Renamed GAUMONT 1948. Closed 11.4.64. (Auditorium demolished. New Odeon opened 12.10.64, 822 seats, above shops in arcade, retaining original facade. Closed 31.5.75. Asian films, renamed Liberty. Closed 31.5.75. Interior gutted. Cascades bingo hall in 1995.)

LEIGH Greater Manchester

PALACE Railway Road. (Opened c7.13 as New Electra Palace, 1300 seats. Taken over by APPH c1920. Renamed Palace.) Taken over 2.29, part of PCT/APPH circuit. 1028 seats. Closed 1.6.57.

LEITH Edinburgh

CAPITOL 24 Manderston Street. Opened 9.28 by Gaumont/GTC, architect: J. M. Johnston, 2600 seats. Closed 22.7.61. (Top Rank bingo from 29.7.61, open in 1995 as Mecca Club.)

LEWISHAM Southeast London
see also Rushey Green

GAUMONT PALACE Loampit Vale. Opened 12.12.32 by Gaumont, architect: W. E. Trent (assistant: James Morrison), 3050 seats. Renamed GAUMONT c1937. Modernised c1960. Closed 27.2.62 by fire. Re-opened 29.7.62, renamed ODEON, 2896 seats. Closed 14.2.81. (Disused. Demolished 1993 for roundabout.)

LEYTON North London

SAVOY Lea Bridge Road and Church Road. Opened 26.12.28, architect: George Coles, 1797 seats. Part of United Pictures Theatres circuit from 1.30.) Under Gaumont management from 7.30 as part of UPT circuit. Renamed GAUMONT 17.2.50. Renamed ODEON 2.3.64. (Taken over by independent c1968, renamed Curzon. Closed c1971. Bingo.

Taken over by Classic, balcony re-opened 26.1.73 as Classic cinema, 435 seats, with Vogue bingo in stalls. Cinema closed 10.3.79. Bingo continued.)

LEYTONSTONE North London

RIALTO 821 High Road and Kirkdale Road. (Opened 1910 as Rink, conversion of skating rink, 1550 seats on one floor. Taken over by Bernstein, re-opened 6.1.27 after alterations, architect: Cecil Masey, as Rialto, 1760 seats.) Taken over 3.28 by Denman/Gaumont, managed by Bernstein/Granada. (Acquired by Granada 3.65. Renamed Granada 25.6.67. Closed 27.4.74. Demolished.)

CENTURY High Road, Harrow Green. (Opened 29.3.13 as Academy, 650 seats. Closed 26.8.33. Enlarged with new facade, architect: F. C. Mitchell, and re-opened 2.10.33, 1100 seats. Taken over by Granada, closed 1.10.55 for renovations, architect: George Coles. Re-opened 28.11.55 as Century.) Taken over 28.7.57 by Denman (London), but continued to be operated by Granada. Closed 5.1.63. (Bingo. Acquired by Granada 3.65. Closed 7.83. Demolished.)

LINCOLN Lincolnshire

CORN EXCHANGE Cornhill, Market Square. (Opened 28.5.10 as Cinematograph Hall, 1750 seats on one floor. Part of Gale and Repard circuit.) Taken over 3.28 by Denman/ Gaumont. (Taken over by independent 1931. Renamed Exchange. Refurbished, re-opened 8.2.54, renamed Astoria, 1008 seats. Taken over/taken back by Rank 2.1.56. Closed 23.6.56. Roller skating rink from 2.57. Bingo from 1972. Closed. McDonalds fast food establishment in entrance from 1982.)

LITTLE SUTTON Merseyside

KING'S HALL. (Opened c1913. Taken over 3.28 by GTC.) Taken over 5.28, part of GTC holdings. Never actually operated by GTC or Gaumont, but leased out until at least 1952. (Closed by fire early 27.1.50. Re-opened 16.12.50. 350 seats. Closed c10.59. Recreation hall. Gymnasium.)

LIVERPOOL Merseyside

see also Aigburth, Allerton, Anfield Bootle, Crosby, Dingle, Kensington, Little Sutton, Paddington, Princes Park, Sefton Park, Tue Brook, Walton and Wavertree

MOUNT PLEASANT PICTURE HALL Mount Pleasant. (Opened 14.12.08 as New Century Picture Hall, conversion of Wesleyan chapel, by New Century Pictures circuit. 850 seats. Renamed Mount Pleasant Picture Hall.) Taken over 3.28 by Denman/Gaumont. Closed 1.12.28 for improvements. Re-opened 26.12.28 as CENTURY REPERTORY THEATRE. Closed 15.2.30. (Auction rooms. Billiard hall. Carpet showroom. Jazz club. Demolished c1972. Multi-storey car park.)

ROYAL HIPPODROME West Derby Road. (Music hall with some film use. Taken over 3.28 by GTC.) Taken over 5.28 as variety theatre, part of GTC circuit. Closed 20.6.31. Re-opened 20.7.31 as fulltime cinema, renamed HIPPODROME, 3200 seats. Closed 16.5.70. (Sold to Liverpool Corp. 28.6.72. Demolished 1984.)

SAVOY West Derby Road. (Opened 23 or 25.2.15. 700 seats. Taken over by GTC c3.28.) Taken over 5.28 as part of GCT circuit. 681 seats. Closed 29.9.56. (Lino store. Car showroom. Offices.)

RIALTO Upper Parliament Street and Berkeley Street. (Opened 7.10.27, architect: Edwin Sheridan Gray of Gray & Evans, 1805 seats. Taken over 3.28 by GTC.) Taken over 5.28, part of GTC circuit. Closed 29.2.64. (Bingo. Antique furniture store. Badly damaged in 1980 by fire during riots. Demolished.)

TROCADERO SUPER Camden Street. (Opened 13.4.22, architects: Rees & Holt, 1347 seats. Taken over by PCT c5.27.) Taken over 2.29, part of PCT circuit. Reconstructed 8.31, 1298 seats. Renamed GAUMONT 18.9.50. Closed 4.5.74. (Snooker club.)

LONDON City of London

for Daily Bioscope, pre-circuit hall, see Chapter 1

LONDON West End

see also Victoria

for suburbs see Acton, Balham, Barnet, Bermondsey, Bethnal Green, Bromley, Burnt Oak, Camden Town, Canning Town, Chadwell Heath, Chelsea, Clapham, Cricklewood, Dagenham, Dalston, Ealing, East Ham, Edgware Road, Edmonton, Elephant and Castle, Eltham Hill, Finchley, Finsbury Park, Hackney, Hammersmith, Hendon, Highbury, Hounslow, Hoxton, Islington, Kentish Town, Kilburn, Kingsbury, King's Cross, Lewisham, Leyton, New Cross, Notting Hill, Old Kent Road, Palmers Green, Peckham, Penge, Putney, Rayners Lane, Richmond, Romford, Rose Hill, Rushey Green, Shepherds Bush, Southall, Stamford Hill, Stepney, Stratford, Streatham, Sutton, Tottenham, Twickenham, Upminster, Walham Green, Wandsworth, Wembley, West Norwood, Wimbledon and Wood Green

SHAFTESBURY AVENUE PAVILION 101 Shaftesbury Avenue. (Opened 19.10.12 by Israel Davis, 750 seats.) Part of original circuit in 3.27. Modernised, architects: Nicholas and Dixon-Spain, and re-opened 18.8.30 as G. B. MOVIETONE NEWS THEATRE, 510 seats. Renamed GAUMONT NEWS THEATRE 1.5.39. Closed during height of Blitz. Re-opened 11.40. Closed 12.40 by bomb damage. (Sold 31.1.55. Demolished. Wingate House and Columbia cinema on enlarged site. Cinema renamed Curzon West End. Open.)

MARBLE ARCH PAVILION, 531 Oxford Street. (Opened 30.5.14 by Israel Davis, architect: Frank T. Verity, 1189 seats.) Part of original circuit in 3.27. Closed 9.40 by war conditions. Re-opened 10.11.40. (Taken over 2.10.52 by independent. Closed 24.3.56. Demolished. Shops.)

PALLADIUM Argyle Street. (Opened 19.3.28 by GTC, former music hall, some variety acts and orchestra retained.) Taken over 5.28, part of GTC circuit. Films ended 23.6.28. (Reverted 25.6.28 to live theatre. Variety and live shows. Sold 12.46 to Moss Empires. Open.)

ASTORIA Charing Cross Road. (Opened 12.1.27 by Lyons and Underwood, conversion of pickle factory, architect: Edward A. Stone, 1650 seats. Taken over 3.28 by GTC.) Taken over 5.28, part of GTC circuit. Closed 4.9.39 on outbreak of war. Re-opened 10.12.39. Closed mid-9.40 by Blitz. Re-opened briefly in 10.40, then from 4.11.40. Modernised and re-opened 6.12.56. Closed 2.10.68. Interior gutted, re-opened 17.12.68, 1121 seats. Closed 28.2.76. (Live theatre. Concert venue. Open in 1995.)

CAPITOL Haymarket. (Opened 11.2.25, architect: Andrew Mather, 1700 seats. Taken over 3.28 by GTC.) Taken over 5.28, part of GTC circuit. Closed 18.1.36 for complete internal reconstruction. (Replaced by Gaumont Haymarket.)

NEW GALLERY 121/5 Regent Street. (Opened 14.1.13, architect: William Woodword & Sons, conversion of restaurant, 800 seats. Taken over by PCT c1919. Closed 1924 for almost total reconstruction. Re-opened 12.6.25, architects: C. F. Nicholas & J. E. Dixon-Spain, 1400 seats.) Taken over 2.29, part of PCT circuit. Closed 30.12.39 by war-time conditions. Re-opened 18.3.40. Closed mid-9.40 by Blitz. Re-opened 8.12.40. Closed. Re-opened 24.7.41. (Taken over 3.1.52 by Regent Film Distributors. Closed 13.9.53. New Gallery religious centre, some film shows. Entrance modernised. Closed 1990. Grade II listed building from 29.5.92. Disused in 1995.)

TIVOLI 65-70 Strand. (Opened 6.9.23, architects: Bertie Crewe and Gunton & Gunton, 2115 seats. Taken over 1925 by Jury-Metro-Goldwyn. Taken over 11.28 by PCT, modernised and upper circle closed, re-opened 27.11.28, 1553 seats.) Taken over 2.29, part of PCT circuit. Closed 25.6.38. Re-opened 8.38. Closed 30.9.39. Damaged 1941 by enemy action. Re-opened 22.2.43. Closed 29.9.56. (Demolished. Department store and offices.)

SUPER 105/7 Charing Cross Road. (Opened 26.8.11 as Pyke's Cambridge Circus Cinematograph Theatre, 690 seats. Closed by basement fire 26.7.15. Re-opened 8.16, renamed Super. Taken over 11.28 by United Picture Theatres.) Under Gaumont management from 7.30 as part of UPT circuit. Fully taken over 25.12.30. Renamed Tatler 16.2.31, operated as news theatre. Feature policy from 12.41. Closed 13.8.50 (Taken over by Jacey, re-opened 23.9.50. Closed 21.7.51. Re-opened 10.51 as Tatler News Theatre. Renamed Jacey 10.2.66. Renamed Jacey Tatler 12.67. Taken over 1976 by Cinecenta. Closed 29.9.76 for tripling. Re-opened 17.2.77 as Filmcenta, 134 & 160 seats [both rear stalls] & 141 [former balcony]. Taken over 30. 8.85 by Cannon. Renamed Cannon Charing Cross Road 6.12.85. Closed 7.1.87. Detripled for Marquee concert venue, open in 1995.).

DOMINION Tottenham Court Road (partly on site of former Court cinema). (Opened 3.10.29 as live theatre, shortly introducing films, architects: William & T. R. Milburn, 2835 seats. Leased for short periods by Universal and United Artists.) Taken over 16.1.33 by Gaumont/APPH. Closed 10.40 by Blitz. Re-opened 12.1.41. Refitted for Todd AO, re-opened 21.4.58, 1654 seats, upper circle closed. Live show use from 8.11.81, with occasional films. (Taken over by Apollo Leisure. Grade II listed building from 10.88. Open as live theatre only in 1995.)

GAUMONT Haymarket. Opened 4.2.37 by Gaumont/GTC, complete internal reconstruction of Capitol building with re-sited entrance, architect: W. E. Trent, 1328 seats. Closed 10.6.59. (Replaced by offices and Odeon Haymarket in basement, open in 1995.)

LUTON Bedfordshire

ELECTRIC High Town. (Opened c1912. 450 seats. Taken over 3.28 by GTC.) Taken over 5.28, part of GTC circuit. (Taken over 3.29 by Southan Morris. Renamed Plaza 5.31. Closed 10.37 by fire.)

PALACE THEATRE Mill Street. (Opened 26.12.12. Taken over 3.28 by GTC.) Taken over 5.28, part of GTC circuit. 1186 seats. Renamed GAUMONT 14.11.49. Closed 14.10.61. (Majestic Ballroom. Top Rank Club for bingo. Front reconstructed. Destroyed by fire in early hours of 28.12.82. Remains demolished 7 & 8.83. Offices and flats in 1995.)

LYDNEY Gloucestershire

PICTURE HOUSE Hill Street. (Opened 1913. Taken over by Albany Ward 1923. Part of Award circuit. Taken over by PCT 9.27.) Taken over 2.29, part of PCT/Albany Ward circuit. 530 seats. (Taken over 5.1.58 by independent. Closed c1964. Demolished. Shops.)

MAIDA VALE North London

PICTURE HOUSE 140 Maida Vale. (Opened 1912 as the Palace, architect: E. A. Stone. Taken over by PCT c1920, renamed Picture House. Transferred 5.27 to APPH.) Taken over 2.29, part of PCT/APPH circuit. 1001 seats. Closed mid 11.40 by war-time conditions. (Carlton Rooms dance hall from 1949, bingo from 1965. Grade II listed building from 5.2.91. Open as Jasmine bingo club in 1995.)

MANCHESTER
see also Chorlton-cum-Hardy, Gorton and Oldham

OXFORD PICTURE HOUSE Oxford Street. (Opened 12.11 by PCT.) Taken over 2.29, part of PCT circuit. (Taken over by independent 8.31. 1150 seats.) Taken over 12.6.60 by Rank, renamed NEW OXFORD. 854 seats. Closed 25.10.80. (Fast food restaurant.)

GAUMONT Oxford Street, corner of Great Bridgewater Street (site of Hippodrome). Opened 21.10.35 by Gaumont, built by Granada, architects: William T. Benslyn & James Morrison, interior decoration: Theodore Komisarjevsky, 2300 seats: 1300 stalls & 1000 balcony. Closed 28.1.74. (Rotters nightclub. Closed. Demolished 1990.)

MANSFIELD Nottinghamshire

ROCK Skerry Hill. (Opened 1.15. Part of Shapeero circuit.) Taken over by Denman/Gaumont 3.28. 760 seats. Closed 29.9.56. (Shop, open in 1995.)

EMPIRE Stockwell Gate. (Opened 1922, former live theatre. Part of Shapeero circuit.) Taken over by Denman/Gaumont 3.28. 823 seats. Closed 14.1.61. (Sold 28.2.62. Demolished c1972.)

MIDDLESBROUGH Cleveland

CLEVELAND HALL Newport Road. (Part of Thomas Ormiston circuit.) Taken over 3.28 by Denman/Gaumont. Closed 1930. Demolished c1936. Bus terminus.)

PAVILION Newport Road. (Opened 1913, former live theatre. Part of Thomas Ormiston circuit.) Taken over 3.28 by Denman/Gaumont. 650 seats. (Taken back c1935 by Thomas Ormiston. Closed 1957. Disco. Closed by fire in 1973. Renovated 1991 for use as rock venue.)

THEATRE ROYAL Sussex Street. (Part of Thomas Ormiston circuit.) Taken over 3.28 by Denman/Gaumont. 1450 seats. (Taken over by independent, renamed Royal 24.11.30. Taken over by Sol Sheckman. Renamed Essoldo 27.4.53. Closed 17.7.61. Demolished. Housing.)

HIPPODROME Wilson Street. (Opened c1912, former live theatre. Part of Thomas Ormiston circuit.) Taken over 3.28 by Denman/Gaumont. 2296 seats. Closed 1.12.56. (Ballroom from 1959. Showboat bingo and club. Both closed by 1987. Re-opened 1991 as club, The Venue.)

GRAND OPERA HOUSE Linthorpe Road, corner of Southfield Road. (Opened c1918, former live theatre. Opened pre-1915, former live theatre. Part of Thomas Ormiston circuit.) Taken over 3.28 by Denman/Gaumont. Closed 6.30 for major alterations including removal of gallery, architects: W. E. Trent & Ernest F. Tulley. Re-opened 30 or 31.3.31 as GAUMONT PALACE, 1700 seats. Renamed GAUMONT c1937. Closed 29.2.64. (Demolished. Shops and offices.)

MILE END ROAD Northeast London

EMPIRE 95 Mile End Road. (Former music hall, cinema from 11.12. Taken over by United Picture Theatres 1.28.) Under Gaumont management from 7.30 as part of UPT circuit. 2000 seats. (Sold to independent 1934. Taken over c1936 by ABC. Closed 3.4.38. Demolished for new Empire.)

MONMOUTH Gwent

PICTURE HOUSE 18 Church Street. (Opened c1916 as Palace, 400 seats, former live theatre. Taken over by Albany Ward. Part of Award circuit. Taken over 9.27 by PCT. Auditorium demolished and reconstructed. Re-opened 5.3.28 as Picture House, 600 seats.) Taken over 2.29, part of PCT/Albany Ward circuit. (Taken over 5.1.58 by independent. Renamed Regal 4.4.71. Closed in 1980s. Grade II listed building from 1990. Taken over by Save Britain's Heritage. Re-opened as Magic Lantern Theatre. Closed. Re-opened as cinema. Closed c1994. Re-opened 28.7.95 as Savoy Theatre for films and eventual live theatre, 450 seats.)

MORECAMBE Lancashire

TOWER Promenade (East End). (Opened 1909. Part of complex of ballroom, bars, restaurant, cafe and gardens.) Taken over 1.10.28 by Denman/Gaumont, 2300 seats. Live shows in summer. Closed 19.4.49 for extensive alterations. Re-opened 6.6.49 as GAUMONT, 1800 seats. Closed briefly in 1955 for reseating (gallery closed), 1200 seats. Closed 30.11.57. Re-opened 1958 for summer season. Closed 13.9.58. (Re-opened summer 1959 with musical show only. Closed late 1959. Sold 10.60. Demolished c8.61. Bowling alley opened in 1963, later divided in half for cabaret use,

closed by flood damage in 1982. Re-opened as bingo hall in 1985, open in 1995 as Gala bingo club.)

MOTHERWELL Strathclyde
see also Wishaw

PAVILION 123 Brandon Street. (Opened 1913, former variety theatre, 1200 seats. Part of Thomas Ormiston circuit.) Taken over 3.28 by Denman/Gaumont. Renamed GAUMONT 25.2.52. Closed 15.8.59. (Majestic Ballroom. Destroyed 20.5.63 by fire. Site cleared 1966. Car park for adjacent Odeon, later bingo hall.)

NEW BRIGHTON Wallasey

TROCADERO Victoria Road. (Opened 1.6.22. Taken over 3.28 by GTC.) Taken over 5.28, part of GTC circuit. 886 seats. Closed 29.9.56. (Supermarket.)

TIVOLI Tower Promenade. (Opened 19.2.23, former live theatre with some film use, 636 seats. Taken over 10.28 by APPH.) Taken over 2.29, part of PCT/APPH circuit. Films and live shows. Live shows only from 1.7.29 to 14.9.29. Films from 19.6.30 to 14.7.30. Live use only from c5.32. (Leased out as theatre. Closed 4.55. Demolished in 1976.)

NEWCASTLE UPON TYNE Tyne and Wear
see also Byker, Heaton and Shildon

PAVILION Westgate Road. (Opened 17.11.13 as Pavilion for cine-variety, former theatre with some films shown. Variety theatre only from 1915. Closed 30.6.17. Re-opened 10.12.17 as New Pavilion, cinema use only, 1600 seats. Taken over 1924 by Thompson and Collins circuit, renamed Pavilion.) Taken over 3.28 by Denman/Gaumont. 1525 seats. Closed for extensive modernisation, re-opened 31.1.61. Closed 3.4.68 for further modernisation. Re-opened 28.4.68. Closed 29.11.75. (Auditorium demolished in 1990. Frontage demolished 5.92. Flats.)

NEW WESTGATE Westgate Road and Clayton Street. (Opened 12.2.12 as the Picture House, architect: Arthur Stockwell, former mission hall, 850 seats. Extended 1913, 1021 seats. Renamed Westgate Road Picture House or Westgate in 1914. Closed 5.3.27 for enlargement and new frontage, architects: Percy L. Browne & Sons. Re-opened 31.10.27 as New Westgate, 1870 seats.) Taken over 3.28 by

Denman/Gaumont. Renamed WESTGATE 8.2.37. Renamed GAUMONT 10.7.50. Closed 29.11.58. (Majestic Ballroom from 26.2.59. Bingo from c1964.)

HIPPODROME Northumberland Road. (Operated as live theatre by GTC. 2453 seats. Taken over 5.28, part of GTC circuit. No apparent film use. Closed 20.5.33.)

GREY STREET PICTURE HOUSE. (Opened 6.5.14 as Newcastle Picture House by PCT, former Victoria music hall and billiard saloon, architects for conversion: White and Stephenson, 927 seats. Renamed Grey Street Picture House from 5.6.22. Taken over 8.27 by George Black. Taken over 3.28 by GTC.) Taken over 5.28, part of GTC circuit. Closed 14.5.32. (Broadloom Mills. Pizzaland on ground floor, TSB above.)

QUEEN'S Northumberland Street. (Opened 8/9.9.13 as Queen's Hall, 1200 seats. Renamed Queen's. Taken over 3.20 by George Black. Taken over 3.28 by GTC.) Taken over 5.28, part of GTC circuit. Closed 23.7.28 for refurbishment. Re-opened 20.8.28. 1413 seats. Closed 15.6.63 for major reconstruction including new roof and installation of Cinerama. Re-opened 9.11.63, 963 seats. Closed 16.2.80. (Demolished 1 and 2.83. Queen's shopping arcade.)

NEW CROSS Southeast London
see also Deptford

KINEMA 325/7 New Cross Road, corner of Clifton Rise. (Opened 7.9.25, architect: Edward A. Stone, 2300 seats. Dance hall attached.) Taken over 3.28 by Denman/Gaumont. 2089 seats. Renamed GAUMONT 16.1.50. Closed 27.8.60. (Rear half demolished for offices, front half converted to supermarket. Front half in 11.93 Furniture House Superstore with Venue nightclub above in old dance hall area.)

NEWINGTON BUTTS Southeast London

QUEEN'S HALL. Taken over 3.28 by Denman/Gaumont. Seems to have been leased to independent. Closed 1930.

NEWPORT Gwent

COLISEUM Clarence Place, Corporation Street. (Opened 22.6.11. Part of Biocolour circuit.) Part of original circuit in 3.27. 1000 seats. Closed 15.4.67. (Taken over by Star. Re-opened 26.9.70. Closed 31.12.70 for twinning. Re-opened 1.3.71 as Studio 1 & 2, 339 & 140 seats. Taken over by Cannon, renamed Cannon. Closed 19.3.87. Disused in 1995.)

NORTHAMPTON Northamptonshire
EXCHANGE 4 The Parade, Market Square. (Opened 2.8.20, former Corn Exchange used as partweek cinema. Taken over c1924 by PCT.) Taken over 2.29, part of PCT circuit. 1916 seats. Renamed GAUMONT 10.4.50. Modernised 1951. Renamed ODEON c3.64. Closed 7.9.74. (Bingo. Open in 1995.)

NORTH FINCHLEY North London
see Finchley

NORTH SHIELDS Tyne and Wear
BOROUGH THEATRE Lower Rudyard Street. (Opened 7.10, architects: Gibson & Steinlet, reconstruction after fire of former live theatre, 2000 seats. Part of Thompson & Collins circuit.) Taken over 3.28 by Denman/Gaumont. 1440 seats. Closed 28.9.57. (Demolished.)
PRINCE'S THEATRE Russell Street. (Opened 7.10.29, architects: Dixon & Bell, 1750 seats.) Taken over 6.31 by Gaumont/PCT. Renamed PRINCE'S. Closed c11.49 for war damage repairs. Re-opened 16.10.50, renamed GAUMONT. (Taken over 5.7.70 by independent, renamed Prince's. Taken over 2.1.72 by Classic, renamed Classic. Closed 18.9.76. Bingo. Old circle opened 1.6.77 by independent as two cinemas, Crown 1 & 2. Cinemas closed 7.82. Bingo continued.)

NORWICH Norfolk
PICTURE HOUSE Haymarket. (Opened 18.2.11.Enlarged in 1929, architect: F. Burdett Ward, 1500 seats.) Taken over 6.30 by Denman/Gaumont, renamed HAYMARKET. Renamed GAUMONT c1954. Closed 15.8.59. (Demolished. Store.)
CARLTON All Saints Green. (Opened 1.2.32, architect: J. Owen Bond, 900 seats. Taken over by Lou Morris. Enlarged and re-opened 8.12.34, 1920 seats.) Taken over 8.36 by County. Taken over by Odeon as part of County circuit. Modernised and re-opened

1.60, renamed GAUMONT. 1515 seats. Closed 6.1.73. (Top Rank Club for bingo, open in 1995.)

NORWOOD South London – see West Norwood

NOTTINGHAM Nottinghamshire
see also Hyson Green
MECHANICS' HALL Milton Street. (Opened c3.16, former concert hall. Part of Shapeero circuit.) Taken over 3.28 by Denman/Gaumont. 1168 seats. Closed 1964. (Demolished. Offices — Burbeck House.)
ELECTRA HOUSE Alfreton Road. (Opened 15.5.13. Part of Shapeero circuit.) Taken over 3.28 by Denman/Gaumont. Called ELECTRA. 800 seats. (Leased to independent c1936. Closed 31.1.42. Re-opened 16.2.42 as Orion. Closed 18.4.59. Demolished. Shops.)
PICTURE HOUSE Long Row. (Opened 5.11.12 by PCT, 560 seats.) Taken over 2.29, part of PCT circuit. Closed 4.1.30. (Sold 1.37, J. Lyons café. Amusements centre, frontage restored.)
HIPPODROME Goldsmith Street/Theatre Square. (Taken over 6.27 by PCT as live theatre. Closed 1.10.27 for reconstruction as cinema and re-opened 22.10.27 [or 7.11.27], 1724 seats.) Taken over 2.29, part of PCT circuit. Renamed GAUMONT 16.2.48. Closed 16.1.71. (Demolished 2.73. Office block & showrooms: Barraford House.)

NOTTING HILL West London
CORONET 103/111 High Street. (Opened c1916, former live theatre, 1010 seats, with some later live use.) Taken over 1931 by Gaumont/PCT, re-opened 17.8.31. Renamed GAUMONT in 1950. Modernised c1970, 515 seats. Closed 27.9.75 for improvements. Re-opened 26.10.75. (Taken over by Panton 27.2.77, renamed Coronet. 399 seats. Grade II listed building from 1989. Open in 1995.)

OLDHAM Greater Manchester
GAUMONT King Street. Opened 14.6.37 by Gaumont Super Cinemas, former Grand Theatre taken over 7.36 and entirely reconstructed internally with facade partly modernised. 1842 seats. Taken over fully 28.2.44. Closed 2.12.61. (Top Rank bowling alley from

15.11.62. Astoria Ballroom. Nightclub from 1973.)

OLD KENT ROAD Southeast London
see also Bermondsey
PICTURE HOUSE 42-44 Old Kent Road. (Opened 1916. Balcony added in 1918. Roof raised, balcony enlarged & auditorium extended, architect: E. A. Stone, and re-opened 11.26, 1993 seats. Part of United Picture Theatres circuit from 1.28.) Under Gaumont management from 7.30 as part of UPT circuit. Closed by Blitz. Re-opened 29.12.41. Closed 27.10.56. (Demolished in road widening c1972.)

PALMERS GREEN North London
PALMADIUM 292 Green Lanes. (Opened 24.12.20. Part of Gale and Repard circuit.) Taken over c4.28 by Denman/Gaumont. 2188 seats. Renamed GAUMONT 26.2.51. Closed 25.2.61. (Demolished. Shops & office block.)

PARIS France
ALHAMBRA Rue de Malte. Opened 26.9.31 as music hall by Gaumont/GTC, architects: Gray & Evans, 2024 seats. Cine-variety. Variety from 10.32. Cine-variety again from 21.4.33. (Under enemy occupation in World War Two. Leased out from 1945.)

PARTICK Glasgow
TIVOLI 53 Crow Road. (Opened 29.4.29, architect: William J. Blain of Denny & Blain, 1918 seats.) Taken over 1931. (Taken over 16.12.67 by Classic, renamed Classic. Closed 30.9.72. (Bingo from 24.1.73, open in 1994.)

PECKHAM South London
TOWER ANNEXE 164 Rye Lane. (Opened 1905 as the Public Hall cinema, former chapel. Reconstructed and re-opened c2.11 as Pyke's Cinematograph Theatre, 780 seats. Renamed Peckham Cinematograph Theatre by 1915. Renamed Tower Annexe 1917. Part of Davis circuit. Taken over 11.26 by PCT.) Taken over 2.29, part of PCT circuit. Closed 6.10.40. Bomb damaged during War. (Auditorium into garment factory. Entrance into shop, later bingo & amusement parlour. Entrance into A to Z Bargain Stores in 1995.)
HIPPODROME High Street. (Opened 1912,

former Crown music hall & theatre. Part of Biocolour circuit. 2000 seats.) Part of original circuit in 3.27. (Demolished Autumn 1928 for new Gaumont Palace.)

TOWER 116 Rye Lane. (Opened 19.11.14 by Israel Davis, architect: H. Courtney Constantine, 2150 seats. Part of Davis circuit. Taken over 11.26 by PCT.) Taken over 2.29, part of PCT circuit. 1938 seats. Frontage modernised 10-11.55. Closed 1.12.56. (Auditorium demolished for open-air car park. Truncated tower left with former entrance as public passageway.)

GAUMONT PALACE 169 High Street, corner of Marmont Road (site of Crown/Hippodrome). Opened 8.2.32 by Gaumont/PCT, architects: Verity & Beverley, 2005 seats. Renamed GAUMONT c1937. Closed in Blitz. Re-opened 23.6.41. Closed 7.44. Re-opened 22.1.45. Closed 3.7.48 for refurbishment. Re-opened 25.10.48. Closed 14.1.61. (Part week bingo as Top Rank Club from 17.5.61. Wrestling on Tuesdays in late 1961. Full time bingo. Auditorium drastically altered. Open as Top Rank Club in 1995.)

PENGE Southeast London

KING'S HALL 172 High Street. (Opened 1920, architect: Cecil Masey. Part of Hyams circuit.) Taken over 17.3.29 by Denman/Gaumont. 1200 seats. Renamed GAUMONT 1955. Closed 27.9.58. (Demolished. Garage/petrol station.)

EMPIRE THEATRE High Street. (Part of GTC from 3.28.) Taken over 5.28, part of GTC circuit. No apparent film use. (Taken over by Moss Empires c12.46. Taken over by Essoldo, opened 9.49 as Essoldo cinema, 1501 seats. Closed 1960. Demolished.)

PERTH Tayside

ALHAMBRA 32/36 Kinnoull Street. (Opened 1924, former live theatre. Part of Thomas Ormiston circuit.) Taken over 3.28 by Denman/Gaumont. 1010 seats. Closed 1956 by fire at screen end. Modernised and re-opened 1956 as GAUMONT, 1288 seats. Renamed ODEON 16.12.62. Closed 1.11.80. (Bingo. Leisureland nightclub. Destroyed by arson late summer 1993. Site cleared.)

B. B. CINERAMA Victoria Street, corner of Scott Street. (Opened 1923. Part of B.B. circuit.) Taken over 12.28 by Denman/Gaumont. 1195 seats. Renamed CINERAMA. Closed 3.2.62. (Bingo. Open in 1994.)

PETERBOROUGH Cambridgeshire

BROADWAY Broadway. (Opened 17.12.10, architect: Alan W. Ruddle, 700 seats. Facade rebuilt in 1913. Taken over 1920 by PCT. Enlarged c1920, 1560 seats.) Taken over 2.29, part of PCT circuit. Renamed GAUMONT 5.11.61. Closed 19.10.63. (Bingo from 31.10.63. Closed 1983. Demolished 1987. Amusement centre, etc.)

PLUMSTEAD Southeast London

EMPIRE High Street and Garibaldi Street. (Opened 1913 by Bernstein, architects: Andrews & Peascod, 900 seats.) Taken over 3.28 by Denman/Gaumont but operated by Bernstein/Granada. Closed c1932 for reconstruction, architect: Cecil Masey, and re-opened as KINEMA. Renamed CENTURY 3.3.52. Closed 24.9.60. (Training centre.)

PLYMOUTH Devon

SAVOY Union Street. (Opened 1921 on site of St. James' Picture Hall. Part of Biocolour circuit.) Part of original circuit in 3.27. 1400 seats. Closed 22.4.41. destroyed by fire bomb. (Site sold by 1952. Flats.)

PALLADIUM 27 Ebrington Street. (Opened 1921, former roller skating rink, 2458 seats.) Taken over 7.28 by Denman/Gaumont. Closed 21.3.41, destroyed by fire bomb. (Site cleared. Dual carriageway.)

ANDREWS PICTURE HOUSE 151 Union Street. (Opened 8.10, 2000 seats. Taken over by PCT.) Taken over 2.29, part of PCT circuit. Closed 1931. (Demolished for new Gaumont Palace.)

GAUMONT PALACE Union Street (site of Andrews Picture House and adjacent property). Opened 16.11.31 by Gaumont/PCT, architect: W. H. Watkins (Percy Bartlett), 2252 seats: 1462 stalls & 790 circle. Renamed GAUMONT c1937. Closed 2.12.61 for subdivision into ground floor ballroom and upstairs cinema extending old circle. Cinema opened 10.9.62 as ODEON, 1043 seats. Closed 9.4.80. (Roller disco from 12.80. Nightclub/rock venue from 1987.)

PORTLAND (Isle of), Dorset
see also Easton

PALACE Victoria Square. (Part of Albany Ward circuit. Taken over by PCT.) Taken over 2.29, part of PCT. Closed c1931.

PORTSMOUTH Hampshire
see also Southsea

HIPPODROME Commercial Road. (Live theatre taken over 3.28 by GTC.) Taken over 5.28 as part of GTC. Cine-variety in 1933. Films on Sundays. 1873 seats. Closed 10.1.41, destroyed by bombing in Blitz. Office block — Hippodrome House.)

REGENT 55 London Road, North End. (Opened 31.3.27, architect: S. Clough, 1908 seats. Taken over 8.10.29 by Hyams & Gale.) Taken over 10.2.31 by Gaumont/APPH. 2017 seats. Renamed GAUMONT 9.3.53. 1616 seats by 1970. Closed 1.9.73. (Demolished 4.74. Safeways supermarket in 1995.)

PRESTON Lancashire

NEW VICTORIA Church Street. (Opened 17.9.28 by PCT, architect: W. E. Trent, 2100 seats.) Taken over 2.29, part of PCT circuit. Renamed GAUMONT 22.9.52. Modernised c1959. Closed 16.6.62 for subdivision into ground floor ballroom/disco and upstairs cinema extending old circle. Cinema opened 28.1.63 as ODEON, 1229 seats. ODEON 2 opened 4.70 in former restaurant, 105 seats. Both closed 10.9.92.

PRINCE'S PARK Liverpool — see Dingle

PUTNEY Southwest London

PALACE High Street. (Opened 1907 as Electric Pavilion by Israel Davis. Taken over c1918 by independent. Renamed Blue Hall in 1920. Renamed Palace c1927. 1430 seats. Part of United Picture Theatres circuit from 1.28.) Under Gaumont management from 7.30 as part of UPT circuit. Closed during World War Two. Re-opened 22.3.42. Closed, then re-opened 28.1.45. Renamed GAUMONT 22.8.55. Renamed ODEON 25.11.62. Closed 11.12.71. (Sold to EMI. Demolished for redevelopment including new ABC cinemas.)

HIPPODROME Felsham Road. (Opened c5.24, former live theatre. Part of United Picture Theatres circuit from 1.28.) Under

Gaumont management from 7.30 as part of UPT circuit. (Taken over 7.35 by ABC. Taken over by independent c1938. 1420 seats. Taken over c1940 by Odeon, re-opened 17.2.41. Closed 14.1.61. Used as location for film *Theatre of Blood* in 1973. Demolished.)

RAMSGATE Kent
PICTURE HOUSE High Street. (Opened 25.3.20.) Taken over by 1929. (Taken over c1935 by independent. Closed 1940 by wartime evacuation. Re-opened 8.43. 600 seats. Closed 4.10.59. Supermarket.)

RAYNERS LANE Northwest London
ODEON Alexandra Avenue. (Opened 12.10.36 as the Grosvenor, architect: W. E. Bromige, 1235 seats. Taken over 5.5.37 by Odeon. Renamed Odeon c1941.) Renamed GAUMONT 26.10.50. Renamed ODEON 27.4.64. 1020 seats. Grade II listed building from 13.3.81. Closed Mondays and Tuesdays from 10.5.81 except school holidays. (Taken over by independent 1.11.81, renamed Ace, open full time. Closed 16.10.86. Listing raised to Grade II* from 6.10.88. Foyer into Grosvenor wine bar, auditorium into nightclub, both from 1991. Both open in 1994.)

READING Berkshire
VAUDEVILLE 47 Broad Street, corner of Union Street. (Opened 8.09, former shop with large garden, 450 seats. Enlarged 1912, 1100 seats. Reconstructed, architects: Emden, Egan, and re-opened 9.21, 1500 seats. Taken over 9.29 by County. 1800 seats. Taken over by Odeon.) Renamed GAUMONT 23.2.53. Closed 30.11.57. (Largely demolished. Timothy White's store, later renamed Boots, open in 1995.)

PAVILION 143/5 Oxford Road, corner of Russell Street. (Opened 21.9.29, architect: Harold S. Scott, 1361 seats. Taken over 1930 by County. Taken over by Odeon.) Improved and renamed GAUMONT 19.1.58. Closed 21.4.79. (Bingo. Snooker hall in stalls with false ceiling, balcony disused — Riley Snooker Centre in 1995.)

REDDITCH Hereford and Worcester
PUBLIC HALL Church Road. (Part of Shapeero circuit.) Taken over 3.28 by Denman/

Gaumont. Closed c1930. Gutted, rebuilt and re-opened 23.11.31 as GAUMONT PALACE, architect: William T. Benslyn (assistant: H. Pittaway), 813 seats. Renamed GAUMONT c1937. (Taken over 16.12.67 by Classic, renamed Classic. Closed c1968. Bingo.)

REGENT'S PARK North London — see
Camden Town

RICHMOND Southwest London
ROYALTY 5 Hill Street. (Opened 24.12.14 as New Royalty by H. J. Mears, architect: Sidney Davis, incorporating 18th century Georgian house for foyer. 1020 seats. Renamed Royalty 10.6.29. Closed 26.10.40 by war conditions. Re-opened 25.5.42. Taken over 3.1.44 by Odeon.) Renamed GAUMONT 26.11.49. Listed frontage. Closed 25.10.80. (Auditorium demolished, new Filmhouse cinema at rear of redevelopment along Water Lane. Former foyer into offices.)

ROCHESTER Kent
MAJESTIC High Street, Star Hill. Opened 15.4.35 by Gaumont-associated company, architects: Harry Weston & Arthur W. Kenyon, 2012 seats. Renamed GAUMONT 3.4.50. Renamed ODEON 21.10.62. Triple from 9.3.74 by creating two small cinemas under balcony, 730 & 120 & 120 seats. Closed 31.10.81. (Demolished 1987. Homes.)

ROMFORD Northeast London
PLAZA South Street. (Opened 20.1.30, architects: Harrington & Evans [W. Evans], 1620 seats. Taken over 4.37 by GCF. Taken over 1943 by Odeon.) Renamed GAUMONT in 1950. Closed 8.9.62. (Demolished in shopping centre development.)

ROSE HILL South London
GAUMONT Bishopsford Road. Opened 17.5.37 by Gaumont, architect: Harry Weston, 1500 seats. Closed 22.7.61. (Top Rank Bingo, open in 1995.)

ROTHERHITHE Southeast London
LION, Rotherhithe New Road and Lower Road. (Opened pre-1915 as Lion Electric. Renamed Lion.) Taken over 3.28 by Denman/

Gaumont. 656 seats. Renamed LION. Closed during WW2 by bomb damage.

RUSHEY GREEN Southeast London
QUEEN'S HALL 141/5 Rushey Green. (Opened 11.12.13, architects: Emden, Egan, 869 seats. Taken over 1920 by Catwood cinemas.) Taken over 3.28 by Denman/Gaumont. 830 seats. Renamed GAUMONT 5.9.54. Closed 14.11.59. (Demolished 7.60. Eros House office block on site of this and adjacent Eros cinema.)

ST. ALBANS Hertfordshire
GRAND PALACE Stanhope Street. (Opened 8.6.22, architects: Mence & Finn [Harry R. Finn], 1400 seats. Part of D. J. James circuit. Taken over 1937 by GCF. Taken over 3.43 by Odeon). Renamed GAUMONT 19.2.50. Closed 27.10.73. (Sold May 1974. Bingo. Demolished c1987. Flats — Chatsworth Court.)

ST. HELIER Jersey, Channel Islands
OPERA HOUSE Gloucester Street. (Taken over by 1914 by Albany Ward. Closed 1921 by fire and rebuilt. Part of PCT circuit.) Taken over 2.29, part of PCT circuit. Mainly live theatre. Under enemy occupation during part of World War Two. Closed 20.12.58. (Live theatre.)

PICTURE HOUSE Don Street. (Part of PCT circuit.) Taken over 2.29, part of PCT circuit. Closed by 1936.

ST. PETER PORT Guernsey, Channel Islands
ST. JULIAN'S THEATRE St. Julian's Avenue. (Operated by Albany Ward by 1915. Taken over by PCT.) Taken over 2.29, part of PCT circuit. Closed 1930 for complete interior reconstruction, architects: W. E. Trent & Ernest F. Tulley. Re-opened 29.6.31 as GAUMONT PALACE by Gaumont/Albany Ward, 758 seats: 570 stalls & 188 balcony. Renamed GAUMONT c1937. Under enemy occupation during part of World War Two. Re-opened 10.45. Closed 15.3.80 for twinning. Re-opened 2.6.80, 157 & 391 seats. Closed 5.1.85. (Bank.)

LYRIC New Street. Taken over by PCT/Gaumont c1936. (Taken over by independent by 1940. 569 seats. Under enemy occupation during part of World War Two.)

SALISBURY Wiltshire

PALACE Endless Street. (Opened 1908 as County Hall. Taken over 1910 by Albany Ward, renamed Palace. taken over by PCT.) Taken over 2.29, part of PCT. Mostly live theatre use. Closed 7.5.31. (Garage from 1937. Demolished. Offices and three shops.)

NEW THEATRE Castle Street. (Opened 1910 by Albany Ward as New Picturedrome and Theatre. Remodelled 1913, renamed New Theatre, mostly live, 800 seats. Taken over by PCT.) Taken over 2.29, part of PCT. Closed 30.4.32. (Demolished. Supermarket.)

PICTURE HOUSE Fisherton Street. (Opened 11.12.16 by Albany Ward, former Methodist Chapel. Taken over by PCT.) Taken over 2.29, part of PCT. 514 seats. Closed 18.9.37. (Playhouse Theatre from 1946. Warehouse. Garrison Theatre.)

GAUMONT PALACE 15 New Canal. Opened 7.9.31 by Gaumont/Albany Ward incorporating Ye Halle of John Halle as vestibule, architect: W. E. Trent, 1675 seats: 1125 stalls & 550 balcony. Renamed GAUMONT c1937. Renamed ODEON 10.8.64. Triple from 26.11.72 by creating two small cinemas under balcony, 120 & 120 seats, plus 471 seats in former balcony. Listed building: foyer always grade I, rest grade II from 1984. ODEON 4, 70 seats, opened c1993 in former restaurant. New ODEON 2 opened 6.4.95 in former front stalls, 278 seats. Former ODEONS 2, 3 & 4 renumbered 3, 4 & 5. All open in 1995.

NEW PICTURE HOUSE Fisherton Street (adjacent to previous Picture House). Opened 27.9.37 by Gaumont/Albany Ward, architects: W. E. Trent, W. S. Trent & R. C. H. Golding, 1313 seats (stadium). Renamed PICTURE HOUSE. Renamed ODEON 27.2.50. Closed 30.12.61. (City Hall concert venue. Major refurbishment in 1985. Open in 1995.)

SALTAIRE Shipley

PICTURE HOUSE Bingley Road. (Opened 17.6.22, 1500 seats. Part of New Century Pictures circuit.) Taken over 3.28 by Denman/Gaumont. Renamed GAUMONT c1945. Closed 19.10.57. (Demolished.)

SEACOMBE Wallasey

MARINA Brighton Street. (Opened 15.7.16, architect: A. Ernest Shennan, 940 seats. Taken over 3.28 by GTC.) Taken over 5.28, part of GTC circuit. 862 seats. Closed 29.9.56. (Disused. Demolished in 1970s. School extension.)

SEFTON PARK Liverpool

PICTUREDROME Smithdown Road. (Opened 1.11, formerly stable, 300 seats.) Taken over 3.28 by Denman/Gaumont. Closed by 11.29. (Penny bazaar. DIY store.)

GRAND Smithdown Road. (Opened 26.7.13, architects: Campbell & Fairhurst, 824 seats.) Taken over 3.28 by Denman/Gaumont. Closed 29.9.56. (Demolished. Petrol station.)

CAMEO Webster Road. (Opened c1925, conversion of church. Altered and re-opened 18.1.26, 690 seats. Taken over by GTC 3.28.) Taken over 5.28, part of GTC. Closed 1929. Re-opened 25.10.37. Closed 5.1.57. (Warehouse.)

SHEERNESS Kent

RIO The Broadway. Opened 21.6.37 by Gaumont, architect: George Coles, 1546 seats. (Taken over by 1941 by Lou Morris. Taken over by Essoldo c1945. Closed c1957. Toy shop. Factory. Disused from 1980. Demolished 1988.)

SHEFFIELD South Yorkshire

ALBERT HALL Barker's Pool, corner of Burgess Street. (Opened 17.6.18 by New Century Pictures, former concert hall with much film use. Closed 13.6.27. Modernised, architects: Chadwick, Watson, and re-opened 25.7.27, 1611 seats.) Taken over 3.28 by Denman/Gaumont. Closed 14.7.37 by serious fire. Work started on clearing site for new Gaumont cinema, architect: W. E. Trent, but land taken over by Sheffield Corporation. (Demolished. Site leased to store owner in 1944. Cole Bros. store.)

HIPPODROME Cambridge Street. (Taken over 3.28 by GTC as live theatre.) Taken over 5.28, part of GTC circuit. No film use. (Taken over by ABC, redecorated and projection box installed, re-opened 20.6.31 as cinema, 2445 seats. Taken over by independent 25.7.48. Closed 2.3.63 by Compulsory Purchase Order. Demolished. Grosvenor Hotel, shops and offices.)

REGENT Barker's Pool. (Opened 26.12.27 by PCT, architect: W. E. Trent, 2300 seats: 1450 stalls & 850 balcony.) Taken over 2.29, part of PCT circuit. Renamed GAUMONT 27.7.46. Modernised 1959. Closed 10.68 for twinning, architects: Gavin Paterson & Son, interior design: Trevor & Mavis Stone. Re-opened 23.7.69, 737 seats upstairs & 1150 seats downstairs. GAUMONT 3 opened 25.11.79 in former restaurant/bar area, 144 seats. Closed 7.11.85. (Demolished for redevelopment including new two-screen Odeon.)

SHEPHERDS BUSH Northwest London

PAVILION Shepherds Bush Green. (Opened 16.8.23 by Davis circuit, architect: Frank T. Verity, 2776 seats: 1450 stalls & 850 balcony.) Part of original circuit in 3.27. Closed 7.44 by World War Two bomb damage. Interior entirely rebuilt, architect: Sam Beverley, and re-opened 25.7.55 as GAUMONT, 2036 seats. Renamed ODEON 25.11.62. Closed 31.5.69 for subdivision into ground floor bingo club and smaller Odeon in old circle extended, opened 7.3.70, 815 seats. Renamed ODEON 1, 1.4.73. Grade II listed building from 16.1.74. Closed 17.9.83. (Bingo open as Top Rank Club, cinema still disused, in 1995.)

SHILDON Co. Durham

HIPPODROME Byerley Road. (Opened c1911 for films and variety. Taken over 3.28 by GTC.) Taken over 5.28 as part of GTC. 1050 seats. (Leased to Thomas Thompson c6.29. Bingo in 1980.)

SHIPLEY West Yorkshire — see Saltaire

SMETHWICK West Midlands

ELECTRIC Cape Hill and Rosebery Road. (Opened 6.11, architects: Gammage & Dickinson. Part of Shapeero circuit.) Taken over 3.28 by Denman/Gaumont. 748 seats. Closed 29.9.56. (Demolished. Post Office.)

RINK Windmill Lane. (Opened 8.4.12, former skating rink. Part of Shapeero circuit.) Taken over 3.28 by Denman/Gaumont. Closed late 1929. (Demolished for new Rink cinema.)

RINK Windmill Lane. Opened 7.7.30 by Gaumont/PCT on enlarged site of old Rink cinema, architect: William T. Benslyn, 1950 seats. Renamed GAUMONT 1949. Partweek bingo in early 1960s. Closed 1.2.64. (Full-time bingo as Top Rank Club, open in 1995.)

SOUTHALL West London

PALACE 14 South Road. (Opened 11.29 on enlarged site of former Palace by United Picture Theatres, architect: George Coles, 2000 seats, one floor.) Under Gaumont management from 7.30 as part of UPT circuit. Renamed GAUMONT 13.3.50. Renamed ODEON 10.12.61. (Taken over 27.6.71 by independent, renamed Godeon. Asian cinema from 31.1.72, renamed Liberty. Grade II listed building from 18.9.80. Closed 1982. Indoor market.)

SOUTHAMPTON Hampshire

HIPPODROME Ogle Road. (Live theatre. Taken over 3.28 by GTC.) Taken over 5.28 as part of GTC. No apparent film use. (Sold c1936. Closed 1939. Bombed 1940.)

EMPIRE Commercial Road. (Opened c1931 by Moss Empires, former live theatre, 2358 seats, booked by Gaumont.) Taken over 12.46 by Gaumont/GTC. Renamed GAUMONT c1948. 2230 seats. Grade II listed building from 12.81. Many live shows. Closed 2.86. (Taken over by City Council. Refurbished and re-opened 1.88 as Mayflower, live theatre. Open in 1995.)

SOUTHEND-ON-SEA Essex

HIPPODROME Southchurch Road. (Taken over 3.28 by GCT. Live theatre.) Taken over 5.28, part of GTC. Cine-variety started 17.4.33. Films dropped from 3.7.33. Closed for modernisation and re-opened 15.1.34 as GAUMONT PALACE, 1588 seats. Renamed GAUMONT c1937. Closed 20.10.56. (Demolished in 1958. Supermarket.)

SOUTHPORT Merseyside

PALLADIUM Lord Street. (Opened 3.1.14, architect: George E. Tonge, 1400 seats. Temporarily closed 20.10.25, circle gutted by fire. Taken over 3.28 by GTC.) Taken over 5.28 as part of GTC. Closed 3.29 by fire. (Auditorium demolished for New Palladium.)

NEW PALLADIUM Lord Street. Opened 1.10.30 by Gaumont/GTC, retaining front of old Palladium, architects: W. E. Trent & Ernest Tulley, 2126 seats. Renamed PALLADIUM.

Renamed GAUMONT 24.7.50. Renamed ODEON 21.10.62. Closed 28.11.79. (Demolished. Supermarket.)

SOUTHSEA Portsmouth

PLAZA Bradford Junction. (Opened 29.9.28, architects: Henry J. Dyer & Sons, 1715 seats.) Taken over by Gaumont/APPH 10.2.31. Renamed GAUMONT 8.5.50. Closed 30.1.65. (Bingo. Gala Club in 1995. Grade II Listed building.)

SOUTH SHIELDS Tyne and Wear

SCALA Ocean Road (second entrance on Mile End Road). (Opened 4.10.20 by Black's, former Royal Assembly Hall with some film shows, refurbished with new facade by architect Pascal J. Steinlet. Taken over 3.28 by GTC.) Taken over 5.28 as part of GTC. 1300 seats. Facade altered in 1938. Renamed GAUMONT 12.3.51. Ocean Road entrance closed in 1960. (Taken over 5.10.75 by Brent Walker, renamed Focus. Taken over by independent, renamed Regal. Three screens from 24.5.80, 329 seats & 2 x 74-seat video cinemas. All closed 26.6.82. Bingo club & amusement centre from 19.6.84, open in 1995 as The Venue.)

SOWERBY BRIDGE West Yorkshire

ELECTRIC Wharfe Street. (Part of National Electric circuit.) Taken over 3.28 by Denman/Gaumont. 812 seats. Closed 11.3.51. (Taken over by independent. Taken over 5.52 by Star. Renamed Roxy. Closed 1 or 2.63. Disused. Bingo from 1972.)

STAMFORD HILL North London

REGENT 1a Amhurst Park, corner of Stamford Hill. Opened 18.2.29 by Gaumont/PCT, architect: W. Sydney Trent, 2172 seats. Renamed GAUMONT 24.1.60. Renamed ODEON 21.10.62. Closed 16.9.72. (Top Rank bingo. Closed. Demolished 4.81. Supermarket.)

CINEMA Clapton Common. (Opened 26.12.25, architect: George Coles, 1800 seats, one floor.) Under Gaumont management from 7.30 as part of UPT circuit. Renamed SUPER in 1947. (Taken over 4.1.48 by ABC. Closed 7.11.59. Bowling alley. Demolished by 1971. Supermarket. Closed except for shops in entrance.)

STEPNEY East London

PALASEUM 226 Commercial Road. (Opened 2.12.12, former Fineman's Yiddish Theatre, 1000 seats. Taken over c5.28 by United Picture Theatres.) Under Gaumont management from 7.30 as part of UPT circuit. (Taken over 1934 by ABC/Regent circuit. To ABC c1935. 920 seats. Taken over 26.3.49 by Southan Morris. Taken over 26.8.54 by Essoldo. Closed 19.3.60. Re-opened 18.10.61, renamed Essoldo. Closed 1.9.66. Asian cinema, renamed Palaseum. Closed 10.85. Demolished.)

TROXY 490 Commercial Road, corner of Pitsea Street. (Opened 11.9.33 by Hyams & Gale, architect: George Coles [assistant: Arthur Roberts], 3520 seats.) Taken over by Gaumont Super Cinemas c8.35. Taken over fully 28.2.44. Closed 19.11.60. (London Opera Centre, rehearsal hall and workshops, from 1963. Grade II listed building from 17.1.91. Reinstated, re-opened 10.9.92 as Top Rank Club for bingo, open in 1995.)

STOKE-ON-TRENT Staffordshire

see also Burslem and Hanley

HIPPODROME Kingsway. (Opened pre-1917, former live theatre. Part of Biocolour Pictures circuit.) Taken over 3.28 by Denman/Gaumont. 1550 seats. Closed 27.12.51 for modernisation. Re-opened 28.7.52, renamed GAUMONT. Closed 14.1.61. (Sold 19.9.62. Demolished. Chinese restaurant.)

STRATFORD Northeast London

see also West Ham

IMPERIAL PLAYHOUSE 1 The Broadway. (Opened 8.10 as Picture Palace. Renamed Empire in 1911. Taken over 1918 by Hyams Bros., renamed Imperial Playhouse.) Taken over 3.28 by Denman/Gaumont, part of Hyams circuit. Closed 1941 by bomb damage in Blitz. (Bingo. Billiard hall. Demolished 1989. Offices.)

BROADWAY SUPER Tramway Avenue. (Opened 22.12.27 by Hyams Bros., architect: George Coles, 2726 seats.) Taken over 3.28 by Denman/Gaumont. Renamed BROADWAY. Renamed GAUMONT 28.11.49. Closed 26.11.60. (Business premises from 25.3.61. Vacant in 10.77. Demolished 3 & 4.90.)

STREATHAM South London

GAUMONT PALACE Streatham Hill, corner

of Ardwell Street. Opened 14.3.32 by Gaumont, architects: [Charles] Nicholas & [J.E.] Dixon-Spain, 2381 seats. Closed 7.44 by wartime bomb damage. Interior entirely reconstructed, architects: T. P. Bennett & Son, and re-opened 18.7.55 as GAUMONT, 1873 seats. Closed 25.3.61. (Interior completely reconstructed for bowling alley, opened 29.1.62. Open in 1995.)

STROUD Gloucestershire

PALACE Russell Street. (Opened 1913, former Empire Theatre. Part of Albany Ward circuit, then Award circuit. Reconstructed in 1927, renamed Palace, 680 seats. Taken over 9.27 by PCT.) Taken over 2.29, part of PCT. Closed 2.2.35. (Demolished for Gaumont Palace.)
PICTURE HOUSE King Street Parade. (Part of Albany Ward circuit, then Award circuit. Taken over 9.27 by PCT.) Taken over 2.29, part of PCT. Closed 1932. Re-opened c11.34 while Gaumont Palace built. Closed c8.35. (Demolished. Shops.)
GAUMONT PALACE Russell Street. Opened 31.8.35 by Gaumont/Albany Ward-PCT, architects: W. E. Trent & W. Sydney Trent, 994 seats, semi-stadium plan. Renamed GAUMONT. Renamed ODEON 11.11.62. (Taken over 16.12.67 by Classic, renamed Classic. Split for bingo on stalls floor and new cinema in former raised rear section, opened 2.3.72, 184 seats. Cinema closed 3.9.72. Taken over by Mecca 11.1.74. Cinema section re-opened as Mecca. Cinema closed by 31.12.76. Bingo only. Closed 22.7.95 as Cascades bingo club.)

SUNDERLAND Tyne and Wear

KING'S THEATRE Crowtree Road. (Part of Thompson & Collins circuit.) Taken over 3.28 by Denman/Gaumont. 1800 seats. (Leased 4.40 by local repertory company, reverted to live theatre. Closed by war-time bombing. Converted to market in 1947.)
HAVELOCK Fawcett Street. (Opened 16.12.15 by PCT [or reconstruction after fire?]) Taken over 2.29, part of PCT. 1504 seats. Renamed GAUMONT 29.5.50. Closed 15.6.63. (Demolished. Offices.)
PALACE High Street West. (Opened 1909 on cine-variety, former music hall. Taken over 3.28 by GTC. 1121 seats.) Taken over 5.28, part

of GTC. 1030 seats. Closed 1.12.56. (Sold 12.58. Taken over 1965 by Council, leased for model car racing in foyer and part of circle in 1968. Foyer into amusement arcade briefly from 1970. Demolished 10.73. Leisure centre.)

SUTTON Southwest London

SURREY COUNTY High Street. (Opened 24.3.21, architect: Captain R. Younghusband. Taken over by APPH by 3.22.) Taken over 2.29, part of PCT/APPH. 1736 seats. Renamed GAUMONT 22.8.47. Closed 4.4.59. (Demolished. Shop in old foyer area, office block on auditorium space.)

SWINDON Wiltshire

PALACE Gorse Hill. (Opened 26.12.12. Part of Albany Ward circuit, then Award circuit. Taken over 9.27 by PCT.) Taken over 2.29, part of PCT/Albany Ward. 867 seats. Closed 23.5.59. (Motor cycle showroom.)
REGENT Regent Circus. Opened 16.9.29 by Gaumont/Albany Ward-PCT, architect: W. Sydney Trent, 1322 seats, one floor. New frontage completed c11.31, architects: W.E. Trent & Ernest F. Tulley. Renamed GAUMONT c1952. Renamed ODEON 2.6.63. Closed 24.8.74. (Top Rank Club for bingo, open in 1995.)

SYDENHAM Southeast London

RINK 6 Silverdale. (Opened 1909 as cinema & skating rink, architects: J. & P. J. Groom & Evan S. Barr. Cinema from 3.6.10, 499 seats, with occasional skating days. Taken over by Army during World War One. Taken over 1924 by PCT, closed 7.28 for improvements & enlargement. Re-opened 22.10.28, 1518 seats.) Taken over 2.29, part of PCT. (Taken over for Civil Defence, then Army use, during World War Two. Never re-opened. Frontage rebuilt as London Electricity Board premises. Demolished 10.95.)

TAUNTON Somerset

GAUMONT PALACE Corporation Street, Castle Way and Tower Street. Opened 11.7.32 by Gaumont/Albany Ward-PCT, architect: William T. Benslyn, 1476 seats: 982 stalls & 494 balcony [or 1487: 989 stalls & 498 balcony]. Renamed GAUMONT c1937. Renamed ODEON in 1969. 1272 seats. Closed 5.9.81.

(Top Rank Club for bingo from 11.81, open in 1995.)

THORNLEY Co. Durham

HIPPODROME East Street. (Opened pre-1915. Part of North of England Cinemas circuit.) Taken over 3.28 by Denman/Gaumont. 1000 seats. (Leased to local company c1939. Given to Easington Rural District Council 13.1.71.)

TOTTENHAM North London

PALACE High Road. (Opened pre-1915, former variety theatre. Taken over c1925 by PCT. 1379 seats.) Taken over 2.29, part of PCT. Closed 28.6.69. (Bingo. Grade II listed building from 9.12.92. Open as Jasmine Club for bingo in 1995.)

TREHARRIS Mid Glamorgan

PALACE The Square. (Cinema by 1910, former Palace of Varieties, music hall. Part of Albany Ward circuit. Taken over by PCT.) Taken over 2.29, part of PCT. (Taken over c1930 by independent, enlarged and re-opened 10.30. 750 seats. Closed 1971. Disused in 1995.)

TROWBRIDGE Wiltshire

PALACE Fore Street. (Opened 1914 by Albany Ward, 635 seats. Taken over by PCT.) Taken over 2.29, part of PCT. 660 seats. Closed 27.2.37. (Demolished for Gaumont.)
GAUMONT 27 Fore Street (site of Palace and adjacent property). Opened 29.11.37 by Gaumont/Albany Ward-PCT, architects: W. E. Trent & W. S. Trent, 1220 seats: 860 stalls & 360 balcony. Renamed ODEON 11.11.62. Closed 20.3.71. (Demolished. Knees store in 4.95.)

TUE BROOK Liverpool

EMPRESS West Derby Road. (Opened 1.7.15 by T. Halliwell Hughes, architects: Campbell & Fairhurst, 850 seats.) Taken over 3.28 by Denman/Gaumont. 954 seats. Closed 12.3.60. (Demolished. Shops and road widening.)

TWICKENHAM West London

QUEENS Richmond Road. (Opened 15.10.28 as The Twickenham, architects: Leathart & Granger, 1141 seats. Renamed Queens 6.40.

Requisitioned and closed 26.10.40. Taken over by Odeon. Re-opened 24.12.45.) Renamed GAUMONT 8.5.50. Closed 1.12.56. (Demolished. Petrol station.)

UPMINSTER Northeast London

CAPITOL St. Mary's Lane and Tudor Gardens. (Opened 10.10.29 by Lou Morris, architect: James Martin Hatfield, 1158 seats. Taken over c1937 by GCF. Transferred 28.2.43 to Odeon. Renamed Odeon in 1948.) Renamed GAUMONT in 1950. Closed 15.7.61. (Bingo. Closed 1973. Demolished. Supermarket.)

VICTORIA Central London

NEW VICTORIA Wilton Road and Vauxhall Bridge Road. Opened 15.10.30 by Gaumont/PCT, architects: W. E. Trent & E. Wamsley Lewis, 2860 seats. Closed c9.40 by war-time conditions. Re-opened 25.5.41. Grade II* listed building from 28.6.72. Closed 1.11.75. (Live shows. Renamed Apollo Victoria 15.9.80. Open in 1995.)

WAKEFIELD West Yorkshire

CARLTON Grove Road. (Opened 29.10.15. Part of New Century Pictures circuit.) Taken over 3.28 by Denman/Gaumont. 1010 seats. Closed 29.9.56.

EMPIRE Kirkgate. (Opened 14.7.21 by New Century Pictures circuit, former live theatre.) Taken over 3.28 by Denman/Gaumont, part of New Century Pictures circuit. 977 seats. Renamed GAUMONT 22.5.50. Closed 30.7.60. (Demolished.)

WALHAM GREEN Northwest London

RED HALL Vanston Place. (Opened 18.12.13, 1600 seats. Taken over c1921 by PCT.) Taken over 2.29, part of PTC. Renamed GAUMONT 8.5.50. Closed 8.12.62. (Top Rank Club for bingo, open in 1995.)

WALLASEY Merseyside — see Egremont, New Brighton and Seacombe

WALLSEND Tyne and Wear

BOROUGH THEATRE High Street East. (Opened pre-1914, former live theatre. Part of Thompson & Collins circuit.) Taken over 3.28 by Denman/Gaumont. 1100 seats. Re-

named GAUMONT c1946. Closed 26.11.60. (Bingo.)

WALSALL West Midlands
see also Willenhall

PICTURE HOUSE The Bridge, Bridge Street. Opened 29.7.20 by APPH, architects: Percy L. Browne & Glover, 1500 seats. Restored 1923 after serious fire damage.) Taken over 2.29, part of PCT/APPH, 1615 seats. Renamed GAUMONT c1948. Renamed ODEON 22.10.65. Modernised and re-opened 26.7.67, 1291 seats. Closed 2.3.71 by major fire. (Demolished. Tesco supermarket in 1995.)

WALTON Liverpool

BEDFORD [HALL] Bedford Road. (Opened 26.12.08. Taken over 3.28 by GTC.) Taken over 5.28, part of GTC, 1100 seats. Closed 23.5.59. (Furniture warehouse extension.)

WANDSWORTH Southwest London

PALACE 60 High Street. (Opened 13.12.20. Taken over by United Picture Theatres 3.12.28.) Under Gaumont management from 7.30 as part of UPT circuit. 1307 seats. Closed c9.40. Re-opened 3.5.42. Renamed GAUMONT 4.8.55. Entrance modernised c1956. Closed 4.2.61. (Bingo from 29.7.61. Closed 1979. Church from 1982. Closed. Nightclub, called The Theatre, from 1992.)

WATFORD Hertfordshire

GAUMONT 65 The Parade, High Street. Opened 3.5.37 by Gaumont Super Cinemas, architect: J. Owen Bond, 2000 seats: 1398 stalls + 602 balcony. Taken over fully 28.2.44. Renamed ODEON 20.9.64. 1948 seats. Mini-cinemas created under balcony, opened 2.6.74, 120 + 120 seats, balcony & original screen continuing as separate cinema, 612 seats. Closed 15.10.83. (Demolished 1985. New shops on front, access road and part of supermarket in former auditorium area.)

WAVERTREE Liverpool
see also Sefton Park

MAGNET Picton Road. (Opened 11.12.14, 1038 seats on one floor. Part of T. Halliwell Hughes circuit.) Taken over 3.28 by Denman/Gaumont. 949 seats. Closed 23.5.59. (Industrial use. Squash and badminton club.)

WEDNESBURY West Midlands

PICTURE HOUSE Walsall Street. (Opened 25.3.15 by APPH, architects: Atkinson & Alexander, 900 seats.) Taken over 2.29, part of PCT/APPH. 851 seats. Closed 8.1.38. (Demolished for new Gaumont.)

GAUMONT 115 Walsall Street (site of Picture House). Opened 10.10.38 by Gaumont/APPH, architects: W. E. Trent, W. Sydney Trent & H. L. Cherry, 1594 seats. Renamed ODEON 9.3.64. (Taken over by independent 30.1.72, renamed Silver. Closed 19.4.74. Bingo.)

WEMBLEY Northwest London

WEMBLEY HALL CINEMA High Road. (Opened 1914. Extensively reconstructed and enlarged, re-opened 12.35, 1050 seats.) Taken over by Rank, modernised and re-opened 23.5.55 as GAUMONT. Renamed ODEON 17.12.61. Closed 18.1.75. (Re-opened as Asian cinema, renamed Liberty. Closed 1981. Demolished. Office block.)

WEST GORTON Manchester — see Gorton

WEST HAM Northeast London
see also Stratford

KINEMA West Ham Lane, corner of Densham Road. (Opened 7.14 as Empire, architects: Andrews & Peascod. Taken over by Bernstein. Altered and re-opened 14.10.25. Reconstructed, architect: Cecil Masey, interior decoration: Theodore Komisarjevksy, re-opened 14.11.27 as Kinema. 1659 seats, one floor.) Taken over 3.28 by Denman/Gaumont but operated by Bernstein/Granada. Renamed CENTURY 23.7.51. (Fully acquired 3.65 by Granada. Closed 5.1.63. (Bingo. Closed in 1994.)

WEST HARTLEPOOL Cleveland

PICTURE HOUSE Stockton Street. (Opened 13.12.20. Part of North of England Cinemas circuit.) Taken over 3.28 by Denman/Gaumont. 1800 seats. Renamed GAUMONT 3.7.50. Closed 19.11.60. (Bingo. Facade rebuilt as Stranton Fairworld Bingo. Demolished.)

WEST KENSINGTON West London

SUPER 235/7 North End Road. (Opened 22.5.22.) Taken over 3.28 by Denman/Gaumont, 1000 seats. Closed 1942 by bomb damage. (Warehouse. Demolished in 1950s. Flats, part of West Kensington Housing Estate.)

WESTMINSTER BRIDGE ROAD South London

CANTERBURY MUSIC HALL 143 Westminster Bridge Road. (Former music hall. Part of Hyams & Gale circuit.) Taken over 3.28 by Denman/Gaumont. 1500 seats. Closed 9.40 by wartime conditions. Re-opened. Closed 1942 by bomb damage. (Auditorium cleared — car park.)

WEST NORWOOD South London

REGAL 304 Norwood Road. (Opened 16.1.30 by A. E. Abrahams, architect: F. Edward Jones, 2010 seats. Leased by Hyams & Gale 24.4.33.) Taken over 10.35 by Gaumont Super Cinemas. Closed by wartime conditions. Re-opened 3.11.40. Fully taken over 28.2.44. Closed 1.2.64. (Top Rank Club for bingo from 20.2.64. Closed 1978. Demolished. DIY centre.)

WESTON-SUPER-MARE Avon

PICTURE HOUSE Regent Street. (Opened 22.3.13, architect: W. H. Watkins, 1088 seats.) Taken over 4.30 by Gaumont/PCT. Renamed REGENT c1930. Renamed GAUMONT 15.11.54. Closed 9.6.73. (Bingo from 25.7.73. Demolished c1985, plaster cherubs saved. Leisure centre & bingo club.)

WEST WICKHAM Kent

ODEON 88 Station Road. (Opened 4.9.33 as Plaza, architects: J. Stanley Beard & Clare, 886 seats. Taken over 1.7.37 by Odeon. Renamed Odeon by 1940.) Renamed GAUMONT 1951. Closed 5.1.57. (Demolished. Rosemallow House with Boots store etc.)

WEYMOUTH Dorset

REGENT St. Thomas Street. (Opened 1909 as Royal Victoria Jubilee Hall and Picture Palace, former public hall. Taken over by Albany Ward. Taken over by PCT. Reconstructed, architect: W. E. Trent, and re-opened 2.8.26 as Regent, 1234 seats.) Taken over 2.29, part of PCT. Renamed GAUMONT 26.2.51. Renamed ODEON c1970. (Taken over 8.2.76 by independent for cine-bingo, renamed New Invicta. Closed 29.1.77. Bingo only from

7.4.77. Closed. Demolished 1989. "Temporary" car park.)

BELLE VUE Belle Vue Terrace and East Street. (Opened 1910 by Albany Ward, former lodging houses. 314 seats. Taken over by PCT.) Taken over 2.29, part of PCT. Closed 29.9.56. (Elim Christian Centre.)

PALLADIUM Town Bridge. (Opened 1912 by Albany Ward, former ironmongery store.) Taken over 2.29, part of PCT. Closed 1932. (Motorcycle showroom and workshop. Nightclub from 1970s, open in 1995.)

WHITECHAPEL East London

RIVOLI 100 Whitechapel Road. (Opened 1.8.21, partly on site of Wonderland, architects: Adams & [George] Coles, 2268 seats. Part of United Picture Theatres circuit from 1.28.) Under Gaumont management from 7.30 as part of UPT circuit. Closed 1940 by wartime bomb damage. (Demolished.)

WHITLEY BAY Tyne and Wear

EMPIRE Esplanade. (Opened 1913. Part of North of England Cinemas circuit.) Taken over 3.28 by Denman/Gaumont. 1200 seats. Renamed GAUMONT 28.8.50. (Taken over 27.11.60 by independent. Closed c1962. Bingo. Ballroom.)

WILLENHALL West Midlands

PICTURE HOUSE Stafford Street. (Opened 19.4.15 by APPH, 736 seats.) Taken over 2.29 as part of PCT/APPH. Closed 2.5.59. (Demolished. Supermarket.)

WILLESDEN Northwest London
see also Harlesden

EMPIRE Church Road, corner of Ilex Road. (Opened c12.20 by Bernstein, architect: Cecil Masey, 1500 seats, one floor. Reconstructed with balcony, architect: Cecil Masey, interior decoration: Theodore Komisarjevsky, and re-opened 27.10.27, 1777 seats. Taken over 3.28 by Denman/Gaumont but operated by Bernstein/Granada. Reconstructed, architect: James Morrison, and re-opened 21.9.36, renamed GRANADA, 1700 seats. Closed 20.10.62. (Bingo. Fully acquired 3.65 by Granada. Closed. Re-opened 14.10.94 as The Comedy Empire, live theatre.)

WIMBLEDON South London

REGAL The Broadway. (Opened 20.11.33 by County, architect: Robert Cromie, 2000 seats. Taken over by Odeon.) Renamed GAUMONT 28.11.49. Renamed ODEON 9.9.62. Mini-cinemas created under balcony, opened 5.11.72, 128 & 107 seats, balcony continuing as separate cinema using original screen, 705 seats. Mini-cinemas closed 6.1.79 for enlargement. Re-opened 8.4.79, 218 & 190 seats. New screen installed in front of circle in 1985. Additional cinemas opened 29.3.91 in front stalls and former restaurant area, 175 & 90 seats. All five open in 1995.)

WISHAW Strathclyde

CINEMA 50 Kirk Road. (Opened 4.20. Part of Thomas Ormiston circuit.) Taken over 3.28 by Denman/Gaumont, 1100 seats. (Taken over 9.12.67 by Classic, renamed Classic. Closed 28.10.71 for twinning. Re-opened 18.11.72, 336 + 134 seats, latter in old balcony. Closed 1985. Balcony cinema re-opened 1986. Closed 7.88. Amusement arcade downstairs, upstairs disused in 1994.)

WOKING Surrey

PLAZA Chertsey Road. (Opened 1913 as Central. 780 seats. Enlarged, front rebuilt, architects: Wilfred Travers & Frank C. Spiller, and re-opened c9.26, 1046 seats. Taken over by London & Southern c1929, renamed Plaza. Taken over c7.37 by Odeon, 914 seats.) Renamed GAUMONT 29.5.50. Closed 13.6.59. Demolished. Supermarket.)

WOLVERHAMPTON West Midlands
see also Wednesfield

AGRICULTURAL HALL Snow Hill. (Opened c9.13, conversion of existing hall with frequent earlier film use, architects: Norfolk & Prior, 1248 seats, one floor. Taken over by 1919 by APPH.) Taken over 2.29, part of PCT/APPH. Closed 19.9.31. (Demolished for new Gaumont Palace.)

SCALA Worcester Street. (Opened 12.13 as the Picturedrome, architect: A. Eaton Painter, 1400 seats. Taken over c1916 by Midland Amusements, renamed Scala. Taken over 1.6.25 by APPH. Closed 11.7.25 for refurbishment. Re-opened 28.9.25.) Taken over 2.29, part of PCT/APPH. Closed 1.12.56. (Supermarket on ground floor, dance hall & wrestling upstairs. Latter converted to bingo.)

QUEEN'S Queen's Square. (Opened 30.9.14 by APPH, architects: Robert Atkinson & George Alexander, 1020 seats.) Taken over 2.29, part of PCT/APPH. Closed 7.2.59. (Opened 15.5.59 as dance hall. Closed 1969. Demolished 1977/78. Bank.)

HIPPODROME Queen's Square. (Live theatre, formerly called Empire. Taken over 3.28 by GTC.) Taken over 5,28, part of GTC. Cinema from 28.9.31 to 27.8.32. Reverted to live theatre. (Taken over c11.46 by Moss Empires. Closed 19.2.56 by fire. Demolished. Furnishing store.)

GAUMONT PALACE Snow Hill and Cleveland Street. Opened 5.9.32 by Gaumont/ APPH, architect: W. E. Trent (assistant: J. Morrison), 1992 seats [but 1270 stalls & 650 circle according to opening programme]. Renamed GAUMONT c1937. Closed 10.11.73. (Demolished. Temporary car park. Carpet store.)

WOOD GREEN North London

GAUMONT PALACE The Broadway, High Road. Opened 26.3.34 by Gaumont/APPH, architects: W. E. Trent & Ernest F. Tulley, 2556 seats. Renamed GAUMONT c1937. Renamed ODEON 9.9.62. Mini-cinemas created under balcony, opened 30.12.73, 149 & 150 seats, balcony & original screen continuing as separate cinema, 814 seats (+ 450 seats in front stalls). Closed 7.1.84. (Mini-cinemas removed, full original auditorium used for bingo as Top Rank Club from 4.9.84. Grade II listed building from 26.3.90. "Gaumont Palace" name reinstated on frontage in 1993. Open in 1995 as Top Rank Club.)

WOOLWICH Southeast London

HIPPODROME Wellington Street, corner of Lower Market Street. (Opened 1924, former live theatre. Part of United Picture Theatres circuit from 1.28.) Under Gaumont management from 7.30 as part of UPT circuit. (Taken over 7.35 by ABC. Closed 1939. Demolished for new Regal.)

WORCESTER Hereford and Worcester

ARCADE St. Swithin's Street. (900 seats. Taken over by PCT.) Taken over 2.29, part of PCT. 850 seats. Closed 1935.

GAUMONT 21 Foregate Street. Opened 28.10.35 by Gaumont/PCT, architects: W. E. Trent & Ernest F. Tulley, 1740 seats. stadium plan. Closed 4.5.74. (Bingo. Open as Gala Club in 1994.)

YEOVIL Somerset

PALACE THEATRE The Triangle. (Part of Albany Ward circuit. Taken over by PCT.) Taken over 2.29, part of PCT/Albany Ward. Closed 1933. (Demolished for Gaumont Palace.)

GAUMONT PALACE The Triangle, Stars Lane (site of Palace Theatre). Opened 15.12.34 by Gaumont/Albany Ward, architect: W. E. Trent (assistant: Ernest F. Tulley), 1384 seats. Renamed GAUMONT. (Taken over 9.12.67 by Classic, renamed Classic. Closed 11.11.72. Bingo.)

YORK North Yorkshire

SCALA 46 Goodramgate. (Opened c12.08 as Victoria Hall by National Electric Theatres. Extended 1910 and entrance hall rebuilt. 1000 seats. Closed 1924. Converted to Palais de Dance by National Electric. Closed by 1927. Re-opened as Scala cinema by National Electric.) Taken over 3.28 by Denman/Gaumont. Closed c1931.

ELECTRIC Fossgate. (Opened 3.6.11 by National Electric Theatres, architect; William Whincup, 600 seats. Part of National Electric Theatres circuit.) Taken over 3.28 by Denman/ Gaumont. 795 seats. Closed 9.8.51. (Taken over by independent. Reseated and redecorated, re-opened 9.9.51 as Scala Super. 717 seats. Closed c4.57. Furniture shop.)

PICTURE HOUSE Coney Street. (Opened 12.4.15, architect: Albert Winspear, 1000 seats. Taken over c1919 by PCT.) Taken over 2.29, part of PCT. 920 seats. Closed 14.5.55. (Demolished. Extension of adjacent Woolworth's store.)

ST. GEORGE'S HALL Castlegate. (Opened c5.21, 1340 seats. Taken over c1922 by PCT.) Taken over 2.29, part of PCT. Re-opened 2.38 after extensive alterations. 1296 seats. Closed 6.11.65. (Auction house. Demolished 1970 except for front, retained through preservation order, entrance to Fairfax House.)

BIBLIOGRAPHY

Articles

"An Internationalist At Home." By Ernest Wamsley Lewis. (*London Architect*, January and March 1972.) About the New Victoria, London.

"United Picture Theatres: The Cinderella Circuit". By Allen Eyles. (*Picture House*, no. 18, Winter 1992/93.). Extensively illustrated.

"W. H. Watkins, A Bristol Architect." By David Ewins. (*Picture House*, no. 5, Summer 1984.) Richly illustrated with photographs of the Barnstaple, Coventry, Exeter and Plymouth Gaumont Palaces, also the Bristol Regent.

Books

Bradford's Rock 'n' Roll: The Golden Years 1959-1965. By Derek A. J. Lister. (Bradford Libraries and Information Service, Bradford, 1991.)

Cinema in Middlesbrough. By J. W. Saunders. (J. W. Saunders, Middlesbrough, 1991.)

Cinemas of Newcastle. By Frank Manders. (City Libraries & Arts, City of Newcastle upon Tyne, 1991.)

Cinemas of the Black Country. By Ned Williams. (Uralia Press, Wolverhampton, 1982.) And 1984 supplement.

A City and its Cinemas. By Charles Anderson. (Redcliffe Press, Bristol, 1983.)

The Dream Palaces of Liverpool. By Harold Ackroyd. (Amber Valley, Birmingham, 1987.)

Enter the Dream-House: Memories of Cinemas in South London from the Twenties to the Sixties. Edited by Margaret O'Brien and Allen Eyles. (Museum of the Moving Image, London, 1993.)

Film Making in 1930s Britain. By Rachael Low. (George Allen & Unwin, London, 1985.)

London's West End Cinemas. By Allen Eyles and Keith Skone. (Keytone Publications, London, 1991.) Includes full illustrated histories of all Gaumont's central London cinemas, including the New Victoria.

Mr. Rank: A Study of J. Arthur Rank and British Films. By Alan Wood. (Hodder and Stoughton, London, 1952.)

The Silver Screens of Wirral: A History of Cinemas in Birkenhead and Bebington. By P. A. Carson and C. R. Garner. (Countyvise/Metropolitan Borough of Wirral, 1990.)

Talking Pictures: The Popular Experience of the Cinema. Edited by Colin Harding and Brian Lewis. (Yorkshire Art Circus/National Museum of Photography, Film & Television, Bradford, 1993.)

Tune Up the Hoover! Cinema Musicians Tell Their Stories. By Jon de Jonge. (Jon de Jonge, Blackpool, 1994.)

ABC

THE FIRST NAME IN ENTERTAINMENT

Allen Eyles

Published in September 1993, this companion volume to *Gaumont British Cinemas* by the same author explores the history of Associated British Cinemas, which formed the largest circuit of picture houses ever to operate in this country and at its peak sold nearly six million tickets every week. Created by Scotsman John Maxwell, it was the exhibition arm of the Associated British Picture Corporation (which made films as Elstree and Welwyn and released them through distribution subsidiaries). Much of the chain survives as part of the MGM/Cannon chain acquired in 1995 by Virgin.

This book examines the creation of the circuit, describes the cinemas that were purpose-built to the designs of staff architect W. R. Glen and others, the major acquisitions of existing cinemas, the booking policy (primarily screening Hollywood films of MGM and Warner Bros. in the boom years of cinemagoing), the live shows and organ interludes, the response to 3-D and CinemaScope, the decline in audiences which led to subdivision into smaller cinemas, closures, and the first step into the multiplex era.

Included is a detailed listing of more than 600 cinemas which were ever part of the ABC chain and the titles of all the main films given an ABC circuit release from 1937 to 1979, plus an array of rare illustrations of major cinemas and company advertising.

"...the overall history of the circuit...is meticulously and interestingly chronicled... ABC The First Name in Entertainment *is a well-produced, informative read and should be on the bookshelf of anyone interested in British cinema"* — Ian Riches, Moving Pictures UK

"Film historian Allen Eyles continues his love affair with British movie theatres with ABC The First Name in Entertainment... *Written with affection...its photographs making one yearn for the return of the golden age of the picture palace"* — Howard Maxford, Film Review

"...the design and decor of the theatres, the prime concern of Eyles' affectionate, elegiac study...In loving detail he describes decorative grilles and side panels, stepped and scalloped ceilings, butterfly-appliquéd curtains and crystalline light fittings" — Philip Kemp, Sight and Sound

160 pages, paperback (200 by 214mm),
127 illustrations (11 in full colour)

Published by the Cinema Theatre Association
Distributed by BFI Publishing   ISBN: 0-85170-430-1
Price £14.99